Sex Panic and the Punitive State

The publisher gratefully acknowledges the generous support of the General Endowment Fund of the University of California Press Foundation.

Sex Panic and the Punitive State

Roger N. Lancaster

UNIVERSITY OF CALIFORNIA PRESS
Berkeley · Los Angeles · London

University of California Press, one of the most distinguished university presses in the United States, enriches
lives around the world by advancing scholarship in the
humanities, social sciences, and natural sciences. Its
activities are supported by the UC Press Foundation and
by philanthropic contributions from individuals and
institutions. For more information, visit www.ucpress.edu.

University of California Press
Berkeley and Los Angeles, California

University of California Press, Ltd.
London, England

Library of Congress Cataloging-in-Publication Data

Lancaster, Roger N.
  Sex panic and the punitive state / Roger N.
Lancaster.
    p.   cm.
  Includes bibliographical references and index.
  ISBN 978-0-520-25565-4 (cloth : alk. paper)
  ISBN 978-0-520-26206-5 (pbk. : alk. paper)
  1. Sex—United States.   2. Sexual ethics—United
States.   3. Sex customs—United States.   4. United
States—Social conditions—20th century.   I. Title.
  HQ18U5L35   2011
  306.70973'09045—dc22   2010020837

Manufactured in the United States of America

19   18   17   16   15   14   13   12   11   10
10   9   8   7   6   5   4   3   2   1

This book is printed on Cascades Enviro 100, a 100%
post consumer waste, recycled, de-inked fiber. FSC
recycled certified and processed chlorine free. It is acid
free, Ecologo certified, and manufactured by BioGas
energy.

For Ritchie and Joe, who try to live well

Present fears
are less than horrible imaginings.
—William Shakespeare, *Macbeth*

Whoever fights monsters should see to it that in the process
he does not become a monster.
—Friedrich Nietzsche, *Beyond Good and Evil*

Rome's life was now an imitation of life: a mere holding on.
Security was the watchword—as if life knew any other
stability than through constant change, or any form of
security except through a constant willingness to take risks.
—Lewis Mumford, *The Condition of Man*

Contents

Acknowledgments

Ideas for this book took shape in a series of invited workshop presentations. The first was "The World Looks at Us: Rethinking the U.S. State," a conference funded by the Wenner Gren Foundation for Anthropological Research, *Critique of Anthropology*, and the Center for Place, Culture and Politics at the City University of New York (October 8–10, 2004). The second was "New Landscapes of Social Inequality," a seminar at the School for Advanced Research in Santa Fe organized by Jane Collins, Micaela di Leonardo, and Brett Williams (March 11–16, 2006). The last was my colloquium presentation on March 28, 2007, at the Instituto de Ciencias Sociales y Humanidades of the Benemérita Universidad Autónoma de Puebla in Mexico during a year of research sponsored by a Fulbright–García Robles grant. I am grateful to various sponsors and interlocutors for giving me the opportunity to outline arguments and to develop ideas.

Many people supplied me with helpful responses to early drafts of portions of this book: Talal Asad, Catherine Besteman, Michelle Boyd, Lisa Breglia, Partha Chatterjee, Melissa Checker, John Clark, Hilary Cunningham, Amal Hassan Fadlalla, Carlos Figueroa Ibarra, Lesley Gill, Hugh Gusterson, Matt Gutmann, Tim Kaposy, Kerwin Kaye, Ann Kingsolver, Catherine Lutz, Nancy MacLean, Jeff Maskofsky, Sally Engle Merry, Pablo Morales, Sandra Morgen, Gina Pérez, Dan Robotham, Tom Scartz, Nancy Scheper-Hughes, Jane Schneider, Peter Schneider, Ida Susser, and Brett Williams. I would like to express special thanks to those who read the entire manuscript at different stages of its development: Andy Bickford, Jane Collins, Micaela di Leonardo, Marcial Godoy, Mark Jacobs, and Mark Pedelty. I especially benefited from close readings and generous feedback from James Faubion and the three readers who served as outside reviewers for the Press: Dorothy Roberts, Michael Sherry, and Jonathan Simon. My editor, Naomi Schneider, gave helpful, supportive guidance throughout. Special thanks to Kate Warne for attentive production editing and to Do Mi Stauber for thoughtful indexing.

George Mason University generously supplied me with faculty study leave that gave me time to research, reflect, and write. My colleagues there have provided me with lively conversation and helpful exchanges over the years, and those conversations clearly mark these pages. I should especially thank Paul Smith, Dina Copelman, and Denise Albanese. Lucas Witman served as my research assistant during much of this project; he proved a thoughtful and indefatigable searcher of libraries and databases. Scott Killen also served as research assistant. Any errors, omissions, or poor word choices are of course my own.

Early (and substantially different) versions of some portions of this book have been published in a variety of places:

"State of Panic," in *New Landscapes of Inequality,* ed. Jane Collins, Micaela di Leonardo, and Brett Williams (Santa Fe, N. Mex.: School for Advanced Research Press, 2008), 39–64.

"Panic Attack: Sex and Terror in the Homeland," in "Terror Incognita: Immigrants and the Homeland Security State," a special issue of *NACLA Report on the Americas* 41, no. 6 (November–December 2008): 31–35.

"Republic of Fear: The Rise of Punitive Governance in the United States," in *Rethinking America: The Imperial Homeland in the Twenty-first Century,* ed. Jeff Maskovsky and Ida Susser (Boulder, Colo.: Paradigm, 2009), 201–12.

"Republic of Fear: The Triumph of Punitive Governance in America," in *The Insecure American,* ed. Catherine Besteman and Hugh Gusterson (Berkeley: University of California Press, 2009), 63–76.

Fear Eats the Soul

The most modern aspect of the spectacle is thus also the most archaic.

—Guy Debord, *The Society of the Spectacle*

To him who is in fear, everything rustles.

—Sophocles, *Acrisius* (fragment)

I began drafting notes for this book when I found myself near the center of a raging sex panic: a combined police, judiciary, and media frenzy triggered by vague and constantly shifting accusations against a gay male schoolteacher I know. It is one thing to understand, in the abstract, that presumptions of innocence, standards of reasonable doubt, and assorted procedures of rational law have been eroded by wave after wave of sex crime hysterias in the United States. It is quite another thing to see scary mug shots of a close friend aired on the evening news. Calling the public spectacle I witnessed unfair or prejudicial would understate matters. Credulous journalists related, without qualification, the narratives of cops, prosecutors, and victims' rights advocates. In the process they conveyed outright misinformation about the defendant and the case. Even facts that would normally count in one's favor—for example, a long and spotless record of employment in the field—were made to sound menacing. Homosexuality, never named, was insinuated—by repeatedly announcing the home address of the accused. (He lived in the heart of a gay neighborhood.)

Sex panics, it suddenly seemed to me, were more or less everywhere, a fixture in and fixation of American culture. I started to pay close attention to other sex cases in the news. Some of these news stories involved nightmarish but isolated events: the rape and murder of defenseless children. Others related serious allegations of serial abuse and systematic cover-up. However, many stories that clamored for public attention involved nonviolent, noncoercive offenses of various types. Minor infractions or petty nuisances were portrayed as ominous threats.

In one case I followed, a man in his thirties was spied through window curtains playing ping-pong in the nude with a pubescent boy; the latter was fully clothed. The man's behavior ought to have raised questions, obviously. But there was nothing nuanced or undecided about the response of law enforcement in this case. The man was arrested, not once but twice, and the result was a lead story on local news stations—a placement that scarcely seems commensurate with any dangers plausibly associated with naked table tennis. Talking heads implored the public to provide "more information" about the arrestee, while self-appointed experts parsed the modus operandi of sexual predators, underscoring the point that there is never any good reason for adults and minors to be nude around each other. No sexual contact of any sort between the man and any minor was ever alleged. And even though the man, who happened to be a police officer, had no previous arrests or convictions of any sort, clarion calls were sounded for greater vigilance, for "fitness evaluations" and more extensive background checks for coaches, teachers, and youth counselors.

PANIC ATTACK

Less about the protection of children than about the preservation of adult fantasies of childhood as a time of sexual innocence, sex panics give rise to bloated imaginings of risk, inflated conceptions of harm, and loose definitions of sex.[1] This book is about sex panics and their relation to other forms of institutionalized fear in the United States today. At first glance the connection might seem a non sequitur: What, after all, could exaggerated fears of pedophiles have to do with the sorts of collective anxieties unleashed after September 11, 2001? Quite a lot, I suggest. The sexual predator is a cultural figure whose meaning is readily transferred to other figures; sexual predation has come to serve as a metaphor for other conditions of injury in the body politic.

It is no secret that the politics of fear have ruled for a long time. For decades tough-talking politicians of both major parties have cultivated voters' fears of crime in order to win elections, keeping the United States in an increasingly disastrous state of panic—and sex is a big part of this perpetual panic narrative. "I wouldn't even be here if it weren't for the politics," Robert Sillen, a gray-haired hospital administrator who was appointed by a federal court to clean up California's prison health care mess, told the *New York Times*. Sillen sees the breakdown of prison medicine as a logical consequence of overcrowding and succinctly describes the political nature of the problem: "No one gets elected in Sacramento without a platform that says, 'Let's get rid of rapists, pedophiles and murderers.' "[2] Where fear is the order of the day, protection is the name of the game. This has become second nature—that's what government is for, isn't it? Law exists to protect the innocent, doesn't it? Sex panics efficiently condense this neo-Hobbesian approach to law and order. They represent an especially salient subset of the ongoing crime panics that, over time, have prepared the public to surrender key rights and guarantees in exchange for security. (Notably, two of the three objects of dread that Sillen names are sex criminals.)

Moreover, the logic of sex panic is essentially promiscuous; its forms disseminate throughout the body politic. Over time the same techniques that perpetually propagate these panics—sensational journalism about child victims, punditry that stokes an exaggerated sense of danger, emotional congressional testimony by victims and their families, collaboration between victims' rights groups and politicians—have been adapted to other causes and have become engines for the production of laws having nothing to do with sex. By such means "road rage" became the object of a public crusade in the 1990s and 2000s, although deaths from rage-related aggressive driving have never exceeded one-tenth of one percent of all traffic fatalities.[3] In Virginia, after casting about for various ways to frame speeding and other traffic violations as serious offenses worthy of harsh penalties—"reckless driving," "aggressive driving"—state legislators eventually settled on "abusive driving," a term eerily evocative of the ubiquitous talk about sex abuse and child protection.[4]

The history of modern sex panics is a closely sequenced one. First came the teen male prostitution scares of the 1970s, followed by AIDS terrors and the satanic ritual abuse and day-care panics of the 1980s. Beginning in the 1990s we have suffered a veritable avalanche. Reportage on violent pedophile predators, the perils of the Internet, the priest abuse scandals, the Michael Jackson trial, and so on made sex crime stories part of the furniture on twenty-four-hour news services, local television news stations, and even newspapers of record.

The pernicious effects of such public panics have been amply noted, and not only by queer theorists and sex radicals. In *The Assault on*

Reason former vice president Al Gore presents a string of nonstop news stories about sex and violence—the O.J. Simpson trial, the JonBenét Ramsey case, the murder of Laci Peterson, the Chandra Levy tragedy, along with assorted disappearances, kidnappings, sexual peccadilloes, and celebrity scandals—as exhibit A in his argument that "something has gone fundamentally wrong" in American public discourse. Such stories rework yellow journalism's familiar dynamics of titillation, scandal, and terror. They blur the difference between major and minor crimes, real and imaginary offenses, grievous injury and social nuisance. They keep the public in a perpetual state of agitation and watchfulness. Certainly, they provide distractions from what rational people have usually regarded as the real news: political deliberations about how to steer the ship of state, whether to go to war, and whose bread should be buttered. But they are not, as Gore suggests, without "impact on the fate of the Republic."[5] These stories provide an infinitely malleable template for the production of recurring narratives about victimization and innocence, the invention of new identities around these terms, and the manufacture of an inexhaustible need for ever more discerning modes of surveillance, supervision, and protection.

SEX! SCANDAL! STING! TELL MORE . . .

True stories of shocking victimization have played a role in the current state of affairs. But fakery also has played no small part in the production of panic as the steady state of serious public culture, as I will show in the chapters that follow. The basic mechanisms of panic can be readily appropriated and manipulated by the opportunistic, vengeful, or mad. As with fake documentaries or fake ethnographies, sex crime fakeries reveal something of the form they mimic and of the conventions audiences have come to crave.[6]

Sometimes the motives of actors in these spectacles are readily apparent. In 1989, when Boston resident Charles Stuart, a white man, killed his pregnant wife, Carol Stuart, also white, he initially told police that a black man had killed her. His false report played off racial and sexual stereotypes older than the Republic itself, triggering what can only be described as a police rampage in Mission Hill, a predominantly black section of town. Police arrested a suspect, whom Charles Stuart then "identified" in a lineup. The case might have wended its way toward a wrongful conviction—had Matthew Stuart not come forward to turn in his brother Charles for the murder.[7] A mainstay of U.S. history, the same phantom black man, out to harm white women and girls, has put in similar appearances in many other places. He is joined in the national morality play by a newer personae dramatis: the white pedophile, who is often homosexual, sometimes worships Satan, and occasionally takes female form.

Sometimes the motives of the actors in our national psychological dramas are murky or convoluted. An ongoing stream of professional puritans, "outed" as philanderers, drug addicts, or closet queens, then forced to do the walk of shame on the six o'clock news, testifies to the profoundly perverse character of some who would pose as guardians of innocence or paragons of moral probity. No doubt, stories about these fallen figures trade in schadenfreude; they allow tellers and listeners to revel in exposing the hypocrisy of others. These sad cases also reveal the capacity for recursive regression in sex panics. Whenever those most zealous about protecting innocence find themselves caught up in scandal, the typical result is not a reconsideration of the politics of fear and protection but panicked calls for greater zeal. "Scandalize the scandalizers" becomes the order of the day.[8]

Consider a prominent political case: conservative Republican Mark Foley chaired the House Caucus on Missing and Exploited Children; he had written legislation targeting suggestive depictions of minors on the Internet. He also sent sexually suggestive e-mail to House pages. The pages were all older than sixteen, the legal age of consent in Washington, D.C., a point sometimes lost in the ensuing brouhaha. But logically, Foley's request for a photo of a seventeen-year-old's erect penis, plus sexually suggestive e-mail sent from his Florida district, could have run afoul of federal child pornography laws or Florida solicitation laws (where the age of consent is eighteen)—had the applicable statutes of limitation not run out.[9] Engulfed in scandal, Foley took a cue from the prevailing script: he denied that he was a pedophile and went into rehab, accusing a priest of having molested him when he was a minor. Neither this move, nor the ambiguous nature of Foley's offenses (which involved no sexual relations with anyone younger than eighteen and were obviously definable as workplace sexual harassment but were not so clearly definable as criminal offenses), quelled the public's rage to punish, if web chatter is any gauge. User comments on the ABC News Web site include references to "shameless homosexual behavior" and calls for federal prosecution. Some writers savor the salacious details or express glee in condemning the fallen representative. One commentator writes: "Anyone ever see 'TO CATCH A PREDATOR' on NBC? If Mark Foley did not have the former House Speaker & GOP Leadership protecting him: HE WOULD & SHOULD BE IN JAIL! The man is a menace to young BOYS everywhere! HE IS A SEXUAL PREDATOR! HE SHOULD BE LISTED AS A SEX-OFFENDER! Sick man, that Mark Foley."[10]

The sense of scandal was much the same with the subsequent case of Senator Larry Craig, a right-wing Republican who was busted on disorderly conduct charges after he made eye contact with an undercover cop, tapped his toes, and fidgeted his fingers under the stall of a Minneapolis airport men's room. Transcripts of the police interview—played repeatedly on CNN and Fox News—show how officers of the law use high-pressure techniques to shame and coerce guilty pleas from toe tappers and finger fidgeters, even though the disgraced senator had neither propositioned the cop nor had engaged in any sexual exhibition or contact with him. It goes without saying that the senator from Idaho had posted a long record of opposition to gay rights and civil liberties, thus the theme of hypocrisy mined in so many editorials and commentaries. What might be less obvious, and thus bears drawing out, is how large the figure of the imperiled child loomed in the background of the case. Such "sting" operations, which entrap men far short of sexual contact, are no longer said to exist to prohibit or patrol homosexual intercourse; they are usually said to protect minors from witnessing sex acts or from being solicited. In fact, children, or even disinterested parties, are usually nowhere near the scenes of "public" lewdness in empty restrooms or remote sections of parks after midnight. Arrests typically target men who "[believe] they are alone or out of view" but who are observed by police using peepholes or hidden cameras, or who are responding to overtures from police decoys. The same authorities pursue heterosexual couples making out in parked cars with much less zeal. When authorities draw such distinctions between public and private, order and disorder, safety and danger, they reproduce mid-twentieth-century patterns of antigay harassment, certainly.[11] They also act in the name of the vulnerable child, whose demand for protection prods the construction of ever more expansive legal and institutional worlds. This imaginary child, examined by a number of academic queer theorists, is a recurring motif in sex panics.[12]

FEAR AND DESIRE IN THE IMAGINATION OF DISASTER

The problem I am trying to describe is both wider and more unsettling than what the Freudian terms "reaction formation"—the denunciation of what one secretly desires—and what other psychic defense mechanisms might suggest.[13] Sex panics display a form of magical thinking that anthropologists have sometimes called primitive and have more accurately described as a contagious or associative logic. That is, sex panics have a tendency to spread uncontrollably; they infuse other questions. Once the specter of sex has been raised, everything—a glance, a posture, a pat on the shoulder—becomes sexual. Scenarios of sexual predation leap into happenings far removed from any sexual scene.

Thus, in the wake of 9/11, sexual fear has colored the imagination of disaster in ways that reveal its misplaced, obsessive, and delirious character. When a 2004 earthquake in the Indian Ocean triggered a tsunami that killed more than 180,000 people, much of the resulting media chatter on twenty-four-hour news programs focused on the fates of a handful of missing white children whose families were vacationing in the region when catastrophe struck. Working to place the region's many thousand orphans in the households of extended kin—on the questionable theory that children are safer with their own uncles or aunts than with strangers—antitrafficking activists then took credit for preventing what never occurred: the wholesale abduction and sexual enslavement of grieving minors.[14]

Later, when Hurricane Katrina hit New Orleans in 2005, among the most sensational stories to be floated on Fox, MSNBC, CNN, and other U.S. news outlets were accounts of the predations of rapists and pedophiles at the Superdome, where city residents were miserably camped after failing to evacuate. The British press echoed the story, and the *Independent* introduced readers to Devan, an eleven-year-old boy who was forced to witness scenes of depravity "no child should witness." "I was scared," Devan is quoted as saying. "I knew that there was rapes going on and they said they were men snatching the boys."[15] Such vivid reports turned out to be entirely imaginary: feverish rumors and hearsay, converted into eyewitness accounts, conveyed as a delirium by journalists. Stories about the unraveling of the social fabric drew presidential notice. George W. Bush announced "zero tolerance of people breaking the law," a comment apparently aimed not only at spectral rapists and dreamed-up pedophiles but even at the real-life people breaking into shuttered stores to take the food and water that were not being supplied by the government. These and other fantastic tales of anarchy and social breakdown help explain the *Army Times*'s shocking headline: "Troops Begin Combat Operations in New Orleans."[16] And as if the travails of Katrina were not sufficiently horrific, authorities then publicly anguished for several days about the possibility that among the hundreds of thousands of displaced people relocated to other areas, uprooted sex offenders might acquire new identities, thus escaping the police surveillance and public scrutiny mandated under Megan's Law. Anxieties run riot in such imaginings and occasionally leave the ground of rational discourse altogether.

BUT IS IT GOOD FOR KIDS?

I am struck by how such imaginings, which conjure the world as a dark and terrifying place, cut against the real interests of children. When I was a boy, children roamed in packs, exploring fields, woods, and lakes. We sometimes encountered perils, no doubt, but in the process we learned how to negotiate danger and freedom. Today the idea that minors should be subject to constant adult supervision cuts against such vital lessons. This supervision appears mandated for ever older ages. A recent ad, sponsored by the National Youth Anti-Drug Media Campaign, invokes lurking "pedophiles" as a reason why parents should supervise their sixteen-year-old daughter's Web activities. Breaking with such parental oversight was once *the* rite of passage into adulthood.

"Playing doctor" and other forms of infantile sexual exploration were also once part of many children's socialization. But today many teachers, parents, and social workers tend to see abuse or violence in the most mundane forms of child sexuality. And because they fervently wish to believe that children are naturally asexual, these adults look for external or traumatic causes for childhood sexual curiosity or activity when it does appear. And so a *Houston Chronicle* headline matter-of-factly announced, "Juvenile Sex Cases on Upswing," citing the case of a ten-year-old boy charged with "aggravated sexual assault," which was said to have occurred about three months before his arrest. The paper quoted the director of juvenile probation for Montgomery County, Texas, as saying, "The most alarming thing here is the fact that so many (local cases) are (youth) of a much younger age—10, 11, 12 years old." He was not criticizing law enforcement for applying adult criminal charges to the trespasses of minors; rather, he was invoking a ubiquitous source of contagion in the new demonology: "Based on what kids say to us, I believe many of these youngsters are affected by unimpeded access to pornography, whether on the Internet or somewhere else." He then went on to suggest that some juvenile sex offenders "are themselves victims of sexual abuse and are repeating with other youngsters what they've experienced at home or elsewhere."[17] Nowhere in the article, or others like it, is there contemplation of how definitions of *sex, abuse,* and so on have come unmoored from plausible usage—thus producing, as Judith Levine shows, an apparent epidemic of "children who abuse."[18]

In the gloomy anxious world of overzealous child protection, it has become the responsibility of adults to anticipate even remote threats to children's safety and to take preventative measures. And where childhood is essentially reconceived as vulnerability, with children as a special class in need of protection, this is true not only when it comes to sex. In 2007 the New York City Council banned the use of metal bats in high school baseball games—on the theory that they are more dangerous than wooden ones but with no evidence that this is actually the case. Council member Lewis A. Fidler, chair of the council's Youth Services Committee and a key supporter of the bill, heaped praise on himself and the city for protecting the imaginary child from hypothetical danger: "We will never know what parents' child we saved by passing this bill today."[19] Such is the recurring illogic that spills across sexual and nonsexual domains.

VICTIMS AND THEIR ADVOCATES

I am struck too by the perverse appeal of the victim role. Nothing, it would seem, causes the individual to stand out against the mass more than a story of suffering, and nothing induces more empathy, goodwill, and other shows of social support than the claim that one has been victimized. Signs of this perverse appeal seem to be everywhere. In Madison, Wisconsin, a white college student staged her own kidnapping, producing such evidence as a knife, rope, and duct tape. The resulting show of state force was anything but a simulation: police combed nearby marshes and woods, with guns drawn, in search of the suspect she had described to the police artist.[20] In Durham, North Carolina, a young black woman falsely accused white members of the Duke lacrosse team of raping her—and in this case a cynical prosecutor whipped up media frenzy to ride the wave of public outrage to reelection, concealing exculpatory evidence along the way, before eventually being disbarred.

The flip side of the victim role is the victims' advocate, who reenacts a key part of what Susan Faludi calls the "guardian myth" of the United States. The retrograde racial and gender politics involved in guardianship could not be clearer. Historically, the guardian myth casts white men as protectors of white women and children; the villains of the piece were depraved red, black, brown, or yellow men. The drama of protection, a key text on the wresting of white civilization from sexual savagery, serves as a foundational national myth.[21] Its logic, deeply embedded in the national psyche, has been taken up time and time again, not only on the Right but also on the Left: by Victorian feminists and late nineteenth-century populists, obviously; by progressives and well-intentioned social reformers of various eras; and by assorted social movements from the late 1960s on. Sometimes the gender and racial roles are reversed: it will fall to white women or black men to protect the innocent—sometimes from the predations of rich white men. This drama will occasionally take homophobic form. After Dashiell Hammett introduced readers to Joel Cairo in *The Maltese Falcon,* the "bad guy" of novels and movies often has assumed the form of the "effete villain," who is subtly or not so subtly characterized as homosexual.

The 2006 Duke lacrosse case was ready-made for agitation among liberals, feminists, and progressives; it shows that sex panics are far from being a right-wing phenomenon. And even after prosecutorial vindictiveness had been fully established, a few progressive friends reminded me that some members of the lacrosse team *were* racists and that neighbors had reported team members' racist taunts on the night that the young woman claimed to have been raped. One colleague tells me he is convinced that *something* happened; another complains that rape shield laws were violated when the press reported a previous charge of gang rape the accuser had made, then dropped. A *Nation* article that specifically critiques what I dub "the victimology trap"—the need to see victims of injustice as pure, innocent, and good—seemingly disapproves of the accuser's subsequent harsh treatment in the tabloids (where she was called a liar): "Neither worthy nor apparently a victim, [the accuser] became fair game."[22]

Such statements remind me of a case twenty years earlier, and of the t-shirts that read "Tawana Brawley was right." In that case the fifteen-year-old black girl's charges so resonated with what we knew about institutionalized racism—and what we then believed about organized sex abuse—that some of her supporters clung to her version of events, even after the accusations were shown to be fraudulent.

These responses suggest something of the erosion of public discourse across the political spectrum: a realignment of core values connecting truth, law, and fairness. They smack of "presumption of innocence for me but not for thee," reversing the ideal of blind justice historically championed, with good reason, by the Left. Whether the white affluent Duke lacrosse players are understood to be good guys or bad guys is entirely beside the point. An accusation alone does not establish whether a crime has occurred. That remains for a dispassionate process of adjudication to decide. Under the best ideals of U.S. law, burden of proof falls to the prosecution, not the defense, and, moreover, that burden is a substantial one: proof beyond reasonable doubt that the accused is guilty. These legal standards stem from neither humanitarian soft-heartedness nor liberal soft-headedness; they serve as important safeguards against the power of the state to lock us up or take our lives. They are critically undermined whenever we side with "the victim" before any legal determination has been made that a crime has actually occurred or when we treat law as a political spectator sport in which everyone roots for the home team.

I dwell on the subject because there is today a strong temptation to regard sexual accusations that seem to convey wider sociological or political truths as more substantial, more credible, than those that do not. This urge to protect potential victims sometimes appeals to scientific techniques; some legal scholars have even argued that sentencing ought to be guided less by the gravity of the crime than by statistical predictions of recidivism.[23] I am profoundly skeptical of this approach. The tethering of punishment to imagined risks and anticipated future victimizations, as opposed to actual deeds and proven harm, would seem to set the law on a slippery slope. For instance, official statistics suggest that recidivism rates are somewhat higher for men who commit sex crimes against male minors than for those who commit them against girls; this statistical effect, based on small numbers, even includes comparisons with fathers who abuse their own daughters.[24] As a result of these associations, a simple scorecard used by parole officers in the California Department of Corrections and Rehabilitation automatically classifies "same-sex pedophilia" as "high risk," and this checkbox can be ticked irrespective of the age of the minor or whether force (or even sex) was alleged in the case. Factoids abound in this fraught area: Men are more likely to *sexually* abuse children than are women; the reverse holds true if the subject is *physical* abuse. Latino men are *said* to have a higher incidence of rape—or, at any rate, of rape convictions—than either black or white men. And so on.

There is good reason to be suspicious of such atemporal truths, which have been severed from the historical conditions and social apparatuses that produced them. For, above all, truth is a tricky business. Sociological truths are compounded by the accumulation of individual cases to yield crime statistics, recidivism rates, racial distributions, and so on—but aggregated facts cannot tell us anything about the facts of a particular case. They also do not speak to the process of their own assemblage. What if the definition of *crime* is becoming bloated? What if accusation, adjudication, and determinations of guilt in the individual cases are systematically skewed by fear or paranoia or the hunt for witches?

The reification of legal justice has deep roots in U.S. culture, of course. Americans have fetishized the law since the time of de Tocqueville, believing that unhappy situations or conflicted relationships could be made right by court order or a judgment for the plaintiff. And throughout American history, the court scene—legal justice—has served as substitute for other forms of social or economic justice. Not coincidentally, it also has served as a platform for the policing of basic inequalities: the outsized role of sexual accusation in race relations is famously depicted in novels like *To Kill a Mockingbird*. But even by U.S. standards, present-day legal fetishism departs from time-honored conventions of jurisprudence. Today there are more arrests, more prosecutions, and more convictions per capita than ever before (see chapter 5)—and still, legal fetishism continues to escalate, to run amok, to spiral out of control. Every tragedy, every horror story, it seems, becomes a social emergency, an occasion for the panicked drafting of new laws, each more exacting than the last. It is thus worth reiterating a few elemental, time-honored principles.

Legal truth is not sociological truth; its "norms" are of a different order from statistical norms, although both involve rule and measure. Even less is it political truth. Rational law, at its best, serves as a hedge against "what everyone already knows"—prejudice. The integrity of legal truth turns on being able to stand against moblike rushes to judgment. Whenever individual legal cases are made to shoulder the burden of either commonly held beliefs or wider social grievances, justice is subverted, by definition. No menace, no emergency, no fear warrants departure from these foundational principles.

FEAR ITSELF: SEXING THE ARGUMENT

Understanding the panic around sex provides a good starting point for comprehending just what has gone so terribly wrong in U.S. society. In this book I claim that the never-ending parade of sex panics provides an important model—part metaphor and part blueprint—for the pervasive politics of fear. In the chapters that follow, I hope to convince readers of several basic propositions. Let me spell out my argument up front, carefully stipulating some of the links among sex, crime, fear, and the waxing of the security paradigm—along with the waning of paradigms related to liberty or welfare—in government.

The wider backdrop of my study is the relationship of fear to government in the contemporary United States.[25] The policies of George W. Bush loom large in this picture. It has been said that in the wake of September 11, 2001, the Bush administration exploited fear in order to hijack U.S. democracy. Policies of preventative detention, torture, extraordinary rendition, and unchecked domestic spying clearly did expand the power of the state and diminished the rights of citizens (and noncitizens). But fear of terrorism, and the various legal and illegal responses to it, built on a series of overlapping scares involving crime: urban disorders in the 1960s, street crime in the 1970s, crack wars in the 1980s, predatory gangs in the 1990s, and terrorists in the 2000s. Each of these crime panics left its mark on U.S. culture and politics. Each precipitated new laws; each fostered a waxing hostility to civil liberties, rights of the accused, and due process; and each prepared the public to surrender ancient rights and legal protections in the name of security. Given the closely sequenced history of these perils, and given the extreme measures adopted in each case, it might be more accurate to refer to a routinization of panic than to a "culture of fear," as the sociologists usually have it.[26]

Put another way, although Thomas Friedman has observed that "9/11 has made us stupid," a wide-angle view suggests that this stupefaction was a long time in the making.[27] The United States has become a measurably harsher, more punitive place since the close of the 1960s because its citizens have become more fearful. Some fears are rational, of course, and horrible things do happen to people. But the perpetuation of a generalized state of panic in the face of falling crime rates remains to be explained.[28] And however fixed the relationship might now appear to be, nothing is natural about the connection between exaggerated fear of crime and excessive punishment (of offenders, suspects, those who might be deemed prone to crime, and others). The rage to punish follows only when other policy options (rehabilitation, redistribution, harm reduction) have been taken off the table. It becomes chronic when perpetually stoked by organized institutional actors. The problem here is a deep one, entwined in ongoing cultural, political, and economic shifts. Democrats as well as Republicans have contributed to this dynamic, which predates September 11, 2001, and will survive any simple changing of the political guard.

There will be objections to my thesis, which traces an ongoing, four-decade shift in U.S. political culture. Haven't Americans always been afraid? And hasn't this fear always set the stage for political repression, war, or communal violence? Fear, admittedly, is nothing new; I claim only that something is new in its institutional forms, uses, and effects. Perpetual fear mongering today produces measurable results: Americans now incarcerate, supervise, and track more people for longer periods of time than do the citizens of any other nation. The racial roots of these historically unprecedented "lock-'em-up" policies have been well documented.[29] I take the analysis further: sex and sexual fears have also figured prominently in the ongoing redefinition of norms of governance. The menace posed by the inscrutable evil of the (implicitly black) rapist, the (implicitly homosexual) pedophile, or the (supposedly irremediable) child abuser prods ever more extreme—and, I will show, increasingly irrational—security measures. This is, at core, what this book is about.

I hope that my overarching argument will not be misunderstood. I do not argue that sex panics have been of primary statistical importance in turning the United States into something resembling a police state. Nor do I argue that sex panic is the central mechanism of modern crime panics overall. Modern campaigns against sexual predation, as I am mapping them, actually got underway somewhat later than did the ongoing "war on crime." Although older ages of consent and enhanced penalties for a variety of sex offenses, plus new laws regarding sexual representation and new technologies, have goosed the numbers of those incarcerated, the avalanche of imprisonments was largely driven by draconian drug laws from the Reagan era and later "zero tolerance" policies for a host of offenses.

What I want to show here, in some detail, is that sex panics have become an important part of modern crime panics and constitute the part that liberals and civil libertarians have been most reluctant to critically engage. This reluctance has occult roots. Because sex crimes are understood as being different from other types of crime,[30] because they are viewed as being both uniquely horrific and uniquely widespread, exaggerated sexual fears have played an important part in stoking outrage and in cementing the prevailing story line around innocence, vulnerability, and victimization. The panic narrative is extended everywhere, is entrenched everywhere, in no small part because sex panics have developed its syntax and deployed its rhetoric into settings far removed from scenes of theft, street crime, or interpersonal violence. This story line reweaves some of the nation's oldest myths into new narratives of identity and danger.[31] It plots news of the national and international scene, passes for analysis in a dumbed-down public sphere, and serves as commercial entertainment for the masses. Chapter 1 sketches the sociology of panic and begins to suggest the role panics have played in shaping the nation; chapters 2 and 3 survey the modern history of sex panics in the United States.

Sex panics also represent the leading edge of the ongoing crime panics that continually prod repressive forms of governance. I will show how evolving sex crime laws embody radical assaults on rights, guarantees, and protections. As cases in point, recent statutes allow for the indefinite detention of convicts *after* the completion of their sentences, a practice hitherto deemed anathema to democratic law. In a growing number of cities and states, new laws throw sex offenders out of work and out of their homes, thus creating a permanent pariah class of uprooted criminal outcasts. Such measures are costly; they have drawn the attention of the human rights community, while even a journal as staid as the *Economist* has noted both the harshness and ineffectiveness of U.S. sex offender laws.[32] These subtractions from the norms of democratic law begin small and grow larger; no one can yet say where the hemorrhaging will end. This is of no mean significance for the rest of us. Chapter 3 shows how fear becomes law, and chapter 4 illustrates these points, for the rest of us, by way of a particular case.

The result of these cumulative trends, I suggest, is a culture obsessed with risk and addicted to panic. Key mechanisms of both the state and civil society have become dependent on the perpetual stoking of fear, the vigilant preemption of real and imagined threats, and the application of ever harsher penalties against ever more minor infractions. Legal norms, which are delineated, circumscribed, and finite, give way to legal normlessness, which is associative and lends itself to infinite replication. I call the resulting system of rule "punitive governance," a term derived from critical race studies and the sociology of crime literature, as well as from the historian Michael Sherry's pointed essay on the "punitive turn" in U.S. culture.[33] Chapter 5 takes a wide-angle view, situating sex panics in the context of broader crime panics. It defines punitive governance and traces some of its effects—in everyday bureaucratic procedures, the burgeoning of the penal state, and scattered surveillance techniques. Chapter 6 examines the war on terror, showing how sexual anxieties have inflected far-flung practices of the punitive state.

Over time these trends have produced new concepts of citizenship and a new sort of national identity. The new model citizen is neither heroic risk taker nor interested stakeholder nor even informed political participant; new model citizens are the survivor, who forever lives in trauma; the aggrieved victim, who cries out for bloody justice; the political subject defined by vulnerabilities and exposure to danger rather than by rights and freedoms. This citizen can call upon the state only to protect or punish, can alternate only between the emotional registers of fear and rage. Completing the pivot from specific instances to general trends, chapter 7 examines the rise of the new victimology in the context of an ongoing cultural shift.

If I am right, punitive governance represents a new political formation, one that increasingly subverts democracy, or at least its loftier ideals, while retaining its trappings. We thus need to know not just what punitive governance is but what it does. Historical research suggests that sex panics are especially likely to erupt during periods of economic stress or imperial crisis. In this regard they share something with generalized nervousness about violable borders, eugenic concerns about racial purity, and anti-immigrant hysterias.[34] On the face of it today's politics of fear would seem to serve as substitute for a politics of economic security: spectacles of criminal victimization divert attention from the violence of everyday business practices. Punitive governance thus buttresses a particularly savage variant of capitalism.

In *The Shock Doctrine* Naomi Klein argues that business interests and free-marketeers can impose their unpopular laissez-faire doctrines only by framing them as responses to disasters or crises.[35] Panic seems implicit in the construction of consent to privatization and deregulation, but what is missing from Klein's analysis, and others like it, is an adequate view of the dark side of social relations, which induces a broad section of the public to view itself as an aggrieved victim of criminal trespass but not of economic exploitation. This sense of insuperable victimization is the bleak medium that allows the slow-moving shocks of racial turmoil and sexual anxieties to produce their effects. How a truncated U.S. political spectrum exaggerates these effects is a key concern of this book: Anyone can see the role played by modern conservatives in whipping up racially and sexually coded fears. But what if liberalism, which begins by positing rights, is the seedbed of panics that result in the erosion of rights? Chapter 8 examines the relationships among capitalism, liberalism, and victimhood.

HOMOSEXUALITY

At the murky core of this book is the stigma of homosexuality. Historically, homosexuality has been associated with—defined as—crime.[36] This association, which spanned popular, medical, and legal cultures, was an important front in the regulation of family life and the production of middle-class values. Today opinion polls, public culture, and everyday experience suggest that overt homophobia is waning—but also that new, exaggerated fears are taking its place. Or do overblown fears of pedophile predators represent new ways of conjuring up and institutionally using homophobia, even while disavowing it as motive?[37] The one does not necessarily preclude the other, nor does it preclude new twists in how racialized sexual anxieties interact with homophobia in the social imagination. In tracing new twists on old plotlines, I am indebted to sociological research on "the culture of fear" and to gay studies scholarship that derived the concept of "sex panic" from the earlier sociological term *moral panic*.[38] My thinking also owes something to Lauren Berlant, whose essays show how the imperiled child has come to occupy center stage in the national morality play and how "narratives of rescue" have become the dominant justification for political action.[39]

The chapters that follow are a mix of fine-grained analysis, robust polemic, personal narrative, and ethnographic writing. The dominant voice is that of a participant in and observer of U.S. culture. I hope that readers will bear with the uneven, sometimes shaky, voice of the writer. How, after all, does one draw attention to the prevalence of minor infractions and the existence of false or delusional accusations in sex crime panics without beginning to sound unsympathetic to those who really have suffered awful abuse? I trust I have not been callous, but I am uncomfortable performing rituals of empathy with the victims, for reasons that will be clearer by the end of this book. Anyway, I hope to keep the text trained on a line of analysis, a trail of evidence, not on whether I am a caring or uncaring person.

Reasoning out the difference between good laws and bad laws would be a challenge under the best of circumstances—but how does one keep cool and composed, how does one avoid sounding shrill, when pondering whether one's own country is becoming a new sort of police state? Reflection on various experiences with panic, policing, and the justice system are crucial to the mix. Nothing, it seems, focuses the mind on abusive state power quite like seeing its action up close and personal. However, I am excruciatingly aware that this statement bears more than passing resemblance to the victimization narratives I rail against: "I have suffered, therefore I know." I worry too that the main thrust of my analysis will become caught up in what it attempts to describe, that my prose will come to constitute a panic about panic: a panic panic. I thus have tried to outplay and outrun that pervasive new plotline that derives authority from injury, insight from grievance. Let the reader judge this effort by the logic of its arguments and its observation of details, not by the wail of protest it embodies.

PART ONE

Sex Panic

If a monster is wandering in the world, we need to catch him,
imprison him, cage him. . . . There are, however, different
ways—none certain—of catching the monster.
—Antonio Negri, "The Political Monster: Power and Naked Life"

"It all seemed darkly funny at first." Or so claims the opening line of
a story published in the *Washington Post,* a story I take as illustrative.[1]
Eric Haskett, twenty-eight, had arrived early for a dinner date with his
girlfriend, Ali Huenger, twenty. Tired, and reluctant to risk falling asleep
while waiting for his date at her mother's home, Haskett napped for a
few minutes in his car, just a few doors down from his girlfriend's house
in Frederick County, Maryland. This innocent napping was to set in
motion a chain reaction involving snoopy neighbors, community vigi-
lantes, the Internet, various modes of surveillance (some plainly unlawful), local police investigators, and no fewer than three FBI agents.

SUBURBAN NERVOUSNESS

According to the *Post* article, the rural-to-suburban neighborhood was
already "on edge from reports [whose reports is not made clear] a month
earlier about a strange car lurking in the cul-de-sacs." And so a few days
after Haskett's nap, Stefani Shuster, thirty-nine, took preventative measures: She sent an e-mail message to her neighbors apprising them of
"an older gray box-style car that has been hanging out at odd times."
She reported that the car's license plate number had been given to police,
who had traced the car to Haskett—and to an address that was also the
home of a registered sex offender, Donald M. Sanders. Sanders had been
sentenced to five years' probation nearly six years earlier for having

sex—apparently, given the probationary sentence, without using coercion—with a fourteen-year-old male. The *Post* writer does not say exactly how Shuster obtained Haskett's name and address using his license plate number, nor does it tell readers whether anyone was investigating what appears to be a violation of privacy laws by someone working for the police or Department of Motor Vehicles. The reporter's tone is light throughout, but the article does offer a glimpse into the mingling of empirical fact with dark fantasy in modern America. It also shows how little it takes nowadays to ignite a full-scale state of panic. In her e-mail message, Shuster speculated about a relationship between Haskett and Sanders, then warned her neighbors: "He [Sanders] is most likely living with and borrowing this car from Haskett. . . . Please pass on this e-mail to as many people as you know in this neighborhood."

Multiple e-mail postings (one resident reported receiving the e-mail twenty times) and impromptu fliers handed out by members of the community at the local elementary school quickly sent word around the area that someone who might be a child molester was stalking the streets. Haskett was a gainfully employed man with no criminal record who was not under any criminal investigation. He had moved into a boardinghouse at about the time that Sanders had moved out. Now Haskett found himself under intense suspicion. It is unclear why local law enforcement, much less the FBI, should have launched investigations into Haskett's activities on the nervous twitchings of a nosy neighbor or even on the rantings of a latter-day electronic mob. "It blew me away that a federal agent was sticking a badge in my face," Haskett said. "*Three* agents, dog—like I'm the ringleader!" After answering questions and assuaging investigators' concerns, Haskett asked how he could clear his name. Logically, he feared losing his job—or worse. Law enforcement officials were not optimistic about repairing his reputation. "They said the best bet is to leave the area," Haskett reported. According to the *Post* article, Sanders had left the area earlier precisely because of this sort of community harassment.

Now one might imagine that participants in this collective hysteria would express remorse at the needless panic they had spread or at the intense anxieties they visited upon their hapless victim. After all, Haskett was a member in good standing of the very community whose urge to protect the vulnerable had precipitated such misguided actions in the first place. Surely, his utter innocence in the face of a gross misunderstanding would invite empathy. Nothing of the sort surfaces in the *Post* story. In the minds of the vigilant citizens, imagined victimization takes precedence over any real victimization. Shuster thus insisted that her intentions were good and gave the soccer-mom-turned-security-mom defense: "I have a family to protect. . . . My original e-mail was to inform people." Another mother, Scottie C. Burdette, forty-five, was more truculent. Hinting at a contagion theory of sexual predation—her "gut feeling" was that Haskett was not a sexual predator, but she thought he might be hanging around with one—she warned: "Don't [mess] with suburbia, because we will chew you up and spit you out."

Of course, it is clear that no one here had "messed" with suburbia. What is not clear, from the *Post* story, is why suburbia should be such a fearful, angry place to begin with.

POISONED SOLIDARITY IN THE HISTORY OF THE PRESENT

Other stories of the post–9/11 period could not be labeled funny, not even darkly so. By this time a most unfunny thing had happened in the American psyche—or at least in that part of the psyche that keeps watch over the neighborhood and monitors e-mail: what I shall call a "poisoned solidarity," defined by fear of others, had become customary. In this inversion of the usual norms of social solidarity, an "I" and a "you" are connected negatively, by mutual suspicion. Such anxiety is relieved, but only a bit, when vented on third parties, outsiders, Others. Associated with this paradoxical form of social glue would seem to be a willingness to believe accusations. I nurture my own suspicion, a working hypothesis based in part on Roger Caillois's ideas about vertigo, which mark the psychic proximity of terror to ecstasy in certain types of games and play.[2] We twenty-first-century Americans seem to be exhilarated by fear; we relish the magical power of the accusation, which, like a psychic atom bomb, flattens all that stands in its way; we savor the heady rush of panic as one might thrill to an amusement park ride.

Panic, for all its destructiveness, is also seductive, productive. See how the heroism of the security mom stands out against the terrors of imagined child victimization? See how the familiar practices of shunning, ostracism, and expulsion have been updated to vouchsafe communal purity in the age of digital communication? It would seem that the monster in the mirror produces and stabilizes a sense of who we are. Perhaps this has always been true for Americans. These social dynamics and psychic mechanisms seem to be intensifying.

Permit me, then, to tell the story of how America panicked, pausing here and there to describe key moments in the process, assess the damage, and map the changing social and political norms. In the next chapter I lay out a general approach to moral panic, its relationship to sex, and its exceptional role in U.S. history. Then, chapter 2, I examine the modern run of sex panics, which began in the 1970s and gained momentum in the 1980s. Next, I take up how Reagan- and Clinton-era sex panics reshaped institutional practices and legal codes. In the final chapter of this part, I examine an anonymous case in depth. What follows, then, are a series of arguments about sex and the anxiety surrounding it—but in the United States stories about sex are never entirely innocent of stories about race, and I shall try to be alert to these changing connections.

CHAPTER I

Panic

A Guide to the Uses of Fear

[W]e are only episodic conductors of meaning, essentially. We
form a mass, living most of the time in a state of panic or
haphazardly, above and beyond any meaning.

—Jean Baudrillard, *In the Shadow of the Silent Majorities*

"Moral panic" can be defined broadly as any mass movement that
emerges in response to a false, exaggerated, or ill-defined moral threat
to society and proposes to address this threat through punitive measures: tougher enforcement, "zero tolerance," new laws, communal vigilance, violent purges.[1] Witch hunts are classic examples of moral panics
in small, tribal, or agrarian communities. McCarthyism is the obvious
example of a moral panic fueled by the mass media and tethered to repressive governance.[2]

The manner in which moral panics operate is the stuff of both archaic and postmodern social forms. Moral panics bear some similarity
to what anthropologists used to call "social revitalization movements":
they represent more or less deliberate attempts to reconstruct social relations in the face of some real or perceived threat or against some
condition of moral decline and social disrepair.[3] Central to the logic of
moral panic is the machinery of taboo: nothing, it would seem, incites
fear and loathing, and initiates collective censure, more rapidly than the
commission of acts deemed forbidden, unclean, or sacrilegious.[4] Another
item from the anthropological curio cabinet seems germane: scapegoating is implicit in the full spectrum of panic's forms.[5] Sometimes the
person designated as the scapegoat is said to embody the moral threat in
some intrinsic fashion. Nineteenth- and early-twentieth-century theories

of degeneration held that some classes, races, or ethnic groups were biologically regressing or declining, and these notions formed the basis for
the eugenics movement and ultimately Nazism.[6] Alternatively, the actions of the designated scapegoat are said to constitute the moral
threat—usually in pernicious, conspiratorial, or occult ways.

For as long as I can remember, unidentifiable evildoers, sometimes
figured as satanists, supposedly have been spiking Halloween candy with
razors or poison. Fear of candy tampering was present at a low level in
the 1960s, grew in the 1970s, then exploded in the 1980s, along with
other imagined threats to children's safety.[7] Needless to say, such seldom
seen, often imaginary folk devils inspire complicated forms of rage.
Manufactured to be tracked, hounded, and pummeled, the scapegoat
can also serve as a repository of secret desires, his or her extravagant evil
a projection and condensation of widely distributed feelings.[8]

Moral panics generate certain well-known forms of political organization. Self-styled leaders of the movement—"moral entrepreneurs"—
convince others that containment, punishment, banishment, or destruction of the person or persons designated as scapegoat will set things right.
This is never the case. Moreover, the acute state of fear cultivated by the
movement's leaders effaces meaningful distinctions between threats real
and imaginary, significant and insignificant. Invariably, then, moral panics tend to escalate.

What Freudians call displacement is a recurring feature of moral
panics: panics often express, in an irrational, spectral, or misguided way,
other social anxieties. At the turn of the twentieth century, panics around
"white slavery" crystallized pervasive anxieties about the economic decline of the Victorian middle class and white skilled workers who were
native born. Social reformers fancifully imagined that white women
and girls were being kidnapped and forced to sexually service black,
brown, and yellow men.[9] In the 1960s the British press anguished about
the socialization of British youth—and thus the future of a Britain
recently divested of empire and great power status—in sensationalist reportage on youth subcultures: the Mods versus the Rockers. (In his land-
mark study of this phenomenon Stanley Cohen popularized the indis-
pensable term *moral panic*.)[10]

As these examples suggest, imagination plays a prominent role in
panic mongering. The object of panic might be an imaginary threat (the
devil, witches) or a real person or group portrayed in an imaginary manner (diabolized Jews, Negro satyrs, plotting homosexuals). And because
alarmed social actors give fantasy free rein in the contemplation of so-

cial ills and moral threats, panics can encompass in a single movement any number of forms of dread and loathing. McCarthyism is generally remembered as the "red scare," but the homosexual purges associated with it lasted longer and wrecked more lives than did the anticommunist witch hunts.[11] "Condensation"—the production of amalgamated, blurred, or composite figures in dream work or symptoms of a disturbance—is a perennial trait of moral panic. The objects of collective outbreaks of fear and loathing are complex entities: part real, part imagined; part one thing, part another.

MEDIA PANIC

Social theorists from Georg Simmel to Jean Baudrillard have suggested that panic is implicit in the structure of mass society. Writing at the turn of the last century, Simmel begins with the basic features of contemporary life: modern metropolitan subjects live among strangers and are constantly bombarded by stimulation. Of necessity, they adopt an indifferent, jaded sensibility, a "blasé attitude." These cool, aloof people in turn crave excitement, intense sensation, and are thus primed for what Todd Gitlin would later call "the media torrent." The mass media—newspapers, movies, and dime novels of Simmel's period—provided the requisite sources of sensation. Now, as then, news that shocks, scandalizes, or evokes fear and dread brings temporary relief from the tedium of modern life. However, these stories also quickly lose their power to excite, reinforcing the blasé attitude and stoking the need for ever more extreme forms of stimulation. In the culture of modernity, then, periods of panic will alternate with periods of social rest, and journalism, especially yellow journalism, plays a key part in setting the rhythm.[12]

For Baudrillard, writing in the late twentieth century, panic is rooted in a different sort of paradox: the circuitry of mass communication itself creates a longing for scenes that disturb or frighten. Baudrillard plants his analysis in a late-modern media-saturated world where everyday experience has been rendered increasingly full of simulations such as television shows, video games, online worlds—virtual realities. "When the real is no longer what it used to be," when reality threatens to disappear entirely behind its simulations, the postmodern subject responds with "an escalation of the true," "a panic-stricken production of the real"—in no small part through news stories that shock, titillate, or horrify. Sensational news serves as evidence of the real. But this news too enters the circle of simulation, which feeds more frantic longing, more frustrated desire—more panic—for the disappearing act of the real. Meaning is exhausted. The circle is closed.[13]

Under any scenario mass media are essential to the dynamics of modern moral panics, so much so that Thomas Shevory prefers the term *media panic*.[14] But not all media panics are the same. Fear and confusion propagate faster through radio and television than by way of mass-produced broadsides or flyers; the Internet is a more efficient means of converting anecdote into evidence than was the Hearst newspaper chain. Paul Virilio succinctly describes the implications of the change-over from type to electronic image: "Following the standardization of opinion that came with the nineteenth century, we are now witnessing the sudden synchronization of emotions. . . . Public opinion is supposed to be built up through shared reflection, thanks to the freedom of the press but, equally, to the publishing of critical work. Public emotion, on the contrary, is triggered by reflex with impunity wherever the image holds sway over the word."[15]

Today alarmist stories and sensational journalism play out in real time. As means of communication have speeded up and expanded, panics too have accelerated and intensified. Media conglomerates, institutional actors, and political factions all have a stake in the production and management of certain kinds of fear[16]; they provoke panic to sell newspapers, to forge "community," to curb dissent, or to foster various kinds of social discipline. All these factors tend toward the production of panic as the normal condition in the contemporary United States. And just as mass media create "publics," media panics tend to forge a certain kind of citizenship and a certain kind of state. When audience-communities become truly alarmed, they demand action, usually repressive action against a perceived enemy. So goes the logic of what Stuart Hall and colleagues have dubbed "authoritarian populism."[17] Panic, then, has become ever more intricately woven into the basic structure of politics and governance; it is a technique for running political campaigns, staging (in some cases contriving) and addressing social issues, and solving problems in a variety of communicative or administrative domains.

A great many—perhaps all—of the social reform movements since Jimmy Carter's presidency have taken the form of moral panics. An obvious example is the victims' rights movement, which promulgates true crime horror stories, advocates harsh criminal penalties, has become a quasi-official branch of law enforcement, and has reshaped judiciary practices across the board. A variant of this approach is embodied in Mothers Against Drunk Driving, an organization founded in 1980 by Candice Lightner after her daughter Cari was killed by a drunk driver. A quick look at the group's methods and aims reveals something of how the logic of moral panic can be applied to genuine, statistically significant problems. MADD draws public attention to the problem of drunk driving by using a communication strategy that puts a human face on highway fatality statistics; the organization succeeded early on at winning passage of the 1984 National Minimum Drinking Age Act, which prodded states to set a legal drinking age of twenty-one. Advocates of this approach point to a decline in fatalities associated with drunk driving after passage of the act, but correlation alone does not establish causation, and statistics from the international Organization for Economic Cooperation and Development do not lend obvious support to the idea that higher legal drinking ages are associated with lower traffic fatalities overall. (In fact, OECD data show that per capita and per vehicle highway fatalities are declining almost everywhere, more rapidly and to much lower levels in many developed countries that have significantly lower drinking ages than the United States.)[18] No doubt MADD's efforts have produced a greater public awareness of the risks involved in drinking and driving that has changed drivers' practices. But many alternative strategies might plausibly contribute to a reduction in traffic fatalities: improving the safety of automobiles, developing mass transit systems, requiring more extensive driver training (presumably to include modules on how alcohol affects driving), or raising the legal age for acquiring a driver's license. In practice, MADD emphasized an approach that played to themes of child imperilment and protection. And in the process what the organization unambiguously accomplished was the retrenchment of a temperance perspective in public life, a redefinition of the rights of adulthood, and an expansion of the domain of childhood.

Threats to child safety are a recurring theme in American public life.[19] During the 2008 Democratic presidential primaries, Hillary Clinton gave her campaign a new lease on life with the "red phone" ad: "It's 3 A.M. and your children are safe and asleep. But there's a phone in the White House and it's ringing." The sociologist Orlando Patterson has suggested that the ad, with its images of "innocent sleeping children and a mother in the middle of the night at risk of mortal danger," has a racist subtext; he compares the ad with scenes of peril from D. W. Griffith's racist epic *Birth of a Nation*.[20] Anything that touches upon the protection or socialization of children can serve as the stuff of panic, of course. But the logic of panic can also be instrumentalized in other, more subtle, ways. When the pharmaceutical giant Merck unveiled Gardasil, its vaccine against the human papilloma virus (HPV), the company was careful to present the new vaccine as a cancer prevention drug, not as a vaccine against a sexually transmitted disease. In the prevailing atmosphere the latter tack would have been tantamount to promoting sexual promiscuity. Instead, Merck's publicity campaign constantly invoked high levels of *male* HPV infection to trump the notion that marital fidelity offered women protection against HPV, which is associated with cervical cancer. In positioning the drug as a protector of girls and young women, Merck used an old story line: virtue, fallen to vice; vulnerable female innocence besmirched by male sexual diseases. Instead of opposing the vaccine, many religious and social conservatives embraced it.[21]

THE FOUCAULT EFFECT IN THE UNITED STATES

Because panics lead to new statutes, organizations, cultural templates, and various durable forms of social organization, their threads are woven into modern social life. Historians have suggested that white fear of violent slave uprisings contributed to the production of a durable culture of fear in the United States. During the eighteenth century, these anxieties were by no means restricted to the South. Fueled during the run-up to the Civil War, these anxieties laid the groundwork for a pervasive culture of *sexual* fear in the South, which was reinforced under Jim Crow.[22] Sexual fears, moreover, have underwritten the development of major state institutions. Radical critics of policing have stressed the role that nineteenth-century moral panics around prostitution and vice played in the definition of crime and the development of modern policing.[23]

Michel Foucault's *History of Sexuality* provides useful conceptual tools for thinking about moral panics in connection with race and class relations. To paint the picture in broad strokes, Foucault treats the role played by sex in class definitions and class struggles at the outset of European modernity. Aristocratic rulers of the old feudal regime had based their right to rule on kinship, descent, *blood*. In contrast, the rising bourgeoisie contested blood right and asserted its right to rule based on fitness, life force, *vitality*. The nascent class cultivated this vitality in myriad eighteenth- and nineteenth-century hygienic practices, and in those practices two methods repeatedly recur: one involves sexual abstention, prohibition—the repression of sex; the other involves the control, use, and productive disciplining of sex.[24]

The entrenched bourgeoisie, whose power today derives from its ownership of capital and the domination of capital over every sphere of economic activity, no longer relies on these procedures, but not so the striving middle class. And when bourgeois values cross the Atlantic, they gain an especially durable purchase. Because the United States lacks both an aristocratic tradition and a strong socialist movement, bourgeois values and identities are stamped indelibly everywhere. The white middle class has repeatedly asserted its claim to be the universal class, the class whose values are life sustaining, by keeping vigil against moral lassitude and by undergoing periodic purifications, renewals, and moral renovations. In these undertakings it has occasionally tilted against the "bluebloods," whose refined tastes and work-free money the middle class equates with sexual decadence, but the main adversaries of the middle class are the nonwhite lower classes (whose profligate sexuality and implicit criminality are held to threaten the social order from without) and white sexual deviants (who threaten the order from within).

The American Left has been no stranger to this middle-class sensibility, which is defined in part by sensitivity to moral and biological threats emanating from the lower classes. Missions of rescue and moral renovation thus have stamped various forms of patrician liberalism and middle-class progressivism. And because U.S. progressives, no less than conservatives, participate in an individualist tradition, liberal activists have tended to see social problems as being rooted in the bad thoughts or bad habits of individuals, not structurally embedded in economic or institutional arrangements. A recurring technique of liberal reformers, then, has been to sound alarms about graphically intense happenings that are statistically uncommon.[25]

Understood this way, moral panic serves as a recurring form of mass mobilization that has shaped U.S. society in distinctive ways over time. Political responses to perceived moral peril—traditions of moral uplift, temperance movements, rescue missions—necessarily embody a different class orientation than do the sorts of movements that built social democracy in Europe or leftist populism in Latin America: trade unionism, farmer-labor alliances, and social-democratic parties based in these movements. Movements of the former type aim to improve the lower classes from without, to imbue the dangerous orders with middle-class virtues; these movements eschew structural analyses in favor of moral pieties or draconian penalties. In contrast, socialist movements, when they are truest to their aims, tilt not against moral but *economic* crisis. They aim not to rescue society's most vulnerable from bad practices but to bring a class to power and to change the logic of the social and economic system.

Control, containment, or betterment of the lower orders is a recurring feature of panic politics in the United States. Yet another option is always possible. Whenever a race/class group perceives itself as being in crisis or in decline, its members can seek to revitalize or renovate themselves by applying the reconstructive logic of moral panic within their own communities. This too has been a recurring feature of American social life, with its periodic rediscoveries of the devil, satanism, and witchcraft in our midst, its episodic waves of revival, awakening, and reform.[26] The white middle classes have repeatedly reinvented themselves in this manner.

SEX PANIC AND SOME PROBLEMS WITH THE CONCEPT

In a 1985 essay on moral panics around sex, the gay studies historian Jeffrey Weeks sums up crucial points: "Sexuality is a fertile source of moral panic, arousing intimate questions about personal identity, and touching on crucial social boundaries. The erotic acts as a crossover point for a number of tensions whose origins lie elsewhere: of class, gender, and racial location, of intergenerational conflict, moral acceptability and medical definition. This is what makes sex a particular site of ethical and political concern—and of fear and loathing." Tracing the rise of the New Right and the explosion of the AIDS crisis, Weeks goes on to sketch how scientists, physicians, legislators, and religious authorities have stoked one kind of sexual anxiety or another to reshape social relations. "The history of the last two hundred years or so has been punctuated by a series of panics around sexuality—over childhood sexuality, prostitution, homosexuality, public decency, venereal diseases, genital herpes, pornography—which have often grown out of or merged into a generalized social anxiety."[27]

Problems no doubt arise with the concept of sex panic, as with any ideal type or heuristic device that attempts to frame disparate social happenings. Bruce Burgett has suggested that loose use of the term *sex panic* trades in a certain view of society as an "organic whole" that is subject to periodic perturbations and crises. The term tends to assume what actually needs to be demonstrated: the existence of a shared emotional response linking variously involved participants.[28] The point is well taken that a one-size-fits-all approach entails distortions. Some events associated with panic occur in the mass media (newspapers, television), others among highly organized groups (specialists, watchdog groups, political organizations), yet others in communities of various sorts (neighborhoods, viewing or reading audiences, general publics). The linkages among these sectors take different shapes in different types of social agitations, and the intensity with which dread propagates is also variable.

But I want to underscore a different point: the notion of moral or sexual panic is not inherently more problematic than that of economic panic. In the sorts of events described by either term, acute anxieties need not be uniformly or universally distributed to make their effects widely felt; they need only be sufficiently distributed among relevant social actors or well-placed institutional actors. Acute anxieties need not even be the "trigger" of precipitous events. During an economic panic holders or managers of stocks, bank notes, debt, or other forms of property initiate a disorderly sell-off based on the belief (which might be panicked or calculated, accurate or inaccurate) that others have been spooked by market conditions and will act to rid themselves of properties whose values are in decline. Actions by some prod responses by others. The ensuing crisis might or might not involve members of the wider public in bank runs, stock dumping, or hoarding. Either way, what is most spectral or speculative about economic panics is also what is most real about them: recourse to a common body of assumptions—to playbooks for how economic actors make decisions under certain kinds of conditions.

Actors in sex panics similarly make suppositions about the responses of others to certain events, representations, or arguments. The crucial links here are not mysterious nor do they require elaborate psychological models to explain them. When politicians draft new laws in response to sensational sex crime reportage, they act on the belief that a broad public's voting behavior either is or will be influenced by such and such events in such and such ways. Agitators, likewise, make certain assumptions about the reactions of others and attempt to reinforce the imagined reactions. In the give-and-take of action and reaction, the dynamics of moral panic are often less spontaneous than are outbursts of economic jitters. In her examination of local moral panics around sex education in U.S. schools, Janice M. Irvine shows how dire scenarios and inflammatory rhetoric serve to "heat up the climate, mobilize citizens, and draw attention to an issue"—that is, to pressure politicians, police, and others to respond to demands for action. In her reading, moral entrepreneurs work from a combination of set emotional scripts and conservative social norms to stage ritualized displays of anger and disgust. Public emotionality in these events represents neither mindless chaos nor psychological meltdown; it is a communication strategy, a normative behavior, and a form of moral suasion.[29]

The question is not whether an abstract, hypothetical "we" feel terror, either in individual or collective psyches. (Since panics reinforce only certain emotional patterns and social norms to the exclusion of others, it seems more accurate to say that a sense of community and its ways of feeling are the products rather than the sources of panic.) Nor is it a question of whether emotions on public display are authentic or contrived. (No doubt they represent a bit of both—with a certain energy produced by the rapid shuttling between the one mode and the other.) The point is that panic exists less within people than between them. Panic brings into being an organizational structure, a movement whose leaders grab headlines and build political clout by magnifying threats and advocating punitive measures. Not everyone need be involved in the production of panic narratives and the consumption of panic effects. All that is required is the interaction of various kinds of social and institutional actors to certain ends. Jeffrey Weeks describes the recurring elements, the general structure:

> The mechanics of a moral panic are well known: the definition of a threat in [an] . . . event (a youthful "riot," a sexual scandal); the stereotyping of the main characters in the mass media as particular species of monsters (the prostitute as "fallen woman," the pedophile as "child molester"); a spiraling escalation of the perceived threat, leading to a taking up of absolutist positions and the manning of the moral barricades; the emergence of an imaginary solution—in tougher laws, moral isolation, a symbolic court action; followed by the subsidence of the anxiety, with its victims left to endure the new proscriptions, social climate or legal penalties.[30]

SEX PANICS OF THE MID-TWENTIETH CENTURY

Estelle Freedman's 1987 essay on the emergence of the "sexual psychopath" as a figure in American popular, psychiatric, and legal cultures aptly illustrates the multilateral relationships among the mass media, law enforcement, citizens' groups, lawmakers, and established professions in moral panics around sex.[31] Retracing some of the links she establishes is worthwhile, as these connect past forms to current trends.

Fritz Lang's 1931 German film, *M*, in which Peter Lorre was cast as a compulsive child-murderer, stoked in the United States a popular interest in sensational reportage on sex crimes, especially murderous sex crimes against children. Thus was born the modern sex fiend. By 1937 the *New York Times*—whose writers were initially reluctant to wade into this journalistic swamp—had created a hitherto nonexistent index category, "sex crimes," to cover the 143 articles it published on the subject that year. That same year, FBI director J. Edgar Hoover called for "war on the sex criminal," asserting that "the sex fiend . . . has become a sinister threat to the safety of American childhood and womanhood." During the 1930s and again after World War Two, newspapers and magazines fanned imaginary brush fires of sex crime. In 1947, Hoover asserted, "the most rapidly increasing type of crime is that perpetrated by degenerate sex offenders" and went on to call for public mobilization. "Should wild beasts break out of circus cages, the whole city would be mobilized instantly. But depraved human beings, more savage than beasts, are permitted to rove America almost at will." Alarms were sounded in *American Magazine* ("Is Your Daughter Safe?" July 1947), *Colliers* ("The City That DOES Something about Sex Crimes," January 21, 1950), *Parents' Magazine* ("What Shall We Do about Sex Offenders?" August 1950), and many other sources.[32]

Local newspapers intensified their coverage of sex crimes. In his account of a mid-1950s sex-crime panic in Iowa, the journalist Neil Miller describes how the "otherwise staid" *Sioux City Journal* "offered a drumbeat of headlines" that played on fears of child kidnappings and child murders: "Link Man Held in Hunt for Boy to Sex Cases" (September 11, 1954; Sioux City); "Whole Town Hunts Boy, 4" (October 19, 1954; Powers Lake, N.D.); "Girl Murdered by Sex Maniac" (November 6, 1954; Norwood, Mass.); "Find Missing Girl's Blouse: Aunt Identifies Stained Garment; Uncle Mum" (November 21, 1954; Lebanon, Mo.); "Nab Suspect in Kidnapping of Youth . . . Jobless Man Admits Crime" (January 10, 1955; Freehold, N.J.); "Rapes and Kills Brother's Wife and Baby" (July 13, 1955; Jamestown, N.Y.). The newspaper demanded a crackdown: "Sioux city must be made the most feared town in America for the sex deviate" (July 12, 1955). An editorial cartoon depicted a small boy and girl walking through a jungle labeled "Our Cities." A threatening panther labeled "Human Depravity" and a giant snake labeled "Sex Perverts" obstructed their path. The cartoon's caption read "Civilized Jungle."[33]

Publicity bred action: arrest rates undoubtedly rose—not for the horrendous acts given prominent media coverage but mostly for assorted sexual offenses of a consensual, nonviolent, or less violent nature.[34] Despite the skepticism of many psychiatrists, new statutes were passed, and the "sexual psychopath" became the shared province of law enforcement and psychiatry. The new sexual psychopath laws built on

Progressive era legislation, which had created separate facilities for "mentally defective" prisoners in some states. During the first wave of sex panics, between 1935 and 1939, five states passed sexual psychopath laws; during the second wave, between 1947 and 1955, twenty-one more states and the District of Columbia passed these statutes. By the 1960s thirty states had passed such laws.[35]

Child rape and murder figured prominently in public discussions of sex offenses. These extreme events triggered mob attacks and the organization of citizens' groups or children's protective associations in a number of cities and towns.[36] They also stimulated wider preemptive measures. The rationale offered for sexual psychopath laws often stressed liberal aims: treatment, not punishment. But because every sex offender was viewed as posing the threat of violence, nonviolent offenders charged with sodomy and exhibitionism could also be incarcerated under sexual psychopath laws. Thus a connection between homosexuality and child murder was drawn; various psychiatric professionals, journalists, law enforcement officials, and popular writers explicitly equated homosexuality with sexual psychopathology and violence, either seizing upon isolated incidents or conjuring stereotypes about the seduction of innocents by oversexed perverts.[37] A *Newsweek* article began thus: "The sex pervert, whether a homosexual, an exhibitionist, or even a dangerous sadist, is too often regarded as merely a 'queer' person who never hurts anyone but himself. Then the mangled form of some victim focuses public attention on the degenerate's work." *Time*, in contrast, actually cautioned against conflation and urged calm, noting that statistics show that "progression from minor to major sex crimes is exceptional"; "only an estimated 5% of convicted sex offenders have committed crimes of violence." Later, presenting the results of a California study, the magazine acknowledged the difficulty in determining the scope and prevalence of sex crimes, since "most sexual acts which violate California's penal code are done in private by 'mutually consenting' adults." But *Time* then ambiguously noted that offenders "rarely repeat their offenses" after treatment—"except for homosexuals."[38]

In some cities media stories about child molestation and sexual deviation prompted roundups of known homosexuals; Neil Miller recounts the 1955 roundup and "treatment" of twenty gay men in Sioux City and surrounding towns after the murder of two children. John Gerassi describes how a male prostitution scandal in Idaho ballooned into a full-scale moral panic that same year; none of the fifteen gay men convicted in the ensuing witch hunt had used force, and some had violated the law only with other consenting adults.[39] The stakes were high in these outbreaks of hysterical homophobia. Long-standing sodomy laws prescribed lengthy prison sentences for men convicted of homosexual intercourse with a consenting adult: up to a year in New York, twenty years or more in fifteen states, and a life sentence in Georgia and Nevada. And broad new sexual psychopath statutes allowed lifetime psychiatric commitment for consensual adult same-sex acts, if the offender's desires were deemed uncontrollable. Treatment for sex offenders included group therapy, drug regimens, electroshock, and frontal lobotomy.[40]

Eventually, sex panics of the 1940s and 1950s subsided. McCarthyism ended, and the sexual and due process revolutions of the 1960s began. Catchall notions of sexual psychopathology were deemphasized or disaggregated, and some states retired the legal category of "criminal sexual psychopath." As part of a general revision of social boundaries around "normal" and "abnormal" sex, the slow process of decriminalizing consensual same-sex acts began. The Kinsey reports, first published in 1948 and 1953, served as important touchstones of this liberalization process, as did the American Law Institute's Model Penal Code, which was formally adopted by the institute in 1962. Sex, in a word, changed, and so did American culture.[41]

Still, sex panics of the mid-twentieth century left a lasting mark on American culture. First, they distilled an amorphous journalistic and legal category, "sex crime." Sex crimes can include such disparate acts as rape, child rape, statutory rape, fondling, a variety of noncoercive acts between adults and minors of various ages, public exposure, consensual sex between adults in a secluded section of a park, public urination, and—until recently—"sodomy." The vagueness of the concept, sex crime, which covers felonies and misdemeanors, facilitates the constant erasure of meaningful distinctions between violent and nonviolent acts, between acts that cause genuine harm and those that are merely socially disapproved.[42]

Second, the timing of events is suggestive of a shift in moral hierarchies and modes of coercion. Sex panics of the new sort took off during the 1930s, 1940s, and 1950s, that is, at about the same time that southern lynch law—which often had been applied against African American men accused of raping white women—went into a decline. Should we say that one regime of repressive violence has been replaced by another? If so, it was not replaced just any old way. The citizens' and parents' associations that came into being during sex panics of the Depression and McCarthy era were white and had vigilante functions, but they were not the lynch mobs of the Jim Crow South; these new mobilizations emerged in northern cities, midwestern and western towns, and along the West Coast. Sensational sex-crime stories of the new sort served to inflame the public to a state of rage, but their language bore only passing resemblance to traditions of racist incitement in southern newspapers. Something had remained the same, and something had changed. The relationship between old and new forms of fear mongering, policing, and vigilantism was—and remains—complex.

Third, then, and by extension, sexual psychopathology laws partially "de-raced" (or perhaps better yet "re-raced") the predatory bogeyman. In her survey of the period's crime studies and state commissioned reports, Freedman notes that sex offenders confined to mental institutions tended to be white men; they were often middle-class professionals. She thus marks the development of a racial double standard. Because black men were understood to be naturally or willfully violent, African Americans accused of rape were seldom held under sexual psychopath laws. They were sent to prisons or executed instead. White sex offenders, by contrast, were coded as "sick." They were confined to mental institutions and subjected to a range of treatments.[43]

This too is an old story with a new twist. In nineteenth- and early twentieth-century medicine, theories of "sexual degeneracy" purported to capture how a person might become "degenerate"—that is, how he might sink to a lower level, becoming unlike his own race or kind. These theories linked ideas about health to ideas about race and progress, and in these imaginings the sickness of the white sexual deviant was contrasted with the criminality of the black man: the former suffered from "too much" civilization, the latter from a "too little."[44] Stephen Robertson shows how newer Freudian theories of psychosexual development allowed psychiatrists to sustain these notions during the Depression and McCarthy era sex panics. The (white) sexual psychopath might respond to treatment because he suffered from arrested development or had regressed to an infantile stage; however, the (black) bestial rapist could not respond to treatment because immature sexuality was a normal trait of African Americans.[45] Mid-twentieth-century sex panics thus intensified certain ideas about race and sex, and their class form recalls something of the dynamic Michel Foucault describes from an earlier era: when sexuality was "medicalized"—brought under the purview of medicine and psychiatry—during the nineteenth century, the new sexual disciplines were applied first to upper and middle classes, then later extended to the lower orders.[46] Perhaps, then, the whiteness and middle-class status of the sexual psychopath suggests not merely that white convicts were treated more leniently than black ones but that a far-reaching redefinition of sexual mores and disciplinings was underway.

Fourth, mid-twentieth-century ideas about sickness and treatment took shape in a definite social context, and this context has proved replicable in many ways. Freedman's analysis suggests that three fears were overtly expressed in mid-twentieth-century sex panics:

- Fear of a roving, predatory, and violent male sexuality—which must be checked, kept in bounds, by new laws, new signposts against transgression—expressed social anxieties about the predations of rootless men during the economic disruptions of the 1930s. The resurgence of such fears in the 1940s signaled the curbing of women's wartime rights and freedoms and the reestablishment of "normal" gender relations.

- Fear of nonconformity in general was especially high during the second wave of sex panics, which occurred during the McCarthy era.

- Fear of homosexual contagion acquired a new salience in discussions of the sexual psychopath.

This last fear bears closer inspection.

Under the new theories of sexual development, with their ideas about normal "stages" and pathological "fixations," the notion of homosexual contagion provided a seductively simple explanation for the occurrence of sex crimes. Thus, in 1938, a popularizer of the new theories wrote that if a boy "happens to be seduced by a homosexual . . . and finds the relationship satisfying, he may become fixated in that direction and it may be next to impossible to change the direction of his sexual drive after that."[47] The authors of a 1948 article in the *American Journal of Psychiatry* claimed that when homosexual adults engaged in sexual relations with teenage minors, "the minors in turn corrupted other minors until the whole community was involved." As evidence of the disastrous consequences of homosexual contagion, the authors cite the case of a boy who killed a younger boy for refusing to perform fellatio on him. Another author states flatly: "All too often we lose sight of the fact that the homosexual is an inveterate seducer of the young of both sexes, and that he presents a social problem because he is not content with being degenerate himself; he must have degenerate companions and is ever seeking for younger victims."[48] Associations of homosexuality with contagion and intimations of murder pile up in popular writings. A police psychiatrist wrote, "The homosexual will murder his victims during an act of sexual frenzy and afterwards rob him," and Philip Jenkins describes how accounts of recruitment were eventually boiled down to what one journalist called "the vicious circle of proselytism": yesterday's young victims become today's sex criminals.[49] The idea that homosexuals were "fixated" at a lower stage of sexual development had important consequences, then: it identified gay men as a variant of the violent sexual psychopath, and it fostered a recurring story line about seduction and recruitment. It thus played a key role in portraying homosexuals as a physical and psychic threat to children.

Mid-twentieth-century sex panics both perpetuated and revised long-standing ideas about race, sex, and vulnerability. They also refined and focused certain institutional mechanisms involving media, citizens, expressible demands, and the state. Sensationalist reportage of statistically uncommon occurrences triggered, as though by Pavlovian response, the formation of vigilant citizens' organizations, demands for police protection, and the writing of laws that failed to discriminate between serious and minor offenses. Key institutional actors fanned the flames of fear: to sell newspapers, to build political careers, to expand the powers of the state. Panic, which is nothing new, attached to sex in a new way, acquired a certain salience, a certain institutional permanence.

In decline through the 1960s, all these elements would be taken up again in the mid-1970s.

CHAPTER 2

Innocents at Home

How Sex Panics Reshaped American Culture

No passion so effectually robs the mind of all its powers of
acting and reasoning as terror.

—Edmund Burke, *On the Sublime and Beautiful*

Fear of lawlessness was running high by the late 1960s, a time of escalating crime rates and social unrest. Full-blown sex panics were slower to develop, but these were already incubating in conservative reactions to the decade's generational conflicts. Sex, manifestly, was in contest: Hippie experimentation with clothing and coiffure bent established gender norms, the antiwar movement confronted social conventions associated with militarized masculinity, and the very idea of free love took aim at the underpinnings of the moral order. Still, sex was only one of many nervous sites along a wider generational divide. Moral entrepreneurs who railed against the feminization of American males were largely restricted to rural backwaters, and, overall, the liberalization of sex laws and the relaxation of rigid conventions were still the main trends.

Outlines of modern sex panic also were taking shape in discussions of race. The 1965 Moynihan Report on inner-city decline sounded alarms about what it deemed the dysfunctional family structure, reversed sex roles, and profligate sexuality of African Americans. The "deterioration of the Negro family" is at "the heart of the deterioration of the fabric of Negro society," the report asserts and then warns that poverty alleviation programs have the unintended effect of undermining traditional marriage, thus tightening "the tangle of pathology" afflicting black America. Such theories of underclass poverty signaled an impending retreat from the period's welfare state liberalism and spurred an important paradigm shift in public rationales for race/class inequality.[1] Ideas about sexuality and its proper disciplining were displacing expressions of overt racism in the construction of moral hierarchies; the resulting distinctions still produced racial pecking orders but without being wholly reducible to race. Such theories also supplied a reusable blueprint for ideas about sex and social breakdown in general. Once sex outside marriage, female-headed households, and flexible patterns of kinship were identified as either symptoms or causes of social disorder, all that remained was to apply this narrative of peril to wider trends affecting white working- and middle-class communities. And this is exactly what happened.

THE RISE OF FAMILY VALUES ON THE RIGHT

Over time sharply rising divorce rates, changing gender roles, and a long-term increase in the number of working mothers positioned the condition of the family as a central concern of politics. Antifeminist campaigns against the U.S. Supreme Court decision in *Roe v. Wade* (1973) and against passage of the Equal Rights Amendment first crystallized pervasive anxieties about the decline of the white heterosexual nuclear family. Crusades against gay rights heated up the rhetoric and sent the politics of cultural backlash into overdrive. These struggles signaled a changing political climate and were the proving grounds of the nascent religious Right.

The positionings of evangelical conservatives expressed a first open, then hidden, connection between racial and sexual politics. Those of us who grew up in the rural South during the 1960s and 1970s recall how the modern religious Right emerged in white fundamentalist churches as an organized backlash against the civil rights movement. In the wake of federal desegregation orders for public schools, conservative churches hastily set up a network of all-white private Christian schools; these schools were often linked, sometimes indirectly, to segregationist colleges such as Bob Jones University. The incipient movement, which began in southern suburbs, small towns, and rural areas, gradually developed connection, coherence, and scale through various preachers' radio and television ministries and perhaps especially through marches in support of the Vietnam War. These developments prepared the way for national organizations such as the Moral Majority and the Christian Coalition.

The nascent movement steadily downplayed its segregationist roots, then found enduring form in its 1970s campaigns against abortion, feminism, and homosexuality. By the late 1970s a movement born in the struggle to preserve segregation had largely "de-raced" its rhetoric, and movement leaders sometimes even attempted to claim the mantle of Martin Luther King, asserting that the rightist family values movement represented a "civil rights movement" for Christians. Still, the link between sexual anxiety and racial imaginings of disorder occasionally surfaced in sermons and homilies. The televangelist Pat Robertson once famously contrasted the idyllic home and family life of Christians with "the flotsam and jetsam of the ghetto where young people don't know who their parents are."[2]

The figure of the white child stood at the center of the transformation from racial to sexual politics, first imperiled by federal desegregation orders and a miscegenational future and later by gay rights and women's reproductive freedom. Apprehensions about the reliability of marital bonds, maintenance of cultural hygiene, and, above all, the stability of "natural" hierarchies and rigid moral distinctions were given expression through homilies on the vulnerability of children. Often, movement leaders staged their propositions not by way of claims, evidence, and logical deduction but by way of an associative logic. Sermons equating feminism with witchcraft or perceiving homosexual conspiracies in asexual children's cartoons were not rhetorical lapses but expressions of this logic. Televangelists' scenarios of divine retribution (hurricanes, earthquakes, terror attacks) for sexual infraction (feminism, homosexuality, abortion) planted squarely in the age of mass communication what anthropologists have sometimes called magical thinking. In the rhetoric of the New Right, sex became the recurring occasion for the conflation of cause and effect and for the projection of a world ruled by fear. In short order sex panic became the enduring technique of the modern conservative movement—its minimal form, its very essence.

The Return of the Predatory Pervert

Overt homophobia was rampant in sexual alarms of the period. Anti-gay incitements were especially pronounced in the mid-1970s, when social crusades launched in the name of child protection gave new life to old themes of predation, despoliation, and contagion. These campaigns would set the terms for later, less overtly homophobic panics to follow.[3] Of course, the new campaigns against homosexuality were very differently situated than those of the mid-twentieth century: they aimed to turn back the clock on gay visibility and sexual tolerance, which many viewed as the most dramatic causes of family breakdown and child imperilment. Two homophobic sex panics of the period stand out.

In the mid-1970s local antigay groups successfully mobilized to repeal gay rights ordinances in several cities across the United States. Marching under the banner "Save Our Children," these groups tilted against "homosexual recruitment" of youth by older gays. The Reverend Jerry Falwell and Pat Robertson made their national debuts in these struggles, and Phyllis Schlafly, a veteran campaigner against the Equal Rights Amendment, also put in appearances. Anita Bryant, the former beauty queen who sparked the original repeal effort in Dade County, Florida, famously explained: "As a mother, I know that homosexuals cannot biologically reproduce children; therefore, they must recruit our children." At a rally in Miami, Falwell told the crowd: "So-called gay folks would just as soon kill you as look at you." Such incendiary propositions depicted antidiscrimination laws as a threat to the safety and well-being of children and vilified gay schoolteachers, in particular, as potential child molesters. Falwell's rhetoric was especially inflammatory, referring to gays as "brutes" or "beasts" while conjuring images of "rejoicing in heaven" at their destruction. (Twenty years later the rhetoric was not much changed. As late as 1997, Falwell roared: "If we do not act now, homosexuals will 'own' America! If you and I do not speak up now, this homosexual steamroller will literally crush all decent men, women, and children . . . and our nation will pay a terrible price!")[4]

In fact, gay men are no more likely to sexually abuse children than straight men.[5] And child molestation is in no small part a family affair: the most common form of child sexual abuse is incest. Research findings vary, but an exhaustive study of sex offenders in prison suggests that nearly half the perpetrators of sexual abuse are family members or close relatives of the victim. Most of the rest are friends or acquaintances of the victim's family.[6] But then, as now, sex panic rhetoric was shaped by ideological imperatives. The religious Right and other social conservatives drew on long-standing stereotypes to conjure sexual threats to children's safety and well-being outside the family and its community. This homosexual menace was loosely construed; it need not involve any direct physical contact. The mere presence of homosexuals in the vicinity of children was alleged to have corrosive, harmful effects. Openly gay adults in the classroom or anywhere in public would confuse children and divert them from the path to normal heterosexuality. If childhood was to be protected, it must be kept free of homosexual contagion.

During the same period exposés about teenage male prostitution and involvement in pornography evoked earlier sex panics and embodied, in another sort of way, the nascent backlash against gay liberation. Actually, male prostitution was an old story, not a new one. Gay history, letters, and literature—including John Rechy's celebrated 1963 novel, *City of Night*—attest to the long existence of a subculture in which sexually mature adolescents and young men receive money for sex. The usual form of these exchanges leaves the younger party's sexual identity intact: he receives cash for submitting to fellatio, not for performing it. Some of these youth will be heterosexual adults. Others will develop gay or bisexual identities, acquiring along the way long-term lovers who serve as mentors. Public interest in this phenomenon has waxed and waned for many decades. But in the 1970s youth advocates floated vastly inflated claims to shock the public into action: large numbers of teenage males were said to be engaged in "hustling." In its 1975 cover story on the gay movement, *Time* invoked parental alarm at gay liberation and cited "estimates that more than 100,000 American boys between the ages of 13 and 16 . . . are actively engaged in prostitution." In 1977 the *Chicago Tribune* ran a much-quoted series on "a nationwide homosexual ring with headquarters in Chicago [that] has been trafficking in young boys." Kenneth Wooden, director of the National Coalition for Children's Justice, testified before the U.S. House of Representatives in 1977 that "most agree that child sex and pornography is basically a boy-man phenomenon." The historian and religious studies scholar Philip Jenkins traces the double effects of such claims: stories targeting gay men offered "a rhetorical weapon of great power" to youth protection activists who were campaigning against child pornography, trafficking, and other forms of exploitation. At the same time these stories were fuel to the fire for antigay activists, who "drew powerfully from the contemporary exposés of sex rings involved in pornography and prostitution." The two movements "inevitably contributed to each other." In concert they fanned the impression that sexual toleration had gone too far and that American culture was spinning out of control.[7]

This revival and intensification of Victorian tropes around sex-as-despoliation was reflected not only in sensationalist journalism but also in period books like Robin Lloyd's *For Money or Love*.[8] But these new depictions represent a curious change in those tropes. Whereas the

despoiled nineteenth-century subject who lacks sexual agency, is traumatized by sexual initiation, and is seduced into a remorseful life was
female, now this stock character was male. In a world reshaped by gay
visibility, then, the need to be alert to threats to his heterosexual future
was not only the responsibility of the teenage male; it also became the
responsibility of parents, teachers, and other adults to be watchful for
signs that his destiny might be compromised.

I note the development of a race/class double standard, in this case a
historically sequenced one. After World War Two male hustling appears
to have been pushed "downscale." Anecdotal evidence suggests that in
large urban areas, it became increasingly identified with black and
brown teenagers from economically marginal families. In midsize towns
and suburbs it was identified with white delinquents—"hoodlums"—
and lower-working-class youth. During this period the practice was
treated largely as police business, a criminal matter, if authorities took
notice of it at all. But during the convulsions of the 1960s, when homeless middle-class "flower children" flooded the cities, male prostitution
came to be identified with white teenage runaways. Hustling thus
moved upscale in sync with the crisis of traditional authority in the
1960s. Authorities subsequently discovered the "epidemic" of (white)
teen male prostitution during the assorted economic crises of the
1970s—a time when the unsettled future of white heterosexual manhood seemed emblematic of the uncertain future of the nation. The rescue of missing children and their restoration to the bosom of the family,
not the punishment of delinquents, then became the prevailing approach, and hustling increasingly fell under the aegis of a new breed of
social workers, children's advocates, and assorted providers of social
services.[9] This new approach resonated well with the emergent family
values politics of the period—outside the safety of the hearth lurks a
predatory homosexual stranger—but it had little to do with the actual
lives of teen runaways, whose experiences with family neglect, violence,
and homophobia typically had caused them to run away from home to
begin with.

Overtly homophobic sex panics of this period turned on the idea that
youth was—or ought to be—a time of sexual innocence. This innocence
was a vulnerable treasure: an idyllic past, an imagined future, capable
of being snatched away at any moment. If such innocence was planted
most firmly in childhood, it could not help but encounter peril during
adolescence. This crisis, and the dread it aroused at a time when teen-

agers were engaging in sexual experimentation at younger and younger ages, stimulated the countervailing adult response: fortify childhood, subject it to greater surveillance, progressively extend the domain of innocence to ever older ages. If there was something old in this notion of innocence, there was something new in its explicit attachment to masculinity. Sexed as male and raced as white, this notion of innocence inaugurates many current conventions for talking about teen sexuality, child sex abuse, and irreparable harm to the person.

The Innocence of the Child

By 1981 political tides had turned decisively to the Right, certain associations had become unimpeachable, and a newly Reaganized *New York Times Magazine* published an excerpt from Marie Winn's book, *Children without Childhood*. Titled "What Became of Childhood Innocence?" the article purports to explain how childhood innocence—largely defined as sexual innocence—was collectively lost in a permissive culture.

> Without a doubt, the upheavals of the 1960s—from divorce and the breakdown of the family, to women's liberation and increased employment—weakened the protective membrane that once sheltered children from precocious experience and knowledge of the adult world. Above all, television, virtually uncontrolled in all but a minority of homes, has caused children to gorge on the fruit of knowledge. . . . As adult culture sloughs off layer after layer of vestigial Victorianism—in books, in rock music, in all aspects of daily life—children are absorbing new information, and that touching trust once synonymous with childhood fades into premature skepticism and uncertainty.

In Winn's account homosexuality and knowledge of it seem to have a special relationship to this fall from grace. Her sixty-five-hundred–word piece contains no fewer than four distinct references to homosexuality, vignettes designed to document the harmful effects on children of its treatment in television shows, movies, youth novels, and public culture in general. Winn quotes a seventh grader as saying: "I watched this special on TV called 'Gay Power,' and they showed this stuff about sadism and how one homosexual takes another as a slave. The scary thing was that it was real, not actors dressing up. And then in school, when some girls had a sleep-over, everybody called them lesbians. It just makes us all nervous about being touched, and some kids are worried that they might turn out to be homosexual." Such placements of homosexuality in arguments about public culture and family life, and the unease they are intended to evoke in readers, do much of the rhetorical work of the piece. And, like the seventh grader worried about homosexuality, most children quoted in the piece are actually adolescents.

Winn's arguments are not the frustrated flailings of a television preacher. The author makes the obligatory nod to Philippe Ariès and other historians whose research shows that "childhood" is a social construct and not a natural category.[10] Children, she acknowledges, once came into adulthood and adult responsibilities at far earlier ages. The "protective membrane that once sheltered children" is thus presented as an artifact of middle-class civilization, not as a natural law. The author's trump card, presented at the end of the piece, is that a failure to patrol the line between adulthood and childhood augurs a lapse into sexual savagery. She concludes (with no evidence to support her claim) that, in a society with less differentiation between adult content and children's worlds, "we cannot fail to observe that child abuse, child neglect, child exploitation are again on the rise, and that the lives of great numbers of children have become more difficult."[11]

Such associations began a new series of agitations around sex and minors. Some would involve the usual suspects: predatory gay men who lurk in spaces outside the family. Aberrant happenings would bolster this framing. When John Wayne Gacy was arrested in 1978, eventually to be charged with the rape and murder of thirty-three adolescents and young men, a succession of news stories planted the homosexual monster at the center of garish sex crime narratives. Other hysterias would encompass large numbers of straight men and—because they work with children—women. Again, a racial dynamic at variance with other crime panics inflects these sex panics. Because so many of these perturbations occurred in suburban, small-town, and rural areas, accusers *and* accused were disproportionately white and middle class. If the old-fashioned heterosexual rapist was implicitly imagined as black, the new predatory pervert, who specialized in outrages against children and obscure predilections, was almost invariably conjured as white.

SATANIC PANIC

The most spectacular of these modern child sex panics were the "satanic ritual abuse" scares of the 1980s. Actually, satanic ritual abuse (SRA) combined several ongoing panics into a terrible maelstrom. Let me describe here some elements that ultimately produced the pandemonium. My account draws on framings by Debbie Nathan and others.

Episodic "satanic panics" would seem woven into the fabric of Christianity. Historically, these panics have been associated with the fear of strangers, suspicion of strange ideas, and the dread of mysterious economic power or uncontrollable social changes. In the wake of the social upheavals of the 1960s and economic crises of the 1970s, rumors of witchcraft and devil worship had fanned across rural Christian evangelical communities. McDonald's magnate Ray Kroc was rumored to have been a satanist; Procter and Gamble's arcane logo was rumored to be an occult symbol; various rock bands were imagined to be winning converts to Satan by embedding secret, coded messages in their songs.[12]

In a more secular vein anxieties around cults—sometimes linked to the occult—had been on the upswing since at least the late 1960s, a period when the young were intensely interested in Hinduism, Buddhism, and eastern mysticism in general. This embrace of "exotic" religions was connected to a much wider generational rebellion, and members of America's white middle classes had reason to fear that their children would reject sexual temperance, the Protestant work ethic, social conformity, and other middle-class virtues. These fears were greatly inflamed when Charles Manson and his followers murdered the actor Sharon Tate in 1969, and again in 1978 when followers of the Reverend Jim Jones committed mass suicide in Guyana. (Accounts of how Jones used his pastoral authority to sexually abuse male and female members of his church circulated widely.)

Some factors that fed into the SRA panic reflected less fantastic concerns. During the run-up to the SRA panic, awareness of child neglect and maltreatment, including sexual abuse, had been growing on several fronts, and rightly so.[13] But from the beginning the rediscovery of child maltreatment betrayed a consummately American understanding of social problems, which framed abuse as an individual illness or moral aberration, distributed equally throughout all social classes. In fact, some parents from every walk of life will occasionally be cruel to their children, but serious abuse and neglect are strongly correlated with poverty, unemployment, and economic turmoil. Barbara Nelson thus shows how mid-1970s legislation around child abuse marked an epochal shift in modes and rationales for state action. In projecting "private deviance" as a "public issue," and in defining abuse as a pressing issue for all social classes, child abuse legislation marked a significant retreat from the systemic, sociological approach of welfare state programs of the immediately preceding period. The new laws addressed "symptoms" while obscuring underlying causes and put a decidedly liberal (not social-democratic) face on the campaign for child welfare. Not coincidentally, this approach also fostered ever broader definitions of abuse.[14]

These skews multiplied when the focus of public attention shifted from physical abuse to sexual abuse. Early on there were distortions in the definition, scope, and identities of perpetrators of sex abuse—which, all studies show, constitutes a very small subsample of child maltreatment overall. Although most feminists recognized that children were more likely to be abused (sexually or otherwise) inside the home than outside it, some feminists were using expanded definitions of *sex, abuse,* and *children* to develop wildly inflated estimates of childhood sexual abuse.[15] And some were equating sex with harm outright.

By the early 1980s antiabuse activism and antipornography crusades, ongoing since the mid-1970s, had spurred the development of an increasingly puritanical sect of cultural feminism—a variant whose rhetoric bore little resemblance to either the sexual liberationists of the early second wave or the antiviolence, rape crisis activists of the late 1960s. In a notable feminist broadside from the mid-1970s, Susan Brownmiller had portrayed rape as paradigmatic of relations between men and women and depicted incestuous child abuse not as the pathological exception but as the normative rule under patriarchy.[16] Rhetorical excesses tended to acquire literal authority, fostering practical consequences. By 1982, Nathan notes, some feminists and child advocates were using definitions of consent and coercion developed around discussions of father-daughter incest—a situation where power inequalities are manifest and extreme—to portray any erotic contact of any sort between unrelated adults (of any age) and minors (of any age, including advanced teenagers) as the moral equivalent of incestuous rape.[17] Others went so far as to define penetrative sex, tout court, as tantamount to rape. Andrea Dworkin thus famously depicted penile intromission as synonymous with violation: "The vagina . . . is muscled and the muscles have to be pushed apart. The thrusting is persistent invasion. She is opened up, split down the center. She is occupied."[18]

Such daguerreotypes of male depravity and female purity divested women and minors of sexual imagination and revived motifs from white

Victorian feminism. They also mirrored trends on the cultural Right. Social conservatives were taking a keen interest in abuse and neglect as signs of personal disorder and symptoms of the "breakdown of the nuclear family," and religious conservatives in particular were invoking sexual dangers to urge a return to traditional feminine ideals of domesticity and motherhood. During the 1970s and 1980s, then, religious conservatives developed a network of Christian psychologists and therapists who often attributed adult emotional problems to childhood sexual trauma.

Sexual danger made for strange bedfellows. Carole Vance has described how active political collaboration between antisex feminists and evangelical Christians began with campaigns against pornography.[19] Feminists supplied the politically expedient argument that sexual representations were inherently debasing and constituted a form of discrimination against women, aiding the passage of antiporn laws in several cities across the country. This collaboration accelerated a wider shift in sexual attitudes among the white middle classes and would prove key to the revival of outsized fears of a violent, roving, predatory male sexuality; such efforts would intensify during assorted child sex abuse panics of the 1980s and 1990s.[20] Meanwhile, interest in criminal victimization broadly defined was spreading on several fronts, and the nascent victims' rights movement was developing its organizational strategy. Stories about horrendous outrages against helpless poster children, conveyed through receptive mass media, would fuel the movement's growth and hone its political clout.

Normal skepticism toward implausible stories might seem a logical bar against the sort of hysterias soon to be unleashed. Sex panics of the 1980s never could have occurred without the spread of new psychological theories that encouraged social workers, prosecutors, journalists, and the lay public to suspend rational skepticism toward outlandish claims.[21] But by the early 1980s some therapists were signing on to trendy pop-psych theories: childhood traumas need not be consciously remembered; they might become "repressed memories" instead, to be recovered under hypnosis or reawakened by some triggering event.[22] Not all therapists subscribed to such theories, but adherence was sufficiently distributed across feminist, conservative, and religious practitioners that bizarre local accusations made by clients at one site could quickly be solicited by naive therapists working in other locales, fostering the appearance of a national crisis. A small interlocking network of therapists and social workers thus produced the bulk of SRA accusations because they worked from the same script (*Michelle Remembers,* an early bible of the repressed memories movement) and used the same suggestive therapeutic methods and interview techniques.[23]

Notions of an asexual childhood innocence figured prominently in the thinking of all these camps. A new generation of social workers was thus primed. Add to these converging factors the pervasive parental anxieties about gay visibility, changing gender roles, working mothers, and the treatment of children in day-care centers. The result? It seemed eminently plausible to many that an extensive underground network of sadistic devil worshippers was sexually torturing large numbers of children in preschools and day-care centers across the country—and that these activities had somehow gone undetected for years, if not decades.

Prominent accusations first erupted in 1982 in Kern County, California, where a relative with a history of mental illness charged that Debbie and Alvin McCuan were abusing their own children. Convinced that they were being tipped to the existence of a child sex ring, authorities used coercive interviewing techniques to solicit from the children accusations that they were tortured, sexually abused, and forced to let animals eat food out of their vaginas. Allegations spread to include the McCuans' defense witnesses. (This pattern would recur in some other cases, notably, in Jordan, Minnesota, where the number of adults accused of satanic sex abuse swelled to twenty-four.) The four defendants in the McCuan case were convicted in 1984 and sentenced to 240-year prison terms each. Their sentences were not overturned until 1996. Accusations and alleged sex rings multiplied, and prosecutors eventually brought charges against forty-six defendants in Kern County.[24] From these ominous beginnings the panic spread to the McMartin Preschool in Manhattan Beach, California, an affluent seaside precinct of Los Angeles (1983), the community of Jordan, Minnesota (1983), the Fells Acres Day Care Center in Malden, Massachusetts (1984), the Early Childhood Development Center in Pittsfield, Massachusetts (1985), the Wee Care Nursery School in Maplewood, New Jersey (1985), and a host of other places, including, near the end of the cycle, the Little Rascals Day Care Center in Edenton, North Carolina (1989).

The Devil Goes to Preschool: The Making of the McMartin Case

The longest-running trial in U.S. history, the McMartin Preschool case, would also prove paradigmatic of its type. I draw much of my summary from a variety of published accounts, especially pioneering research done by Debbie Nathan and Michael Snedeker, who cowrote the definitive book on satanic ritual abuse.[25]

The case began in the fall of 1983 when Judy Johnson claimed that her son had been sodomized by Ray Buckey, a twenty-five-year-old teacher at McMartin who was also the son of its administrator, Peggy McMartin Buckey. In the weeks that followed, Johnson's allegations became increasingly bizarre. She claimed that Ray Buckey and other teachers had dressed as witches to abuse her son, that Ray Buckey "flew through the air," and that Peggy McMartin Buckey had stuck scissors in the boy's eyes. Johnson's accounts involved a goat, a lion, an elephant, and day trips by train and airplane to other sites for sex abuse and torture. Her son showed no signs of physical abuse, and Johnson would later be diagnosed a paranoid schizophrenic, but her accusations set in motion an elaborate chain reaction. A police search of Buckey's home turned up "evidence"—a rubber duck and copies of *Playboy*. After arresting Ray Buckey, the Manhattan Beach police chief sent a letter to parents naming Buckey as a suspected child abuser. The letter asked parents to ask their children whether they had witnessed or been victims of abuse, helpfully naming several variations of sexual abuse. Persistent questioning by panicked parents produced more accusations, and a major part of the police investigation was handed over to Kee MacFarlane of the Children's International Institute, a clinic for the treatment of child abuse.

In its early coverage of the story, the mass media essentially inflamed the public, fanning fear of ritual abuse (along with detailed salacious descriptions) across the country. *Newsweek* reported, without qualification, that "some of the children are now strong enough to relate" details of "the Naked Movie Star game." The article continued: "The horrors may only have started with sodomy, rape, oral copulation and fondling. For years, the authorities now suspect, parents had unwittingly delivered their children to an outlet for child pornography and prostitution." Noting a string of similar accusations that were erupting at other day-care centers, the magazine quoted Gary Hewitt of the Center for Missing Children, who opined that the problem is "much bigger than anyone wants to believe." Pondering how such elaborate horrors could have gone on for many years at a day-care center with an excellent reputation, *Newsweek* suggested that "staff members terrorized their young charges into silence with threats by example—mutilating pet rabbits or squeezing to death young birds." *Time* uncritically recounted the story of how a horse was slaughtered in front of students to intimidate them—this, at a busy day-care center, where parents were coming and going at all hours. The magazine went on to warn that "parents were too trusting, assuming that separation anxiety was the reason their children cried when dropped off at school." "Brutalized" was the emphatic headline on one *Time* story. Another article matter-of-factly referred to "the 125 children who were molested at the McMartin School."[26]

The McMartin furor stimulated congressional hearings, and the *New York Times* uncritically reported Kee MacFarlane's testimony before the House Ways and Means Subcommittee on Oversight and the Select Committee on Children, Youth and Families:

> A nationally recognized expert in the treatment of sexually abused children testified today that she suspected that there was a wide network of "child predators" and that although evidence was circumstantial, it seemed to indicate a conspiracy to operate day care centers as a cover for child pornography.... [MacFarlane] stunned the audience when she said, "I believe that we're dealing with a conspiracy, an organized operation of child predators designed to prevent detection.... The preschool, in such a case, serves as a ruse for a larger unthinkable network of crimes against children. If such an operation involves child pornography or the selling of children, as is frequently alleged, it may have greater financial, legal and community resources at its disposal than those attempting to expose it."[27]

Such claims and their uncritical reportage sparked political initiatives to redefine the legal burden of proof and to diminish the rights of the accused. In the *New York Times* Brooklyn District Attorney Elizabeth Holtzman wrote of "a cloak of immunity" for child molesters, claiming that legal requirements for corroborative evidence, in addition to children's testimony, has the effect of "encouraging [molesters] to continue to sexually abuse children—so long as they do it secretly."[28] Long-standing legal conventions—the right of the accused to face the accuser in open court; the right of the defense to conduct a rigorous cross-examination—were said to further traumatize already-traumatized children, constituting extensions of the original acts of abuse.[29] Debbie Nathan underscores how such framings undermined rational law and stoked the magical power of the accusation: "By 1986, in many states, hastily reformed criminal statutes made it unnecessary for children to come into court; parents could act as hearsay witnesses, or kids could testify on closed-circuit TV, giving juries the automatic impression that defendants had done something to frighten the child. And once a person stood accused, the community often decided that *something* must have happened. Any remaining skeptics were blasted for 'condoning child abuse' and some were accused themselves."[30]

By spring 1984 a grand jury had handed up indictments against seven people—Ray Buckey, Peggy McMartin Buckey, Peggy Ann Buckey (Ray's sister), Virginia McMartin (Ray's grandmother, who had founded the preschool thirty years earlier), and three other McMartin teachers—on 115 counts of child abuse. Additional counts were tacked on later, eventually bringing the total as high as 354 counts involving as many as 369 alleged victims.[31] Hinting that they were investigating a criminal conspiracy of enormous scale, police informed the media that thirty more people linked to McMartin were also under investigation.

The Trials

Pretrial hearings lasted more than a year, as attorneys for the defendants mounted an aggressive defense. On the stand child witnesses related stories that involved sex abuse, satanic rituals, secret underground passageways, secret rooms, excursions to far-flung sites, the actor Chuck Norris, animal sacrifices, orgies, and the mutilation of corpses. These stories were graphic, incendiary, bizarre, and often inconsistent. They held up poorly under cross-examination.

Supposedly, McMartin, a preschool with a long uneventful history and an excellent reputation, had been a front for the production of child pornography by a satanic sex abuse ring. Local investigators, the FBI, and Interpol had cast a global dragnet, searching cars and houses in far-flung locations while reviewing thousands of photos and porn flicks in an effort to locate pornographic pictures of McMartin children. Police even offered a substantial monetary reward, no questions asked, for anyone who could produce a single incriminating photo. But no child pornography was ever found. No semen or blood was found anywhere on the premises of the school. No sacrificed babies, no mutilated corpses, no remains of sacrificed animals were ever discovered. Nor was any corroborating evidence of satanism ever found. The closest thing to a witch's or warlock's outfit ever proffered was the graduation gown police found when they searched Ray Buckey's home. Determined to prove the existence of underground tunnels and dungeons, parents began digging around the school; after a few days they were joined by an archaeological team funded by Gloria Steinem. But no tunnels were found. Even *Newsweek*—an early promoter of the hysteria—highlighted the "absence of evidence" and could see that the case had begun to fall apart.[32]

By fall 1985 charges had been dropped against all but two of the original defendants, Ray Buckey and Peggy McMartin Buckey. Logically, Debbie Nathan observes, the case could have been dismissed outright. But uncritical reportage of the charges continued in most of the mass media. In 1985, for instance, ABC's evening tabloid 20/20 had run a report claiming that satanic crime and day-care sexual abuse were epidemic.[33] Local television stations in California continued their incendiary coverage of the case.

As a graduate student at Berkeley during this time, I observed to friends that the events said to have occurred at McMartin and other preschools simply could not have happened. Teachers and staff were alleged to have ritually abused students in open, unlocked classrooms at a busy preschool. The charges themselves were more suggestive of "a toddler's notion of unspeakable transgression . . . than . . . any known profile of adult sexual perversion," as Margaret Talbot subsequently put it.[34] Large circus animals were involved in several of the children's stories—surely a sign of flights of the imagination. And then there were the physically impossible acts: impracticable copulations, corporeal flight, undetected day trips by air balloon (or later, at Little Rascals, by spaceship). More often than not, someone would remind me that terrible things happen to children or insisted, "We have to believe the children." A few times I was given the logically suspect argument that the more fantastic elements of the children's stories, while probably untrue, nonetheless revealed an underlying truth—that some terrible trauma had in fact occurred. Children, after all, don't lie about child abuse. Prosecutors pressed on, and judges allowed the scaled-back case to move forward.

The first trial got underway in 1987. Prosecution and defense closely questioned Kee MacFarlane of the Children's International Institute. It came out that MacFarlane's interviewing techniques, which used hand puppets and anatomically correct dolls, were profoundly biased, to put it mildly. Guided by the conviction that any denial that abuse had occurred was itself evidence of abuse, MacFarlane and her associates had asked leading questions and used coercive interviewing techniques to cajole accusations from 384 of the four hundred children they interviewed. One child was asked, helpfully, "Can you remember the naked pictures?" Children who said that they recalled no abuse were asked to speculate: "Let's pretend and see what might have happened." Children were fed the desired answers to questions. The adult questioners provided details that they asked the children to confirm. Young children who supplied stories of abuse were rewarded with hugs; those who did not were harassed: "Are you going to be stupid or are you going to be smart and help us here?"[35]

The jury voted to acquit on fifty-two of the sixty-five remaining charges; it remained hopelessly deadlocked on thirteen charges, all against Ray Buckey. (A majority of the jury had voted to acquit on all thirteen charges.) McMartin Preschool parents, child protection groups, and victims' rights advocates demanded a new trial, marching in Manhattan Beach under the banner "We Believe the Children." Goaded by afternoon tabloid television shows—*Geraldo* and *Oprah*—and prodded by public opinion surveys, which showed that overwhelming majorities believed the accusations (90 percent of those who followed the news, in one telephone poll), prosecutors slogged on, refiling charges against Ray Buckey on eight counts involving three children.

At the second trial the defense team put MacFarlane on the witness stand. The second jury never heard evidence that Judy Johnson was disturbed when she made the original accusations or that she had made similar allegations against her estranged husband, her son's father. In the end the second jury deadlocked on all eight counts, leaning toward acquittal on six. And so the McMartin case died not with a bang but with a whimper.

By the end of the process Ray Buckey had spent five years in jail awaiting trial on crimes no rational person would believe ever occurred. Hundreds of children had made similar accusations against hundreds of adults nationwide. More than seventy people were wrongfully convicted during the ensuing hysteria and later exonerated. Their trials reveal much the same script, outlined by Debbie Nathan as follows: An unreliable accuser makes outrageous charges; letters to parents and sensational media coverage kindle communal fears; suggestive or coercive interview techniques—or hypnotherapy to recover repressed memories— produce more false accusations; families of the victims, aided by crusading therapists and social workers, are recruited into tightly bound support groups that disallow questioning of the abuse scenario and function as public pressure groups; publicity-savvy prosecutors press forward, despite the lack of corroborative evidence; potentially exculpatory evidence is withheld; and the defendant goes to trial under conditions that resemble the classic witch hunt.[36] These cases shattered untold lives, wrecked unblemished careers, bankrupted countless families, and fostered a durable culture of paranoia.

For some the tribulation continues. Bernard Baran, a working-class gay man, was only nineteen in 1984 when he was accused of ritual sex abuse at a day-care center. He then spent twenty-two years in a Massachusetts prison, where he was repeatedly raped and beaten, sustaining eye injuries and broken bones. A long campaign by supporters and attorneys has shown how overt homophobia, junk science, coercive child interviews, incompetent counsel, and the concealment of exculpatory evidence produced a guilty verdict on eight implausible counts, resulting in three consecutive life sentences. Still, prosecutors were slow to relent. Baran's conviction was overturned on the ground that he had received incompetent counsel, and he was released on bail in 2006—to face the possibility of being retried on the same charges. In June 2009 the district attorney finally dropped all charges.[37]

In Arkansas three teenagers who listened to heavy metal music were convicted of raping and ritually murdering three eight-year-old boys in 1993. High-pressure police questioning produced a confession from one of the accused, who was himself then a minor. Inflammatory media coverage and a moblike atmosphere did the rest. New DNA evidence has established that the teens were not present at the crime scene. Expert forensic analysis concludes that the grisly dismemberments were the postmortem work of wild animals, not ritual abusers. As this book went to press, the "West Memphis Three" had spent more than fifteen years in prison, one on death row. Attorneys have petitioned for the men's release or retrial.[38]

RESIDUES: WE ARE ALL SUSPECTS NOW

"Satanic ritual abuse" has been thoroughly discredited.[39] But in history timing is everything, and these latter-day witch hunts came at a crucial historical moment of cultural retrenchment and political backlash. The decay of New Left social movements played an important part in setting the stage, and the blending of leftist and rightist logics intensified the effects of sex panics. The professionalization of moral entrepreneurs in key fields facilitated the work of building permanent institutional and legal structures in the wake of SRA.

Thanks to the careful research of Elizabeth Loftus and others, most professional psychologists and memory researchers now recognize that the notion of repressed memories is fatally flawed on two counts.[40] A trauma—precisely because it is traumatic—most likely will be remembered, not forgotten or unconsciously repressed. And the "recovery" of repressed memories, through therapy under hypnosis, is impossible to distinguish from the implantation of such memories.[41] Still, despite the American Psychological Association's repudiation of repressed memories, notions of repressed memories and their recovery under hypnosis persist to this day in popular culture, among some therapists, and sometimes in legal form. As late as 2005 the *New York Times* posted a friendly "Conversation with the Author" piece that focused on a promoter of recovered memory psychoanalysis; in it the author aired claims that as many as 1 in 6 boys and 1 in 3 girls experience sexual abuse. In 2004 the Reverend Gerald Robinson, a Roman Catholic priest in Toledo, was arrested and charged with the murder of a nun committed twenty-four years earlier, in large part as the result of a then-unidentified woman's recovery of the familiar satanic ritual abuse memories. He was convicted in 2006, even though his DNA did not match male DNA recovered from the murder victim's underwear and fingernails. And Florida still allows exceptions to its statute of limitations on child abuse for accusers claiming "repressed memory."[42]

More alarming than the stubborn persistence of "recovered memories" in some quarters is the general residue of 1980s pseudoscience: some vague and highly subjective definitions of sexual infraction. From the early 1980s Diana Russell was using loose definitions of *children* (to include adolescents), *sex* (to include tongue kissing), *incest* (to include cousins), and *abuse* (to include experiences remembered as pleasant) in sociological studies.[43] A popular incest recovery book, whose language has been reproduced in other quarters, encourages adults with ill-defined maladies (dysfunctional relationships, depression, addiction, low self-esteem) to inspect their childhood experiences for forgotten occurrences of sex abuse, which is defined as broadly as "being forced to listen to sexual talk," being "held in a way that made you uncomfortable," and "being bathed in a way that felt intrusive to you."[44] Such phrases might describe traumatic events or innocuous ones, and the conflation of one with the other has been fertile ground for false accusations.[45] Leering is sometimes classified as a form of sexual abuse. When researchers and child advocates lump together "unwanted hugs," "attempted kisses," "a pat on the buttocks," and "a touch on the leg" with "the terribly damaging ordeal of child rape," they erode standards of discourse and do a real disservice to victims of child abuse, as Neil Gilbert has suggested. And as Ian Hacking has shown, if one draws childhood so broadly as to include adolescents up to the age of eighteen, and if one further encourages respondents to classify as abusive a broad spectrum of sexual and nonsexual interactions with both adults and other minors, one can indeed produce large numbers of "abused children."[46]

It is not simply that strained, highly subjective, after-the-fact definitions permeate the burgeoning world of recovery, survivor, and self-help manuals; they also obtain in the realm of official and quasi-official practices. In a news story about a Southern California molestation case against a twenty-eight-year-old substitute teacher, a police spokeswoman is quoted as saying: "We're not going into details, but the contact was so subtle that some of the victims may not realize they were victims." Hyperbole too can be construed as child abuse. In New York City a hip-hop disk jockey was arrested and charged with endangering the welfare of a child after on-air rants against a rival DJ that included theatrical, over-the-top talk about abusing the rival's four-year-old daughter.[47]

Meanwhile, what might count as evidence of child sexual abuse for the vigilant teacher or social worker has come to include any number of innocuous behaviors, as Margaret Talbot shows in her thoughtful review essay about the consequences of 1980s sex panics. Joseph Tobin, a professor of education, recounts his university classroom discussion of a high-spirited four-year-old girl who liked to kiss her male preschool peers; about half his students thought that such behavior "should alert us to the possibility of sexual abuse." Nowadays suspicions of abuse can be aroused when children express curiosity about sex, use profane language, sketch anatomically correct drawings, masturbate, attempt to catch a glimpse of naked adults, play doctor, or engage in sexual play with other children. Talbot sums up the resulting culture of child protection as one defined by anxiety and paranoia: "Our preoccupation with people who actually do assault children has made us wary of people who never would assault them. These days we are all suspects."[48]

Upon learning that I was writing a book on the topic, acquaintances have sometimes volunteered stories about their encounters with the everyday sex panic. A registered nurse recounts how his niece got brainwashed at summer camp when an overzealous counselor's lessons on sex abuse encouraged the girl to construe her father's every hug as sexual. A straight white professional describes his response to the fear of strangers: "I'm afraid of seeming too interested in other peoples' children. . . .

Even making faces at them, when they make one at me, can elicit strange looks from the parents—particularly if I'm alone. I generally just try to ignore them now." A black schoolteacher, witness to periodic outbreaks of sex panic at her school, describes her daily ritual to ward off misfortune: she keeps a diary of events in her classroom, paying close attention to any interactions with troubled or disruptive students. "It's my insurance policy," she says, "evidence of what happened."

Protecting Innocence, Making Monsters

Because they allied antagonistic social movements against a phantasmic threat, Reagan-era sex panics had important cultural consequences. They buttressed conservative Christian notions of immaculate childhood sexual innocence while joining forces with neo-Victorian feminist accounts of sex as trauma. They distilled diffuse anxieties about sex and children into the pervasive perception that all children everywhere are at perpetual risk of sexual assault. In the resulting culture of hypervigilant child protection, the denial of childhood sexuality and the perpetual hunt for the predatory pervert are opposite sides of the same coin: the innocent and the monster, the perfect victim and the irredeemable fiend.

As the feminist and queer theorist Gayle Rubin correctly predicted while SRA fantasies were still raging, the long trajectory of these and other sex panics would leave indelible marks on American professional and legal culture.[49] They spawned expansive new subfields of pseudoscience—fanciful psychological profiles of abusers, whimsical diagnostic tools said to predict future predation or recidivism. They powerfully contributed to the consolidation of an ever more comprehensive culture of child protection, thus extending the purviews of both long-standing official bureaucracies (child protection services) and newer, quasi-official ones (victims' rights advocates). In 1975 the United States had 25,000 clinical social workers; by 1990 their ranks had swollen to 80,000, and by 1999 the number was approaching 100,000.[50]

It seems logical to surmise that child sex abuse went underreported in the past. But what to make of new levels of reportage, solicited by an ever growing institutional apparatus? Nationally, reports of child sex abuse leaped from 6,000 in 1976 to 113,000 in 1985 and 350,000 in 1988—a fifty-eight-fold increase in twelve years. Sex abuse allegations became a nuclear weapon in child custody cases. In 1987 a Michigan psychologist and lawyer reported that 30 percent of his state's contested child custody cases involved such accusations. *Time* had changed its tune on the McMartin case and was quoting an attorney's advice: "You're asking for trouble if you give your child a bath without someone else's being there. . . . And you never, ever, sleep in the same bed."[51]

A push-pull mechanism was thus primed, with material incentives built into both sides of the system's operation. On the "push" side: child protection services providers, social workers, and other functionaries have a vested interest in defining the nature of the problems they treat broadly and in discovering hitherto undetected or undetectable cases, thereby making work, enlarging their ranks, and expanding their domain. On the "pull" side: in the context of an ongoing valorization of crime victimhood, claims of child sex abuse became an all-too-logical channel for the expression of vague suburban anxieties, middle-class resentments, and assorted personal grievances.

Panic Becomes the Norm

These sex panics have led to new terminologies and produced new ways of speaking and thinking about children.

- A blanket "no touching" policy has replaced the touchy-feely ethos of the 1960s and early 1970s, which held that everyone, especially children, needs a good hug every now and then.

- The basic Freudian insights—that children are sexual beings and that myriad human relationships, including relations between parents and children, can have an erotic dimension without any overt sexual activity ever occurring—have been rebuffed, rendered unthinkable or dangerous. In the prevailing argot, such ideas would "sexualize" children, and this, in the prevailing mind-set, could only be a precursor to abusing them.

- Commonsensical propositions, easily uttered before the 1980s—children sometimes develop crushes on their teachers; adolescents sometimes seek out sexual relationships with adults precisely because the latter are more mature, more experienced, and more sophisticated—have become suspect.

- Research findings that buttress the association of sex with trauma are accorded official status and are freely invoked by activists, lawmakers, and judges. Research findings contrary to the prevailing line sometimes are ignored or even censured.

When Bruce Rind and two colleagues performed a meta-analysis of fifty-nine studies based on college samples, they concluded that available data did not support the notion that sex between adults and minors invariably caused harm or was always experienced as traumatic. The researchers also found that degrees of harm varied, depending upon the age and gender of the minor, whether the sex was consensual or coerced, and the child's family environment. Many males actually recounted their experience as positive or beneficial. The research, published in the American Psychological Association's *Psychological Bulletin,* drew a unanimous vote of condemnation by the U.S. House of Representatives. (The vote was 355–0, with 13 members voting "present.")[52]

- As a result of such denials, suppressions, and expurgations, *innocence*—a euphemism for child sexlessness—has become the new watchword, apparently more valued than children themselves. And offenses against this childhood innocence have become a crime capable of inflaming opinion, inciting juries, and inspiring rash actions. The improbable suggestion that the cult leader David Koresh was sexually and physically abusing children triggered the Justice Department's order for the disastrous assault on the Branch Davidian compound in Waco, Texas, in 1993. In fact, as the FBI well knew at the time, Koresh was in no condition to abuse anyone; he had been seriously wounded in an earlier shootout with the Treasury Department's Bureau of Alcohol, Tobacco and Firearms. The resulting conflagration killed seventy-nine people, including twenty-one children.[53]

- The protection and promotion of childhood innocence has taken various forms since the 1980s. Conservatives have sponsored a nationwide virginity movement, while some schools have withheld sexual information and sex education from adolescents. Meanwhile, wider demographic evidence suggests that American children are anything but protected: more than 1 in 6 live in poverty. Before the 2010 health care reform, about 8.4 million children—11.4 percent of all children—had no health insurance; many more had minimal coverage or were underinsured, with poor, black, and Latino children overrepresented in these statistics. Assorted national and local welfare reforms have reduced state subsidies available to poor mothers and children, ultimately producing a sharp rise in infant mortality rates in many parts of the country.[54] The obsession with one thing (sexual innocence) would seem to serve as a substitute for or distraction from the other thing (child welfare writ large).

- *Pedophile*—a term that had no clinical standing before the 1960s—has become a household word, the special object of fear and loathing, a term applied to an ever broader range of desires and predilections. Whatever its etymological origins or textbook definitions, the term has often functioned as a stand-in for the archaic term *pederast*—a man attracted to adolescent boys—and gained standing when homosexuality was "de-medicalized," removed from the list of mental illnesses. *Pedophile* then came to include heterosexual child molesters and has been applied loosely to statutory rapists. The term continues to spread: there are now "female pedophiles"—and sometimes, at least implicitly, even "child pedophiles."

In going about the work of protecting children, institutional actors also do something else: they set up definitions of *childhood, innocence, sex, abuse,* and so on, in ways that hitherto would have been deemed implausible.[55] The totality of these effects is more than the sum of its parts. Reagan-era sex panics produced a comprehensive new mythos of the person, the person's susceptibility to trauma, and how an individual is shaped by experience. Pick up virtually any pop psychology text or, for that matter, a large sampling of high feminist academic treatises, and you'll likely encounter a certain dark picture of childhood: encircled by sinister forces, menaced by innumerable threats, stalked by shadowy evildoers. Read virtually any issue of any newspaper and you'll encounter all the myriad ways innocence can be snatched from the young. In these definitions, "innocence" will serve as a perpetual catalyst for activism and intervention. Threats to this innocence will spur new variants of the collective wariness sociologists have glossed as "crime-consciousness."[56] It becomes every citizen's responsibility to be alert to the dangers embodied by strangers. Panic becomes the norm, duty, law.

SECURING CHILDHOOD

Judith Levine, Janice Irvine, and other feminists have argued that the established culture of child protection—with its fetishization of virginity and its constant battery of alarmist messages that equate sex with danger and risk—actually harms children psychologically and socially.[57] It certainly disallows pleasure, autonomy, and discovery. A British study has found that in the United Kingdom, where sex panics rival those of the United States, the irrational fear of strangers has driven children indoors, contributing to a sedentary lifestyle and a fear of the outside environment.[58]

In escalating panics around sex, children too have become objects of public wrath. Minors who fail to conform to adult fantasies of sexual innocence may be labeled "SACY" (sexually aggressive children and youth) and can be subjected to many of the same forms of prosecution, supervision, and surveillance prescribed for adult sex offenders. Various sources on child abuse blandly cite figures—up to 41 percent of child sex abuse perpetrators are said to be juveniles, with adults younger than thirty overrepresented among the remaining adult perpetrators—without inquiring how nonviolent, noncoercive sex acts between minors (or between mature teenagers and young adults) came to be classified as abusive.[59] Levine has cataloged some instructive stories: In New Hampshire a ten-year-old boy was charged with two counts of rape after touching two girls "in a sexual manner." In New Jersey a neurologically impaired twelve-year-old boy who groped his eight-year-old brother in the bathtub was required to register as a sex offender under Megan's Law. In Pennsylvania an eleven-year-old girl was convicted of rape, while newspapers buzzed with reports of a "child sex ring" in which children taught each other how to have sex.[60]

Several hundred programs nationwide treat juvenile "molesters" younger than twelve. Some are as young as two. Of course, children can be aggressive, even violent. And in the process of juvenile squabbling and cruelty, children sometimes do horrendous things to other children. Occasionally, these things involve sex. One would hope social workers and other clinicians well trained in psychology would gently, rationally, and appropriately intervene in the worst of these rare cases. But, as Levine shows, the trouble is that the "experts" on "children-who-molest" turn out to include the same characters who produced the SRA panics in the 1980s. "Today, teachers and social workers, undereducated in psychology and overtrained (often by law enforcers) in sexual abuse, tend to see sexual pathology and criminal exploitation in any situation that looks even remotely sexual."[61]

In one suburban community school officials called the cops when a seven-year-old boy smacked a classmate's bottom. "I thought they were going to take me to prison," the boy said later. "I was scared." Even barring

draconian scenarios involving social workers, police, and courts, a punitive and puritanical culture has invaded early childhood education. In
Virginia alone, 255 elementary schoolchildren were suspended in
2007 for offensive sexual touching or "improper physical contact against
a student." In Maryland 165 elementary schoolchildren were suspended
for "sexual harassment" the same year, including three preschoolers, sixteen kindergarteners, and twenty-two first graders.[62] Children-who-
molest, children-who-harass, children-who-abuse are mostly children
who fail to validate adult fantasies of childhood innocence. And those
fantasies are becoming increasingly fantastic.

Age of Consent

During sex panics of the 1970s, 1980s, and 1990s, definitions of *child,*
sex, and *abuse* expanded, and new ideas were codified in a wide range of
legal reforms. Not least among these reforms were revisions to statutory
rape and age-of-consent laws. "Statutory rape" refers not to rape or
coerced sex but to sex with a willing partner; "age of consent" or "age of
majority" refers to the age at which a willing participant is deemed legally
capable of giving consent to sex. As Carolyn Cocca shows in her careful
study, *Jailbait,* statutory rape laws, with their historically changing rationales and definitions, provide a recurring battleground for struggles
around the meanings of childhood, sexuality, and marriage. Sequenced,
these laws and the struggles around them provide a thumbnail sketch of
how sex, power, and authority have been organized in different social
epochs.

In the colonial period statutory rape laws were concerned not with
consent but with the virginity of marriageable white girls. Because female
chastity was a precious commodity, coin of the realm for the kin-based
patriarchal system, "statutory rape was a property crime."[63] In practice
these laws applied neither to boys (whose virginity was not a prized
commodity) nor to nonwhite females (who were deemed incapable of
purity).

When independent working-class girls and young women flocked to
work in cities at the end of the nineteenth century, their greater economic and social freedoms were viewed as akin to prostitution. Middle-
class social reformers, religious conservatives, and Victorian feminists
concocted elaborate moral uplift schemes—codes of virtue and vice designed to steer women away from casual dating and other forms of
heterosocial mixing deemed likely to result in seduction. States raised

ages of consent—for a time, as high as twenty-one in Tennessee. Again, Cocca notes, these revamped laws protected the virtue of white females; some southern states specifically excluded black females from protection under rape laws.[64]

In the wake of the sexual revolution, and in the throes of growing waves of sex panic, the logic of statutory rape laws underwent another sea change: In the 1970s and 1980s, consent, not virtue, became the laws' stated criterion, and the prevention of sexual abuse became their key rationale. Some states raised ages of consent, and laws were rewritten to make them gender neutral. Offenses were graded, based on the age of the victim, with lesser penalties applying when the victim was of a more advanced age. In partial recognition of the sexual agency of advanced adolescents, many states also adopted age-span provisions, although these vary greatly from state to state. Under age-span provisions, if two lovers are close in age and at least one is an advanced minor, the older party either has not committed a crime or has committed a lower order of crime than if the age span is wider.[65]

The gradation of offenses—an approach supported by most feminists and liberals—seems a logical step. But as Cocca points out, the problem is that the new legal language "viewed sexual activity with a person under 10 or 12 and with a person under 16 or 18 as two manifestations of the same crime." In practice "what is clearly child abuse and what may be a consensual sexual relationship can both be prosecuted as sexual abuse under statutes titled 'statutory rape,' 'child molestation,' 'sexual assault,' or 'sexual battery.'"[66] This is no small matter. At the outset of these reforms in the 1970s and 1980s, penalties were generally revised downward; then, beginning in the 1990s, punishments for all these acts became increasingly onerous, sometimes including retroactive sanctions. Thus statutes designed to distinguish offenses and to sort degrees of harm in theory have blurred them in practice.

Such problems were exacerbated by a second wave of consent law reforms in the 1990s that were undertaken in the name of child protection. During Clinton-era agitations around the "epidemic of teen pregnancy," conservatives in some states piled on harsh new penalties for sex with near-adults if intercourse resulted in pregnancy, and the prevention of teen pregnancy became a new rationale for severe penalties for statutory rape overall. In some states variants of the new laws preserve the marital exception, suggesting that marriageability and "virtue," after all, still haunt the notion of consent. As Cocca suggests, the new laws thus combine colonial period statutory rape laws with late

Victorian laws against seduction. They effectively define advanced adolescents—as old as seventeen in many states—as children incapable of giving meaningful consent to sex.[67] These laws codify, expand, and carry forward the very logic of the preceding child sex panics.

A Georgia case that received national attention highlighted the excessiveness of many current sex laws. Genarlow Wilson, an honors student and star athlete, was seventeen when he was caught on videotape having oral sex with a fifteen-year-old girl at a New Year's Eve party. Convicted of aggravated child molestation in 2003, he received a mandatory minimum prison sentence of ten years. (Other male classmates videotaped at the same party accepted plea bargains that required them to register as sex offenders for life.) Wilson was black, as was the "victim" (who repeatedly asserted that the fellatio was consensual), and many Georgians, black and white, believed that race was a factor in the prosecution and punishment.

Outrage around the case prodded the Georgia legislature to rewrite the law, downgrading sex between minors to a misdemeanor offense punishable by no more than one year in prison. But the legislature declined to apply the law retroactively to Wilson; legislators were apparently persuaded by prosecutors' claims that retroactive application would free many more prisoners who had been incarcerated under similar circumstances. The Georgia Supreme Court eventually stepped in, ruling that Wilson's sentence was "grossly disproportionate" to the crime and ordering his release from prison.[68]

Another case, which received less publicity, called attention to different incongruities: Matthew Limon had just turned eighteen when he gave consensual oral sex to an adolescent boy who was nearly fifteen. Both were residents at a school for developmentally disabled youth in Miami, Kansas. At the time the state's "Romeo and Juliet Law" prescribed a reduced penalty—a maximum of fifteen months—for statutory rape when the case involved two teenagers of the opposite sex, with the "offender" younger than nineteen and the "victim" at least fourteen. Because his "victim" was male, Limon had no recourse to the Romeo and Juliet Law; he was prosecuted instead under the state's criminal sodomy laws. And because the mentally challenged young man was a "repeat offender," a registered sex offender—when he was fifteen, he had been found guilty of sodomy for engaging in consensual sexual relations with a boy his own age—he received a long prison sentence: seventeen years and two months.

Two sets of laws, one for heterosexuals and another for homosexuals, would seem a clear violation of the Fourteenth Amendment, with its guarantees of equal protection under the law. But the Kansas Court of Appeals upheld Limon's conviction. And even after the U.S. Supreme Court vacated the conviction in the wake of its 2003 ruling in *Lawrence v. Texas,* which struck down the nation's remaining sodomy laws, the Kansas Court of Appeals still refused to reopen the case. In late 2005 the Kansas Supreme Court finally reversed Limon's conviction. He was released after serving five and a half years—more than four times the maximum sentence he would have received had his partner been a girl.[69] Limon's eventual release from prison marks an important victory in the fight for equal protection under the law. Same-sex acts are now covered under Kansas's age-span provisions. But as with the Wilson case, the Limon case leaves intact laws that put kids in jail for consensual sex.

American Exception

The U.S. approach to these matters is unique among industrialized democracies. In Europe commonplace noncoercive sex between minors might be cause for parental concern, but it is not framed as cause for legal intervention. And ages of consent are typically lower than in most U.S. states. In Spain the age of consent is thirteen; in Hungary, Austria, Kosovo, Estonia, and other countries, it is fourteen (sometimes with provisions prohibiting deception or stipulating that the younger party be sufficiently mature). In France, Sweden, Poland, and other places, it is fifteen. Some countries are expressly permissive while also providing safeguards. Since 1990 Holland's graduated age system acknowledges the sexuality of adolescent teenagers, but it also recognizes their immaturity and relative weakness vis-à-vis adults. Thus minors aged twelve to sixteen can legally consent to sex with an adult who is not their parent or an authority figure (e.g., their teacher)—but either the teens or their parents can bring charges if there is evidence of sexual exploitation, as verified by the Council for the Protection of Children. The Dutch state navigates a zone of ambiguity and draws conditional lines, but the crucial questions pertain to coercion, exploitation, and abuse.[70]

In the United States the crucial questions pertain to innocence and its preservation. The resulting laws deny ambiguity and prescribe harsh penalties for even minor infractions. High ages of consent, elaborate age-difference schemes, and laws against sex between minors have not actually prevented teens from having sex at younger ages. But such laws do accomplish a certain other work, which not coincidentally also produces work for an expanding apparatus of child protectors. They shore up shaky categories, purify an imaginary world of childhood, and intensify the policing of everyday life. They manufacture new victim and villain identities, and they produce more criminality because they define more acts as criminal.

SEX PANICS OF THE 1990S AND BEYOND

By the late 1980s the SRA/day-care panics were burning out. But the broad civil, media, and government apparatus left in their wake did not cease to sound alarms about sex. Rather, institutional actors and advocacy networks revised their story lines, refined their focus, and streamlined their techniques.

Whereas the 1980s had witnessed gothic horrors and macabre accusations coaxed out of the heads of small children, the 1990s institutionalized the true crime story of the solitary child who, in actual reality, befell a terrible death at the hands of a repeat offender, a certified monster. A string of first-name victims—virtually all of whom were white—would serve as prods for perpetual alarm, righteous anger, and citizens' crusades for tougher laws: Adam, Jacob, Megan, Amber, Jessica, Carlie, Samantha. Groups like the Center for Missing and Exploited Children and Parents of Murdered Children, along with far-flung elements of the victims' rights movement, worked with journalists to keep sex crime panics in the news and with government to keep them on the political agenda. Meanwhile, newly minted television shows like the Fox Broadcasting Company's *America's Most Wanted* worked the beat, turning crime and punishment into a commercial spectacle while urging on the public a constant state of citizen vigilantism. (Still in production, *America's Most Wanted* reenacts crime scenes and urges the audience to call in with tips on the whereabouts of fugitives.) Network reportage on the bizarre atrocities committed by Jeffrey Dahmer, the cannibal-torturer who was arrested in 1991 and charged with fifteen counts of murder, gave new substance to the (homo)sexual monster story. In a new wave of sexual alarm the lone predator was portrayed as an ordinary risk to life and limb, and the singular event was portrayed as a common occurrence. These images, this rhetoric, have proved more enduring than the overly homophobic appeals of the 1970s or the hysterical witch hunts of the 1980s.

Occasionally, these horror stories would overlap with other plotlines: not the sacred child, martyred by a monster, but the monster-child, an unnatural product of sexual contagion. By the time the Manzie case received national attention in 1997, the new conventions were so firmly in place that the story practically wrote itself: "Prey Becomes Predator," "Victim Turns Victimizer."

Teen Kills Boy—Who's to Blame?

Sam Manzie of Jackson, New Jersey, then fourteen, had met Stephen Phillip Simmons of Long Island, forty-three, in "Boys," a gay chat room of America Online. In the summer of 1996 the two arranged a rendezvous at the Freehold Raceway Mall in New Jersey and then spent the night at Simmons's home in Holbrook, Long Island. Between August and December the two met several more times in New Jersey. When Manzie's parents discovered unfamiliar long-distance numbers on their phone bill, they confronted Simmons by telephone, telling him not to talk to their son. However, at this time they did not suspect a sexual relationship. After a series of escalating violent outbursts by Sam during the next year, the Manzies hired a counselor for the teen. In treatment Sam Manzie disclosed his relationship with Simmons. On August 28, 1997, as required by law, the counselor notified authorities that an underage minor was having sex with an adult.[71]

Authorities needed little more than a statement from Sam Manzie; Simmons had two previous convictions, one for second-degree sodomy and the other for sexual assault and lewd behavior with a minor. Or they could have obtained online chat records detailing trysts and matched them with documented motel visits. Either tactic would have been more than adequate to secure an arrest warrant. Instead, detectives enlisted Sam Manzie in a "sting operation" to help gather evidence against Simmons. Prosecutors installed equipment in the Manzie home to monitor the teen's phone calls to Simmons. Initially, Sam Manzie assisted the police. But on September 21 the adolescent smashed the monitoring equipment in his home, alerted Simmons that he was being investigated, and stopped cooperating with prosecutors. Authorities quickly arrested Simmons and attempted to take Sam Manzie to a hospital for psychological treatment. The teen refused to enter the hospital. On September 24 Sam

Manzie's parents went to court to try to have Sam committed to a hospital, but the judge refused, observing that the treatment Sam was already receiving was superior to that which he would receive in court-mandated confinement and recommending daily counseling and a "positive approach" instead. Three days later San Manzie's eleven-year-old neighbor Edward P. Werner came to the door selling candy as part of a school fund-raiser. Sam Manzie robbed, raped, and strangled the boy, leaving his body in the nearby woods.

Under legal definitions of sex abuse, Sam Manzie was a child, but he would be tried as an adult for the murder and eventually was sentenced to seventy years. Explaining his transformation "from a victim to a monster" (as one academic article puts it), ABC's *20/20* reported that Manzie "snapped after a homosexual affair with an older man he had met in an Internet chat room." Statistically insignificant events were linked to other statistically uncommon events to produce a "pattern": Newspaper articles invoked the "cycle of abuse" (abused boy becomes violent abuser), "brainwashing" by manipulative pedophiles, and the perils of the Internet. Phyllis Schlafly railed against the American Civil Liberties Union and liberal judges, citing Sam Manzie as a youth who "had fallen prey to homosexual conduct prompted by the internet." Writing in *Time,* the columnist Lance Morrow fantasized about the "retaliatory rage" of the "lynch mob," a fantasy apparently directed against Simmons. In colloquial language the *Asbury Park (N.J.) Press* laid the blame squarely on Simmons: "Without a 'chicken hawk' stalking him, Samuel Manzie . . . probably would have been just another 15-year-old boy trying to cope with his developing sexuality."[72]

More logically, the sequence of events suggests that Sam Manzie may have snapped because he was pressed to participate in an extensive investigation of Simmons—and because parents, counselors, and police subjected the fifteen-year-old to virtual house arrest while bombarding him with messages equating sex, especially homosexuality, with violence. Facts that were downplayed in media discussions at the time include Sam Manzie's record of emotional instability—he had been under psychiatric treatment on various occasions—as well as Simmons's record of mental illness, which included suicide attempts and various admissions to the Veterans Affairs Medical Center in Brooklyn, New York. And there were other complicating factors. At the time of the murder Sam Manzie was taking the antidepressant medication Paxil, a drug that has never been officially approved for the treatment of people younger than eighteen.[73] The teen had reason to be depressed: he was taunted as "Manzie the pansy" by his peers.

No casual observer could sort and prioritize the various factors involved in a crime like Sam Manzie's. What is certain is that the case is typical only of itself: it points to no social trends, no statistical probabilities, and no rationally assessed risks. It became a major media event not because it was newsworthy but because of the ideological work it was induced to perform: See what happens when minors surf the Internet unsupervised? See how catastrophic is the despoliation of childhood innocence? In short, the story became instructive in media venues only through a process of selective editing and telling, which produced an "official story," a panic narrative. In the process the tale was tailored to fit one of the oldest homophobic narratives available, that of homosexual contagion ending in murder.

Writing in *Wired Magazine,* Steve Silberman puts matters in broader perspective: "The truth is, gay teenagers and older gay men have always found ways to meet, despite every law against it. Those interactions, fraught with risk on every side, comprise a kind of initiatory process for young gay men—one made necessary by the scarcity of believable gay role models for youth in films and on TV, and the fact that it's not cool to walk down the hall of high school with your best buddy, holding hands and going steady."[74]

Sam Manzie's own words are complicated and contradictory. About six months before the murder, he is reported to have logged on to Cyber Angels, a child abuse hotline, to plead for help. But he told Long Island police, "Ever since I was about 12 years old I had this fantasy about meeting an old guy who would take me to his house to have sex with me." Of his meetings with Simmons, he told investigators, "I know what he did was wrong, but it was an enjoyable experience." From prison he wrote to Simmons, who was in jail awaiting trial on charges of abusing Manzie: "I'm thinking about you every day. . . . I look forward to communicating with you more in the future: letters while you're in prison, phone calls and visits when you get out." His testimony at Simmons's sentencing hearing was emphatic: "I would like to shed some light on my relationship with Simmons. It was a good one. . . . Please keep in mind that he never forced me to do more than I wanted to, and please keep in mind that I never regretted the relationship."[75]

Helping an emotionally fragile gay teen deal with his sexuality in a homophobic world would be difficult under the best of circumstances.

(I do not want to be misunderstood here. Simmons, who was himself mentally ill, was not "helping"—but he also was not the primary source of harm in this case.) In the Manzie case, it would seem, official therapeutic and law enforcement practices helped turn a difficult situation into a disastrous one. But this is not the official story.

CHAPTER 3

To Catch a Predator

New Monsters, Imagined Risks, and the Erosion
of Legal Norms

I will show you fear in a handful of dust.
—T.S. Eliot, *The Waste Land*

In the wake of September 11, 2001, came a renewed round of intense reportage on the Catholic Church sex abuse scandals. Those reports illustrate something of how proportion and measure are distorted in sex panics. There were horror stories of rape or unconscionable abuse perpetrated by men of the cloth. But there were also grown men in their midthirties or forties who wept before television cameras, recounting the trauma of a brush to the crotch or a groping said to have happened twenty years before.[1] Journalistic interest in the subject synchronized with the conduct of several high-stakes lawsuits by trial attorneys, and a recurring cast of victims' rights advocates gave prosecution-friendly media interviews. Such journalistic techniques blurred with reportage on the Michael Jackson accusations and the Kobe Bryant case. Jackson, in particular, was characterized as a "sexual predator." And although no child pornography was discovered in police raids of Neverland Ranch, a coffee table art book found in Jackson's home was publicly described as being consistent with material that might be found in a pedophile's possession.[2]

THE PRIEST PROBLEM

It is not just that major crimes were conflated with minor ones in the priest abuse scandals. These conflations constructed the menacing image of the "pedophile priest," a term that has been repeatedly invoked in news accounts and public discussions. The John Jay Report paints a more nuanced picture. (This report was commissioned by the U.S. Conference of Catholic Bishops and is based on a survey of dioceses and religious communities conducted by the John Jay College of Criminal Justice.)[3]

The percentage of Catholic priests who had at least one sex abuse accusation made against them between 1950 and 2002 is unacceptably high but relatively small: 4.2 percent of all diocesan priests in ministry and 2.7 percent of all religious priests in ministry during the same period. Child molestation and rape figured large in public discussions of the problem, but a majority of the priests credibly accused of abuse can be classified as ephebophiles, not pedophiles; that is, their victims were adolescent teens—mostly boys, often fifteen to seventeen years of age—not prepubescent children. The accusations tabulated by the John Jay team vary considerably in their severity. Among the most common forms of abuse alleged were touching, either over or under clothing, sexual talk, disrobing, masturbation, or the cleric's giving oral sex. Serial offenders made for spectacular headlines, and indefensible church practices, such as secrecy, not reporting credible accusations to the police, paying hush funds to victims, and transferring known abusers to new parishes, have rightly been spotlighted as enabling some offenders to repeatedly abuse minors. But a majority (56 percent) of the accused priests had a single accusation against them, and another substantial group (27 percent) had two or three accusations. Many of these priests appear to have acted impulsively to begin with, and may have responded to counseling, or they may have discontinued abuse out of feelings of remorse. A small number (149 priests, or 3.5 percent of those with any accusations against them) were responsible for a substantial percentage (26 percent) of all alleged abuses. News reports sometimes portray an ongoing epidemic of abuse by priests, but accusations declined sharply after 1980.[4]

I review the statistics not to diminish the seriousness of the issues involved but to show how the catchall notion of the pedophile priest, like the monstrous image of "the criminal," conceals differences of degree and kind. As Philip Jenkins has noted, these differences "may seem trivial . . . [but] to speak of a 'pedophile priest' implies that the victims are younger and more defenseless than they commonly are and that offenders are severely compulsive and virtually incurable."[5] Refusal to see distinctions is, of course, part of how panic works. This refusal allows misrepresentations to enter, unqualified, into the public record. It cultivates a willingness to believe allegations, no matter how improbable.

It also invites a presumption of guilt to seize the minds of prosecutors, journalists, and jurists alike.

The Boston case of Father Paul Shanley is extreme but revealing. In 2002, as trial attorneys pressed for settlements in civil cases at the peak of the priest abuse scandals, the Boston press buzzed with reports that Shanley had admitted to past rapes; that he had received a psychiatric evaluation that concluded that "his pathology is beyond repair"; and that he was a founding member of the North American Man/Boy Love Association. Independent journalist JoAnn Wypijewski was virtually alone in picking through these misrepresentations.[6] So Shanley was shaped in the image of a pedophile monster. In fact, Shanley's journals and letters recount that he had had a great deal of noncoercive sex with teenagers and young men—some of whom, Wypijewski notes, eventually won sex abuse settlements from the church based on claims that they had had sex with Shanley while they were in their twenties.[7] No doubt Shanley's relations with teenagers and young men in his professional counsel were inappropriate and unacceptable. Some of these relations violated statutory rape laws. Some of the alleged involvements may have violated more serious child abuse laws. But inaccurate statements, conveyed in sensationalist reportage, created a prejudicial environment for Shanley's trial on other, very different charges: the former priest was accused of repeatedly raping a young boy for several years in the 1980s, beginning when the child was six.

At twenty-seven Shanley's original accuser in the case had a long history of mental illness, drug abuse, and violent outbursts. He and three other men, all of whom knew each other, began having "flashbacks" only after reading news reports of Shanley's past involvement with adolescents in the 1960s and 1970s. Represented by the same trial lawyer, all four men collected settlements from the Catholic Church in 2004. All four accusers also were originally part of the criminal case against Shanley, but prosecutors trimmed charges before trial—apparently out of concern about the weakness of the case. They nonetheless pressed forward. During the eventual trial the prosecution claimed that the single remaining plaintiff had immediately repressed his memory of every attack, which allowed him to greet Shanley anew without fear, as though nothing had happened, over several years. Such claims would seem implausible. In the end, Shanley was convicted in 2005 based on testimony about "recovered memories," that troubled relic from the SRA panics; prosecutors produced no corroborating evidence or testimony. In fact, testimony by others who worked at the school at the time when the events were said to have taken place strongly suggested that the alleged rapes did not occur. Hoary standards of "reasonable doubt" seem to have eroded in the Shanley case.

No doubt, prosecutors, victims' rights advocates, and the public at large were feeling a keen sense of frustration: the statute of limitations had run out for many priest sex abuse crimes committed in the 1960s and 1970s in Massachusetts and other states. Perhaps some felt that a man like Shanley ought to be convicted of something. But under classical norms of jurisprudence, a defendant is to be judged based on some specific act that he is charged with committing, not based on what others did or on other things that he may have done. Legal grandstanding and media frenzy in this case produced what might well be described as a show trial, that is, a trial staged for purposes of shaping or satisfying public opinion. Worse, prosecutors also established a statewide precedent for testimony based on "repressed memories," which has been excluded from evidence by judges in some other states. In 2010 the Massachusetts Supreme Judicial Court, the commonwealth's highest, upheld Shanley's conviction, asserting that repressed memory was supported "by a wide collection of clinical observations and a survey of academic literature."[8]

RISK FACTOR

Tales of predatory victimization bred yet more tales of wanton evil. Even before some of the sensational priest accusations and trials had begun to wind down, the national mass media were giving extensive play to a string of gruesome crimes involving child abduction, rape, and murder, thus giving the impression that statistically rare occurrences were epidemic and that predatory recidivists were wreaking havoc across the heartland. Two unrelated but closely timed kidnapping/sex/murder cases in Florida involving violent repeat offenders drew especially intense national attention.[9]

I stress the exceedingly rare nature of such occurrences. In any given year hundreds of thousands of children are reported missing. The Center for Missing and Exploited Children often claims they number in the range of 750,000. But the overwhelming majority of these "missing" children are home within twenty-four hours. (Most "missing" minors had lost simply track of time—or, following an old American tradition, had briefly run away from home.) Child custody disputes account for much of the remainder. Teenage runaways and throwaways account for another substantial sector. Most of the three thousand or so child abductions each year involving nonfamily members do involve family acquaintances, pose low risk of violence, and are usually quickly resolved.

In a nation whose population is roughly 300 million about one hundred high-risk abductions of children by strangers occur every year, and about half end in murder. You would not know it from news reports or political deliberations, but the incidence for all varieties of child disappearance and abduction is down significantly from the 1980s (along with most other forms of violent crime).[10] In real terms, then, a child's risk of being killed by a sexually predatory stranger is comparable to his or her chance of being struck and killed by lightning (1 in 1,000,000 versus 1 in 1,200,000).[11] In raw numbers, the fifty abduction-murders rank far below more common causes of child death: disease or congenital illness (36,180), motor vehicle accident (7,981), drowning (1,158), accidental suffocation or strangulation (953), fire (606), firearm accident (167) —or death at the hands of a family member.[12] The U.S. Department of Health and Human Services estimates that about fifteen hundred children die every year as a result of abuse or neglect. One or both parents is deemed responsible in 70 to 80 percent of these deaths. And less than 1 percent of all child deaths caused by abuse or neglect are attributed to sexual abuse.[13]

McCarthy era agitations around sex crime had revolved around just such anomalous child fatalities, and a resurgent focus on individual predations signaled the yellowing of investigative journalism in the 1970s, paving the way for new cycles of sex panic. Subsequent waves of fear and loathing were conveyed by new modes of communication. In the late twentieth and early twenty-first centuries, intense competition among twenty-four-hour news services such as CNN, Fox, and MSNBC drew sensationalist stories to the fore, fudging the difference between local and national news stories. Unusual events thus became the nation's collective, real-time ordeals, and personal horror stories served as instructive morality plays. Meanwhile, institutional backscratching by police, victims' rights advocates, and reporters became more intense than ever. Media practices that developed around the AMBER (America's Missing: Broadcast Emergency Response) Alert system, established by the 2003 PROTECT Act, dovetailed with this "tabloidization" of the public sphere to blur the difference between policing, vigilantism, and journalism. Once law enforcement officials determine that a minor has been kidnapped, AMBER Alerts interrupt regular television programming, are broadcast on electronic highway signs, can be beamed to mobile phones, and may be printed on lottery tickets. The net result was (and remains) a steady drumbeat of news stories about rare but highly inflammatory events that invite every citizen to live in a state of watchfulness, preparedness, and alarm.[14]

The power of such reportage to distort perceptions of everyday risk was driven home to me one day when I was visiting my parents. A string of stories about children snatched from parking lots had been playing non-stop for several days on Fox News. Many of these child snatchings had happened in Wal-Mart parking lots, no doubt the most expansive and heavily used parking system in the country. As Fox aired yet another AMBER Alert story, my parents contemplated, and then decided against, a quick trip to Wal-Mart with my young niece. They deemed the excursion too risky and would not venture into the parking lot with a small child in tow.

With the same unsound approach to numerical data that turns a statistical blip into a "crime wave," victims' rights advocates agitated for new laws while organizations like the National Center for Missing and Exploited Children worked to capitalize on the resulting confusion. They called for more policing, more surveillance, more monitoring—for surveillance cameras on every street corner and in every parking lot. Such demands highlight the consolidation of new political norms: fear as the normal condition, vigilance as the model for good citizenship, panic as the prod and rationale for lawmaking.

The model evildoer in narratives of child predation is the strange "sexual predator," the rootless, violent "repeat offender." This ignominious figure's ability to arouse fear, rally citizens, and inspire legislation is based not on any significant statistical facts but on the outrage and revulsion his invocation stirs. Stranger assault is the least common form of child sexual abuse.[15]

Advocates for laws to register, publicize, and monitor sex offenders after their release from custody invariably assert that those convicted of sex crimes pose a high risk of recidivism. But according to a U.S. Department of Justice study that tracked male sex offenders (men convicted of rape or sexual assault, including child molestation and statutory rape) who were released from prison in 1994, only 5.3 percent had been re-arrested (and 3.5 percent reconvicted) for another sex crime within three years.[16] A Human Rights Watch study of North Carolina sex offender registrants found low recidivism rates: The overwhelming majority of the five hundred registrants randomly sampled—98.6 percent—were one-time offenders; that is, the offense for which they were registered was their first and only conviction for a sex offense. No offender living in the community for ten to twelve years after release had been reconvicted. "Of the 36 percent of the sample (183 offenders) who had been out of confinement for more than 5 but fewer than 10 years, only 2.19 percent (4 offenders) had been reconvicted"—all four for "indecent liberties with a minor," an offense that involves neither violence nor coercion and need not even involve sexual contact.[17]

Advocates for the rights of sex offenders and their families point out that official recidivism rates are significantly lower for convicted sex offenders than for burglars, robbers, larcenists, drug offenders, and so on. And, contrary to prevailing narratives, repeat offenders and/or strangers are responsible for only a small percentage of new sex crimes, including sex crimes against children.[18]

No doubt, a small number of violent repeat offenders, serial rapists, and child stalkers are among those listed in the burgeoning registries of sex offenders. But a great many of the offenses listed in public sex offender registries are either less violent or nonviolent. Degrees of culpability and harm vary greatly in these offenses; indeed, many would not be classified as sex offenses under European laws, which set significantly lower ages of consent than do U.S. laws. As one anonymous writer suggests, the "typical" registered sex offender is a less freakish figure than the official narrative suggests.[19]

Contrary to the common belief that the Megan's Law registries provide lists of child molesters, the victim need not have been a child or minor and the perpetrator need not have been an adult. First-degree rape is always a registry offense. Statutory rapists—who are not rapists at all, insofar as their crimes involved neither coercion nor violence—may also be listed, depending on the state (and depending on the definition of the offense). In some states statutory rapists and child abusers may be minors themselves. Some states require exhibitionists and peeping toms to register. "Forcible touching" is a registry offense, and this designation may apply even to adolescent boys who "copped a feel," as it was called on my junior high playground. A sizable majority—67 percent—of the North Carolina registrants randomly sampled in the Human Rights Watch study had been convicted on the relatively mild and nonviolent offense of "indecent liberties."[20]

ACTUARIAL ILLOGIC

One might well hope for a classification system that distinguishes menace from nuisance, with rational criteria for sorting violent, repeat offenders, who belong in prison or require close supervision, from nonviolent, one-time offenders.[21] But as Gayle Rubin once observed, American thinking admits little nuance when it comes to sex.[22] And the criminologist David Garland notes how redefinitions of *risk* in recent lawmaking turn assorted lawbreakers into, simply, "wicked individuals" who lose "all legal rights and moral claims": "Politicians often speak in the language of risk only to bowdlerize its terms and confound its logic."[23]

The federal Wetterling Act of 1994 requires convicted sex offenders to register with authorities upon release, parole, or probation. The act mandates annual registration for a ten-year period for some sex offenses, and lifetime registration on a quarterly basis for others deemed more serious. Megan's Law, which in 1996 required local law enforcement authorities to develop community notification procedures, roughly sketches notification protocols at three levels, supposedly corresponding to the risk of recidivism: low, medium, and high risk. Some states have responded to these federal mandates by establishing two levels of registry and notification, others four. Many states purport to parse out "low-," "moderate-," and "high-risk" offenders, but exact criteria for these classifications vary from state to state. In some states judges consult a checklist to decide whether a convict is deemed high, medium, or low risk. In other states these designations do not mark "risks" at all but distinctions based on the crime for which the person was convicted. For instance, in some jurisdictions "high-risk" offenders were convicted of *either* sex crimes involving the use of force *or* any sexual offense against a child aged twelve or younger, without regard as to whether force, penetration, or trauma was involved. "Moderate risk" typically refers to people convicted of crimes that involved neither the use of force nor children younger than twelve. "Low-risk" offenders can include those convicted of offenses as minor as public urination (if construed as indecent exposure), public masturbation (a common solicitation technique in male cruising areas), "mooning," or prostitution. Before the U.S. Supreme Court struck down the nation's remaining sodomy laws, some states required registration and community notification for people convicted of consensual adult sodomy.

In practice, what has happened is that the language of risk lends scientific credibility to inconsistent labeling practices that are anything but scientific or predictive. Gradations first haltingly elaborated to distinguish degrees of harm have subsequently become the rationale for blurring these distinctions, and in many locales mid- and lower-level nonviolent offenders have become subject to the same community notification procedures as violent repeat offenders: Web listings, the distribution of electronic notices or paper flyers. This is associative logic, magical thinking, the logic of panic. Such notions of risk align with much older ideas about danger, taboo, and ritual pollution.[24]

The swelling ranks of convicted and registered sex offenders doubtless include many innocent people, falsely accused, tried in the press, then wrongfully convicted by incensed juries. A study of exonerations of defendants convicted of serious crimes suggests that inflammatory charges, such as murder or cross-racial rape, raise the risk of wrongful conviction.[25] The risk to those wrongfully accused of child abuse would seem especially high.

The rhetorical flourishes of the moral entrepreneurs who alternately produce and capitalize on sex panics are revealing. In Florida, after a minor's abduction from a parking lot was caught on videotape, a state legislator appeared before cameras to cry "no more" in a weeping rage so fearsome that one would have imagined her own child had been snatched and brutally killed. The case at hand was an especially heinous act; the proposed legislation, however, applied broadly to a host of minor or nonviolent sex offenses. So goes the associative logic of panic.

Oprah Winfrey—whose career was shaped in significant ways in the 1980s when she floated different claims of her own experiences with childhood sexual abuse—staged a similar performance on her syndicated television talk show, launching a national "Child Predator Watch List" and offering $100,000 rewards for information leading to the capture of various fugitives. "The children of this nation ... are being stolen, raped, tortured, and killed by sexual predators who are walking right into your homes. How many times does it have to happen? How many children have to be sacrificed? What price are we as a society willing to continue to pay before we rise up and take to the streets and say: Enough. Enough. Enough!"[26]

Winfrey's pitch, delivered personally on her Web site, traded in many of the tropes that have come to substitute for politics in a tabloidized public sphere: the ritual enactment of outrage, the vow to undertake a quasi-religious crusade, the evocation of secretive conspiratorial evil-doers who plot against long-suffering common folk. . . . It is worth noting that Winfrey's nation of beleaguered innocents, violated in their own homes, bore striking resemblance to lynch-mob incitements of the Jim Crow era that invariably depicted white women and children being menaced, in their very homes, by black rapists. As though to exorcise ghosts of the "black beast," Winfrey's Web site featured a multiracial cast of mug shots. Despite the alarmist rhetoric, the sex crimes with which the men were charged varied considerably in terms of harm or intensity: Some indeed were accused of having raped children, others of having noncoercive sex with teenage minors, others of inappropriately touching minors of various ages. Some were not actually wanted by authorities for having committed any offense other than failing to register as sex offenders.

Winfrey's was only one of many such expansive cris de coeur from the period. The prosecutor-turned-journalist Nancy Grace kept similar narratives going nightly on CNN. NBC's *Nightline* marketed "To Catch a Predator," a pseudonews event aired during sweeps week. In this recurring format journalists pose as minors in online chat rooms to entrap adult men. So extensive was coverage of this beat that "an MSNBC afternoon news summary . . . once jokingly called itself 'all pedophiles all the time.'"[27]

BOY SEDUCED INTO SORDID BUSINESS

Meanwhile, the *New York Times* weighed in with extensive reporting of the case of Justin Berry. Berry began operating his own sexually oriented Web cam at the age of thirteen, reaping hundreds of thousands of dollars over the years. Online fans paid to watch Berry, a white boyish adolescent, remove his clothing and masturbate. The teen also arranged private meetings with some of his clients and eventually developed an expansive Web-based business in porn, video, and performance. *Times* reporter Kurt Eichenwald helped get Berry out of the business at nineteen. Eichenwald helped arrange immunity for the young man on a long list of charges in exchange for testimony against his clients, thus blurring the difference between policing and reportage while giving the imprimatur of serious journalism to ongoing panics around sex, minors, and the Internet.

The *Times* article tells the tale of a straight-arrow kid who was lured into Web porn by predatory perverts. "I didn't really have a lot of friends," Berry is quoted as saying, "and I thought having a Webcam might help me make some new ones online, maybe even meet some girls my age." Berry's loneliness, combined with ready access to Internet technology,

supposedly made him easy prey. This account of lost innocence resonates with mid-twentieth-century fears of homosexual contagion, but it
does not mesh with unreported facts of the case, dug out by the indefatigable Debbie Nathan, nor was it confirmed by Nathan's subsequent
interviews of Berry's peers. Far from being friendless, Berry was popular enough to be elected president of his freshman class in high school.
Chat logs with his age-mate friends suggest that Berry was confident,
even cocky, about being (in his word) a "camwhore." His first sexual
encounter with an adult he met on the Internet (which was said to have
traumatized the youth) was not a coupling but a threesome involving a
twenty-five-year-old man and a close age-mate friend of Berry's, "Vic."
Vic, who wore "exotic clothes, eye-shadow, and fingernail polish" to
school, openly adored Berry, and the two would later make sexual videos
together.[28]

The *Times*'s account repeatedly asserts that great emotional harm
came to Berry as a result of his victimization by pedophiles. It refers to
"molestations at the hands of multiple men." But neither Berry's online
relations nor his meetings with adult men—some of whom were quite
young when they became involved with him—appear to have involved
the use of force. No doubt there was trauma in Berry's young life. But the
more logical source may have been what Eichenwald refers to as a
"troubled relationship" that Berry had with his father; police records
show reports of physical abuse. (Berry's father, who disappeared after
insurance fraud charges were brought against him in connection with
massage clinics he ran, would later host the minor's porn business from
Mazatlán, Mexico.)[29] Certainly, Berry came to suffer the effects of social stigma. But this stigma is perhaps best characterized as the shame
of having engaged in homosexual acts. In early 2003, as gossip about
his gay porn spread, Berry had become the butt of homophobic jokes
and was beaten up by another boy. Clearly, Berry was ill served by having more money and more autonomy than any adolescent should enjoy;
he developed drug problems. But millions of American teenagers ex-
periment with drugs, and most have never been abused, molested, or
involved in online pornography.[30]

However badly Eichenwald's journalism aligned with facts and logic,
it meshed with the mechanisms of mass hysteria. The reporter actively
promoted this dynamic. In a move reminiscent of the worst witch hunts
from the satanic ritual abuse years, Eichenwald produced an expert from
the right-wing fundamentalist Family Research Council to explain the
presence of people who work with minors among those who supplied

credit card numbers to Berry: "These people go into these professions, like teacher and pediatrician, to get themselves close to kids. . . . Their desires drive their careers."[31] Actually, there is no reason to believe that pedophiles are more common in child-related professions than in other areas of work, nor are there any serious studies that suggest that "getting themselves close to kids" is a sexual motive for becoming a pediatrician or schoolteacher.

In broad strokes Eichenwald depicted the Internet as the medium of a far-flung conspiracy: It has created a "virtual community of pedophiles," supposedly transforming child pornography from a "smallish trade" to a fast-paced, rapidly expanding industry. Such talk spurred a congressional hearing on the perils of the Internet. There, Eichenwald matter-of-factly asserted an unsubstantiated claim that child porn is a $20 billion-a-year industry. (This would mean that the market for child pornography is about the size of Hollywood's annual worldwide box office revenues.) Not to be outdone, another witness at the congressional hearing claimed that Internet predators were using Web cams and instant messaging to lure, meet, and prey upon children as young as eighteen months.[32]

With Berry in tow, the journalist went on a whirlwind media tour, appearing on *Oprah, Larry King Live,* and *Paula Zahn Now.* Internet predators, Eichenwald told an attentive Oprah, are "the most manipulative people I have ever encountered in my life, working day after day after day on a child, to get that child to do what they want." "Your kid," he warned parents, "is going to be lured into this. . . . Every webcam in every child's room in America should be thrown out today."[33] So goes the familiar story of virginal innocence and homosexual predation, a story line given new urgency by new communications technology. But there are other stories to be told. Among them, Debbie Nathan straightforwardly suggests, is a story more deeply rooted in the actual lives of Berry and other teens. It is the story of a world where "the line between gayness and straightness is much fuzzier for young people than for their elders—yet where boys, especially, are under grinding pressure to insist, while they're testing that line, that they're not really exploring their erotic impulses, they're just doing it for the money. Or worse, because they were duped."[34]

THE REVULSION OF SOCIETY

Not so long ago, during the 1960s and early 1970s, rehabilitation was the normative goal of criminal justice.[35] The law acknowledged gradations of offense, and jury members theoretically aspired to a dispassionate view of harm. The need for procedural barriers against police brutality, forced confessions, and prosecutorial misconduct was widely acknowledged and enshrined in important Supreme Court rulings. And so long as a "welfare model" of crime control ruled, pity, not panic, was the prevailing legal attitude toward nonviolent pedophiles. That was before legal and popular cultures took a sharply punitive turn, a shift that occurred sometime after the turbulent year of 1968 but sometime before Ronald Reagan took office in 1980—a period that corresponds to the politicization of crime, especially sex crime.[36] Today, many Americans no longer give lip service to enlightened ideals of justice; they aspire only to measures that protect, punish, and preempt. This will to punish is evident on a wide range of fronts. But nowhere are reason, judgment, measure, and pity more lacking than in ongoing panics about sex.

In the early years of the twenty-first century, alarmist reportage and overwrought calls to action fanned acts of vigilantism. These calls played out as the backdrop to everyday life.

- Signs posted at my sister's YMCA urged perpetual vigilance: "If you have any reason whatsoever to believe that any child is being sexually abused here, remember—You don't have to 'prove' anything. Just report your suspicions to us and we'll take over from there."

- Anonymous bilingual broadsides posted in Washington, D.C., identified a registered sex offender as "Child Rapist" / "Violador de Niñas." Actually, the man had been convicted not of raping a child but of having noncoercive sexual relations with a fifteen-year-old minor who was less than one year short of the district's age of consent.

- In Florida a disabled thirty-eight-year-old man committed suicide after neighbors distributed flyers labeling him a "child rapist." Physically, mentally, and socially impaired, the man was not actually a rapist, statutory or otherwise. Eighteen years earlier he had exposed himself to a nine-year-old girl. It goes without saying that the leafleters expressed no remorse at their actions.[37]

- In Maine two registered sex offenders were tracked to their house using the Megan's Law listings on the Internet and shot to death. Their murderer got into the house by pretending to be a police officer who had come to warn them of a vigilante plot.[38]

anyone ever convicted of a sex offense to obtain green cards, tightens sex offender registration requirements, and makes failure to register or update one's registration a felony. Sections of the new law, each named for a different child victim, include provisions for DNA collection and a pilot program to use global positioning to keep an eye on sex offenders. Ex post facto law is usually viewed as inimical to democratic norms, but the Walsh Act also gives the U.S. attorney general the authority to apply its provisions retroactively.

A 2005 Gallup poll suggests how heavily sex crimes weigh in the public imagination. Gallup found that fear of child molestation topped a list of public safety concerns: two-thirds of Americans were "very concerned" about child molestation in their local community, a figure that is almost double the rate of concern for terrorism (36 percent) and significantly higher than the rate for violent crime (52 percent). Almost universally (94 percent), poll respondents favored sex offender registries, while two-thirds were unconcerned that such registries might erode civil liberties. Six in ten people who were aware of public sex offender registries had visited their state's Web site—and two-thirds of all respondents said that it was at least somewhat likely that a convicted sex offender was living in their neighborhood.[42]

As in the 1940s and 1950s, then, horrific but statistically uncommon events foster a sense of dire emergency, a need for draconian laws, and demands for exceptions to the luxury of democratic legal norms. But sex panics of the early twenty-first century represent an extension of a more or less continuous series of panics that have played out, in different modes and to different degrees, for far longer than their predecessors. Fostered by new modes of communication (milk carton ads, twenty-four-hour news channels, the reality-based television crime drama that involves viewers in a perpetual manhunt) and new means of communication (the Internet, e-mail listservs, text messaging), contemporary sex panics have occurred at a pace that is both faster and more constant than those of the mid-twentieth century. In addition to producing new layers of statutory law, contemporary panics have produced an expansive and more or less permanent civil, government, and media apparatus dedicated to the production of a constant state of panic. In the process, ongoing sex panics have shifted the basis of legal debates away from ideals of informed argument and toward expressions of raw emotionality.

At last count, forty-four states either have passed or have pending laws that would require some sex offenders to be monitored for life with electronic bracelets and global positioning devices. Since 2005 the U.S. Congress has been considering a bill that would electronically track some sex offenders—the Jessica Lunsford Act, or "Jessica's Law," named after the Florida girl who was raped and murdered by a repeat offender in 2005. Ten years into Megan's Law, New York revised its rules, requiring "moderate risk" sex offenders to register for life, not for ten years, as required under an earlier law, while extending the registry period for "low-risk" offenders to twenty years. Meanwhile, a bipartisan effort in Ohio would require some sex offenders (and, by extension, their family members) to post green license plates on their cars. Nine states now allow or require castration before some sex offenders can be released from prison.[43]

Part of what defines the current wave of sex panics is the desire to discover, publicize, and perpetually punish even minor infractions. Journalists and parent groups sometimes advocate expanding Megan's Law listings to require lifetime registration and community notification for all convicted sex offenders, including people arrested for having sex with consenting adults in public restrooms or parks. In 2005 the Maryland legislature considered (but did not pass) a bill that would require electronic monitoring of virtually all sex offenders. That same year New York's Republican governor, George Pataki, issued an executive order (later ruled illegal) remanding all sex offenders to civil confinement in locked mental asylums upon their release from prison.[44]

THE RETURN OF AN INSTITUTION

Pataki never did get the civil confinement bill he wanted. But when the liberal Democrat Eliot Spitzer became governor, New York became the twentieth state to resurrect that odd institution from the 1950s. The law—which Spitzer said he hoped would become the "national model"—now permits the indefinite confinement of sex offenders after their prison sentence is served. Assembly speaker Sheldon Silver, a Democrat who supported the measure, was quoted as invoking all the familiar tropes: "Like every parent, I have strong feelings about how to punish sexual predators for robbing children of their innocence." Predictably, the new law was widely touted as applying to the "most dangerous" sex offenders, those deemed most likely to commit new crimes. In fact, it applies to a wide range of offenses. Even minors, or those convicted of nonviolent offenses such as giving indecent material to minors, could be subject to civil confinement. The new law even creates a strange new legal category, "sexually motivated felony," which applies to "those who intended to commit a sex crime but did not."[45]

The New York law closely follows the logic of the U.S. Supreme Court's decision in *Kansas v. Hendricks* (1997): Civil confinement is not deemed punitive if psychological treatment is provided. That is, it does not violate democratic legal norms and their aversion to preventative detention or indefinite sentences. But the New York law also replicates the *Hendricks* decision's inherent illogic. As one legal scholar puts it, "Either sex offenders are too sick to go to prison in the first place, or they are too dangerous to be released from prison after the set term limit, and sentences should be lengthened. The current state of the law allows lawmakers to have it both ways."[46]

Even as Spitzer was steamrolling his civil confinement law through the state legislature, the *New York Times* was running a three-part series on the glaring failures of the practice:

- Such laws invariably catch up minor offenders or confine offenders long past the point at which they might be dangerous. (In Wisconsin a 102-year-old man who wears a sports coat to dinner and suffers memory lapses remains confined.)
- Civil confinement is applied to a mixed group that sometimes includes nonviolent exhibitionists but not violent, garden-variety rapists.
- Psychological "treatment" for civilly confined sex offenders is largely unscientific, based more on therapeutic fad and conjecture than on any body of informed evidence or double-blind studies.
- Inmates face a legal catch-22: One condition of release is the successful completion of therapy. But since therapy typically requires a complete recounting of past crimes—including those unknown to authorities—many detainees logically refuse therapy and do so on the advice of counsel.[47]

The three articles might have provided the occasion for deeper reflection on the fetishization of child innocence and its inverse, the imagination of monstrosity, in popular and legal cultures. Surely, one of the striking features of the politicization of sex crimes is that minor nonviolent offenses against underage teens and children are often treated far more harshly than the serious, violent crime of rape against adult women. Rapists, it would appear, are simply not monstrous, at least not to the same degree as child fondlers.[48] In reality, the three articles had no discernible effect on deliberations of the new law. And even in the otherwise exemplary *Times* series, the reporters' language sometimes seems haunted by ghosts from mid-twentieth-century sex panics. Monica Davey and Abby Goodnough blur homosexuality with sex offense or lack of control: In the first article they report that "sex among offenders is sometimes rampant." In the second they describe a scene apparently meant to disturb: "Two men took their shirts off, rubbed each other's backs and held hands, while others disappeared together into dormitory rooms." In the third they matter-of-factly report that "those driven by deviant sexual interests" (this is sometimes, but not always, a euphemism for men who are attracted to male minors) are most likely to recidivate—without taking into account the ages of victims, and without parsing distinctions between pedophilia and exhibitionism or between violent and nonviolent offenses.[49]

THE WHITENESS OF THE SEXUAL PREDATOR

The race of the sex criminal remains the exception to the rule of how crime is usually "raced," in both in public imaginings and law enforcement practices. In keeping with the racial double standard of the mid-twentieth century, which coded crime and generic sexual violence as "black" and homosexuality or specialized sexual perversion as "white," and in keeping with the racial geography of the satanic ritual abuse panics, the national statistics recorded in the *Times* series reveal that a majority of those held in civil commitment nationwide are white. (Virtually all are male.) The same holds for Megan's Law registrants nationwide.

No doubt African American men are overrepresented in sex offender registries, a point carefully demonstrated by the legal scholar Daniel Filler.[50] But what the data also show is that the racial distribution of registered sex offenders is far less skewed against African Americans than are incarceration rates. In the states for which racial data were available, blacks are 1.35 (Texas) to 14.35 (North Dakota) times more likely to appear in sex offender registries than whites, with a median rate of 1.9. (North Dakota is the far outlier in this data set.)[51] Compare this median figure with the much wider racial disparity for incarceration rates. Recent national estimates have found black men to be seven times more likely than white men to be in prison.[52] And in every state surveyed save one, whites were an absolute majority of registered sex offenders. This is not the usual profile of those caught up in the U.S. legal system.

Department of Justice statistics show that at roughly the same time that Filler was gathering data on sex offenders, 32.7 percent of all prisoners sentenced to one year or more nationwide were white; 42.4 percent were black, and 19.2 percent were Latino.[53] New sex offender laws may be applied disproportionately, but they are not applied primarily against African Americans. (See appendix 1.)

The data suggest the need for a nuanced view of race and sex dynamics in the contemporary culture of fear. Modern sex panics, the forms of communal control they produce, and the overreaching laws they precipitate are not the racially motivated rape panics of yesteryear. (The white woman or girl is not necessarily their principal imagined victim.) Modern sex panics are not even directly comparable with present-day anxieties about violent crime. (That is, in modern sex panics the black man is not necessarily the imagined predator, the statistically preponderant object of fear and loathing.) Or perhaps another way to look at it is this: If ongoing sex panics are considered as a subset of contemporary crime panics, the territory they map is not coextensive with fear of violent crime in general. Their purpose is not racial domination in the usual sociological sense of the term.[54]

Race is involved, in the sense that modern sex panics emerged from the worldview of a race and class group. Mid-twentieth-century sex panics produced the implicitly white sex fiend as the target of an early war on sex crime; the most ferocious ventings of anxiety occurred in places like Sioux City and Boise. After a hiatus lasting from the close of the 1950s through the early 1970s, sex panics resumed in new forms, and from the mid-1970s through the 1980s, the new perturbations swept white suburbs and small towns. More waves followed in rapid succession. These spasmodic occurrences might seem to be episodes of nervous collapse, but they are also productive and constructive: they help the white middle class to feel a sense of community, exert a sense of sexual hygiene and moral discipline, define itself against Others, and stake its claim to being the universal class, the one whose sense of danger, morality, and justice will serve as norm for all of society. If one effect of modern sex panics is racial domination, then, this effect is achieved by means more subtle than simply directing another set of laws against black men. What happens here resembles the sort of moral fortification practices analyzed in the field of critical whiteness studies. Whiteness was fabricated in opposition to blackness, of course, and brute force is how that opposition was structured historically, but the moral superiority of whiteness was maintained by way of shared practices designed to fortify and purify white communities. These communal practices have been as mild as white weddings, dietary reforms, or assorted prohibition movements and as harsh as shunnings, witch hunts, and other forms of communal violence directed against internal deviants.[55]

A long-standing variant of moral fortification, homophobia, seems more clearly implicated than racism in the forms and logics of modern sex panics—and this has something to do with both the imagined victim (often the boy child) and the implicit "whiteness" of the perpetrator in sensational sex crime stories. But the pedophile monster both is and is not the lurking homosexual predator of times past. Or perhaps this too might be put another way: The figure of the modern sexual predator occupies the space formerly associated with the homosexual in the social imagination. As the queer theorist Lee Edelman has suggested, "the pedophile," now portrayed as *the* threat to children's safety and well-being, evokes homosexuality's imagined antisocial sexuality, its wholly negative relation to reproduction, children, family, and the future.[56] The terror he evokes draws sustenance from all the evil that American culture once unambiguously attributed to the homosexual, whose depraved condition was imagined, contrarily, to be both congenital and contagious.

Today the homosexual is no longer so far beyond the pale as he was during McCarthy-era repression or even in 1970s backlash and 1980s AIDS alarms. So long as he has sex in his own home under conditions resembling heterosexual monogamy, he has moved from the outer limits of stigmatized and immoral sex to a zone of tolerated, if contested, sexualities just outside the charmed circle of normal sex (to crib a phrase from Gayle Rubin).[57] By dint of these movements and shifts, then, contemporary sex panics are not simply duplications of the overtly homophobic sex panics of the past—although, I hasten to add, the relationship between one kind of fear and another is volatile, unstable. The recent relative tolerance will sometimes lapse into homophobic hysterics outright. Often-repeated claims about the incurability of the sex offender whose preference is for males clearly mark the genealogy of the pedophile, and free-hand theories about "the cycle of abuse" (abused children become adult abusers) echo yesteryear's notions of homosexual contagion (the "vicious circle of proselytism"). In this zone of terrible ambiguity, something has remained the same, while something else, something more, is in the making: the invention of new monsters and victims; the production of new ideas about childhood, sex, and the integrity of the person; the development of new middle-class norms and phobias; and the deployment of an expansive new machinery for marking, supervising, and regulating deviants.

Shall we say, then, that in a society committed both to a war on crime (with its mass incarceration of black men) and to ridding itself of racism (through formal adherence to a regime of civil rights), the feared figure of the white pedophile is necessary? His outsized function appears to have both psychic and territorial dimensions in the emergent social formation. Perhaps part of the psychic work he performs is to absolve the guilty conscience of racism at a time when so many other fears are focused on the black gangbanger or the brown border menace. The territorial work the white pedophile performs is of course linked to geographies of race and class: He circulates fear of crime beyond the inner city and into the outer suburbs. He thus fosters security measures and watchfulness in places far removed from any crime scene. He anchors the culture of control firmly within the far-flung redoubts of the white heterosexual middle-class family.

He also does something more. If we think of the white sexual predator as a social construct—a type of person who no doubt exists, and no doubt causes harm, but whose monstrous image is an oversized expression of white middle-class fears—and if we recall that the white middle class invariably projects its concerns as universal ones, then we are in a position to see not only how small-town rites of purification and suburban dramas of protection supply the working materials for the elaboration of national norms but also how overt references to the racial origins of those norms can be progressively erased in the resulting imagined community. *Whiteness* and *straightness* may not even be the right words anymore for the type of rectitude that is staged in moral panic. Today virtually anyone can assert his belonging to the national moral community by taking up the logic of sex panic, by lashing out against the sexual monster. As the cultural anthropologist Lorna Rhodes has shown in her moving and disturbing fieldwork among "supermax" prisoners, even those most radically excluded from social citizenship assert their commonality with national moral standards by persecuting sex offenders in the name of the victimized child.[58]

STATE OF EXCEPTION

In *State of Exception,* the Italian philosopher Giorgio Agamben theorizes executive power in modern states as the power of exception, the power, in an emergency, to bypass normal legal procedures, to suspend constitutional rights, and to issue impromptu laws. In the immediate context of the USA Patriot Act and the war on terror, and against a wider backdrop framed by domestic and international crises, Agamben ominously notes "a continuing tendency in all of the Western democracies": "The declaration of the state of exception has gradually been replaced by an unprecedented generalization of the paradigm of security as the normal technique of government."[59] By degrees exception becomes the norm. Modern democracies are becoming "protected democracies."

Agamben's exposition provides a useful starting point for thinking about current trends in the United States, and it will be clear that I have kept his work in mind. Much of what happens in the realm of governance today is premised on the existence of this or that emergency, some state of affairs so menacing that exceptional measures at once protective, preemptive, and punitive are said to be in order. But *State of Exception* is marred by gaps. Curiously absent from Agamben's analysis is any reckoning with irrational, imaginative, or phantasmic elements in the developments he describes. This, it seems to me, makes the exceptional state seem far more rational than it is. And Agamben's depiction of law as an abstract, self-generating system subject to periodic perturbations tends to remove law from its historical contexts. The notion that the exceptional state both exceeds and lies at the perpetual font of law poses a conundrum of the sort that invariably amuses structuralists and poststructuralists. But it is difficult to see how placing the exception at the "threshold" or "edge" of normative law sheds light on how any particular set of laws works as a system or how it breaks down during a crisis.

What Agamben's textual study of legal documents and political theory ultimately fails to disclose is how deeply embedded undemocratic trends are in both government and civil society and how these trends are involved with deeper institutional and political-economic shifts. Far from being restricted to the presidency, the "security paradigm" and its associated forms of action, as I have been describing them, are distributed across executive, legislative, and judicial functions of government. Far from being confined to organs of government proper, the state of panic is spread across a style of journalism, a mode of activism, a kind of civic ideal, and a way of thinking. And far from resulting in a suspension of law or in rule by edict, perhaps the most pernicious effect of these pressures on legal norms is that they subject the law itself to a slow, constant revision; they lodge exceptionality inside the rule, where it remains in force long after any crisis has passed.

Few would argue that sex crime laws have been as toxic to democratic legal norms as were the signing statements issued by President George W. Bush, which produced a legal netherworld populated by "unlawful enemy combatants" subject to policies of indefinite detention and torture. I point out only that sex crime laws have circumscribed the lives of far larger numbers of people who "cannot be integrated into the political [or social] system."[60] This process has happened over a much longer period of time, and it continues to intensify. In this process, sex offenders are progressively stripped of rights not because they are "unclassifiable" and thus relegated to the lacunae of normal law but by dint of the development of a classification system that lodges them in closely written definitions of law. This production of categories of people who have diminished rights has happened not by undemocratic or unlawful means but by means of a process that is effectively poisoned while remaining democratic and lawful. The state of exception passes when crises end and edicts are retired. But the state of panic, which is abnormal, comes to be written at the heart of law, which provides norms.

LAW WITHOUT BOUNDS

The usual rules do not apply to the development and deployment of the new laws. Normally, statutes of limitations set maximum time limits for the filing of charges in noncapital criminal cases—and with good reason: memories fade or change. Barring extreme cases, such as murder, the state has no interest in pursuing or prosecuting defendants for events said to have transpired long ago. But sex law is not normal law, and from their beginnings sex laws have constantly announced themselves as exceptions to the rule of normal law. Successive revisions to federal law have extended the statute of limitations for many sex offenses involving child victims, including nonviolent crimes, to the life of the minor.

The new laws represent not just a temporal expansion but also a spatial one. Historically, the scope of laws has been coterminous with the borders of the states that passed them. States seldom claimed jurisdiction over events beyond their boundaries. But a strange thing happened to traditional concepts of sovereignty and citizenship in the aftermath of wave after wave of sex panic: new sex crime laws attach to the body, the person, in unprecedented ways. Evolving sex trafficking statutes extend the long arm of earlier laws, which primarily regulated interstate travel and U.S. maritime jurisdiction. These laws make it a crime to travel abroad for purposes of having sex with a minor or, even less purposefully, to have sex abroad with a person who is younger than eighteen years old. These statutes apply without regard for the age of consent in the traveler's home state or the traveler's destination.

The protection of minors from abuse and exploitation is a legitimate concern of law. But part of what happens in campaigns against trafficking and crusades for child protection is that the lurid spectacle of extreme predation has the effect of obscuring everyday, workaday exploitations. An all-too-easy rage to track down and do away with the wicked man substitutes for the greater challenge of addressing the root causes of poverty, dislocation, and homelessness. This seems to me to be symptomatic of a perverse relationship between the regulation of sex crimes and the deregulation of economic life: moral indignation substitutes for the promotion of child welfare writ large at a time when the privatization schemes mandated by the International Monetary Fund, the business practice of relentlessly squeezing of supply lines down to factory and field, and assorted social and economic turmoil associated with what we euphemistically call globalization are aggravating the underlying conditions associated with capitalism's most predatory forms. These more systematic sources of coercion in the world of sex work go unaddressed, as the feminist sociologist Julia O'Connell Davidson has convincingly shown in her studies of sex work and child trafficking.[61]

The techniques used in sex panics have proved replicable in other domains, and sex offender laws have come to serve as a model for new laws and juridical practices. The marking and shaming of convicts by means of public registries seems an especially popular technique. A victims' rights clearinghouse in New Mexico posts an online database of everyone convicted in the state of driving while intoxicated. Several states publish online listings of methamphetamine offenders, while lawmakers in Texas, Nevada, and California have introduced initiatives to create public registries of those convicted of domestic violence. Mimicking the form of Megan's Law listings, Florida and other states maintain Web sites that give the personal details (photo, name, age, address, offenses, periods of incarceration) of all prisoners released from custody.

David Garland notes that such practices reverse the logic of various expungement laws from the 1960s and 1970s, "which made it illegal to disclose information about an ex-offender's criminal record after a certain time had elapsed." He goes on: "The assumption is that there can be no such thing as an 'ex-offender'—only offenders who have been caught before and will strike again. 'Criminal' individuals have few privacy rights that could ever trump the public's uninterrupted right to know."[62]

Other techniques have proved equally replicable: templates for the drafting of broadsides, molds for the casting of new statutes. I note here an ongoing shift toward legislation on a first-name basis. Historically, laws that bore names bore the surnames of their authors: Mann, Taft-Hartley, Humphrey-Hawkins, McCain-Feingold. Since the early 1990s Americans have increasingly named laws—which are supposed to be impersonal, detached, aloof—after individual victims, usually a child or young adult. These laws are typically referred to in familiar form: not the Megan Kanka Act, but "Megan's Law." First-name laws put the victim, or presumed victim, "in front of" the law, as the legal scholar Jonathan Simon has aptly put it, and this placement reinforces the idea that justice is a personal matter, a settling of scores between victim and offender.[63] Victims' rights advocates argue that such personalization (personification) of the law represents a democratization of justice: such laws involve activist civil society in campaigns to draft legislation, symbolically represent plaintiff citizens at the bar of justice, and reinforce intuitive concepts of justice. But in a deeper sense this mode of personalization has all the sound and fury of democracy while shifting the norms of governance in undemocratic (or at least hitherto unconstitutional) directions. Personalization bends lawmaking to the passions of the populace; it reinforces punitive trends to strip away rights of the accused and protections for the convicted; and it ratifies the power of the special case to steer the general rule. Whereas the use of surnames lends gravitas to laws and policies, the use of first names condescends to the public and has the effect of infantilizing the law and patronizing the public. Stoking raw emotions, it prepares the public for political manipulation: Who but a moral monster would oppose a law, no matter how draconian, named for a murdered child?

Consider the bizarre legal trajectory of a moral panic touching indirectly upon sex and violence. In 2003 the Florida state legislature intervened in a painful dispute between Michael Schiavo and his in-laws, passing "Terri's Law." Terri Schiavo had been kept alive in a persistent vegetative state for more than thirteen years when her husband had the feeding tube removed. Terri's Law specifically empowered Governor Jeb Bush to order the tube reinserted. After the Florida Supreme Court struck down the law and another tube removal was imminent, the federal government intervened in 2005. The "Palm Sunday Compromise" gave federal courts jurisdiction over the case, and George W. Bush flew to Washington from Texas, where he had been vacationing, to hastily sign the bill into law.[64]

The Schiavo case is usually understood to have been a campaign by religious conservatives and pro-life activists, who equated removal of the feeding tube with euthanasia and euthanasia with abortion. And so it was, but what is striking about these events is how closely they follow the script of sex panic and the cult of child victimhood. The campaign for government intervention was spearheaded by Terri Schiavo's parents, who assumed the role of the victim's family. Congressional Republicans and right-to-lifers deployed the usual tropes of moral alarm. Allegations were floated that Michael Schiavo (decidedly *not* "family") was a violent spouse abuser, and some made dark insinuations about his motives for wanting to remove the feeding tube. The family's complicated ordeal was packaged as one more outrage against the innocent. Videotapes and posters of the comatose woman put a face on the suffering.

Well in advance of Terri's Law and federal intervention in the case, a growing body of sex crime laws had prepared the way for just such use and abuse of lawmaking. It cannot quite be said that Aimee's Law, Megan's Law, Jessica's Law, or the Adam Walsh Act were special statutes passed for individual people or particular cases. But they did push legal norms toward reactive, ad hoc lawmaking around special cases. Their naming, their valorization of victimhood, their conflation of horrifying anomalous events with pervasive risks, the techniques of suasion used to pass them, not to mention the special provisions they applied against ex-convicts who had already served their sentences, deeply eroded fundamental legal principles. Many such laws have to do with sex crimes, others with federal involvement in the search for missing adults (Bryan's Law, Kristen's Act, Jennifer's Law), others with routine appropriations for mundane undertakings.

When seventeen-year-old Brett Chidester committed suicide after experimenting with salvia, a hallucinogenic sage used by Mazatec shamans in Oaxaca, Mexico, the boy's parents campaigned for a ban on the drug. Chidester's mother provided material from the boy's diary to argue that salvia had influenced the boy's feelings that "our existence in general is pointless." The Delaware legislature promptly passed "Brett's Law," banning the herb.[65]

While first-name laws are becoming a normal technique of governance, still other statutes take commemorative form, populating the legal landscape with icons of misfortune. By degrees the social drama boils down to stories of innocence and victimization. The state is cast as the parental figure who will save the imperiled child. By increments exception becomes the rule, emotionality replaces reason, and special provisions become ordinary. This happens not through the suspension of the law but through a hollowing-out of law's essence.

CLEANSINGS

Assorted laws in twenty-two states and hundreds of municipalities restrict where a sex offender can live, work, or walk. Where a sex offender lives has no known bearing on whether he will commit new crimes.[66] But in twenty-first-century sex panics, residency restrictions have proved especially popular, promoted by citizens' groups, victims' rights advocates, crusading journalists, and politicians in a wide variety of settings. First, a growing number of cities and states passed ordinances prohibiting registered sex offenders from living within one thousand feet of schools or parks—effectively evicting them from many towns and communities. Then, as expelled sex offenders began filtering out of restricted zones into unrestricted areas, states and municipalities began to actively compete with each other to pass ever wider perimeters of exclusion (2,000 feet, 2,500 feet) and to concoct ever more comprehensive definitions of which offenders would be evicted from their homes.

California—in 1947, the first state to impose a statewide sex offender registry and in 1982 the epicenter of the SRA/day-care panics—signed on to the new wave of sex offender legislation with zeal. In 2006, 70 percent of Californians who went to the polls voted to pass Proposition 83, loosely dubbed "Jessica's Law." Proposition 83 banishes all registered sex offenders (felony and misdemeanor alike) from living within two thousand feet of a school or park and mandates lifelong electronic tracking of all felony sex offenders (whether deemed dangerous or not) through the Global Positioning System (GPS). The two-thousand-foot buffer effectively evicts all convicted sex offenders from California's cities, scattering them to remote or rural areas. Among the legally dispossessed, who face the option of removal or imprisonment, was a man convicted of having consensual relations with his fifteen-year-old girlfriend when he was sixteen.[67] Another offender perpetually circulates the streets of the Bay Area, where there are no places he can live. He and his wife must move their trailer constantly to avoid violating a rule tacked on by the Department of Corrections and Rehabilitation, which prohibits sex offenders from being in the same noncompliant place for two hours. His original registry offense was indecent exposure: mooning his sister-in-law during a family argument.[68]

Consider the scene in Cedar Rapids, Iowa, where a state law, passed overwhelmingly in 2002, barred virtually all sex offenders from living within two thousand feet of a school or day-care center: twenty-six men crowded into twenty-four rooms at a motel, one of the few residences legally available to them in the town. Some offenders were driven across state lines—where neighboring states and municipalities then rushed to pass similar ordinances. One person shuffled into the sheriff's office, because he knew nowhere else to go. Others, thrown out of their homes, were driven underground: They slept in cars, under bridges, or in abandoned buildings.[69]

In Deltona, Florida, forty-nine-year-old Juan Matamoros, along with his wife and two sons, were forced to move out of their home because Matamoros had been convicted in Massachusetts twenty-one years earlier for "lewd and lascivious behavior." He says he had had too much to drink while celebrating the birth of his daughter and was seen urinating at the side of a parked car.[70]

In Miami, where both city and county laws prohibit sex offenders from living with twenty-five hundred feet of a school, day-care center, or park, five men took up residence under a bridge, the Julia Tuttle Causeway. The authorities charged with monitoring sex offenders allowed this because they could find no other place for the men to live. Javier Diaz, thirty, was among those rendered homeless; he was sentenced in 2005 to three years' probation for lewd and lascivious conduct involving a girl younger than sixteen. Because he lived under the causeway, Diaz had "trouble charging the tracking device he is required to wear; there are no power outlets nearby." Diaz elaborated: "You just pray to God every night, so if you fall asleep for a minute or two, you know, nothing happens to you." That was 2007. By 2009 the number of sex offenders living under the Tuttle Bridge had risen to sixty-six; some later counts put the number as high as 140.[71]

Such scenes raised safety questions, and many concluded that the laws had gone too far. So in 2009 Iowa retained its ban on sex offenders' living within two thousand feet of a school or day-care center but scaled its application back to a smaller subset of sex offenders: those convicted of more serious crimes. At the same time, however, the state imposed stringent new daytime rules on where any offenders might set foot and raised the fees it charges sex offenders to register with authorities. In

2010 Miami-Dade commissioners followed suit and passed a new sex offender ordinance that created a single countywide standard. The new ordinance had the effect of repealing twenty-four competing sex offender statutes passed by Miami and various other municipalities within the county. Authorities then began relocating homeless sex offenders to new motels, apartments, and campgrounds. Civil libertarians hailed the new comprehensive law as a step in the right direction but noted that it did not go far enough. Florida state law still prohibits all sex offenders from living within a thousand feet of a school, day-care center, park, playground, bus stop, or other places where children gather. And the new Miami-Dade law still prohibits sex offenders from living with twenty-five hundred feet of a school; it simply eliminates the profusion of other laws that kept sex offenders from living within 2,500 feet of various other places that children frequent. "It's the end of the Julia Tuttle, but it's not the end of this kind of place," said Patrick, described as "a registered sex offender who has lived under the rat-infested bridge for three years." "There will be another Julia Tuttle, another place where people will put us so that we are out of sight and out of mind."[72]

When Hurricane Gustav approached New Orleans in 2008, the state's evacuation plan sorted human beings into four categories. Medical evacuees were taken to special shelters. Those with their own transportation were instructed to seek out shelters run by churches or the Red Cross. The poor, the indigent, and those without cars were warehoused by the state. Sex offenders were left to fend for themselves.

The classification of sex offenders as unfit for rescue in the event of an emergency, the devising of exceptional laws to deal with them, and various efforts at purging them from their communities all reenact the logic of "social death," a term introduced by the sociologist Orlando Patterson to describe the condition of slavery. As James Waller summarizes, three features define social death: "Subjection or personal domination, excommunication from the legitimate social or moral community, and relegation to a perpetual state of dishonor." The concept has been applied to the situations of black prisoners under current conditions of mass incarceration, the legal limbo inhabited by terror suspects who have been classified as "unlawful enemy combatants," and the position of Jews in Nazi Germany, whose social death was a forerunner of genocide.[73]

The teenager who had sex with his underage girlfriend; the older man who is fond of performing fellatio on sixteen- or seventeen-year-old males; the flasher, the masher, the social nuisance alongside the real menace; the wrongfully accused beside the rightfully convicted: these people have become a phantom, fugitive population, shadowy flickerings in the deepest night. Such scenes, played out in towns and states across America, suggest that something is broken in U.S. culture and law.

These scenes also suggest that a new system of governance is in the making. Thirty-five years of virtually nonstop sex panics have traumatized the public with imaginings of risk, danger, and harm. These alarms foster a conception of the state that stresses its role as protector and punisher, stimulating the production of laws that undermine democratic legal norms in durable and pernicious ways: the protection of innocence trumps a presumption of innocence, and the public's right to security trumps the time-honored idea of limits to punishment. Growing numbers of citizens are marked, registered, and transferred to a space outside society but within the law. The state of panic becomes the normal state of affairs.

Miscarriages of justice, authoritarian tendencies, and undemocratic laws are nothing new, of course; the United States has always failed to achieve its own lofty standards of freedom, due process, fair play, and the like. But how would you recognize the point at which quantitative changes amounted to a qualitative difference? The culture of sexual fear, which has permeated a wide swath of public political culture today, resembles the psychological milieu of the late Weimar cinema, whose dread of the city, fear of strangers, and celebration of the safety of the hearth anticipated the coming of fascism.[74]

CHAPTER 4

The Magical Power of
the Accusation

How I Became a Sex Criminal and Other True Stories

The sacralization of the child thus necessitates the sacrifice
of the queer.

—Lee Edelman, No *Future: Queer Theory and the Death Drive*

When I was thirteen, it seemed to me that my life had come to an end.
Students in my eighth-grade class started a rumor that I, and several
other boys (the exact constitution of this group varied from telling to
telling), had been caught "fagging off" in the bathroom. A veritable mania
quickly swept the school, and for several weeks it seemed that my homosexuality was all anyone could talk about. Such was my first encounter
with sex panic. These and other experiences have conditioned my deep
interest in the subject.

Here, then, I tell some stories about events I have lived through, the
first a tale of youthful inexperience, the last a tale of adult travails. I propose that because they reveal something of the texture of events, from a
close vantage, these stories serve as empirical evidence, as ethnographic
material to be productively examined. (See appendix 2.) No doubt the
simpler task here would be to document wild accusations and grave
injustices, but it seems to me that this strategy leaves intact the motor
that drives hysterias: the extreme account, the personal horror story.
Anecdote alone is a poor teacher, and so I punctuate the two episodes
that bracket this narrative with a brief reflective interlude on microhis-
torical shifts and unstable meanings, also seen from the vantage of a
certain life trajectory.

PART 1: I AM OUTED

When it was rumored that I had been spied in sexual congress in a public restroom, nothing could have been further from the truth. At thirteen my disposition toward sex was reticent, to say the least. But this is not to say that I was not already disquietingly aware of the draw of other boys' bodies. In sixth grade, anticipating the routines of seventh, I had experienced a stomach-wrenching terror. Physical education was a requirement in junior high, and after gym class everyone was supposed to take a shower. What if the sight of other naked boys got me excited? What if I got an erection?

Of course, I had had some visual and manual play with other boys from church and in the neighborhood. These private games of "you show me yours, I'll show you mine" were de rigeur; almost everyone played them, so far as I could tell. But as late as eighth grade I was still inexperienced in the ways of sex, if by "sex" one means intromission or even acts leading to emission. Perhaps I was a slow lad, but I did not even know how to masturbate yet, much less how to perform any other acts of gross indecency. And up until this moment my only experience with the word *fag* had come by way of Archie Bunker's foul mouth on the CBS sitcom *All in the Family* (whose writers, in their mockery of Bunker's bigotry, also introduced my peers to a veritable minithesaurus of derisive terms: *pansy, fairy, queer*). It did not take much work with a dictionary for me to figure out that I was being called a homosexual. A bit more work with the *Reader's Digest,* whose editors had recently published a piece on how to cure homosexuality, put me on to some useful distinctions and filled out the picture.

Having done my homework, I set out to determine, first, exactly what I was said to have been seen doing, so imprudently, in a busy junior high boys' room and, second, who might be the source of such gossip, which was obviously based on some sort of misunderstanding or misidentification. So vivid were the details, so emphatic the certitude of rumor, that I imagined somebody must have seen something; somehow, it never quite dawned on my adolescent reasoning that nobody had seen anything, that the whole thing was a collective delirium. My first query turned up a number of sex acts, some of which the human anatomy might plausibly admit, others that seemed (and still seem) quite improbable. I can't say that I was not intrigued by the idea of attempting the more mundane copulations, but I did not—could not—let on. My second query yielded no single source for the rumors. It eventually unearthed no fewer than a half-dozen eyewitnesses who swore they had walked into the boys' room—in some versions it was the locker room—catching me, en flagrante, engaged in some sort of group sex with a shifting cast of other boys.

The Wonder Years

And so I was catastrophically outed even before I had a real chance to be in the closet. For the long duration of eighth and ninth grades, I was a pariah, an untouchable, a social outcast. Tenth grade was not much better, for stigma followed me into the lower reaches of high school.

I am not sure I can adequately convey just how low I ranked in the adolescent pecking order, surely among the cruelest and most unequal of all social worlds. It would not be much of an exaggeration to say that I was taunted every hour of every day spent on the school bus or at school. Denial had no effect; in fact, it only inflamed my accusers. It was a "well-known fact" that I was queer, that I had done such and such. To assert otherwise offended common decency. Why, you could tell just by looking at me that I was not "right," as one girl apodictically put it. That I can still remember this remark might give an idea of how cutting it was. Nor could reason prevail: "If I were going to fag off, would I do it at school, in a place likely to be discovered?" "Well, that's not our problem; you *did* it." Girls slapped me, and boys beat me up, whenever I was so bold as to confront my tormentors. When I fought back, I was subdued by a swarm of my peers. I was not allowed to speak in public; I would be shouted down, reproved, publicly harangued for stepping out of place. Anyone so foolhardy as to defend me quickly found himself engulfed in the same torrent of stigma. Who would defend a fag but another fag? Schoolteachers and administrators were aware of my treatment, much of which happened in the classroom and all of which happened on school grounds or buses, yet they never intervened to put a stop it. Actually, I think they thought this sort of rough treatment was good for social hygiene. Or perhaps even they feared, quite logically, what would happen to them if they attempted put a stop to what was happening.

Long before I became an adult, I thus came to understand the magical power of the accusation. Some accusations, by force of their mere utterance, also constitute proof of transgression. Standing so accused, I learned too what it was like to be the scapegoat, the punching bag, the whipping boy. I think I know the helpless rage prisoners must feel. I came to identify with every class of reject, deject, pervert, and loser. I conjured Columbinesque fantasies of retribution. I thought about, but never attempted, suicide. For many years I understood this outing—before there was such a term—as the formative experience of my life. Perhaps I still do.

I survived as outsiders have always survived, by becoming more a spectator than a participant in the world around me, by developing a contemplative attitude toward events, and by escaping, ever more deeply, into the world of words, books, ideas. I read broadly, preferring imaginative, exaggerated literature of the sort accessible to adolescent boys. I wrote poetry and essays with a youthful enthusiasm. In placing words just so, I aimed to capture how sights and sounds struck the senses on a given evening. If I could not control or even much affect the events that were swirling around me, I could at least control the selection, order, and presentation of words used to describe the world, to make it *be,* on the page, in a certain sort of stylized way. Writing, in no small part, was compensation; I suppose it still is.

This world of ideas and aesthetic enthusiasms not only gave respite from my immediate sufferings; it also promised broader cosmopolitan possibilities beyond the horizon of a rural proletarian adolescence. My survival strategy has served me well over the years. I know now what I could not have suspected then: that my experiences with the totalitarian nightmare of adolescence were in no sense unique. But even today I imagine that my tormentors might come back to get me. And you can't convince me that fascism, complete with registries, badges of shame, and concentration camps, won't break out at any moment.[1]

In a Different Register

That is how I sometimes write. But when I am feeling bold, empowered, self-possessed—shall I say, cocky?—I write in a different mode. For eighth grade turned out to be not the end of life but a particularly dreadful station along the way. Things got better in high school, at first slowly, then dramatically. In the later grades the meanness of adolescence begins to wane, and gradually, by way of some metamorphosis as mysterious and as regular as that which characterizes the life cycle of cicadas, high schoolers begin to emerge as adults, more familiar with the inevitable blows of life, hence more tolerant, more understanding. I too eventually emerged from my protective shell, to learn how to connect with others.

And by this time other things had become apparent to me. I could not help but note how tormented were my tormentors, how the most outspoken ruffians would try to sweet-talk, even beg, me in private settings to suck their cocks—which, they could readily demonstrate, were already hard at the thought.

The Incident

It was not just in private settings that these undercurrent sentiments would break out; they sometimes took astonishingly visible form, and I, like a novel's invisible narrator, would duly note them, if only to myself. One day a particularly vigorous bit of rough play broke out in the locker room at school. Some athletes, black and white, were snapping their towels, popping the less athletic boys as they showered after ninth grade PE. Now, as any schoolboy knows, a really hard snap with a wet towel can sting and burn, leaving a red mark on your back or buttocks. Normally, the strong would inflict such treatment upon the weak. But on this occasion, instead of submitting to the sadism of everyday life, the freaks and geeks fought back, with Tommy—a delicate asthmatic with black hair, blue eyes, and fine features—in the vanguard. Tommy, a notorious sissy, gave as well as he got. This, I think, surprised the footballers. His laughter, which was perhaps a bit hysterical, proved infectious. Such was the din of battle that it drew both coaches into the locker room (a place they almost never ventured). "Hey, guys, knock it off, quiet down, get to class."

These unusual happenings all registered an impression on me, but the queerest detail I recall from that day is this: Tommy's penis, always large, was growing larger, heavier, and more substantial. So visible was his excitement that I thought someone would surely say something—but many of the athletic boys with whom he struggled also were becoming tumescent. The more arduous the struggle, the more visible their erections became. No one, neither bullies nor bullied nor even coaches, ever said a word about this.

INTERLUDE: SCATTERED SCENES

And so I have never thought of childhood as a time of innocence, nor could I ever entertain the incredibly stupid thought that kids do not lie about sex, a subject that, for adolescents at any rate, is the singular subject of attraction, repulsion, delirium, and power. But there are other true stories to tell, points of history and biography that contextualize my skepticism toward absolutist claims about the shifting meanings of childhood, youth, and maturity and the numbers that serve as signposts along the way.

Start with the long sweep of history. Customary ages of consent used to be much lower than they are today. Until the end of the nineteenth century, English common law set the age at ten.[2] Historically, in the rural South children from poor families married young, and rural folk, far longer than city-dwellers, resisted the modern American tendency to set sexual adulthood at eighteen (or higher: some contemporary youth advocates occasionally propose pushing the age of consent for some forms of sexual expression to as high as twenty-one).[3] I am a product of this cultural time lag. My mother was fifteen when she married my father, who was seventeen. And it was not a shotgun wedding. My parents would be the first to say that this was not ideal. Both were still immature, impetuous, headstrong. Over the years they endured several breakups and reconciliations. But this is hindsight. Their lives with fractious families living in rural poverty also were not ideal, and they hoped to escape these conditions, romantically, by forging a new life together. Meanwhile, folk wisdom was still dispensing bits of advice: Marry young, and you will raise each other. Or, sometimes, the asymmetrical version: marry a girl young, and raise her to your liking.

Even during a much later period, three fourteen-year-old girls in my junior high class were dating grown (if somewhat immature) men who were in their late teens or early twenties. During homeroom the three girls sat together, freely discussing their boyfriends' pig-headedness, their most recent breakup or reconciliation, the new monster truck Johnny Mack had bought, or the condition of Danny-Boy's tobacco seedlings after a frost. Two of the girls sported frosted hair—to make them look more mature, I suppose—and one already wore an engagement ring. Today their boyfriends would be labeled dangerous pedophiles, but in the early 1970s these courtships were known to parents and others and were considered to be within community norms. Two girls eventually married their older beaus, one at the beginning of high school, the other just after graduation. I would not argue that this sort of arrangement is ideal. It seems to me that the girls were cheated out of some of the useful experiences of growing up in the modern world: having a series of courtships, a series of breakups, sexual exploration with more than one person one's own age. But I do not see how any of the participants would have come out better off had the law become involved. And anyone listening in on the girls' conversations would realize that their adult boyfriends were not calling the shots.

My own experience suggests that the line between late adolescence and early manhood is a fuzzy one. When I came out of the closet, I was eighteen, a college freshman. But I looked younger than my age and thus got to know a number of men whose decided preference was for mature adolescents. I preferred the company of older men because they made better conversation and brought more experience to the bedroom than did my peers. When my parents disowned me, and honest work as a dishwasher would not pay the bills, these men's gifts and monetary contributions constituted an important source of support.

Still, I was far from being "barely legal," as they say nowadays, and there was some confusion about what *consent* might mean under the expressly homophobic laws of the time. Although my state's crime-against-nature statute defined homosexual intercourse as a felony, word on the street had it that law enforcement broadly protected young men until they turned twenty-one, defining them as victims of statutory rape if they engaged in relations with an older man. So in my mind I made double felons of my boyfriends, many of whom were in their mid-thirties. In some countries, sodomy laws indeed did set higher ages of consent for homosexual acts than for heterosexual intercourse, but this was not the case in my home state. Actually, court rulings there allowed judges to convict boys as young as twelve of crime against nature—so I became a sex criminal, even before I knew.

Like butch-femme or hustler-john relationships, intergenerational relationships were a long-standing paradigm of American gay life until recently. Equipped with fake IDs, teens as young as fifteen or sixteen sometimes were difficult to distinguish from young men who did not quite look their age ("twinks"). Their admirers (chicken hawks) were scarcely numerous, but they were a visible part of gay life in the late 1970s, when I arrived on the scene. (I should note here that, to the best of my knowledge, I have never met a textbook pedophile, someone whose sexual object of choice is a sexually immature child, and the chicken hawks I knew as a youth all condemned relations with children, as well as relations involving the use of force, deception, or exploitation, as they understood these terms.) No doubt opportunities for exploitation existed in these settings. But because participants in these relationships frequented the same bars and shared gossip through overlapping networks, they were subject to the norms of the subculture. Mature minors, young adults, and mature adults alike took a decidedly dim view of sugar daddies who mistreated their "boys." And whether the younger party was younger or older than eighteen, there was an explicit expectation that the older partner would mentor the younger, helping him to acquire education, skills, savvy, or other forms of cultural capital. It does not seem self-evident to me that deeply criminalizing this sort of relationship, banishing it from subcultural oversight and regulation, benefits minors. Although I was not a minor, my first significant relationship was of this general variety. I learned a great deal from my lover, a ruggedly handsome New Yorker who was ten years older, more cosmopolitan, and certainly better educated than I was. The relationship began when I was barely nineteen and lasted for ten years.

Many lives joined in such relationships already were far from ideal. Some of these couplings provided the younger party—who was often a teen throwaway or disowned young adult—with affection and stability, not to say housing and nourishment. But because they combined parenting effects with amorous love, these relationships sometimes had the effect of freezing the younger partner into a sort of perpetual dependent adolescence. Doted upon by older men with resources, "kept boys" did not always turn out well.

Matt's story is extreme and atypical. He had hit the streets of New York when he was not quite sixteen. Solicited by many admirers, he alternated between the East Village punk scene, where he hustled, and being a kept boy. He inverted the absolutist fundamentalism of his upbringing and read books on satanism and listened to the devil's music: Lou Reed, David Bowie. Matt hung out on the street where Patti Smith and Robert Mapplethorpe lived, hoping to catch a glimpse of the famous couple. And he consumed more than his fair share of club-scene drugs. Rather than grow up—rather than lose his "tragic youthful appeal," as his final letter put it—Matt committed suicide on his twenty-first birthday. No one, he wrote, would much care what happened to an aging pretty boy, so better to go out now with a bang. Some journalists and youth advocates might chalk his death up to years of abuse at the hands of older men: an extreme version of the Justin Berry story, as it was presented in the *New York Times*. But it was homophobic parents who put Matt on the street, and it was his last lover—a sad rich old man whose politics were so conservative that they bordered on the fascistic—who tried to keep him grounded while he was alive, who mourned him after his death, and saw to it that he had a decent burial.

In the late 1970s, as now, there was some variability in how parents treated sexually active gay teens, perhaps especially in the small-town rural South. Some prayed or called the minister. Some called the police. Others threw their kids out of the house. The details were the stuff of gossip. Bill, a gangly working-class kid with a malformed leg, was thrown out at fifteen, then taken in by Alan, thirty-eight. Alan saw to it that Bill got a GED. Even after the relationship ended, the two remained friends, and Alan put Bill through cosmetology school. Bill turned out to be a good hairdresser and went on to make a good living in the profession. I cannot see how his life would have turned out better had Alan been dubbed a pedophile monster and hauled off to prison.

Some families took matters in stride. Ted's parents, exasperated by their sixteen-year-old's precocious, flamboyant, and increasingly wild antics, had allowed him to move in with his boyfriend, a conservative forty-five-year-old. They hoped the latter would be a stabilizing influence. He was. He kept Ted in high school until he earned his diploma, an outcome all observers had deemed unlikely at the time. This stability did not last long. Upon turning eighteen, Ted ran away from both lover and parents, to hit the streets of San Francisco. But then, later, the relationship did resume. After a year or so Ted returned to his older lover. I do not know whether it would be right to say that Ted's boyfriend exploited him or vice versa. But I am skeptical of the idea that either party could have been induced to love someone his own age.

The lives of gay people, including gay teens, have changed dramatically since the 1970s. But if the law no longer criminalizes homosexuality, and if overt expressions of homophobia are considered unacceptable in large portions of society, this is not to say that sexual anxieties have lessened or that accusation has lost any of its occult power, only that these anxieties have acquired new sources of potency. Lee Edelman describes how unspoken assumptions animate the zeal to protect childhood innocence. The fault of the pedophile, "as 'everyone' knows, defaults, faute de mieux, to a fear of grown women—and thus, whatever the sex of his object, condemns him for, and to, his failure to penetrate into the circle of heterosexual desire."[4] Writing in a lesbian and gay studies quarterly, Kevin Ohi puts matters more bluntly: "The discourse around child abuse has given stalwart homophobes ... a seemingly unassailable venue for homophobic ecstasy in the guise of inflamed righteousness."[5] In this condition of ardor lawmakers and law enforcers seem on principle unable to distinguish what is actually harmful from what merely offends, what is not ideal from what warrants punishment. They also sometimes lose track of the difference between homosexuality and child abuse, lie and truth, guilt and innocence.

PART 2: STRANGER TO THE LAW

Taking a studio apartment in Central City during a sabbatical leave had seemed the perfect opportunity for me to explore the interior of the country, a region that was terra incognita to me, and, it so happens, to reestablish an old friendship with Joe and his partner Ricardo. I was at the pair's condo apartment when someone unexpectedly knocked on the door about midevening. Collectively, we were about to become not party to a statistic but to what the statistics elide. Statistics, after all, capture only the official version of events. This will be an unofficial report. I have tried to forget these events, a poor practice for a writer. I cannot—or rather, will not—remember the date, lest I have to mark unhappy anniversaries. But I cannot forget the details. They haunt my nightmares and demand some sort of airing.

Falsely Accused

It had already been a dark week for the couple. Ricardo, an ebullient, gregarious junior high school teacher, had been summarily sent home first thing one morning pending an investigation into his "classroom activities." Joe, a quiet and introverted civil servant of leftist sympathies, called me in to help think through what was happening. And so perchance I would become an involved witness and scribe.

The three of us pored over the formal notice Ricardo had been given, taking some solace in the phrase "classroom activities." Since so many widely reported allegations of teacher misconduct involve claims about off-campus activities, we foolishly imagined that nothing serious could be alleged to have happened inside the classroom. We also took some comfort in the liberalism and tolerance of Pleasantville, where Ricardo worked. A suburb of his Central City home, the town had a broad human rights ordinance protecting gays and lesbians from various forms of discrimination. Still, on the advice of the teachers' union, Ricardo had obtained legal representation.

Then, in short order, the phone calls began: first from the school district, then from Child Protection Services, last from the police. Acting on the lawyer's instruction, Joe and Ricardo used their answering machine to monitor these calls and avoided delivery of certified mail; they immediately conveyed the recorded phone messages and certified mail notices to the lawyer, who responded promptly with phone calls and faxes to the various parties involved, offering to set up prompt meetings at which counsel would be present. These were described as standard measures to preserve one's legal rights, including right to counsel. As the lawyer explained, if one answers a call from investigators or signs for delivery of certified mail, one can be summoned straightaway for an interview, allowing school authorities or social services to conduct interviews without counsel's being present and to prejudge the case at less than legal standards of evidence. By the end of the week, then, Ricardo knew that an ominous spectrum of authorities were conducting separate investigations—but into what? Like Joseph K. in Kafka's *The Trial*, he still had no idea who had accused him of what.

On Friday, as a diversion from these unknowable troubles, I had taken Joe and Ricardo out for dinner. Afterward, I was visiting with them in their home when the knock came. I say "knock" here with some qualification. Cops do not really knock at the door, polite visitors asking nicely to be let in. They batter the door in an effort to rattle your sense of security at home and to let you know who's in charge. Ritchie had gone upstairs and Joe froze, so I went to the door. "Who's there?" "Police—open up. We'd like to talk to you." I peered through the peephole, which was blocked. (I am told this is not an uncommon tactic.) For all I knew, robbers were at the door. I tried to keep some presence of mind. "I'll have to see some kind of identification," I said, vaguely mindful of procedures and rights. The peephole remained blocked. "I can't see anything through the peephole," I said. I heard some hushed conversation on the other side of the door—I imagine the police were trying to decide whether I merited disclosure or whether they should batter down the door—then some sort of document (I couldn't actually read it) became visible through the hole. But I could make out several blue-clad figures in the hallway outside: seven or eight cops, an armed SWAT team.

Exchanging glances with Joe, I opened the door a crack. One cop asked if they could come inside. I said that I would prefer to talk to them through the doorway, to which another replied: "Do you really want to conduct this business in front of your neighbors?" When I paused, preparing to ask Joe what to do, a large male officer with a carrot-colored buzz cut pushed through the doorway, saying, "Well, guess what? We're already in." As a middle-class, native-born citizen, I was shocked by this abrupt invasion—but I did not dare protest.

One officer asked Joe and me for our names, which we gave, before they asked if anyone else was present. When Ritchie came down the stairs, an officer told him he was under arrest. "What for?" he asked. "Aggravated sexual assault." And so it was with a protracted *"Whaaaat?"* that Ricardo learned the nature of the nightmare into which he was being plunged.

A ritual of humiliation goes with arrest. The suspect is told to empty his pockets and to remove his jewelry and shoestrings, then he gets his hands cuffed behind his back. No one read Ricardo his Miranda rights, a staple of television police procedure. Downstairs, as Ritchie was being loaded into the patrol car, Joe drew near to catch his attention. With a small locking gesture in front of the lips, Joe reminded Ricardo of the basic rule: no talking without your lawyer present. This gesture enraged the red-headed officer, Smith, who turned out to be the investigating detective from Pleasantville. He began yelling that Joe—and I, as I stood by—could be arrested for interfering with police business. "I'm just trying to tell him good-bye," Joe offered. "Well, you haven't been patted down; you could be carrying a concealed weapon." "Look, I'm harmless," Joe replied, arms outstretched, jacket open to the winter elements. I might have imagined that Joe's Christlike pose would further infuriate Smith, but he seemed to take it as a gesture of submission. Joe and Ritchie would learn more about gestures of submission as this ordeal played out.

Sirens ablaze, the small caravan of patrol cars disappeared into the night.

Deprived of Rights

And so, even though his lawyer was in contact with the police, Ritchie was arrested on a fugitive warrant at his home in Central City. In hindsight the unnecessary arrest—which came at the beginning of a weekend—apparently was intended to increase the pressure on Ricardo. Perhaps it was all based on a common theory about how gay men respond to stress. Or perhaps it was based on real-world knowledge of what jails and prisons are like, especially for gay men accused of crimes against minors. In any event Central City jail conditions are notoriously unpleasant—its prison conditions even more so. Meanwhile, back in the apartment, Joe and I waited for the customary phone call. It never came.

After a bout of hyperventilation Joe numbly pulled himself together, found a prominent ad in the telephone directory, and called a lawyer to represent Ritchie at the arraignment hearing on Monday morning. (Central City was across the state line from Pleasantville, and the lawyer

Ritchie had been consulting was not licensed to practice law in both states.) The new lawyer made two trips to the Central City jail but was never allowed to see his client. He was not surprised by this; he noted that attorneys are seldom given access to their clients before arraignment. So Ritchie did not know until Monday morning that Joe and I had lined up a lawyer. Until then, on the advice of a public defender, Ricardo had been prepared not to contest Pleasantville's request for his extradition, a decision that would have involved his transfer from Central City's jail to its prison, perhaps for several days of rough treatment, before his eventual transfer to Pleasantville.

Joe and I were in the courtroom Monday morning. The judge read charges and set bail, arraigning a stream of mostly black men. When at last Ritchie came before the bench, the judge read the charge—sexually assaulting a thirteen year old. Upon hearing this, one of the marshals, a young white man with a rural southern accent, let out a loud whooping utterance: "Ohhh, *ma-an!*" I cannot quite capture the tone and nuance of his exclamation, which played awkwardly to the crowd assembled in the courtroom; it was a curious mixture of opprobrium and prurience, with excessive body language that suggested he might either hit or high-five someone. This has always struck me as one of the more telling details of the arraignment hearing.

The other curious detail was this: After Ritchie's lawyer asked that bail be set, the judge—who had released on their own recognizance swarms of men charged with domestic violence, set bail at a few hundred dollars for a stream of accused drug dealers, had dealt harshly only with the female sex workers, whom she generally sent to detention pending trial—peered over the rims of her reading glasses to intone: "This is a very serious charge." It appeared to me that the lawyer took a step back, hammered by the magical force of the accusation. "Your honor," the lawyer replied after catching himself, "the facts are not in evidence." And so it was that bail was ultimately set. It was not a trivial bail. Joe and I scrambled to secure it and did so with the help of friends just before the close of business. Had we missed the deadline, Ritchie would have been sent to Central City's infamous prison, to await either bail or eventual transport to Pleasantville.

This treatment, I believe, is called "softening up" the accused. It was not over.

Ritchie went home on Monday afternoon. He continued to cooperate with the authorities; his lawyer had arranged for Ritchie to voluntarily appear at the Pleasantville Police Station on Wednesday, supposedly for questioning. The first thing the police did was to separate Ritchie from his lawyer. "I was asked by [Detective] Smith if I was willing to answer questions or make a statement," he reports. "Naturally, I asked for my attorney to be present. Once again, I was denied access to legal counsel. I was told that my lawyer could come in to see me any time he wanted." Outside, his attorney, who was asking to see Ritchie, was not allowed in; he was told that Ritchie could call for him any time he wanted. Behind the scenes and out of sight, Ritchie was then handcuffed, arrested, swabbed for DNA, and photographed, this time by the Pleasantville authorities. A magistrate denied his requests for an attorney to be present and summarily ordered him held without bail. After sitting in the waiting room for the better part of an hour, Ritchie's lawyer eventually ventured behind closed doors and into the bowels of the building to make inquiries, finally arriving at the magistrate's chamber. The magistrate lashed out when asked why he had denied bail without hearing from Ritchie's lawyer. "Because it's within my power to do so," he spat, leaning hard into the iron bars that separated the dispenser of justice from those in the antechamber. For a moment I thought he was going to have us all—the lawyer, Joe, and me—ordered held without bail.

The lawyer arranged for a bail hearing before a judge the following day. "I harbored no illusions about police techniques," Ritchie relates. "Still, I was shocked by what the prosecutor claimed at the bail hearing. He said that a fugitive warrant had been issued because my principal had described me as a person with 'no family' and 'no roots' in the community." In fact, Ritchie had lived with Joe for the previous fifteen years; they had lived together in the Central City area for twelve. Ritchie had taught at Pleasantville Junior High School for eight years—longer than the principal had worked there. Ritchie and Joe had owned the condo for seven years. "No roots," "no family": how easily these words come as accusations against those denied the right to official kinship.

The prosecutor objected to the bail request, suggesting that Ritchie, a Mexican American who was born in California, might flee to his "home country." The judge was not amused, drily noting that "California is an American state, last time I checked. My wife and I were there on vacation a couple of years ago, and we used American currency." And so bail was set, for a substantial sum, with a series of conditions: no travel, no contact with any minors.

At the bail hearing Ritchie first learned the details of what he had been accused of: touching a male student on his inner thigh or on his buttocks. Joe reports that, in the lobby outside the courtroom, Ritchie's attorney puzzled at the wording in the charges: such ambiguous touching, which involved neither genitals nor digital intromission, did not constitute sexual assault.

Tried in the Press: The Media Spectacle

By Friday, when Ritchie was released on bail from the Pleasantville Detention Center, his name, address, and photograph had been published in local newspapers and aired on local television news shows. I call attention to details of the reportage—which anyone who follows the news has seen played out dozens of times in dozens of local news stories—because they illustrate how journalism today essentially operates as a propagandistic extension of policing and prosecution. Journalism is panic, officially induced state-sponsored panic, in the reportage of sex crime accusations.

The story recounted by talking heads and newspaper reporters was nothing more than a press release drawn up by the police, dutifully conveyed, sometimes word for word, as "news." It erroneously reported that Ritchie had been arrested in Central City, then transported to Pleasantville. A truthful news release about how he had arranged a walk-in would have undermined the narrative about a rootless uncooperative sex criminal that police wished to bullhorn into the wider community. On some channels victims' rights advocates worked fist in glove with prosecutors, discussing the "special difficulties" children face when reporting teachers who abuse them. Such advocacy assumes that there is a victim in advance of any legal determination. As I see it, the public role of victims' rights advocates is to ensure that no defendant ever gets a fair hearing in the press, which of course reduces the chances that he will receive an unbiased hearing in court.

Ritchie was falsely reported to have been uncooperative with police investigators. I take this to mean that he would not confess to something he had not done and insisted on protecting his right to counsel. Police investigators therefore sought "additional information" from the community. As the authorities would have the public believe, Ritchie's bad behavior had forced reluctant police to go to the public for help. This sort of appeal is a common police tactic, which reporters apparently did not think twice about relaying to viewers and readers. It is an effort to turn citizens into spies for the police. Open calls to complain like this terrify me: Who knows what attention-seeking fabrications such invitations might solicit?

Not one reporter initiated a call to Ritchie's attorney, who might have corrected police misrepresentations and provided some balance. Only one reporter called Ritchie's house to seek comment from Ritchie—or anyone who happened to be home. Joe referred the reporter to Ritchie's attorney.

But not everyone was buying the allegations. While Joe was trying to raise bail on Friday, Ritchie was in the Pleasantville Detention Center, where stories about Ritchie's arrest were playing full blast on the television. Ritchie, a former La Raza activist, would later deadpan: "I was surprised to learn that I am white." News reports had described him as Caucasian. The menacing-looking photograph distributed by police to reporters did not much resemble Ritchie, and apparently no one in jail recognized him from the scary mug shot. But he reports that, as the news was playing for the umpteenth time, a newly arriving detainee, a heavily tattooed gang leader, called out: "That's bullshit, man. I don't believe any of it." Ritchie, still apparently unrecognized, approached the gangster to ask, "So how do you know anything about this Ricardo Jimenez?" "My cousins went to Pleasantville Junior High; they had classes with him. They say that's not what he's about."

Bugged or Paranoid?

When Ritchie returned home, he was initially terrified to be seen in public, afraid to stand in front of the condo building to smoke a cigarette. "What if someone tries to hurt me?" He began to calm a bit when Joan, a retired neighbor, greeted him and Joe in hallway. She began weeping, inquiring earnestly, "What the hell are they doing to you guys?" "I wouldn't have picked her for a sympathetic neighbor," Joe confided, "but it's times like this you find out who your friends are."

A police car was perpetually parked on the corner across the street, perhaps monitoring traffic, perhaps monitoring Ritchie and Joe. Then the strange telephone service began. Calls to certain numbers, especially to far-flung members of Ritchie's family, registered suspicious background noises—hums, buzzes, scratchy reception. A few times Joe had me listen in from the upstairs extension. We could find no crossed wires in the condo basement, and the noise seemed to me consistent with a clumsy wiretapping. When I was a student activist with socialist and civil rights groups, the state bureau of investigation had twice tapped

but a valued colleague with family and friends. Twenty teachers from Pleasantville Junior High came to show their support. They were almost all women, black and white, young and old. Five of Ritchie's siblings traveled to Pleasantville from out of state; former college professors came, as did an assortment of Central City friends. Joe's parents attended. As he passed through the lobby on the way to his chambers, the judge looked nervously around the room.

During the trial the student's testimony offered yet another version of what had happened; this version conformed with what the prosecutor had described erroneously in her final pretrial arguments as the accuser's evidentiary hearing testimony. Now the student claimed that Ritchie had reached inside the student's pants and touched the adolescent's penis—in a full classroom, without causing a disturbance. In a bizarre turn the student also engaged in a long argument with the prosecutor about the gist of his testimony at the preliminary hearing, denying some statements he did make and claiming to have said things that did not appear in the official court transcript. His behavior on the witness stand was so exaggerated and confrontational that even schoolteachers in the outside hallway, who glanced through the window in the door to the courtroom, discerned it: "Why look at that," said one teacher. "He's throwing his hand out, he's serving attitude."

Three student witnesses for the prosecution, all girls, told stories that did not square with another, but one girl clearly had rehearsed her part. Improbably, she echoed the exactly the same phrase, "thirty seconds," that the male student used in his pretrial testimony. She also claimed to have seen Ritchie run his hand down the student's pants, moaning the boy's name over and over in a full classroom, a caricature of the archetypal homosexual fondler of children.

Outside in the waiting room the four teens were as jolly as could be, playing games, laughing, moving around in groups of two or four. "It's children's day at the courthouse," intoned Joe's mother, a former junior high school teacher with strict disciplinary standards. "They don't seem very traumatized," said a sociologist who had been one of Ritchie's instructors in grad school. This was an understatement. In fact, they seemed oblivious to the seriousness of what was happening and to what was at stake. Indulged by their mothers, who were also present, all four seemed to have regressed to earlier stages of childhood; they exhibited behavior appropriate for seven or eight year olds, not thirteen or fourteen year olds. Joe's mother, in particular, was not amused when the accuser, a rather large adolescent of nearly fourteen, settled into his mother's lap and laid his head on her neck.

Ritchie's testimony was simple and consistent. He categorically denied ever touching a minor in an inappropriate manner. He went on to recount events that had occurred over several months. His accuser had been an unfocused and disruptive student since the beginning of the school year; his behavior had required constant management. The student's behaviors, which had been apparent from his demeanor at the evidentiary hearing and at the trial, suggested that he suffered from attention deficit disorder, attention deficit–hyperactivity disorder (ADHD), or an emotional disturbance. Early on, then, Ritchie had engaged colleagues in discussions of the boy's problems. He had shared notes with other teachers and had called in the school psychologist to observe the student's behavior in his classroom. And he had attempted for months— unsuccessfully—to call a meeting with the student's parents. (The parents were consistently unresponsive and evasive.)

Ritchie had been methodically building the case for referring the student for psychological evaluation, a process that required a number of preliminary steps. Ritchie's testimony was fully corroborated by other teachers, the school psychologist, paperwork, and telephone records. A few days before the accusations started, Ritchie had, in fact, gotten through to the boy's parents, and a meeting seemed imminent. And the day before the principal sent Ritchie home without explanation, Ritchie had given the student an after-school suspension, at which the student had exploded: "I don't have to listen to you! You're not going to be giving orders around here much longer!"

The three other students who testified against Ritchie constituted a clique, organized under the strong-willed girl whose "thirty seconds" had matched the testimony in the preliminary hearing. Ritchie had been applying increasingly strict disciplinary pressure against the girl, as she was underperforming and failing to do her assignments. A couple of days before the accusations started, he had scolded her for not doing her homework and for being impudent about it.

A scale drawing of the classroom showed an extremely poor setting for sexual abuse: along one long wall was a continuous row of large windows that opened onto a busy sidewalk. The door had a glass window.

Ritchie's attorney decided not to put his own child witnesses on the stand. I am not entirely convinced that this was the best strategy, but it was certainly the most cautious one. "Kids can be unpredictable," the lawyer explained. "We prefer not to use them." The media spectacle and repeated interviews by prosecutors might have planted ideas in some kids' minds. The constant repetition of stories, constant discussion among the students, might have planted stories that no one had actually witnessed but that some now might believe. Besides, in a case in which one witness says he or she saw something, the testimony is not necessarily refuted by the word of a witness who says he or she did not see it.

During his summation Ritchie's lawyer noted that the student's story had shifted and changed throughout the legal proceedings. Moreover, the stories told by the three teenage girls were strikingly inconsistent with each other. The prosecution thus was a far cry from establishing guilt beyond reasonable doubt. Is it credible that the hyperactive and unruly adolescent who appeared in court, who was taller and heavier than Ritchie, sat still for a fondling—in a full classroom? Surely, Ritchie's account, amply corroborated by other competent adult witnesses, provided the context in which the student's always shifting accusations were hatched. No child abuser draws attention to the child he or she is abusing, least of all the attention of other teachers and the school psychologist. The defendant was being prosecuted for doing his job and for doing it well, Ritchie's lawyer concluded.

The prosecutor, in turn, improbably depicted Ritchie's efforts at getting a referral and setting up a parent-teacher conference as the track-covering stealth of a criminal mastermind. "Children don't conspire to lie about sexual abuse," she asserted. She also acknowledged that the boy probably suffered from ADHD and attempted to turn this to the prosecution's advantage, as an explanation for why the accuser never told the same story twice.

Wrongfully Convicted

The judge acknowledged that the students' accounts were logically inconsistent, which would seem to fulfill the reasonable doubt standard for acquittal. Then he made a statement that probably would fail basic standards of evidence as set forth in first-year law school textbooks: "But even if I discount two of the witnesses, there's always the third." It is unclear which "third" testimony he meant—perhaps the echo of the improbably precise phrase "thirty seconds." Addressing Ritchie, the judge then simply posited a statement of belief or, rather, disbelief, without explaining how he arrived at such a judgment of a model teacher, a citizen with a spotless record—indeed, a decorated veteran, honorably discharged: "I don't believe you."

The judge then continued with a stream of imponderable assertions, saying (perhaps more for his own amusement than for the edification of anyone in the courtroom): "The irony is that this charge would not normally entail any jail time." Irony, of course, always involves a subtext, a meaning not understood by participants in the action. The characters in a drama say things that they understand to have one meaning but that the audience will understand to have another. I have often wondered at this assertion of irony—who is the unknowing actor? Who is the audience? Where is the hidden meaning? Whence comes the irony?

The judge found Ritchie guilty—it is still not entirely clear to me what the transgression was, since the allegations shifted and changed from moment to moment—and sentenced him to ninety days in jail.

Justice Deferred

What can be said? Presumption of innocence, standards of evidence, burden of proof: All have shifted.

Ritchie immediately appealed the judge's ruling. This move effectively voided the first ruling and set the stage for a de novo trial. After consulting with several lawyers, Ritchie and Joe quickly learned that the appeal also provided the prosecutor with an opportunity to simply drop the misdemeanor charges and seek Ritchie's indictment by a grand jury on felony charges. One lawyer gave this a 99 percent probability. To understand Ritchie's decision-making process in what followed, it is necessary to elaborate on what happened just after the prosecutor had inadvertently introduced a new version of the accusation.

In the final round of pretrial hearings, Ritchie's attorney reviewed the misrepresentations in the prosecutor's briefs (many), noted the prosecution's attempts to circumvent the judge's rulings (several), touched upon the prosecutor's manipulations of the media (including talking to reporters after the judge had expressly forbidden it). Ritchie's lawyer reviewed how his client had been unnecessarily arrested and denied access to his attorney. Citing legal precedents from the state supreme court, he concluded that the prosecution's actions might give rise to the appearance of prosecutorial vindictiveness. After this hearing, Ritchie reports, "the prosecutor and his co-counsel got extremely upset and yelled at my attorney, storming out of the room. 'You've crossed the line,' co-counsel spat; 'Now you've gone and made it personal. Now it's personal.'"

American court standards have become notoriously biased in favor of the prosecution. But what does one do when the game of law gets personal? Had Ritchie pursued his appeal, he concluded, he would have opened the door for yet more rounds of prosecutorial vindictiveness. "I had already been wrongfully convicted once. What if the prosecutor brought back the felony charges? And what if I couldn't convince the jury that I wasn't a child molester? In the worst-case scenario, for the truth to eventually prevail, I might have had to spend several years in prison filing appeals and begging reviews." If the cumulative costs of the first trial—roughly $100,000—nearly bankrupted a middle-class couple, the costs of a second trial would likely have been considerably greater. Joe put it this way: "It's like they're blackmailing you to accept injustice."

And so, under duress, under clear and direct threat, and with his attorney under personal attack by the prosecutor and her assistant counsel, Ritchie withdrew his appeal. He served the sentence (forty-five days on a ninety-day sentence) for a crime he did not commit. Joe, who had never been separated from Ritchie in fifteen years, visited him almost every day, bringing along a succession of friends, including me. Friends mailed Ritchie packages of reading material almost daily.

Inside the Belly of the Beast

There were little mercies in these gray events. When Ritchie met the sheriff's deputy at the courthouse to turn himself in and serve his sentence, he said, "I suppose you're going to handcuff me now." He had been handcuffed twice in two previous arrests. "I don't see how that's necessary," the deputy replied. "After all, you've been waiting here for me." It was a small mercy not to be handcuffed. Then, as Ritchie was being processed at the jail, the nurse asked him a standard set of questions: "Are you taking drugs?" "No." "Were you molested as a child?" "No." "Have you ever molested a child?" "No," Ritchie sobbed. "But that's what they say. That's what they put me in here for." This was the only time he ever wept in front of anyone other than Joe. Presumably, the interviewing nurse could have brought in the psychologist, on the pretext that Ritchie was in denial. (The prosecutor had asked for mandatory psychological treatment as part of the sentence, but the judge did not require it.) Instead, miraculously, she quietly empathized: "Well," she said in a low voice, "there's a lot of that going on these days."

There were also a great many injustices. "The white guards go easier on the white prisoners," Ritchie explains, "but they're harsh with the black and brown prisoners. The black guards sort of look out for the black prisoners; they're not nice at all to the white and brown prisoners. In fact, some of the guards are related to some of the prisoners—they're brothers-in-law or cousins or what have you. But there are no Latino guards. So all the guards pretty much dump on the Latino prisoners all day. We're at the bottom of the pyramid."

Jail conditions? The Pleasantville Detention Center prides itself on being one of the more progressive jails in the country, with low levels of violence and few rapes. It achieves these results by having a high guard-to-prisoner ratio and relatively small dormitory-style suites. Staff members are pleasant enough to family visitors; Joe says that he was never treated badly and was sometimes given additional time for visits through those glass windows that separate inmate from visitor.

But that's the face the jail turns to the outside world. Inside, where Ritchie was housed in the protective custody unit, he had no access to fresh air and sunshine, just an interior recreation room with a couple of windows, to which he supposedly had access three times per week. But since recreation is not one of the guards' priorities, prisoners can go days on end without seeing even a beam of sunlight. Imagine it: no trees, no birds, no green or moving things; just gray putty-colored concrete everywhere. Ritchie reports that it is always cold in the jail, and with only an orange jumpsuit and no bedcovers, one spends a great deal of time shivering. The food failed to meet even basic nutritional needs. Ritchie says he ate everything that was served and purchased snacks at the canteen (an option for those whose family or friends deposit money for cash credit). But he still lost more than ten pounds in forty-five days, in addition to the ten pounds he had already lost when grief and injustice were eating him alive.

Ritchie was not a big guy when the ordeal started. He looked like a tired sad little boy when it ended.

Piecing the Puzzle Together

After Ritchie got out of jail, the state he lived in compelled him to register as a sex offender for ten years. (A conviction at the felony level would have meant lifetime registration.) But this was not the end of the story. He had new tribulations to endure, new discoveries to make. After a pro forma hearing, in which he denied yet again all the shifting allegations against him, Pleasantville Child Protection Services declared Ritchie to be a "child abuser," to be so listed for eighteen years. And there was still business with the Pleasantville School Board. Initially, the superintendent would not accept Ritchie's resignation, pressing instead to fire him. But there was an upside to these new rounds of struggle. The procedures of the school board and Child Protection Services required the disclosure of information that had hitherto been denied Ritchie and his attorney. Meanwhile, other news was coming out. And so only after Ritchie got out of jail did some pieces of the puzzle begin to make a certain kind of sense.

First was the judge's inexplicable decision. What causes a judge to discount plausible, consistent testimony in favor of changing, inconsistent testimonies? The answer did not become apparent until some weeks after the trial. Unbeknown to the wider legal community, the governor, a centrist Democrat, was hatching a scheme to promote the liberal judge who heard Ritchie's case to a higher court while the Republican-controlled legislature was in recess. After this fait accompli, the judge, an old-stock white Protestant, would face legislative review as a sitting judge, not a mere nominee. At the time of the trial the judge was aware of these plans; he was aware that he was then under, and would continue to be under, intense political scrutiny. Finding Ritchie not guilty almost certainly would have triggered a second media circus—and would have invited Republicans to closely inspect the judge's decisions over many years.

Then there was the question of what had happened when. The teachers who worked with Ritchie's class at Pleasantville Junior High understood that the complaint had originated outside the school, with Child Protection Services. According to several teachers, the police did not actually have a complainant willing to press charges until after they had arrested Ritchie and the media had begun to publicize his arrest. On the teachers' retelling, the police then used the arrest and media fanfare to induce the male student's immigrant parents to cooperate. Other cases nationwide show that prosecutors and police use carrots and sticks to induce parents to cooperate with them. Sticks include the threat of a Child Protection Services investigation: Who but bad parents would resist naming the person who had molested their child? Carrots include offers to help parents with various troubles, including immigration issues, a not-insignificant offer in the wake of September 11.

The newly revealed record at Child Protection Services showed that, indeed, the allegations originated with the girl who led the three-girl clique. She had made these accusations during regular meetings with her social worker. (The girl had a social worker because of emotional problems she had developed when her mother left her in the care of relatives for two years.) Notably, this initial record at Child Protection Services involved vague accusations and homophobic innuendo substantially different from what came out in testimony during pretrial proceedings and at trial.

The school's newly revealed records included handwritten transcripts of interviews with every student in Ritchie's class. These transcripts showed that only four students had made negative statements of any sort, the same four who had appeared at the trial. More significantly, the vague assertions and disgruntlements contained in these transcripts meshed poorly with the accusation on file at Child Protection Services and with later versions contained in the arrest warrant and in pretrial and trial testimony. (I count five distinct versions of the accusation over time.) The defense might logically have presented such details as evidence—and noted the failure of other students, including students sitting immediately around the male student, to corroborate events said to have occurred in the middle of class. But prosecutors narrowly define "exculpatory evidence" (which they are legally bound to share), and judges too tend to take the narrowest possible view of such evidence. The school district had resisted turning over the transcripts of these interviews, and a judge had denied the defense's pretrial request for these records. "You don't get much in the way of disclosure there," said one defense attorney, reflecting on the state's conservative courts.

'Twas the Banana That Did Him In

Perhaps what is most alarming about the school transcripts is not that they were withheld from the defense but the manner in which they were conducted. The principal had developed a list of ten questions, which every student was compelled to answer. The questions, and the sequence in which they were asked, can only be characterized as leading. For instance, several questions focus on bananas: Did the teacher bring bananas to class? What did he do with the banana?

In fact, Ritchie recalls, he once used a banana from his lunchbox as prop in a gag. Holding it like a pistol, he had said in a cartoon voice (the mock-desperation of a teacher besieged by energetic students), "Watch out! This banana's loaded and I'm not afraid to use it!" The banana bit had been received with great hilarity at the time. And most students tell the same innocent banana story. A few, however, apparently felt pressed by the questioners to say something negative—that Ritchie had eaten the banana in front of class during a break or that "he showed us his food." But in one student's version Ritchie had threatened to shove the banana up someone's ass.

School authorities also focused on another incident involving food. Did the teacher ever withhold food from the class as a punishment? Ritchie explains that, at a party, he had allowed one slice of pizza per student—not to withhold food from anyone but, quite the contrary, to ensure there would be enough to go around. Did the teacher ever say or do anything to make you uncomfortable? One student reported that Mr. Jimenez told the class that they stank. Ritchie puzzled over this one a long time. He finally concluded that it was a reference to his hygiene lesson, an exercise so effective that the school nurse had come to Ritchie's class to take notes.

Clearly, the principal had interviewed one or two hostile students, collected their allegations, and then constructed a series of questions based on their assertions. As the questionnaire progresses, then, the interview becomes occasion for eliciting a story line and for airing every conceivable complaint a child might have against an adult authority figure. These interviews were not taped or video-recorded; instead, the principal, a secretary, and another staff member all cosigned each document, apparently indicating that all were present at the interview. The signatures no doubt are intended to give these improvised procedures the imprimatur of legitimacy. But, in fact, they underscore the opposite. The school unleashed amateurs with no qualifications to conduct such an investigation. Administrators played at being child psychologists, and staff members played at being police investigators, in violation of every standard of child interview. Their clumsy techniques actually planted stories, pandering to prejudice and poisoning the atmosphere for subsequent interviews. It is unclear how common such practices are. Courts in only a handful of states guarantee the right to a fair and untainted pretrial child-interview process.

One interview, however, seems pivotal. The girl who initiated allegations at Child Protection Services pointed to a specific incident: "He brought that other man to the museum," she said. That other man's sinister presence among minors is offered by the girl as proof that Ritchie "was out of control, completely out of control." The phrase "out of control," sometimes invoked by adults in their admonitions of badly behaving children, is thus given back to adults in a language they might understand. And the image of the Other, the strange man, brought in to lurk inexplicably among minors, already speaks in the language of sex panic.

This is where I come into the picture, another piece of the puzzle.

I Am the Other, the Strange Man Who Lurks

Three weeks before all hell broke loose, Ritchie had asked me to be one of the adult monitors accompanying students on their field trip to a local museum. I eventually agreed. I was away from home and had free time. And, besides, like many gay men my age, I had thought for some time about adopting a child. I was encouraged to view the outing as an opportunity to test my patience with children. "I'm not so sure you really want kids," Ritchie had warned me. "See how you like dealing with ten junior high school students for a day."

I took my ten kids on a tour through the science museum. It so happens I had the boy and the clique of three girls in my charge, a fact that dawned dizzyingly on me when I saw them all together at the courthouse and buzzed alarmingly in my head when I read the girl's interview. For most of the tour the boy had hovered at my elbow, tugging at my shirtsleeve. "Meester, meester, what's theese? What's that?" he asked of every exhibit at every stop. He struck me as being slightly effeminate, the sort of boy that other kids make fun of. He also struck me as being neurologically impaired, as though an electrical storm were raging in his brain all the time. I spent 90 percent of my time responding to his questions. I tried to spread my attentions more broadly—after all, how often do mostly working-class school kids get a tour of a museum with a college professor?

Flattering myself for my community service, I was eager to do my part. But the three girls always stuck to the back of the group, always seemed to be at an elusive distance. And when I tried to draw them in, the clique-leader tried to bait me, telling me, "You have an earring, just like Mr. Jimenez." The girls continued to hang back from the rest of the group, whispering and conversing in Spanish. I couldn't quite make out their conversation against the hubbub of the museum, but I could catch the occasional familiar pejorative: *Raro, puto, maricón.* After the three girls pulled the boy over and said something to him, he no longer haunted my elbow and tugged at my sleeve but kept a distance, too.

And so, I suspect, it was *I* who triggered this sex panic, my mere presence the occasion for an outbreak of pandemonium. My only protection was the nature of the museum itself, which was teeming with visitors and surveilled by cameras everywhere.

I have often reflected on the weird byplays of sexual, racial, and class politics, which make me think that we all live, unknowingly, atop a social tinderbox capable of bursting into a great conflagration at any moment. The linchpin of the piece, the effeminate boy with ADD/ADHD, could avoid the charge that he was gay only by keeping the hot potato of stigma in motion: by passing it along to someone else. His ever expanding lie also proved a convenient way to get rid of a strict demanding teacher. And perhaps it also played well with his religious immigrant parents. The girls, all from immigrant families too, had discovered the secret weapon capable of leveling everything in its path, had found a language that speaks with equal facility to both religious conservatives and liberal social workers: the language of sexual peril.[6] The invocation of my presence at the museum, which trades in "what everyone knows" about homosexual pedophile rings, serves to clinch the case. The principal, a white, suburban, Republican soccer mom with nominally feminist pretensions, was all too ready to believe that children are imperiled and that the gay brown man was a logical source of danger. For the judge it was nothing to sacrifice the interests of a gay brown man—or was it a white gay man, as the official documents claim?—to advance his career. Police investigators and prosecutors, of course, build their careers on convictions, not exonerations. Cases of this sort are especially useful in propelling careers. Across the United States ruthless prosecutors use practices of the sort I have been describing, according to studies by Angela Davis, Edward Humes, and others.[7] And when was the last time you heard of a prosecutor being brought up on charges of prosecutorial vindictiveness or withholding evidence?[8]

This was a tainted and sickening process, evocative of witch hunts and satanic ritual abuse panics of the past. It begins with an adolescent whispering campaign. The record documents a steady progression of accusations: the earliest, at Child Protection Services, are vague, gossipy; in fact, they miss the legal mark entirely (as did the allegation in the arrest warrant). The school transcripts are no clearer. "He was always trying to get close to the boys," says one of the four hostile students. "They *say* he was always trying to touch boys," says another. Over time the vague accusations of disgruntled students became criminal charges fashioned by unqualified interviewers, irresponsible investigators, and overzealous prosecutors. ("Did he touch you?" "Where did he touch you?" "How often did he touch you?") Homophobic gossip, innuendo, and supposition—all of which appear in the school transcripts and were repeated by children in court—played an obvious part in the legal proceedings. "Everybody knows Mr. Jimenez is gay," the boy said on the witness stand. "You can ask anybody."

The highly publicized arrest was crucial in whipping up hysteria and prodding parents to the cause. Even so, teachers at the school reported at the time that Ritchie's class remained split, with a majority insisting in loud classroom and hallway arguments that nothing illicit or immoral had happened. Then came a pair of crucial interventions: the principal sent a memo instructing teachers to intervene to stop such arguments (because, in cases of child abuse, nothing is more damaging to the victim than being disbelieved), followed by another memo erroneously advising teachers that they were legally required to cooperate with police investigators but could be subject to legal sanction if they spoke with the defense attorney or his investigators. After these memos appeared, students were forbidden to say what had *not* happened, and teachers were instructed that they could assist only the prosecution; meanwhile, amateur sleuths, police, and prosecutors had unlimited access to Ritchie's classroom, and the defense had none. Nothing, then, checked the progression of gossip, innuendo, and whispers to legal charges derived from sexual fantasy. The result was manipulation all around: of adults by children and of children by adults.

I know what happened, because I was there at the inception. And I know, as I have known since I was thirteen, exactly what children are capable of.

Keep Me on Candid Camera

By the end of the journey I was feeling dreadfully homesick and remarked on the unpleasantness of Pleasantville and its environs: a heartland of darkness where neo-Victorian feminism meets postmodern religious fundamentalism, a zone of assimilation into American nightmares. "Actually," Ritchie responded, "what happened to me here could have happened anywhere." He elaborated a bit: "I used to give my students lessons on how to avoid sex abuse. Basically, I told them, 'Don't let anybody touch you in a way that makes you uncomfortable.' I still think these were good lessons. I still think sex abuse is a serious issue.

But something has gone wrong with how the issue is taken up and communicated. This blinds everyone to facts and reason." He then added, "And this turns loose the demons of prejudice."

On another occasion, as the seven o'clock news report droned on about the positive effects of surveillance cameras on students' classroom behavior in an Orwellian school district, Ritchie commented, "But that's not the real story." I was surprised that he spoke up; this was a light dinner, and we have tried to put unpleasant events behind us. "There's not a teacher in America who hasn't wondered what would happen if a student or group of students concocted a story claiming physical or sexual abuse," he continued. "If there had been a camera in my classroom, I wouldn't have been charged, and I wouldn't have gone to jail. What the teachers in this school system really like is the assurance that there's an unimpeachable record of what they do, not what the students do."

And so we reach the nadir of punitiveness in U.S. law, a complete reversal of burden of proof. The accused must prove their innocence—and not just beyond reasonable doubt but beyond a shadow of a doubt.

The New Citizen

I have thought a lot about the body language and demeanor of various participants in Ritchie's ordeal, a multihued cast, with each character enacting distinctly American fantasies of protective zeal: the police detective, seething with rage at the bad man and venting contempt for everyone around him; the judge from Central City who, after releasing a series of men accused of violent crimes on scant bail, if any, peered over her glasses to intone, "This is a very serious charge"; the angry magistrate, whom I would have thought capable of assaulting us had he not been secured behind window bars; the prosecutor—who was often flustered, invariably ill prepared, quite possibly in violation of the law but always aggressive and confident (and rightly so, given the workings of the system).

But of all the images registered on my jaded retinas, one stands out. A few days after he got out of jail, Joe and I took Ritchie for a walk, one of those urban excursions that features dogs on leashes and waves to familiar faces. We had gone no more than a block when I noticed two Latinas—sisters? a mother and daughter?—eyeing us and excitedly whispering to each other while frantically and repeatedly clutching a small boy to their skirts. They had no doubt seen news stories on television or read stories in the Latino press. And posters of the sex criminal living down the street had been distributed at the elementary school around the corner. They seemed to believe that a terrible danger was in their midst. And yet they did not flee; they froze, agitatedly, in place. As I caught wisps of their excited whispering, I realized in a flash that they enjoyed playing out this spectacle. They savored the drama it brought to their bare existence—the terror of the monster, the thrill of heroic vigilance.

The Social Costs

The women's gestures seem to me emblematic of how successive waves of sex panic have cultivated a new model of citizenship, a new ideal of civic participation. The new citizen, so engaged in rites of protection, is not without her opposite, the individual deprived of citizenship, divested of rights, and "laid bare," as in Giorgio Agamben's discussion of "bare life."[9] Ritchie used to be the kind of man who could not pass by a baby stroller without peering inside and making inquiries of the parent or parents: "How old is he?" "My, what a strong grip—she's very developed for her age!" Community, if such a word has positive meaning, is the product of thousands of such daily acts. But in Ritchie's ordeal, something of community's substance has been diminished. Now he avoids strollers and eye contact with parents. Now he does not make friendly chitchat with passers-by on the street. Pleasantville, moreover, lost a model teacher who had developed an important part of the district's math and science curricula and whose immigrant and working-class students, against all odds, had gone on to notable educational successes over the years.

Joe too has been affected. He would not call 911 when he witnessed a burglary in progress in his own condo parking garage; he is unable to deal with the police. And when a small boy fell down face forward on the street across from him, I watched Joe take a step forward, as though to pick the boy up—then stop dead in his tracks. Someone else came to the aid of the wailing boy, but my mind flashed on the news story of the Englishman who froze as a child drowned in a pond. He was terrified of being dubbed a pedophile if he waded in to rescue the girl.

As for me, I can no longer discern my exact relationship with the law—or, rather, I cannot orient myself to the idea of Law, cannot say for sure what I really think of it or its relationship to justice. (Law, surely, is not justice itself but only a means of attaining it. We thus distinguish just and unjust laws, as between merely procedural legality and actually fair process.) I experience this lack of orientation along the lines of that multiple personality disorder, postmodern fragmentation. Part of me wants Law to serve as a model for good and right and measure and reason, as in the classical Hellenic tradition. The progressive good citizen in me thinks of Law as the model for social redress, and this tradition too has deep cultural roots. It is everywhere in the Old Testament. The Marxist in me is skeptical of such claims. One reads Marx in vain for positive uses of terms like *law* and *justice* or even depictions of history as the court of durable verdicts. After all, how could Law, which exists to protect property, ever serve as a model for social good? The existential queer in me believes the Law is there to flush me out of the bushes and into the open, to render me exquisitely vulnerable to social regulation—or worse.

And yet, the thing remains: What does anyone persecuted by the law want, if not validation by some higher Law? What does the victim of injustice demand, if not justice?

The Punitive State

As nightfall does not come at once, neither does oppression.
In both instances, there is a twilight when everything
remains seemingly unchanged. And it is in such twilight that
we all must be most aware of change in the air—however
slight—lest we become unwitting victims of
the darkness.

—Justice William O. Douglas

In the twilight years of the Bush-Cheney administration, a number of writers took the view that something had gone terribly wrong in U.S. society. Public intellectuals and prominent scholars discerned "the end of America," "the last days of the republic," "the subversion of democracy," and the specter of a new form of totalitarianism.[1] Some of the period's broadsides dated the undemocratic turn to the Supreme Court's intervention in the 2000 presidential elections, which stopped the Florida vote recount and thereby installed an unelected president in the White House, or to the days after September 11, 2001, when the Bush administration issued a series of signing statements and executive memorandums designed to trump congressional and judicial interpretations of the Constitution, or to other spectacles of official lawlessness that dominated the news of the day. Near the end of this period of excess, Zbigniew Brzezinski, a hawkish geostrategist (and Jimmy Carter's national security adviser), wrote that "the 'war on terror' has created a culture of fear in America."[2] A dispassionate review of ongoing social trends suggests the need for a longer view. In this part I develop this view, moving the book's focus on sex panics into a wider perspective on the modern fear of crime and connecting both to the eventual war on terror.

Let me sketch my general arguments about the relationship of sex, crime, and terror, parts of which I have already made and that I will develop further in what follows.

THE ARGUMENTS

First, heightened anxieties about crime predate (and in many ways lay the groundwork for) modern sex panics. Fear of crime was ascendant from the late 1960s, a time of spiking crime rates, urban unrest, and race reaction. Sex panics emerged (or, rather, reemerged) later, during the mid- to late 1970s, a time of waxing nervousness about the fate of the white heterosexual nuclear family and its attendant moral hierarchies. The timing of these developments was consequential: crime and sex panics bridge the gap between social backlash and economic retrenchment. They play a key role in turning the United States into a more conservative nation than it had been previously.

Second, although sex panic involves a different racial and geographical pattern than does fear of crime overall, the two converge at crucial points: the valorization of the victim, who is seen as wholly innocent and whose interests are understood to be wholly antithetical to those of the criminal wrongdoer; the stigmatization of the offender, whose guilt becomes a permanent, irremediable condition of his being and who therefore must be marked or set apart from the rest of society; the application of criminal sanctions to growing numbers of behaviors ("defining criminality up"); and the elaboration of laws and surveillance practices designed to anticipate, preempt, detect, and punish lawbreaking. Sex panics have pushed these logics in new directions, dispersed them into new spaces, and taken them to extremes, but that is to say that they extend, intensify, and reinforce wider trends.

Third, David Garland, Jonathan Simon, and other criminologists and legal scholars have described the resulting system as a "culture of control" and have shown how crime control has become the central "pivot for governance" and struggles around it.[3] I call the emergent system of social controls "punitive governance" to emphasize its connection with perpetual punishment, a presumption of guilt, unending vigilance, and modes of citizenship that would have been understood as premodern forty years ago. I stress the role of fear in organizing power and regulating social relations under this regime, and I mark the inherent instability of this system. If moral panics involving crime, sex, and terror have made the law progressively harsher and more exacting, they also periodically push governance to the point of excess or breakdown, giving rise to abuse, overreach, and other illicit forms of power.

Finally, it might seem that the culture of fear is in retreat today. But the authoritarian political culture that I am tracing is no simple or unitary phenomenon. An increasingly repressive political culture has found support in assorted campaigns against urban unrest, street crime, drug users, gang activity, pedophiles, and so on. The erosion of rights and liberties accelerated in the wake of terror attacks on New York and the Pentagon and during the global war on terror. This is to say that a repressive approach to crime and disorder has waxed over a forty-year period, emerging from multiple sources (sometimes in opposition to each other). In consequence, crime-control techniques are now durably embedded in a wide array of institutional practices, and they have gradually reshaped the landscape in ways both obvious and subtle. Piecemeal, the system of panic, punishment, and preemption has become part not only of legal practices but also of the economic system. As a result punitive trends survived periodic turns to the center-left under presidents Jimmy Carter and Bill Clinton, as well as long-term changes in racial and sexual politics. This decadeslong reconstruction of U.S. society has been advanced by Democrats no less than by Republicans, by liberals almost as often as by conservatives.

CHAPTER 5

Zero Tolerance

Crime and Punishment in the Punitive State

Beware of those in whom the will to punish is strong.
—Friedrich Nietzsche, *Thus Spake Zarathustra*

If one stands only a step back from the periodic changing of the political guard, perhaps the most impressive social trend in post-1960s America has been the rise of what academic critics have called the "carceral state."[1] In plain English the carceral state is a type of political organization in which three conditions obtain. First, incarceration becomes the preferred sanction for a growing number of infractions. Second, official bureaucracies and civil society collude to intensify enforcement, enhance penalties, and keep the prison system growing. Third, a bloated prison system begins to supply norms for other institutions of government: surveillance becomes routine, and a crime-centered approach shapes the activities of functionaries working in offices unrelated to the penitentiary.

The Rise of the Carceral State

A few basic numbers will reveal the gravity of what has happened in U.S. society. In the 1960s rates of incarceration in Western democracies generally ranged from 60 to 120 per 100,000 inhabitants. These rates tended to decline until about 1990 and then posted modest to substantial increases thereafter, depending on the country. For example, in postfascist Italy incarceration rates declined from 79 per 100,000 in 1960 to 57 in 1990, before climbing again to 107 per 100,000 in recent estimates. Similar patterns have been posted in other Western European countries. The decline was especially steep in Finland, which began with high crime rates and a penal system built on the Russian model, and, after decades of humanitarian and social-democratic reforms, now posts one of the lowest incarceration rates in Europe. Not coincidentally, since its prison system is correctional in the best sense of the term, not dehumanizing, it provides no breeding ground for anger, resentment, and recidivism.[2] Finland posts one of the lowest rates of serious crime in Europe, a rate much lower than that of the United States.[3] Even after slight increases in the past few years, Finland's rate of imprisonment is 67 per 100,000.[4]

Britain has followed a different course. Under Tony Blair's Labourites, even more so than under Margaret Thatcher's Tories, the state pursued an ever more punitive approach to crime. An obvious measure of this punitiveness is the passage of more laws with more exacting punishments. Nick Cohen has derisively described New Labour's overhaul of the criminal code in the *New Statesman:* under Blair the government found 661 new reasons to lock people up.[5] As a result the British rate of imprisonment doubled, from 70 per 100,000 in 1966 to 154 per 100,000 in 2010. That is to say, Britain's current rate is a bit higher than U.S. rates in the 1960s.

But the United States stands out even in comparison with the British model.[6] In less than thirty years the United States more than quadrupled its total prison population. The rate of imprisonment has soared to 753 per 100,000 in 2010. The United States thus imprisons five to ten times more people per capita than do other developed democracies. The country now ranks first in the world both in both the rate of imprisonment (1 in every 99 adult residents is behind bars) and in the absolute number of people imprisoned (2.3 million). That is more prisoners than China, a strong-arm state with more than four times the population of the United States. It is more than Russia, once the gendarme of Europe, a culture whose fondness for locking people up both predates and postdates the Stalinist period. With only 5 percent of the world's population, the United States claims about 25 percent of the world's prisoners.[7]

PUNITIVE AMERICA

That this remarkable social transition, so inimical to the spirit of a free society, occurred under formally democratic conditions—indeed, was prodded by electoral pressures to "get tough on crime"—mocks any grand conception of democracy in America. The most basic facts call to mind the gauge Jean-Paul Sartre and Maurice Merleau-Ponty once applied to the loftier claims of Soviet socialism in 1950: "There is no socialism when one out of every 20 citizens is in a camp."[8] If we take the French existentialists' measure as a general guide, then what, plausibly, could be said of the character of American democracy under prevailing conditions?

If recent incarceration rates remain unchanged, 1 in every 15 Americans will serve time in a prison during his or her lifetime. For men the rate is more than 1 in 9. The weight of these numbers falls disproportionately on black and brown men. For African American men the expected lifetime rate is roughly 1 in 3: 32 percent of black men will spend some portion of their lives incarcerated, compared with 17 percent of Latino males and 5.9 percent of white males. Twelve percent of African American men aged twenty to thirty-four are currently behind bars.[9] Such figures have no precedent, not even in the postslavery period, when southern states first organized systems of compulsory prison labor as a substitute for slavery, or during Jim Crow.[10]

The U.S. criminal justice system metes out stiffer sentences, longer incarcerations, and more onerous terms of release and surveillance to far, far more people than any of the nations Americans like to think of as their peers.[11] As a result a large percentage of people in U.S. prisons today—even many inmates serving extremely long sentences—were not convicted of a violent crime. Many were convicted for offenses against public order or morality: they are drug offenders of one sort or another. Others serve long sentences for property crimes that once would have drawn a short term, a fine, or a suspended sentence.[12] Another expanding class of criminals has been created by states that have raised the age of consent. (Many of the resulting criminals—statutory rapists—are themselves young men, barely adult.) The image of the "repeat offender" looms large in the public imagination, but data from the Bureau of Justice Statistics show that the great run-up in the prison population comes as the result of an increase in first-time incarcerations.[13]

The criminologist David Garland describes this system of control in the bleakest of terms. The present prison system "serves as a kind of reservation system, a quarantine zone," where "purportedly dangerous individuals are segregated in the name of public safety." In form, number, and arbitrariness it "resembles nothing so much as the Soviet gulag—a string of work camps and prisons strung across a vast country, housing [more than] two million people most of whom are drawn from classes and racial groups that have become politically and economically problematic. . . . Like the pre-modern sanctions of transportation or banishment, the prison now functions as a form of exile."[14]

And once the system gets its hooks into a person, it is loath to let him go. Nearly five million Americans are on probation or parole. Added to the 2.3 million behind bars, this means that 1 in every 32 adults—3.2 percent of the adult population—is actively caught up in the long reach of the penal state.[15] (This figure does not account for all 705,000 registered sex offenders, most of whom are no longer on parole or probation, and many of whom are registered for nonviolent, noncoercive first offenses.) Extended periods of parole, with their mandatory meetings, reporting conditions, and drug tests, virtually assure future infractions. As a result the number of people in prison today for parole violations alone is the same as the total U.S. prison population in 1980.[16] This is not how the parole system was intended to work, but it is a gauge of the growing punitiveness of all procedures associated with law enforcement, even those formerly conceived as having a rehabilitative effect.

Only two states, Vermont and Maine, allow prisoners to vote. Thirteen more states allow all ex-convicts to vote as soon as they set foot outside prison. In the rest of the states some form of felony disenfranchisement is the norm. Most states strip ex-cons of the right to vote and bar them from holding work-related business licenses while on parole or probation. Some states extend this effective loss of citizenship beyond parole or probation—and in a shrinking handful of states this disenfranchisement remains in effect for life, thus creating a more or less permanent caste of criminal outcasts. More than five million Americans (1 in 41 adults) have temporarily or permanently lost their right to vote; black men (roughly 6 percent of the adult population) represent more than a quarter of this figure.[17]

Such numbers have stark implications for the integrity of the political process. In many states where closely contested elections are common, Republicans have used felon disenfranchisement to purge the voter rolls of minority voters (and to intimidate or confuse other minority voters). Even assuming a clean count of ballots, this disenfranchisement of black citizens likely made all the difference in the 2000 presidential elections and in other close races.[18] Consider: If 2.3 percent of the adult population is barred from voting by law, and if a similar number of voters stay away from the polls because they mistakenly believe that they have been disenfranchised—for example, for a misdemeanor conviction or not realizing that their probationary period has ended—then a considerable portion of the public has been excluded from democracy.

By design this penal system churns the poor and marginal, rendering them all but unemployable, thus poorer and ever more marginal. No legitimate theory of corrections, crime, or social order justifies this approach, which can only be understood as vindictive. This spirit of vindictiveness—the idea that law exists not to correct or balance but to punish—obviously animates the continuing popularity of capital punishment in the United States. Until the 5–4 Supreme Court decision in *Roper v. Simmons* in 2005, the United States even allowed the execution of minors. And although the Supreme Court has barred states from executing the mentally disabled, nothing prevents pro–death penalty states from defining mental disability more narrowly than less vindictive states.

Spectacles of Punishment

Jokes are made about these matters: "Book him, Danno!" "Three strikes, you're out!" Jingles and ditties celebrate this punitive approach to law: "Don't do the crime if you can't do the time." Everyone knows that race and class disparities pervade, even motivate, this unjust work of the justice system, but many Americans accept these monstrous conditions with handy platitudes ("It's because of the breakdown of the family that so many black men are in jail") or attribute responsibility to the final link in a causal chain ("He shouldn't have violated the terms of his parole"). A handful of courageous activists, lawyers, journalists, and organizations advocate for prisoners' and ex-convicts' rights, but few politicians wish to take on these matters as a primary cause.[19]

Americans, it would appear, adore punishment; they have become obsessed with it, addicted to it. Politically ambitious prosecutors have long relished the theatrical staging of "perp walks" for the evening news: unnecessarily manacled defendants are paraded like captured quarry before a crowd of photographers and videographers. Such values have leached into the broader world of commercial entertainment. Network police dramas, afternoon programs devoted to courtroom scenarios, and an entire cable channel, Court TV (now rechristened TruTV), put the "show" in "show trial" and reinforce this image of law as a punitive spectacle. Much of what reality television programs serve up is the spectacle of punishment, gratuitous humiliation: *Cops* and *Judge*

Judy, obviously, but less obviously, judged competitions like *American Idol* and *Survivor*—"The tribe has spoken."

Among the images endlessly circulated on the Web are police mug shots of celebrities, arrestees, or convicts. These fire the public's appetite for ever more public, ever more humiliating, and ever more stigmatizing forms of retribution. Some judges make convicts wear signs, post notices in their front yards, or perform some other public ritual as part of their punishment. Such forms of humiliation, in excess of fines paid or time served, are usually associated with archaic legal practices, but their application is growing, not diminishing, in the modern state.

Nowhere is the spectacle of crime and punishment more extravagantly enacted than in the case of sex crime, and on *Dateline NBC's* "To Catch a Predator" series, a sweeps week staple, journalists partnered with cops to push the theater of cruelty to new lows. In 2006 Louis William Conradt Jr., a fifty-six-year-old district attorney living in Texas, was accused of making online advances to an adult decoy pretending to be a thirteen-year-old boy. The decoy attempted to lure Conradt to the "sting house" where, in the usual sequence of events, a certain ritual is enacted: The show's host, Chris Hansen, confronts and humiliates the suspect. Then, after Hansen tells the suspect he can leave, the cops move in to make a dramatic arrest. Even arrestees who offer no resistance are tackled, thrown to the ground, and violently subdued by swarming officers. But when Conradt did not show up at the designated house, the producers instead arranged a police raid on the district attorney's home. As police and the television crew stormed the house, Conradt shot and killed himself. One of the participating police officers is reported to have told the NBC producer, "That'll make good TV." In fact, the episode aired in 2007, and the series continued through 2008.[20] In the guise of producing public service exposés and undertaking investigative journalism, NBC has not blurred but erased distinctions between journalism, law enforcement, and the gratuitous arousal of its audience's baser instincts.

There is no direct relationship between Americans' fascination with the police blotter and real-world conditions of crime and depravity. Although crime rates have fallen dramatically since the early 1990s, crime reportage has actually risen in inverse proportion. Half the lead stories on local news broadcasts are crime stories. As much as 50 percent of local news airtime in some locales is now devoted to crime reportage: prurient stories about sex abuse, lurid tales of gang violence, breathless accounts of callous predation.[21] While the so-called liberal news media have profited from sensational coverage of the overblown crime beat, right-wing political interests have manipulated it, stoking fear of crime and predation to win elections—and, more enduringly, to reshape the social contract. This new social contract involves ever more sticks and ever fewer carrots. The current zeal for punishment turns on the perpetual cultivation of outsized fears.

Punitive Governance

The United States has become a measurably harsher, more punitive place—so much so that we need a new term to convey how government relates to citizens and how citizens participate in an increasingly truncated political process. I draw the term punitive governance from various fields of study that try to map this change in social climate: international studies (Michael Sherry's important essay on "the punitive turn" in U.S. culture), the critical race studies literature, and especially sociological studies of policing and imprisonment.[22]

The much older term *punitive justice,* which is usually associated with what is said to be primitive or communal violence—lynchings, for instance—is obviously of some relevance here. Punitive justice expresses anger, resentment, or vindictiveness, in contrast to preventative, reformative, or restorative ideals. It also tends toward "time-saving" forms: only abbreviated adjudication procedures, if any at all, stand between accusation and punishment. Moral philosophers since Plato have generally held this urge to punish in low esteem: The visceral satisfaction taken from vengeance stirs the baser instincts, clouds judgment, and incites mobs. It attaches, in ways that demean or diminish, to the character of those in whom the will to punish is strong. In the classical canon, then, punitiveness has not been regarded as a defensible foundation upon which to build a rational system of justice. Indeed, it has been viewed as contrary to the basic intent of reasoned law.[23] "Revenge," wrote Francis Bacon, "is a kind of wild justice; which the more man's nature runs to, the more ought law to weed it out."[24]

As I am using the term, punitive governance involves first and foremost a dramatic shift in long-standing liberal ideas about the burden of proof. Instead of being presumed innocent until proved guilty, a common law concept, the accused today is presumed to be guilty—or, at any rate, is thought to be predisposed to commit offense. From this presumption follows a series of ever more stringent laws and disciplinary measures. In practice no parsing of the offense ever seems sufficiently thorough, no punishment is ever quite enough, and no monitoring regime ever proves sufficiently vigilant. Punitive governance is punitive justice codified, writ large, and suffused throughout a wider body of practices.

Of course, the punitive element has always been pronounced in U.S. law. The pillory, stockade, and scarlet letter cast long shadows in U.S. history. Moreover, the spectacle of punishment is often associated with "democratic" or popular concepts of justice. But this is only one side of the story. The U.S. Constitution has always prohibited torture ("cruel and unusual punishment"). And as James Q. Whitman reminds readers, once upon a time Europeans viewed the U.S. prison system as a model of humane and enlightened practices, not as the scandal of the Western world. Foreign governments sent visiting delegations on tours of U.S. penitentiaries to learn how to better manage their own penal systems. De Tocqueville extolled the mildness of punishment in America.[25]

The usual historical accountings thus trace the ebb and flow of contradictory impulses in the land that married fervent puritanism and cruel slavery to the cool deliberations of the Enlightenment. U.S. history runs in cycles, it is said: private interest oscillates with public action; the party of memory gives way to the party of hope; reactionaries alternate with progressives.[26] In this telling of the big story historians typically have expressed a rooting interest in the triumph of reason over unreason and freedom over oppression. Lynch law stood for decades as a caricature of law, but the arguments against mob violence, torture, and extrajudiciary murder eventually prevailed. Every war or international crisis has unleashed government censorship, political repression, suspensions of rights, and even mass incarcerations, but with the passing of each crisis the United States eventually has reestablished civil liberties. In this optimistic version of history, then, the tension between reaction and progress can be decided in only one direction. Whatever its long twists and circuitous turns, U.S. history is the story of the gradual extension of more rights to more people, the slow victory of reason over violence. The more vigorous tradition of rights, guarantees, and protections ultimately curbs traditions of communal violence; the better traditions of reasoned law check the magical power of the accusation.

The entrenchment of punitive practices at the center of governance today poses a striking challenge to the progressive story line. First is the question of duration and scale: the crime and sex panics that erode civil liberties today have lasted far longer than any wars or crises in U.S. history. The worst of McCarthyism lasted about a decade; today's punitive trend, as I have been describing it, has held sway for more than thirty

years. And then there is the question of codification. Present-day punitive trends are buttressed less by rash acts of Congress, presidential
edicts, or suspensions of law than by gradual ongoing redefinitions of
law itself alongside steady erosions of those very principles intended to
measure, moderate, or curb the law—to protect the citizen from excessive punishment or unreasonable enforcement. In these gradual revisions
of law, carried out by formally democratic means, the difference between democratic consent and rule by terror becomes increasingly compromised.[27] Last is the issue of concurrence. Social conservatives and
the usual parties of reaction have been at the vanguard of many of these
changes, obviously. But what is most remarkable is the role played by
social liberals and progressives of various stripes in fostering a consensus
that government exists, essentially, to protect the innocent. This tendency was present all along in liberalism, which construes the rationale
for government action narrowly, as intervention to correct excess or redress abuses; it was pushed to current extremes in no small part by waves
of sex panic beginning in the 1970s.

In other words the equation that sets vindictiveness in tension with
reason seems increasingly out of balance. The law itself has turned
punitive, vengeful—and openly so. This imbalance has not remained
strictly confined to correctional procedures or even state functions; it is
prodded by new conceptions of risk, new accounting procedures, and
new technologies. It is tied to the development of a new civic culture,
which broadly distributes responsibility for safety and prevention, law
and order. A multicentric ethos of punishment emanates from schools,
corporations, congregations, and families, progressively reorganizing
what has been called, with hope, "civil society."[28]

Meting It Out

Even efforts to roll back some of the most odious features of punitive
governance express a certain residual vindictiveness. Such, it seems, is
the price of passage. Consider recent developments in Florida.

The good news is that Florida has recently opted to "leave the 'offensive minority' of states that uniformly deny ex-offenders [voting]
rights," as Republican governor Charlie Crist put it. Upon being released from prison, offenders deemed nonviolent—up to 80 percent of
Florida's ex-convicts—are now eligible to have a more expeditious restoration of their right to vote and to earn work-related state licenses.
But this development bears closer inspection. The bad news is that it

falls far short of an outright repeal of the Jim Crow rules that were manifestly designed to disenfranchise as many black voters as possible, rules that were subsequently enshrined in the state constitution during the turbulent year of 1968. Voting rights restoration is not an automatic, paperless process: every restoration requires the agreement of three of the four members of the Clemency Board, and convicts released from prison cannot vote until they receive official notice from the board that their rights have been restored.

The situation is worse for the burgeoning population of ex-convicts, estimated at 628,000 (the state's official estimate) to 950,000 people (the estimate given by civil rights, civil liberties, and prisoner advocacy groups). Florida's new rules still require these ex-cons to take the initiative, gathering paperwork and collecting documents, some of which are decades old. Moreover, a late amendment to the rules requires those arrested or convicted a second time to wait an additional ten years to apply to have their rights restored. (Second arrests can occur at police discretion, and second convictions can result from unintentional parole violations.) And even those convicted of nonviolent offenses have to demonstrate that they have made restitution to their victims—a curious requirement, given the prevalence of "victimless crimes" among non-violent offenses and, moreover, a difficult requirement. "Many ex-convicts can't pay restitution because they can't get a job. That's a big deal," notes Aziza Botchway, an attorney for the American Civil Liberties Union. Meanwhile, people in some categories, including sex offenders, remain ineligible for expedited review and will probably never regain voting rights.[29]

Punitive governance is especially evident in southern states, where the legacies of Jim Crow still inflect myriad law enforcement practices and social conventions. But punitiveness is not just a feature of states of the former Confederacy; northern states have their own versions. These are often pecuniary in nature.

In progressive Wisconsin, for instance, only defendants earning less than $3,000 a year in 2008—which was far below the national poverty line—were eligible for a public defender. Other jurisdictions set eligibility for a public defender at income levels below the minimum wage. Then there are various "cost-recovery policies." According to a report published by the American Bar Association, at least seventeen states charge application fees to people seeking court-appointed attorneys, thus undermining or qualifying the defendant's Sixth Amendment right to counsel.

These include Colorado, Connecticut, Massachusetts, New Jersey, Oregon, Vermont, and Wisconsin. In California, Los Angeles County assesses fees, as does King County (Seattle) in Washington.[30] Note that these charges are assessed against people who are already poor or indigent or who have lost their jobs or become unemployable as a result of arrest or conviction.

Indeed, "almost every encounter with the criminal justice system these days can give rise to a fee," reports Adam Liptak of the *New York Times*: application fees, copayments for public defenders, court costs, restitution, and contributions to various high-minded funds: "In Washington State, people convicted of certain crimes are . . . charged $100 so their DNA can be put in a database. Private probation companies charge $30 to $40 a month for supervision. Halfway houses charge for staying in them. People sentenced to community service are required to buy $15 insurance policies for every week they work. Criminals on probation and parole wear global positioning devices that monitor their whereabouts—for a charge of as much as $16 a day." Such piling on of fees and charges neatly marries a primal rage to punish to the modern mania for privatization of government functions—privatized justice as punitive justice. Liptak goes on to note that progressive Washington State "has one of the longest lists of fees assessed to criminals, and it is diligent in trying to collect them." It also withholds the right to vote from people who have not paid their debts. Beverly Dubois was sentenced to nine months in jail for growing marijuana. Subsequently disabled in a car accident, Dubois "makes payments of $10 a month toward what was once a $1,610 debt—$1,000 for a county 'drug enforcement fund,' a $500 'victim assessment fee' and $110 in court costs. 'I still don't know who the victim was,' she said. Her efforts notwithstanding, her debt is growing because of the 12 percent interest assessed annually by the State of Washington. As of September, it stood at $1,895.69. 'I will never have it paid off in my lifetime,' Ms. Dubois said."[31]

In the Name of the Victim

Punishment looms large in modern U.S. culture. "To an extraordinary degree the rhetoric of punishment is being drawn on to resolve basic administrative problems," suggest Theodore Caplow and Jonathan Simon in a review of prison population trends. They give a harrowing example. In Florida both liberals and conservatives supported a ballot initiative campaign to shift the financial burden of prosecution from localities to the state. How did this basic bookkeeping procedure carry the day? Commercials featured the families of murder victims lamenting that the death penalty could not be pursued in their loved ones' cases—because a county could not afford capital prosecution with its lengthy appeals and procedures.[32]

EXTENDING THE CARCERAL

Harshness is not simply built into the penalty phase of the justice system. Coercive techniques pervade the world of law enforcement, and these are used as measures of first resort. Once the exception, heavily armed SWAT (special weapons and tactics) teams have become the rule: shows of state force deployed—often clumsily, sometimes erroneously, and occasionally to disastrous effect—against the citizenry in the routine service of warrants.[33] Other police practices break with established traditions of fair play. The customary "one free phone call" from jail is not always granted, and lawyers sent by the families of arrestees are not always allowed to see their clients, who can thus be held for days on end without any access to counsel or the outside world. Defense attorneys tell me that these are not uncommon practices. The whole point of such techniques, as I understand them, is to create a sense of isolation and helplessness in the detainee, thereby "softening him up" and breaking his will. Police officers and jail guards with whom I have spoken understand this principle well enough. Cops and prosecutors use these techniques, strategically and without sanction, to circumvent legal protections against capricious policing.

More public aspects of the justice system are similarly coercive. Prosecutors strategically pile on charges as a substitute for scrupulous investigation. Rather than risk conviction on a higher charge, most defendants will plead guilty to the lesser charge. Americans are accustomed to television courtroom dramas, which feature exhaustive investigations, presentations of complex evidence, and impassioned closing arguments. But in the real world about 95 percent of felony convictions are settled with a plea bargain.[34] This is not, as is often imagined, a sign of leniency but of punitiveness.

Lawless Law

The notorious 1999 case from Tulia, Texas, where a racist and unscrupulous special prosecutor manufactured drug charges against forty-six people, forty of them African American—a substantial percentage of the town's black adult population—is doubly disturbing. Submitted to the usual routines of harsh policing, unable to afford competent legal representation, told that the jig was up and they might as well cooperate, and unwilling to believe that they would receive a fair trial, thirty-one of the innocent defendants simply pleaded guilty to false charges.[35] The details of the Tulia case give a disturbing picture of what law has come to mean for millions.

The skids on the road to Tulia were greased by democratic means, not despotic ones. One peculiarity of the U.S. system is that most state judges and prosecutors are elected, not appointed. The U.S. justice system thus is uniquely subject to populist rages. Since the white backlash against urban disorders at the end of the 1960s, voters have clamored for tough prosecutors and judges. In the process Americans have accepted an increasingly lawless law. Overzealous or vindictive prosecutors are seldom brought to heel, even when they conceal exculpatory evidence. Successive revisions to criminal codes have defined more and more acts as criminal while enhancing penalties associated with crime in general, thus codifying sanctions that violate the cardinal rule of law, the idea that punishment should be commensurate with the crime.

In the face of gradual erosions—no-knock warrants, looser definitions of probable cause, weakened rules against unreasonable search and seizure—the protections embodied in the Bill of Rights seem like relics from happier times. One seldom hears any more what used to be the point of pride of U.S. law, at least in my public high-school civics lessons: the idea that it is better to let a few guilty people go free than to imprison a single innocent person.

Lawlessness, unleashed as law, has proved difficult to keep within bounds. And in their zeal for punishment, the anticrime warriors have become alarmingly indifferent to the guilt or innocence of the accused. Scores of innocence projects in dozens of states show that. They document, beyond reasonable doubt, that prosecutors can be vindictive, that police investigators sometimes conceal exculpatory evidence, that crime laboratories serve up erroneous results—and worse. A study by the University of Michigan Law School examined 328 cases in which defendants convicted of murder or rape were later exonerated. This study did not include the thirty-five people wrongfully convicted in Tulia, Texas, then pardoned, and more than one hundred people falsely convicted after being arrested by police in the rogue Rampart Division of the Los Angeles Police Department (LAPD), or more than seventy child-care workers wrongfully convicted in sex abuse hysterias.[36] The study concludes that thousands, "perhaps tens of thousands," of innocent people are languishing in U.S. prisons.[37]

CRASH (Community Resources Against Street Hooliganism) was the tough-sounding name of the LAPD's antigang squads. The jarring, Orwellian acronym, not to mention the unit's skull-and-crossbones insignia, should have signaled from the start that something foul was afoot. Before it was disbanded, members of the CRASH unit in the Rampart Division, which serves an area east of the Olympics area of Los Angeles, systematically sent black and Latino youth to prison on trumped-up charges, planted evidence, and perjured testimony. Police officers had also engaged in a pattern of unnecessary arrests, unprovoked beatings, illegal shootings, murder, witness intimidation, cover-up, and, in general, acts of terrorism. They had even moved in on the lucrative drug trade. Police in the Rampart Division essentially functioned as an especially ruthless gang on the streets of LA—or, one might say, as a terror cell that operated for a while with legal impunity.

It is often said that, in combating the evils of gangs, such police units fall under a sort of mimetic spell, involuntarily copying the miasmic violence they set out to fight. This sort of argument was made a lot during the cold war: the United States, in its zeal for fighting the good fight against Soviet communism, was in danger of mimicking Stalinist methods. I have never liked this form of argument, and I think it is especially pernicious now. Such an argument invariably begins by positing an unthinkably evil nemesis. Against this evil alter stands a precious, innocent, and true self, one that predates the struggle, a self to whom one becomes, by degrees, untrue. But there is nothing innocent about this innocence, nothing true about this truth. Such an argument leaves uninspected and uninspectable the anticommunist and "zero tolerance" policies that led—quite logically, if you ascribe to them—to such business as McCarthyism, the Vietnam War, and police-state hooliganism. This argument fails to explain how a public obsession with law and order, stoked by sensationalist journalism and reinforced by both political parties, rewards overreaching cops and fosters a culture of police impunity. It thus precludes any genuinely self-critical reflection: even when we do terrible things, it was not us, it was really them—the bad guys—who did it, who forced us to do it.

The rogue Rampart Division, of course, is not the norm; it was an extreme case—so extreme that it demanded remedy, lest the entire system of aggressive, preemptive, race-targeted policing be delegitimized.

What goes unchanged is the weight of race and class in the criminal justice system. In Los Angeles, as in Tulia, a majority of the defendants who would later be exonerated had pleaded guilty to trumped-up charges. And what go unaddressed are the everyday police tactics with which many white Americans have become quite comfortable. Joshua Marquis, district attorney for Clatsop County, Oregon, describes the public policy calculation behind this attitude. Responding to the University of Michigan study of wrongful convictions and subsequent exonerations, Marquis said, "We all agree that it is better for 10 guilty men to go free than for one innocent man to be convicted." But then he added, "Is it better for 100,000 guilty men to walk free rather than have one innocent man convicted? The cost-benefit policy answer is no."[38]

Maximum Security, Perpetual Surveillance

A staggering fourteen million Americans are arrested each year, excluding traffic violations—up from a little more than three million in 1960. (That is, the arrest rate as a percentage of the population has nearly tripled: from 1.6 percent in 1960 to 4.4 percent today.) Still, the majority of solid citizens who will never have a serious run-in with the law might imagine themselves immune to the logic of punitive governance. This would be incorrect. "Crime control," Caplow and Simon conclude, "has become the dominant model for government."[39] The presumption of guilt, with its rage to punish and assorted monitoring practices, is most dramatically at work in law enforcement and the legal justice system, but it has also come to pervade the provision of social welfare, public housing, student loans, and many other functions of government. Today a host of public institutions takes on police functions, acting to retroactively punish actual infractions, to zealously discover new offenses, and to actively anticipate imagined crimes.

Consider some of the ways the will to punish has gradually been extended beyond the gates of the prison:

- Presumably, a college education would put youth who have had a brush with the law on the straight and narrow path. But college students with drug crime convictions of any sort may be denied government-insured student loans, Pell Grants, and other forms of financial aid for education. (Some might become eligible for such loans after completing an authorized drug rehabilitation program.) Instituted in 1998, this eligibility requirement was interpreted broadly by the Clinton administration, which construed it as applying not only to convictions concurrent with a student's education but also to any drug conviction in the past.

- Nationwide, residents of public housing can be summarily expelled if they or any coresident member of their family are convicted of a crime. No doubt some public housing residents desired and even agitated for such a policy, an extreme measure that amounts to a formalization of collective punishment. The policy dates to the Clinton administration and was devised in the throes of gang wars and drug panics. As with the screening of student loans, this approach has never been retired.

- "Zero tolerance" policies in schools across the United States mean that children can be permanently expelled for even simple possession of a single marijuana cigarette. Elaborated in the name of child protection, such policies rewire our understanding of education. They turn schools into an extension of prisons and actually sacrifice children on the altar of child protection.

- Voter identification requirements have replaced lifelong felon disenfranchisement as the voter suppression method of choice. At least 11 percent of voting-age citizens are said to lack the requisite identification papers.[40] In its 2006 ruling in *Purcell v. Gonzalez,* the Supreme Court found that states may impose voter identification requirements, even if these have the effect of disenfranchising some qualified voters. The logic embedded in the Court's ruling is revelatory. Justices cited the fear of voter fraud—which has been shown to be extremely uncommon—as providing a compelling state interest in preserving the integrity of elections. The Court solidified and expanded this reasoning in its 2008 decision in *Crawford v. Marion County Election Board.* By a 6–3 majority the Court rejected arguments that Indiana's law requiring voters to produce government-issued photo identification imposes an undue burden on the poor, indigent, aged, or members of minority groups. These rulings represent a reversal of established ideas about democratic participation. If the Court had applied the logic of the *Crawford* ruling in 1966, it is unclear whether it would have thrown out the poll tax. This is the logic of punitive governance in a nutshell. The real voter is disenfranchised in order to thwart the largely imaginary lawbreaker.[41]

- In San Diego welfare applicants must submit to warrantless searches of their homes, including exploration of their cabinets, dressers, and closets. Any evidence of illegal activity uncovered in these rummagings can be used as evidence in criminal prosecution. This practice—a departure from Fourth Amendment protections against unlawful search and seizure—has been upheld by the U.S. Supreme Court, which, in a bizarre ruling, asserted that these "home visits" are not searches. The assumption that welfare applicants might be hiding income that would disqualify them from benefits thus becomes the occasion for a devil's bargain: the poor must surrender key rights and protections in order to receive social benefits.[42]
- In the wake of ongoing sex panics, even the timeless pleasure of watching children play has been rendered a suspicious activity. Many elementary schools now post high-security fences around their perimeters, causing places of learning to resemble nothing so much as penitentiaries. Playgrounds and urban parks too have become garrisons. At one playground in San Francisco a security guard refuses entry to adult strollers who show up without children in tow, and solitary adults are also told not to loiter outside the playground.[43]

Punitiveness and preemption have progressively redefined practices in an array of fields. Black and brown people have always known that they could not walk through certain neighborhoods without facing police harassment. But try asking airport immigration officers why they need to know what you were doing in Mexico. Even if you are a white, middle-class, native-born Protestant, you will instantly see what I mean. Or, just try taking a laptop into the Library of Congress for the first time; after several hours of bureaucratic hassle, it will become apparent how new assumptions have rebuilt the social landscape, such that security measures significantly impede any legitimate use you might enjoy of the public facility.

New technologies speed punitive governance. Walk the streets of New York City or Washington, D.C., and municipal surveillance cameras will likely photograph your goings and comings. Should a crime occur in your vicinity, you will become an instant suspect when police review the video files. Drive the highways of Maryland, and a camera attached to an unmarked patrol cruiser may scan your license tag, running it through state and federal crime databases—while also checking to see that you have passed your emissions inspection and paid your parking tickets. In Maryland, Virginia, Wisconsin, and other states, police may also attach a Global Positioning System device to your car to monitor your movements—without your permission, of course, but also without obtaining a warrant or court order. Legally cross the border, passport in hand, and data on you and your travels will be automatically collected, to be stored for fifteen years—seventy-five years if you are not a citizen—for perusal by a range of intelligence and law enforcement agencies. Run a Google search on certain subjects, and your activities may very well be noted. Send an especially heated e-mail to a friend, and your message might get swept up in the National Security Agency's indiscriminate "data mining" of electronic communications.[44]

The sorting and filtering of multiple databases means that the presumption of guilt is now widely distributed. Or, as Jeremy Crampton has noted, surveillance, once directed against individuals deemed dangerous, is now applied at the level of the entire population, whose "dangerousness" is inferred from activities not in themselves unlawful or dangerous (checking certain books out of the library, visiting certain Web sites, walking certain streets, taking a vacation abroad).[45] Should you think these invasions of privacy insignificant—"But I've done nothing wrong, so I've got nothing to worry about"—imagine being interrogated by the police, and perhaps being mentioned in the local news, solely because your DNA showed up at a crime scene.

This punitiveness shapes the behavior of voters and the way citizens understand their citizenship. Ballot initiatives to "get tough" on crime, to assess additional punishments for infractions, or to "crack down" on various imagined abuses of government services have proved popular, and over the years voters have vented ballot-box rages at sex offenders, welfare cheats, and convicts of various stripes. Increasingly, ballot initiatives and punitive laws have been directed against illegal immigrants. Undocumented border crossing is a misdemeanor offense, and being present in the country without papers is a violation of civil, not criminal, law, but such points seem moot in ongoing hysterias. Depending on the state, county, or municipality, undocumented workers may be denied social, educational, or medical services; they may be denied drivers' licenses; they may be prohibited from congregating (often in the name of public safety); they may be screened by local police, who now function as an extension of Immigration and Customs Enforcement in some jurisdictions; and undocumented workers may be denied housing under hodgepodge zoning laws that prohibit unrelated unmarried people from living in the same house. At the national level the increased enforcement of immigration laws has sharply realigned the ethnic makeup of the federal prison population, according to a study by the Pew Research Center: Latinos now make up 13 percent of the general population, one-third of federal prison inmates, and 40 percent of those convicted in federal courts. (More than 70 percent of those convicted were not U.S. citizens, and more than 60 percent of those were sentenced for immigration offenses.)[46]

The Dragnet of Everyday Life

It is not just in the sphere of government proper that the logic of punitive governance flourishes. Punitive assumptions about risk, prevention, and safety now pervade wider civil, corporate, and familial practices, reshaping the social landscape in tangible ways, as Jonathan Simon shows in *Governing through Crime*. Private monitoring practices extend the long arm of the state. Visit a Family YMCA for the first time, and the receptionist will take your photo. Purchase the kind of Sudafed that actually works, and the druggist will take down your driver's license number.

Americans are accustomed to background checks for employment, credit, rentals, and security clearance; these are reasonable measures, no doubt. But now even small-scale employers can, and do, run Google checks on prospective employees. And more intrusive "security clearances" have become mandatory for ever wider areas of employment. An investigative news report in the wake of 9/11 turned up ex-convicts—including, ominously, sex offenders—working in the fueling, luggage-handling, and janitorial sections of airports. Just how the dread of ordinary crime and sex offense might square with fears of terrorism was never explained, but the news report was widely waved as evidence of inadequate airport security. Airports responded by firing workers and tightening their employee screening.

And the screening only begins with background checks and security clearances. Simon catalogs the basic design of modern office complexes and other workplaces; his inventory includes secure key-card entry systems, video surveillance technologies, elaborate performance monitoring procedures, security guards, and security specialists. In an earlier era Marx famously described the split between "the labor contract," with its appearance of freedom, and the factory, whose working conditions resembled forms of authority found in the prison. Today, the irony Marx underscored seems lost. "Surveillance and punishment," writes Simon, are "the inevitable and ever-widening penumbra of the contract" itself.[47]

Drug panics have fueled get-tough approaches and intense surveillance in widely distributed sites. Some industries require periodic drug tests of all workers, not just those who are driving, working with heavy machinery, or distributing medications. You don't have to have this or that job, the logic goes, so you might expect to give up some privacy as a condition of employment. But minors do not have the right to refuse to go to school, and many will participate in some extracurricular activity or other. At least one public school requires periodic drug tests not only of athletes (a practice that became common after Reagan-era drug panics) but also of all students wishing to participate in any extracurricular activity. Although no one could cite evidence of serious drug use or distribution at the school, Simon notes, the Supreme Court deemed the drug tests acceptable, reasoning that "the nationwide drug epidemic makes the war against drugs a pressing concern in every school."[48] And so, again, the imagined threat trumps traditional arguments for privacy. Remote undocumentable risks become tantamount to dire emergencies. The need to flush out and expose lawbreaking, even when it has no visible victims, has become something no one questions.

Notions of child safety and protection have consistently shifted what might count as responsible public speech in a preemptive direction, and in this shift families—once the strong bastion of privacy law—have become instruments of punitive governance. For many years public service announcements have hammered home the condescending message that parents must take responsibility for closely monitoring their children for signs of drug or alcohol use. Some ads have recommended that parents search their children's rooms, and others have urged parents to submit their children to home drug tests. The idea that parents ought to exercise vigilance in a wide range of matters has become widespread. V-chips and parental control settings on Internet browsers allow parents to restrict what their children see or read. One seldom hears the case made that such practices poison the relationship between parents and children—or that minors, in order to become responsible full-fledged adults, require certain zones of privacy and freedom. Parental responsibility for surveillance and prevention is reinforced by judicial practices that punish parents for their children's misdeeds. Some states even require parents to report to the police if they discover that their teenage kids are having sex—and make it a crime for them not to do so. Missis-

sippi's Child Protection Act of 2009 defines as abuse a parent's "toleration . . . of the child's sexual involvement with any other person." The
so-called child-centered family thus has become the crime-centered
family, as Simon calls it: an apparatus designed for surveillance, detection, and discipline.[49]

Citizens Watch over Armored Suburbs

Long before 9/11, watchfulness had become a civic duty. Beginning in
the early 1970s, Neighborhood Watch organizations broadly disseminated a cultural logic of reflexive wariness. I vividly recall an experience
with this sense of confrontational insecurity in the late 1980s. As I drove
slowly in search of a friend's home one afternoon, peering at incon-
sistently placed house numbers in a new subdivision, a neighborhood
vigilante stopped me and demanded to know what I was doing. When I
protested, she insisted, without fear of contradiction, that my right to
drive on a public roadway was trumped by the residents' desire for
safety.

Gated communities and what Naomi Klein calls "armored suburbs"
extend and intensify this logic, which progressively rebuilds the social
and physical landscape.[50] And it is not just within the gates of such
modern fortresses that the rebuilding is underway. Even in the "open"
city, security cameras perch at the entrances to new condominiums and
remodeled apartment buildings. Presumably, these cameras protect the
residents from break-ins, but such devices are double-edged: the resulting video records can be (and have been) subpoenaed in residents' divorce cases—or as evidence in criminal cases against a resident.

A cursory survey of sundry technologies and everyday practices
turns up more of the same. It shows that how we live has been ubiqui-
tously, ambiguously reshaped by security concerns. Cul-de-sac layout
has become the norm in many suburban housing developments; devel-
opers market such residences as "safer" than those on through streets.
But there is no evidence that disconnected clusters of housing are safer
than the alternatives and good reason to think that the traffic-unfriendly
design poses real navigation difficulties for ambulance drivers, firefight-
ers, and other emergency service providers. Sport utility vehicles clutter
the highways—visible evidence of America's love affair with safety, or
at least its illusion.[51] But in addition to consuming more fuel and materials than ordinary cars, SUVs actually make the roads less safe for
the rest of us. Global Positioning System devices and other monitoring

equipment built into cars and telephones give consumers the perception of security. But they also allow the driver or talker to be tracked and monitored.

People now tend to speak in the language of the security state. Last winter, when a homeless man found his way inside my apartment building to sleep in the stairwell, a resident posted a notice on the bulletin board. Taking the tone of a police memo, the announcement referred to "security breaches" and "incidents." Residents were reminded to "be vigilant."

THEORIES OF THE PUNITIVE SOCIETY

The punitive trend would seem to confound modern theories of law.[52] In theories dating to the origins of modern sociology, no less than in the classical canon of humanism, it is understood that brute punishment is "primitive." How, then, to frame the resurgence of a punitive orientation in the justice system, the spread of a preemptive paranoid approach throughout other areas of social life?

Emile Durkheim draws distinctions thusly: "Repressive law" is associated with the "mechanical solidarity" of small-scale societies. Under this arrangement people go along and get along because they are similar to each other. They perform the same labors, live the same routines, and think in much the same way. Accordingly, primitive law aims to repress differences and punish nonconformity. Examples of this type of law include penal law, sanctions that damage or kill the lawbreaker, and punishments for blasphemy, defilement, or other offenses against the group. In contrast, nuanced sanctions that have the effect of restoring disrupted social relations ("restitutionary law") are associated with the "organic solidarity" of complex cosmopolitan societies. In the latter arrangement goodwill and neighborliness are negotiated among people who perform different kinds of labor, have different styles of life, and express different ways of thinking. Under organic conditions law thus aims not to enforce conformity but to regulate ordered differences, to structure diversity, and to maintain an equilibrium. The calibration of penalties is a key feature of restitutionary law, which includes contract law, civil law, and constitutional law. In Durkheim's accounting, then, punitive law should diminish in proportion to restitutionary law as civilization advances. A similar process of amelioration logically should occur according to Norbert Elias's conception of the civilizing process. As standards associated with self-restraint and shame become higher, cruel punishments should decline.[53]

But where fear has run amok, where panic has overrun the body politic, all such sociological bets are off. Even Durkheim allowed that the march of civilization is beset by crises, breakdowns, or losses of meaning (anomie), and Elias understood all too well that the banishment of unpleasant topics from polite society, which is part of the civilization process, opens up spaces where civilization runs in reverse. Sex panic would seem a paradigmatic example of this paradoxical process: a more civilized sensitivity to child maltreatment unleashes the barbarism of current sex offender laws. Fear of crime too produces this boomerang effect: the savagery of primitive violence solicits "civilized" brutality.

In this space a much darker sociology might be planted. When fear becomes the normative condition, it inaugurates a broken social order based on mistrust, resentment, and ill will. The pervasive assumption that anonymous, lurking others cannot be trusted undermines goodwill and feeds a sort of poisoned solidarity: We shall all be diligent in monitoring each other for signs of transgression.[54] This rage to surveil and punish reverberates, internalized, in the psyche. It preaches an authoritarian, fear-based ethics that Vygotsky once described as the "policeman of the soul."[55] Of course this worldview mandates preemption. Coercion is the only language the bad man will understand.

Fear induces a dread of the other, a tear in the social fabric, and a propensity toward violence. Violence, masked as retribution, cannot be seen as aggression, nor can the harm it inflicts ever be acknowledged. The emergent republic of fear thus constructs an essentially negative sense of community, nation, and social good. Once established, this negativity becomes self-perpetuating. Citizenship becomes tantamount to vigilant surveillance, a conception Americans once ridiculed as a defining feature of totalitarian societies. Law becomes an obsessive-compulsive process—the closing of imaginary loopholes, the proscription of ever more closely circumscribed behaviors. Procedures once deemed anathema to democratic governance become first thinkable, then necessary, and at last unavoidable.

Punishment in the Name of Well-being

The system I have been tracing maps onto the regimes of power described by Michel Foucault in *Discipline and Punish, The History of Sexuality,* and other works but only partially so. Or, rather, the emergent system of power represents an unanticipated amalgam of those regimes, their extension into new territories.[56]

The form of power Foucault designates as sovereign is essentially the right of the ruler to seize things: time, property, or bodies. By the classical age this right of the king to punish, torture, or kill had been limited, at least theoretically, to states of emergency—to instances when the sovereign or the state was imperiled by enemies from within or without. In contrast the regime of discipline aims to correct or rehabilitate. The "gentle punishments" of Enlightenment law aim to induce the miscreant to mend his ways. Bio-power follows suit. As Foucault sketches it, this mode of power is neither deductive (in the sense of subtracting life or enjoyment) nor correctional (in the usual sense of straightening out crooked ways) but productive, as it aims to invest in life. Biomedicine, psychology, and other disciplines that promote well-being intervene in life, not from without but from within. Obviously, state actors and other authorities use the life sciences to secure the integration of individuals into economic systems, and they use demographic techniques to manage populations. More subtly, bio-power induces individuals to work on themselves through various forms of self-care, self-improvement, fitness schemes, and so on.

Foucault acknowledges that bio-power is sometimes organized in terms of racisms and sexual phobias. Congenital criminals, evolutionary throwbacks, sexual perverts, and racial degenerates were among the earliest inventions of the life-investing disciplines, and the hunt for the biopolitical monster is a recurring feature of bio-power. Still, within the model Foucault sketches, the modern state logically should continue developing forms of power that are more invasive but also gentler and more rational, more effective but also kinder and more nuanced. In my reading this has not happened, at least not in the United States. Or, rather, this process *was* happening for many years, then suddenly reversed course. The result is a curious admixture of social forms. The middle term in Foucault's suit—the correctional approach—all but disappears. Restraints on power associated with "disciplining" give way to "punishment" and the rage for more and more of it. But the punitive state is not simply a retreat to premodern practices. The role of the sovereign is not played by the king; rather, ongoing social crusades are undertaken on behalf of the population, its biopolitical health, and well-being. Today, it is the populace—or a segment of it, speaking on behalf of the rest—that claims society is in peril and thus assumes the right (democratically expressed by elected officials, lawmakers, and judges) to inflict increasingly public and spectacular punishments on a variety of enemies within and without.

Anxiety (Dis)Order

Should we, then, name a fourth regime of power: panic? If so, this regime would be the mutant offspring of sovereign power and bio-power. Its practices would tether technical advances in bio-power and cybertechnology to increasingly irrational undertakings, twenty-first-century technologies to nineteenth-century concepts. I emphasize the uniqueness of this regime. Archaic tyrannies and antecedent totalitarianisms, of course, also were based on fear but in a different fashion. Elites terrorized the masses directly, to extort their acquiescence. And ancient regimes sometimes directed pogroms against witches, Jews, perverts, and others—but these horrors too seem different from the present orchestrations of anxiety. The modern state of panic traffics in fear, not as a special effect, nor to stand down adversaries, nor as a safety valve for the release of pent-up social pressures, nor even to terrorize subjugated peoples but as the justification for its own existence, as ballast and support for its rule, as the very definition of its democracy, and as the social cement that holds things together. Power flows through the nervous system of a body politic paralyzed by dread. Ruled and rulers are equally trapped in fear.

Panics and hysterias have broken out from time immemorial, wherever humans have lived under conditions that allow for rumor. And in the past those who would intimidate opposition, unseat authority, or ride fear into power have manipulated gossip, scandal, and collective disturbances. But that is to say that panic was power in an abnormal condition, in a process of siege, crisis, mischief, or instability. Panic was the wild card of the ancient regimes, an instrument to be selectively applied but also the harbinger of systemic breakdown. Panic could never before constitute a steady state, a durable regime of power, a universal tendency toward hypochondria, obsessive-compulsive behaviors, and deliriums, because reliable techniques for its communication and perpetuation did not exist. Not so today. Never before have so many mechanisms existed for panic's stoking, democratization, modulation, and institutionalization. The present system's default mode does not correspond to power in any previously existing normal condition.

Risks remain in this twitchy, mass-mediated system, of course, as Paul Virilio notes. One risk is that the besieged will be "buried alive . . . behind their protective enclosures." Another is the accidental release of a "terror that is unspeakable and counterproductive" for its anonymous managers.[57] In the chapters that follow, I will continue to explore this strange state of affairs: how punitive excess went global during the war on terror; how the public came to see itself as perpetually imperiled; and how this business might be integrated, either efficiently or inefficiently, into economic systems.

CHAPTER 6

Innocents Abroad

Taboo and Terror in the Global War

The shrill voices of those who give orders are full of fear.
—Bertolt Brecht, "The Anxieties of the Regime"

American culture metabolized the outrages of September 11, 2001, in a pattern evocative of the sex and crime panics. Depictions of despoiled innocence, sensational journalism, and calls to citizen vigilantism were followed by preemptive measures, the devising of lists and registries, and the erosion of fundamental rights and procedures. The resulting war on terror projected America's forty-year punitive trend onto the international stage, replete with images of tough-talking sheriffs straight out of the Old West, "wanted" posters, and steely ultimatums.[1]

AMERICAN INNOCENCE, LIVE

On September 11 and for weeks thereafter, live nonstop news coverage stoked a sense of collective trauma, fanning fear into the hinterlands, far beyond the sites of any logical terror targets. The monstrous images on the screen and voiceover narratives fed a mass-produced sense of threat and catastrophe. Talking heads aired rumors of other attacks underway, then pondered the safety of U.S. nuclear power plants, water supply systems, and mass transit. The chattering class even wondered aloud whether the United States would survive. And as these scenes and narratives played and replayed for days, by means of a repetition at once morbid and perverse, television audiences relived the terror, panic, and thrill—the spectacle—of 9/11.[2]

As Corey Robin, author of *Fear: The History of a Political Idea,* has noted, prominent political writers openly savored this experience of terror, which they expected would prod the nation from passivity to action. According to the *New York Times* columnist Frank Rich, 9/11 was a wake-up call, jolting us out of a "frivolous if not decadent decadelong dream." His colleague David Brooks treated fear as a morning "cleanser," and George Packer of the *New Yorker* claimed that the terror attacks brought us a heightened state of awareness: "Alertness, grief, resolve— even love." Packer approvingly quoted an investment banker who was fleeing the conflagration of the World Trade Center: "I'm not in shock. I like this state. I've never been more cognizant in my life." If this state of panic gave citizens purpose, meaning, civic-mindedness, and knowledge of good and evil, then what was to be avoided was not so much another terror attack as a return to the complacence that had preceded it. "Perhaps this is what some in our society seek," Robin concludes, "to be in thrall, perpetually, to fear."[3]

In the throes of events the public was enjoined to be vigilant: report suspicious packages, suspicious activity. Praise for the tipster initially greeted a story that a citizen had reported to authorities the sinister plotting of Muslims in a Georgia diner. But it later turned out that the three medical students had no ties to terror cells, no bombs in their car, and had expressed no ill will toward the United States. Hate crimes against Muslims and Arab Americans, not to mention everyday acts of discourtesy, spiked. In Arizona a disturbed gunman enacted fantasies of vengeance by going on a shooting spree against Muslims, ultimately murdering a Sikh gas station owner whom he had misidentified as Muslim.[4]

Critics have noted how public narratives about September 11 excluded treatment, or even acknowledgment, of the Islamists' political aims, effectively rendering the horrific events of the day as the criminal acts of inscrutable "evildoers" (George W. Bush's favored term for describing the terrorists). In the prevailing version the attacks simply were leveled against America's goodness. Moreover, public narratives invariably rebuffed even friendly suggestions that some measure and proportion be applied in understanding the fiery devastation of 9/11. As Paul Smith, a professor of cultural studies, has noted, the suffering of Americans was to be understood as unique and was not to be compared with the suffering of any others.[5] Discreet silences further sharpened the picture of a wholly innocent, victimized nation: discussion of the U.S. role in cultivating, organizing, and funding Islamist terror cells, including al Qaeda, during the Soviet occupation of Afghanistan was mostly excluded from the serious public sphere.[6]

SEX AND TERROR AND BUSINESS AS USUAL

Both official and unofficial narratives of 9/11 contained subtle echoes of the familiar sexual anxieties. Public portrayals of an immaculate nation's "lost innocence" resonated with long-standing cultural motifs associated with child abuse, and the naming of the new Department of Homeland Security, with its intimation of a national hearth under siege, reverberated eerily with the logic of the earlier sex panics. Similarly, the organized response of citizens' groups drew on familiar tropes: in the name of family and victimization, families of the victims of 9/11 organized to press for compensation, monitor congressional hearings on intelligence failures, serve as a pressure group in lower Manhattan redevelopment plans, and seek redress in various criminal trials having little or nothing to do with 9/11. Assorted actions by various of these groups have sometimes tilted rightward, other times leftward but have always traded in the dominant cultural logic of the victims' rights movement, which derives a sort of sacral authority from aggrieved victimization.

The logic of the one panic dovetailed with that of the other in less subtle ways, too. The sexuality of the 9/11 terrorists—whose devotion to an extremist Wahabi politics allowed them to drink and cavort at Hooters as part of their "cover"—was the object of some media attention. For a time speculation that Mohamed Atta was homosexual was a staple of the yellow press.[7] *Predator,* a term generally used to describe pedophiles who stalk children, was the favored euphemism for *terrorist,* and Jerry Vines, twice president of the Southern Baptist Convention, stirred news stories when he called the prophet Muhammad a "demon-possessed pedophile."[8] The rhetorical association of one disapproved thing with another is old hat, but new connections between sex and terror developed after 9/11. When the Patriot Act first became law, civil libertarians worried that aggressive new surveillance tactics would not be restricted to the detection of terror plots but would gradually be applied to everyday, routine law enforcement. In fact, nothing was gradual about the Patriot Act's extension into sex. Almost immediately, Homeland Security was boasting that new border screening measures were keeping pedophiles out of the country, and the Justice Department was defending Internet "data mining"—which never caught any terrorists at work—as a means to detect child pornography and to catch online sex predators.[9]

WAR ON ~~CRIME~~ TERROR

From within so much forgetfulness and trauma came new rationales for steel and strength. Various pundits took up arms against a host of troubles by trying on the mantle of empire. Not since Rome had one nation possessed so much power, they suddenly discovered. A chafed, restive, and increasingly dangerous world would benefit from the benevolent exercise of American tutelage—or so it was said.[10] It was also said that we, citizens of a free democratic nation, had no choice but to surrender some ill-defined portion of our freedoms in exchange for security. A political agenda thus acquired the imprimatur of necessity—and who can argue with necessity?

Soon came the announcement of an indeterminate "war on terror," a war in which the rules of the Geneva Convention would not apply to the treatment of "unlawful enemy combatants," a specious legal category hastily devised to skirt the procedures of both international conventions and criminal law. The United States invaded and occupied Afghanistan, then launched a preemptive war of occupation against Iraq, whose government was falsely portrayed as possessing weapons of mass destruction and as having conspired with al Qaeda in the days leading up to 9/11. In the conduct of these wars and other international campaigns, the United States abrogated long-standing human rights conventions. Legal memos attempted to redefine *torture,* and the Bush administration authorized the use of some forms of torture. And as part of an expanded policy of "extraordinary rendition," intelligence operatives kidnapped foreign citizens and extradited them to secret CIA prisons overseas or to foreign intelligence services in other countries for interrogation using more extreme forms of torture.[11]

Back home, the Bush-Cheney administration exploited the occasion to get new laws through Congress, expand police powers, and engineer new relations between the state, its citizens, and noncitizens. Federal agents rounded up and detained more than twelve hundred immigrants (often on the word of neighbors), holding them for extended periods without charges, without access to counsel, in solitary confinement. Under the National Security Exit-Entry Registration System, male immigrants aged sixteen to forty-five who were from twenty-five Arab, Muslim, and South Asian countries were required to register with the U.S.

n." These ideas re-
olonists, of course.
l reformers, politi-
entiments have be-
ing media, govern-
ned will serve as a
e state.

s twitchings of the
meets the cold hard
no number of legal
er provide sufficient
er entirely superable,
cur, in part because
and risks to it are in-
evil expand like an
neighborliness turns
bricious. Subjected to
distinctions between
just this slippery and
lose all meaning but
rate into unsanctioned

U GHRAIB

later, Seymour Hersh in
xual abuse, and torture
o distinguish sanctioned
nsued, as did soul search-
wondered "how much
s of Abu Ghraib was in-
imagery available on the
ing out Webcasts of them-
ed much of the establish-
Internet. Others noted the
from Pier Paolo Pasolini's
Catholic fantasy depicting
Of course, there is a hitch:
by the director's adoration

government once a year. Registrants were photographed, fingerprinted, and interrogated under oath by Immigration officials. No terrorists were located through either of these procedures, but thousands were deported on various immigration law violations.[12] Meanwhile, the Patriot Act centralized federal agencies associated with policing and expanded government powers of surveillance. Mysterious "no-fly" lists were devised. Government prosecutors brought high-profile charges against accused terrorist conspirators—sometimes on scant evidence (e.g., a defendant was heard to express a vague but enthusiastic wish that harm would come to the United States), sometimes on evidence that could only be described as entrapment (i.e., undercover agents encouraged conspiracy to commit criminal acts). In some cases defendants pleaded guilty to substantial charges rather than risk execution on capital offenses—or reclassification as "unlawful combatants." In Detroit a U.S. district judge released a defendant after throwing out his terrorism conviction; the judge was acting on an unusual request from the government, which by then had opened an investigation of the former lead prosecutor.[13]

The Bush administration launched a broad domestic spying program, widely monitoring Americans' e-mail communications, Internet activity, phone calls, phone records, and financial transactions. Secret legal memos released after Bush left the White House reveal much grander declarations of executive power, asserting that the president could deploy military forces inside the United States (in violation of the Posse Comitatus Act) to pursue terrorists and to conduct warrantless searches and seizures (in violation of the Fourth Amendment). Memos further asserted that "First Amendment speech and press rights may also be subordinated to the overriding need to wage war successfully," that the president could order eavesdropping without warrants, and that Congress lacked any power to intervene in the treatment of detainees or to limit the president's authority to practice secret rendition.[14]

Measure and proportion proved elusive on other fronts, too. With the launching of Operation Predator in 2003, the Department of Homeland Security's Immigration and Customs Enforcement (ICE) unit expressly linked sex, terror, and immigration policies. The stated purpose of the initiative was to rid the country of immigrant child molesters and sex offenders, thus restoring integrity to an immigration system widely viewed as broken while also capturing U.S. citizens who violate federal sex laws while traveling abroad. The problem, say immigration lawyers, is that ICE has also swept up people who pose no conceivable threat to safety and welfare. Because ICE agents review Megan's Law registries to identify sex offenders, the quirks and imprecisions of one system of enforcement confer to the other. One long-term Mexican immigrant, convicted years earlier on statutory rape charges stemming from his relationship with his girlfriend when he too was a minor, faced deportation as a sexual predator. Another immigrant urinated behind a garbage can in an alley; he was convicted of indecent exposure and rounded up for deportation hearings. MaryLu Cianciolo, an immigration lawyer, told the *Chicago Tribune*: "In Operation Predator, the purpose is to rack up the numbers and say, 'Oh, we've deported thousands of dangerous sex offenders.' . . . Some of them are dangerous sex offenders. But some of them aren't."[15]

The domestic war on terror upended sacred rights and ancient privileges of citizenship. José Padilla was effectively stripped of U.S. citizenship to be held indefinitely without trial as an "enemy combatant." The government preempted a Supreme Court review of the decision to detain a U.S. citizen without charges by eventually bringing criminal charges against Padilla in federal court. But the criminal charges made no mention of the original accusation—that he was part of a conspiracy to detonate "dirty bombs" in the United States. Videotapes and other evidence suggest that Padilla was extensively tortured during his detention.[16]

Lynne Stewart, the court-appointed attorney for Sheik Abdel Rahman (the blind cleric who was convicted in the 1993 World Trade Center bombing), and her translator were convicted of aiding and abetting terrorists. In fact, Stewart and her translator broke no laws. They were convicted of violating prison communication rules laid down by the prosecutors. The Stewart case is disconcerting in many ways: during the trial prosecutors played secretly recorded conversations between the attorney and her client—and, moreover, charged the radical lawyer with interfering in their efforts to tape these privileged conversations.[17]

Other cases raise equally serious questions about procedure, process, and vindictiveness. After Sami Al-Arian was acquitted by a Florida jury of the several terror and conspiracy charges against him, he entered a plea bargain to one relatively minor charge (providing nonviolent services to people associated with a terrorist organization), with the feds agreeing that he would not be subjected to further prosecution or called as a witness in other cases. In fact, federal prosecutors have continued lobbing subpoenas and heaping charges against the Palestinian professor, whose travails eventually spanned five and a half years in a half-

the victims," "Fear th
verberate over a long
They echo in alarms s
cal progressives, and
come trapped withou
ment, and social mo
perpetual resource fo

A certain magic w
body politic, where t
facticity of risk: no
safeguards, and no p
barriers against harn
and real acts of terr
new frontiers of inn
finitely conceivable.
uncontrolled process
to dread, and solidar
such heat and press
law and lawlessness
skittish space, wher
also where sanctione
forms.

IS IT PORN YET?

In April 2004 *60 M*
the *New Yorker*—de
of Iraqi detainees by
from unsanctioned f
ing or some sembla
of the sexual tortur
spired by the vast re
Internet—and which
selves, try to emulat
ment's reaction to th
similarity of the sho
film, *Salò*, a gay con
how fascists, given t
Pasolini's leftist pass

of young well-formed working-class toughs and subproletarian hustlers—a desire fully conveyed in every frame of the film.

The unnerving correspondence of Pasolini's voyeuristic fantasies and the *tableaux vivants* staged by the torturers at Abu Ghraib, I venture, says a lot. It gets at the tense and volatile relationship between taboo (which, if Georges Bataille was right, holds violence in check) and violence, between attraction and repulsion, between fantasy and power.[22] It suggests something of the prurience of a culture that meticulously examines and sternly condemns sexual infraction. It reveals something of the complex motives involved in the rage to punish, the precariousness of the distinction between licit and illicit violence, and the conditions under which evil becomes banal. One such situation of banality is well enough known: Adolf Eichmann "not only obeyed *orders*, he also obeyed the *law*."[23] Another circumstance, sometimes invoked to explain human rights abuses in war and civil strife, has to do with the breakdown of law and order: If war releases the animal inhumans, as they say, then this is because soldiers at war carry out their duties on the perpetual edge of panic. Soldiers at war can be allowed a kind of reprieve from the taboos and conventions of everyday existence because they act in extremis.

This is where the trouble ends—but it is not where the trouble begins. And so I carefully mark two points: Whatever one might make of human nature and its capacity for violence, state violence is no collective instinctual urge, held in check by taboos; it requires systematic cultivation, implantation, and indoctrination. Even panic responses, on this count, are prepared over the longue durée by a culture that communicates through certain circuits, conditions certain responses, and stokes certain emotions. Breakdowns of rule and order are structured by an elaborate apparatus.

In view of how this apparatus works, we should worry less about the allure of images than about the way talk of this allure gets caught up in public discourse. Narratives about the "attraction of violence" or the "mimetic appeal of pornography" make for poor explanations precisely because such notions are so deeply embedded in American beliefs and anxieties. After all, the orchestrators of events at Abu Ghraib also believed in the efficacy of images; they thought that nothing could be more degrading than simulated submission to the power of the phallus. They too were caught up in the panic around sex, with its fetishism of innocence, its fascination with despoliation, and its systematically solicited rages against the bad man. When the resulting images are criticized from the same perspective that gave rise to them (spooky murmurings about the mysterious power of images), what ensues is a recursive regression— a perpetual ratification of the idea that gave rise to the action.

HO, HUM, ANOTHER ACT OF EXTRAORDINARY BRUTALITY

We can read in the Iraqi photos a Rorschach of lawful lawlessness, an extension and intensification of business as usual in the United States, one of many points where sanctioned violence degenerates into unsanctioned violence. For the torture of prisoners of war at Abu Ghraib, in Afghanistan, and at Guantánamo is only a slight extension of the mistreatment of Muslim prisoners in the Brooklyn Detention Center after 9/11. And that episode was only an elaboration of the everyday indignities (many involving sexual cruelty) heaped on black and brown men in the systematic, workaday world of the U.S. prison system.

The torture of Muslim prisoners in New York included mockery, name-calling, beatings, ramming unresisting prisoners into walls, unnecessary strip searches, and unnecessary cavity searches—one of which involved the insertion of a flashlight in the rectum of a prisoner. Such practices are not entirely exceptional in U.S. prisons, as the reporter Fox Butterfield has noted. In some states "inmates are routinely stripped in front of other inmates before being moved" to a new unit or prison. At the Maricopa County jail in Phoenix inmates "are made to wear women's pink underwear as a form of humiliation." At a maximum security prison in Virginia, inmates have reportedly been "forced to wear black hoods" and report being frequently beaten and forced to crawl on all fours in front of jeering guards. In some states prison guards allow, effectively oversee, and sometimes even exploit, systems of sexual slavery.[24] Add to this catalog of American horrors the various forms of sanctioned and unsanctioned human rights abuses documented by Amnesty International and Human Rights Watch. These include beatings and chokings; the unconscionable use of extended solitary confinement in maximum security and "supermax" prisons; the systematic mistreatment of juvenile and mentally ill detainees; the inhumane use of restraints, electrical devices, and attack dogs against detainees, prisoners, and members of ethnic minorities; and other patterns of police and prison guard brutality.[25] Torture, endemic in U.S. prisons, spread beyond its limited scope after 9/11, ushering in a new world of secret evidence, secret detentions, summary deportations, and extraordinary rendition.

Here is how the retired warden of the Brooklyn Detention Center spoke of the torture of Muslim prisoners that occurred on his watch: "There was no game plan, such as we're hearing about now in Iraq, to break their will. . . . There was no collusion." Of the apparently spontaneous brutalities that happened under his command, he says, defensively, that in the wake of 9/11 "people were feeling very patriotic. The city and the country felt victimized and felt threatened by what had happened. Of course many people, my staff included, had neighbors and friends who were killed in the attack."[26] This is our clue—what we need to know to make sense of extralegal practices spanning the prison-industrial and military-industrial complexes.[27] This is what we need to know to understand how evil becomes banal.

The spontaneous brutalities in New York, shadowy extrajudicial law enforcement practices nationwide, the nauseating business at Abu Ghraib, similar practices at Guantánamo, and the chronic overreaching of presidential power in the open-ended "war on terror" are all fueled by a kind of helpless, inarticulate moral rage at the world. This is the rage of a people who feel victimized and threatened and thus construe their acts (which of necessity sometimes will be preemptive) either as righteous self-defense or as the defense of imperiled innocents. An insignia, inscribed by magic marker on some anonymous prisoner's arm at Abu Ghraib, says it all: "RAPEIST" (sic). Here again, rationales turn to sex, crime: sex crime.

The choice of this particular sobriquet is no accident. Private First Class Lynndie England, whose jaunty thumbs-up and bright smiles adorned some of the most sensational photos from Abu Ghraib, told investigators that guards put prisoners on leashes to intimidate them; they were trying to get prisoners to confess to raping a fifteen-year-old boy.[28] Perhaps this is revealing of converging currents in U.S. culture. Whether a fifteen-year-old boy was actually raped or not is beside the point. Where ongoing sex and crime panics combine with terror panics, the abusiveness of the abuser becomes a justification for the abuses that flow, ever more abundantly, from the font of the state. (Besides, says the voice of moral equivalence, it's not really abuse if you do it to an abuser.)

MEANWHILE, AT FALLUJA

The photos from Abu Ghraib pushed other events off the front pages, one of which was the assault on Falluja. At Falluja the U.S. military laid siege to a substantial city and killed, by its own count, more than seven hundred people, mostly civilians. And this was only the first sustained assault on Falluja. In subsequent assaults U.S. troops cut off water to the city and blocked food supplies, turning virtually the entire population into refugees; the military then razed the city. Every step in this process meets the strictest definition of a war crime. There was little outcry at these acts, which violate international treaties and agreements to which the United States is party. But, then, the razing of Falluja did not involve sex (or its simulation or its depiction).

NOW EVERYONE TRADE PLACES

The distinction between legitimate and illegitimate violence is a difficult one, at best, as is the difference between following and ignoring a rule. Putting a postmodern spin on these difficulties, Jean Baudrillard once notoriously argued that Watergate was not a scandal at all but a trap laid by the system to catch its adversaries in a diversionary moral panic.[29] Diversion, in all its senses, is no doubt part of what moral panics do, but I develop a different sort of argument, one that still distinguishes between law and crime while seeing both as part of a system.

It should be clear enough that any cultural system that equates punishment with justice will foster complicated forms of sadism. And any institutional system that inculcates intense fear and rage will produce technicians who periodically depart from standard operating procedures. But that is not all. Certain cultural-institutional systems, by the nature of their functioning, not only necessarily generate excess; they also possess the uncanny ability to recapture and reinvest that excess in the operational logic of the system itself. When actors caught up in moral panics around sex, crime, and terror themselves become objects of a moral panic, the friction of the one panic within and against the other then becomes a resource for the intensification of the punitive state. Of course, the ruse of liberalism, on socialist readings, is just this: to draw attention to scandal, individual pathology, and worse abuses, thereby diverting attention from the workaday functioning of the larger social system. The curious dynamic I am describing here reproduces this diversionary tactic but also causes it to mutate into illiberal, punitive form. Today this dynamic has become so deeply embedded in both the ordinary machinations of government and the subterranean assumptions of its citizens that even efforts to right things fall prey to its logic.

Prove your innocence. The innocence projects that I mentioned in chapter 5 have used new DNA evidence to exonerate hundreds of men previously convicted of rape and murder. These efforts have revealed much about everyday miscarriages of justice but less about how the rage to punish has shifted the burden of proof, eroded concepts of due process, and produced a burgeoning population of prisoners who are doing time for nonviolent offenses. Some fear that the projects' emphasis on innocence actually reinforces the pervasive fetishization of that concept and is fostering a perverse assumption among judges and juries, that it is the responsibility of the accused to prove his innocence, not the responsibility of the state to prove his guilt. Already, those accused of certain crimes (and presumably still protected by a presumption of innocence) have no right to refuse DNA tests in many states—and New York's then-governor Eliot Spitzer cited exoneration as a rationale for radically expanding the state's DNA database.[30] Thus abuses of state power are being recaptured by the logic of a system that generated them. Extending its reach to the molecular level, the punitive state becomes a stronger, more discerning, less escapable contraption. Privacy, along with the right to it, evaporates.

Scandalize the scandalizers. A recent headline, typical of its genre, announces a citizenry's shock and consternation: "Foes of Sex Trade Are Stung by the Fall of an Ally." As New York State's attorney general, Eliot Spitzer had broken up prostitution rings and called for new laws to punish prostitutes' clients. As governor, he had ramrodded an assortment of new sex crime laws through the state legislature—then got caught patronizing a high-priced call girl.[31]

Call it "abuse." When the outrages of Abu Ghraib hit the press, the first words out of President Bush's mouth, even before determinations of law, responsibility, and so on could be made, were punitive: "The guilty will be punished." Scenarios of child sex abuse—the specter that haunts so many conceptions of innocence and wrongdoing—reverberated eerily in discussions of the photos. Although the international press mostly described the depicted events as torture, U.S. government officials and the U.S. press largely preferred the word *abuse.* Recurring stories about Arab males' "fragile egos" infantilized the victims of these tortures and fed back to the empire its commonplace understandings of sexual trauma and the subversion of heterosexual manhood. Dhia al-Shweiri told the AP he preferred Saddam Hussein's torture to the fifteen minutes of humiliation he said he endured at the hands of Americans. Al-Shweiri explained that he had not been sodomized but that he was ordered to strip naked, bend over, and place his hands on the wall. "We are men. It's OK if they beat me," said al-Shweiri. "Beatings don't hurt us; it's just a blow. But no one would want their manhood to be shattered."[32]

Sacrifice some punishers. Military tribunals addressing troops' behavior at Abu Ghraib meted out punishments for lower-ranking offenders, not for higher-ranking officers, much less for the administration officials whose memos and findings had authorized departures from Geneva Convention protections against torture. The negative sociality of the punitive order was enacted, ratified, secured. The glee on the faces of the prison guards, who relished meting out humiliation and punishment, became consternation on the faces of the public, who took grim satisfaction in judging the wrongdoers. Predators became quarry, bullies became bullied, guards became prisoners, and the thirst for punishment was quenched—a bit. The prison guards cycled back into the beastly machinery they once guarded, with the result that society will be kept pure—or at least indifferent to its own impurities.

CHAPTER 7

Constructing Victimization

How Americans Learned to Love Trauma

It is the abused who become the abusers, whether politically
as well as psychically may depend on contingencies of social
and political history.

—Gillian Rose, *Mourning Becomes the Law:
Philosophy and Representation*

Some elements of the current scene are more deeply embedded in American culture than others. Americans have long imagined themselves to be a nation of innocents. Narratives of rescue are a recurring feature of U.S. social movements, and rites of protection fashioned the pioneer nation around red, black, and brown threats to white women and children long before there was a republic. But the modern institutions that recycle these cultural artifacts do not much resemble the institutions of the McCarthy period, much less those of the progressive, Victorian, or colonial eras. Even those patterns that seem most durable in current trends thus beg further explanation, unless history is imagined as the unfolding of a pageant, a unilinear history of self-identical forms and unchanging subjects.[1]

How, then, do such elements wax or wane, convey different political content, or morph into altogether new forms at different moments in history? Understanding how the present state of affairs came to be requires not only a historical accounting but a historicist one, an examination of the various social sources of anxiety and some untangling of the changing relationships among victimization, fear, and punitiveness. So, first, let me map some of the theoretical paradigms that have attempted to explain the metastasis of punishment in U.S. culture. Then let me trace the long public wail of the victim against shifting institutions of race, class, and sex—the better to plant theory in history, the better to shape the explanation to the contours of the thing explained.

SOME EXPLANATIONS FOR THE PUNITIVE TURN

Observers have put forward a number of explanations for "the punitive turn" in American life: the normalization of harsh measures as the policy of first resort, accompanied by the surge of a vengeance orientation in domestic and international affairs.[2] These accounts shed light on transitions still underway; they also miss something of what they purport to describe.

Social conservatives argue, implicitly or explicitly, that the punitive turn developed as a logical response to high crime rates associated with the turbulent 1960s and 1970s.[3] This framing correctly marks the historical moment when crime issues began to be politicized, but as a wider sociological explanation the conservative argument merely represents the story of the punitive turn told in its own terms.

The real story of crime and punishment in the United States is more complicated than the prevailing conservative version admits. Certain crime rates actually began climbing during the socially tranquil mid- to late 1950s, when "juvenile delinquency" scares first aired. Crime rates then rose dramatically during the 1960s through the early 1970s; they remained roughly flat, at an elevated level, from 1972 until 1992.[4] No doubt the perception, from the late 1960s on, that crime was out of control has fostered the growth of a get-tough, law-and-order approach among policy makers and especially among white middle- and working-class voters. And no doubt the scarifying experience of criminal victimization has served as a perpetual point of recruitment for the punitive crusade. (Old joke: "What's a conservative?" "A liberal who's been mugged.") But perception and experience bear closer scrutiny. Fear of violent crime in the 1970s was buttressed by substantial statistical data and common experiences of victimization, while the sensational sex panics that played an important role in the punitive turn in the 1980s were buoyed by imagined dangers and an exaggerated or misplaced sense of risk. And many of the most punitive laws actually were passed after 1992, a time of rapidly declining crime rates.

There were always viable alternatives to the law-and-order approach. In countries of the North Atlantic, including the United States, penal models stressing rehabilitation, reform, and welfare had gained ground steadily from the late nineteenth century on, and by the mid-twentieth century these were the prevailing approaches almost everywhere. In the wake of liberal legal reforms of the 1960s, the prison population was slowly shrinking, and alternatives to incarceration were being developed. Michel Foucault brilliantly traces the shift from punitive to welfare models of social control in *Discipline and Punish*—although nothing in Foucault's analysis could predict what soon followed in the United States: the resurgence of punishment as a spectacle; the return of a punitive orientation, specifically designed to subtract from life or enjoyment rather than to produce well-being. The real question, then, is how rehabilitation came to be discredited and how the punitive "lock 'em up" approach—which diverts funds from health, education, and social services, uproots social support networks, devastates poor minority communities, and imposes other enormous social costs—came to be acceptable.[5]

Ironically, the Left helped prepare the way for this turn to the Right. Leftist activists from the civil rights, black power, and antiwar movements had leveled heavy criticism against the criminal justice system, and rightly so. Patterns of police brutality were readily discernible triggers of urban unrest and race riots in the late 1960s, and minorities were overrepresented in the prison population (although not as much as today). Summing up New Left critiques, the American Friends Service Committee's 1971 report, *Struggle for Justice,* blasted the U.S. prison system not only for repressing youth, the poor, and minorities but also for paternalistically emphasizing individual rehabilitation. Rehabilitate the system, not the individual, the report urged—but the point got lost in the rancorous debates that followed. As David Garland carefully shows in *The Culture of Control*, the ensuing "nothing works" consensus among progressive scholars and experts discouraged prison reform and ultimately lent weight to the arguments of conservatives, whose approach to crime has always been a simple one: Punish the bad man. Put lawbreakers behind bars and keep them there.[6]

Social conservatives also claim that the dramatic growth of the carceral state, combined with intensive policing and "zero tolerance" policies, is responsible for the substantial downturn in crime rates since the early 1990s. Again, this is the punitive culture rationalizing its own existence. In fact, cause-and-effect relationships are notoriously difficult to pin down when it comes to policing, incarceration, and crime. Consider the long historical trajectory: Violent crime rates were high in the early nineteenth century—much higher than during the 1970s and 1980s. These rates declined until the 1950s, and explanations for this long-term reduction abound. Some historians say crime rates fell because Americans became more religious; others say the rates fell because new industrial modes of life encouraged social conformity. Some attribute the decline to the benefits of public education and new bureaucratic modes of socialization. Others see in the crime figures a general, long-term "civilizing process." As Michael Tonry and Joan Petersilia point out, virtually no one who studies these matters attributes this historic, much-researched decline to innovative policing strategies, sentencing provisions, or the institutionalization of a modern criminal justice system.[7] Similarly, few serious criminologists credit harsh penal policies with the substantial downturn in crime rates since the early 1990s. By reasonable estimates, locking up millions of people for long periods may have contributed to as much as 27 percent and as little as one-tenth of the overall reduction in crime.[8] But what factors account for the other 73 to 90 percent?

In *The Great American Crime Decline* Franklin Zimring convincingly argues that no single explanation for long-term trends will suffice. The sharp rise and steep fall of street crime in U.S. cities has to do with a complex interplay of cultural, social, economic, and demographic factors, some quite subtle. For instance, data comparing visible crimes with nonvisible crimes suggest that simple infrastructural improvements—better street lighting—have a considerable effect on crime rates. Among the more compelling combination of factors usually cited: There were once a lot of young men in prime crime-committing age brackets, and many were angry poor black youth. Crime rates eventually fell when the demographics shifted and the crack wars burned out just as the 1990s economic boom arrived. The boom caused unemployment to drop and brought more or less stable work to social sectors that previously had been excluded from the job market. But even this complex story is only a guess, a partial explanation. Crime rates actually went up in the late 1980s, when demographic models might have predicted a downturn. And comparisons with the United States' neighbor to the north are instructive. Canada never posted rates of violent crime comparable to U.S. levels; it never signed on to mass incarceration as a crime-control strategy; it experienced no crack epidemic from which to recover; nor was it party to the economic boom of the 1990s—yet Canada's crime levels also declined after 1992, at rates approaching the U.S. decline.[9] Why? No one is sure.

Policing Racial Hierarchies

An important strand of analysis picks up where the conservatives leave off, stressing the role of racism in the development of a burgeoning prison state. Loïc Wacquant thus divides U.S. history into four epochs of racial domination, each characterized by its own "peculiar institution": slavery (1619–1865); Jim Crow (South, 1865–1965); the ghetto (North, 1915–68); and the hyperghetto and prison state (1968–).[10] Wacquant's periodization captures many important facts. The extraordinarily high levels of black imprisonment speak for themselves, and harsh public talk about crime—like stories about welfare abuse, black family pathology, and so on—often serves as a front for the expression of racism. Discriminatory policing accounts for much of the racial disparity in prisons. Blacks make up only 13 percent of drug users but more than one-third of drug arrestees, more than half of those convicted on drug charges, and 58 percent of those ultimately sent to prison on drug charges. And when convicted, an African American can expect to serve almost as much time for a drug offense as a white person would serve for a violent offense.[11] Needless to say, had the mania for incarceration devastated white middle- or even working-class communities as it has black lower- and working-class communities, the steep increase in the prison population would have proved politically intolerable quite quickly.

But the prevailing punitiveness has affected not only African Americans, and it involves not only mass incarceration. The incarceration rate for brown-skinned people, who have suffered racial discrimination at the hands of white America but not slavery, is also relatively high (and climbing). The confinement and processing of illegal immigrants has become especially harsh.[12] And although white men are imprisoned at a substantially lower rate than either black or brown men, there are still more white men in prison, in both raw and per capita numbers, than at any time in U.S. history. In mid-2007 there were 773 white males in prison or jail for every 100,000 of their number in the population overall; this was roughly one-sixth of the rate of 4,618 per 100,000 for black males but more than three times the total average rate of male confinement that obtained from the 1920s through 1972.[13]

Even if one accepts the compelling premise that a primary effect of the carceral state is racial domination, something more—or perhaps something else—would seem to be at work in the logic of punitiveness.

This "something else" begins to become visible when one turns from crime panics in general, whose villains are implicitly raced as black, to sex panics in particular, whose villains are typically raced as white. This something else also appears in a succession of high-profile investigations or trials aired as infotainment. Former U.S. representative Gary Condit, the mass media's chief suspect in the 2001 Chandra Levy disappearance case; Martha Stewart, the business magnate accused of insider trading but convicted instead in 2004 of lying to investigators and obstruction of justice; Scott Peterson, the adulterous fertilizer salesman sentenced to death in 2005 for murdering his pregnant wife, Laci Peterson; and former U.S. representative Mark Foley, who resigned his House seat in 2006 after revelations that he had sent sexually suggestive e-mail to congressional pages, have little in common other than their whiteness.

Mass incarceration of nonwhite men is one aspect of punitive governance—an especially salient one, to be sure. But a broader perspective is necessary, as Jonathan Simon has shown: punitiveness emanates from multiple points in networks spanning numerous institutions.[14] A crime-control model has reshaped even white middle-class experiences of school, employment, family law, new technologies, and neighborhood. Its spread has been especially pronounced in those institutions that touch upon child socialization, sexuality, and the cultivation of personal discipline. Even if white, middle-class America were to repent its racist drug laws, its tacit support for racial profiling, and its acceptance of racially targeted law enforcement, much of the apparatus of punitive governance still would remain in place because much of it is designed to fortify, circumscribe, and discipline the white middle-class suburbs.

Paranoid Style, Institutional Exigencies

Some have seen in the punitive turn a new twist on a familiar need for demonized enemies. Deprived of the communist menace abroad by the winding down of the cold war, Americans sought new outsized enemies at home: the inveterate criminal, the violent sociopath. The need to make war on depraved enemies does seem deeply ingrained in U.S. political culture. Even progressives use this rhetoric. Franklin Delano Roosevelt famously called the Great Depression "the moral equivalent of war," the Johnson administration declared a "war on poverty," and so on. But this view, it seems, omits a number of important questions. What Richard Hofstadter once dubbed "the paranoid style" in U.S. politics might be always there, waiting backstage, to be trotted out in a new Halloween costume at a moment's notice, but historically this paranoia waxes and wanes according to political, social, or economic exigencies that require further elucidation.[15] And in any event the modern "war on crime" actually started neither after détente nor after glasnost but (as I will shortly describe) during some hot years of the cold war. If anything, the emergent criminal menace condensed and displaced, without replacing, other racial, sexual, and political enemies; it rearticulated them in new forms, wove them into a new garb, and patterned a new social formation after them.

Others discern a more or less continuous tendency toward institutionalization in U.S. history. It turns out that during the 1940s and 1950s, Americans were institutionalized at a slightly higher rate than they are today, but the institution was the psychiatric asylum. As that vast system of social control was dismantled, a new one was built up—in its place, the argument goes. It is clear enough that many "individuals who used to be tracked for mental health treatment are now getting a one-way ticket to jail," as Bernard Harcourt has aptly put it.[16] Today schizophrenics, manic-depressive psychotics, and those who suffer from major depression or other severe mental illnesses are four times more likely to be in prison than in a psychiatric hospital; removing these people from the penal system would probably result in at least a 16 percent reduction of the overall prison population. The placement of substance abusers in treatment programs rather than in prisons would remove a much larger percentage.[17] What is not so clear is how to compare the logic of treatment (which once applied to both mental hospitals and penitentiaries, after all) with the punitive logic of today's carceral state or how to ponder the very different populations subjected to these two cultures of control. Wards of the psychiatric institution were older, less poor, and much whiter than wards of the carceral state—and half were women (as opposed to roughly 7 percent of the prison population today).[18] In no small part, the psychiatric institutions of decades past were places where families confined women deemed troublesome or disorderly. If the prison has replaced the mental hospital, it has not simply replaced it.

Reserve Labor in the "Garrisonized" Economy

Some sociologists and political economists have described the growth of a self-sustaining "prison-industrial complex," sometimes linking it to strategies for containing and controlling a population of surplus laborers. The result is an elegant model of race/class control under contemporary capitalism. Let me unpack this model a bit.

A "labor surplus" exists wherever supply exceeds demand. Business either cannot or will not employ all available hands. Obviously, some labor surplus is useful for capital. Reserve labor can be called upon to break strikes; its very existence dissuades labor unrest and helps keep wages down. Business owners thus will always prefer to squeeze more labor out of already-employed workers than to hire additional laborers.[19] But too much unemployment poses a problem. Idle hands can become disorderly, dangerous. Chronic unemployment can lead to social unrest. How to manage this problem? Historically, U.S. capitalism has offloaded unemployment onto African American communities, which were closely circumscribed and heavily policed. And for much of the twentieth century, the military draft absorbed, diverted, and socialized millions of unemployed youth, especially black youth. In other words, much of what Marx called the "reserve army of labor" was actually billeted in the army.

The end of conscription in 1973 required a new institution to "warehouse the precarious and deproletarianized fractions of the black working class," to borrow a phrase from Loïc Wacquant.[20] Michael Sherry crunches the numbers: as active duty military personnel decreased from more than 3 million in 1970 to 1.41 million in 2002, the population of inmates sentenced to maximum terms of one year or more increased from 200,000 to 1.345 million.[21] It has been estimated that during the 1990s, America's zeal for incarceration shaved two percentage points off the unemployment figures. If the prison population is factored into unemployment statistics, U.S. unemployment rates actually equal or exceed the rates of the supposedly sluggish social-democratic economies of Europe.[22]

Meanwhile, during the same period factories were pulling up stakes and moving abroad in search of less expensive labor and lower production costs. As secure unionized jobs in the industrial sector declined, stable work associated with law enforcement—policing, guarding prisons, private security—expanded. During this extended period police fraternal orders and prison guard unions perpetually (and successfully) lobbied for harsher laws and tougher enforcement, which had the obvious effect of creating more jobs in the prison-industrial complex. As a result in the new punitive state more and more labor is employed in the work of containing and controlling surplus labor. Today total expenditures for the prison, policing, and justice system—the prison economy—begin to approach expenditures in the military economy.[23] Roughly 4 percent of the civilian labor force is employed by the penal system or works to put people in prison.[24] If one adds to these numbers those employed in private security positions, plus those whose work responsibilities include the monitoring and guarding of other laborers, the results are striking. In an increasingly "garrisonized" economy, 1 in 4 or 5 American laborers is employed in what Samuel Bowles and Arjun Jayadev call "guard labor." (This is more than double the rate the authors document for Sweden.)[25]

The rapid expansion of the carceral state, along with the spread of punitive measures across the social and economic systems, represents a sort of dystopian Keynesianism. This political economy is arguably even more dystopian than the military Keynesianism of the liberal welfare state, which kept the U.S. economy on a war footing for much of the twentieth century, for nothing in the new model actually diminishes the likelihood of war. In essence, penal Keynesianism solves two economic problems: it creates jobs while guarding the unemployed. This dual function gives the prison-industrial complex deep entrenchment in the present social formation. But as advocates of this view generally recognize, this dual function serves as explanation for the rapid increase in prison numbers only when other means of solving these economic problems are excluded from consideration. Americans *chose* to invest in prisons, not day care, schools, jobs, or housing—why?

How America Changed

All these analyses describe crucial pieces of the puzzle, but the explanation I propose here (which has been propounded in part by others) is of a different order: punitiveness itself has waxed in U.S. social life. All the other factors follow from this punitiveness, which in turn follows from fear. Put another way, in a more or less continuous stream of crime, sex, and terror panics, a complex set of cultural values related to forbearance, forgiveness, rehabilitation, and second chances has progressively ceded ground to an equally complicated set of values that revolve around vigilance, accusation, detection, the assertion of guilt, and spectacles of punishment.[26]

The punitive trend has advanced according to different logics with changing institutional supports at different moments in an accelerated history of the present. To recap from David Garland's summary: In the

1960s rising crime rates and urban turbulence fostered the perception that crime was everywhere. As fear became routinized, crime became politicized. The mass media played a role in coordinating this trend. By the 1970s television dramas, news reportage, and political entrepreneurs all were focusing on the plight of the victim; these approaches reinforced visceral emotional responses and gave everyone a sense of personal investment in crime control. So primed, the white middle classes turned away from enlightened, educated ideas about rehabilitation and humane punishment ("penal welfarism") to embrace harsh penalties and long prison sentences ("expressive punishment"). By the 1980s myriad social actors were participating in the development of new security arrangements: private security, defensive designs, crime-conscious routines, and the development of crime-deterrent technologies. Fear of crime became reflexive, ingrained, and habitual. Once implanted in everyday life, the crime-control worldview proved resistant to change and continued to grow even after crime rates declined in the 1990s. Fear of crime gradually has been institutionalized, and the open society, which is mobile and porous, has given way to the crime-control society, which is closed off, locked down, and strives to keep strangers at bay. Punishment, which had been gradually deemphasized in favor of rehabilitation, staged a spectacular and unanticipated comeback.[27]

The increase of punitiveness at the expense of forgiveness has been particularly acute among the white middle and working classes, while punitive measures have been applied disproportionately against the poor, racial minorities, and the sexually suspect. But these latter sectors are not exempt from the punitive trend, insofar as their members respond to the same body of cultural assumptions as their straight white compatriots and insofar as their interests buy into an increasingly carceral state. Fear of crime, which in itself can be quite logical, supplies the grappling hooks that give punitive governance an increasingly illogical hold on minds and actions. Sexual anxieties tighten fear's grip and extend it into the recesses of childhood, family life, and other everyday institutions. Other points of this hold involve material interests. The ranks of America's urban police forces, which were virtually all white in the 1950s and 1960s, are now integrated and in many cases are representative of urban demographics. Forty percent of federal prison employees are nonwhite.[28] And so the psychological, cultural, and material conditions for the punitive state are spread almost everywhere, but buying and selling, giving and taking are distributed unevenly, skewed in certain directions.

THE CULTURAL SHIFT

Americans clamor for punishment because they have learned to be always afraid and to be afraid of risks so remote as to defy reason. They feel comfortable venting vindictive rages that only a few years ago would have been deemed shameful because an elaborate institutional apparatus has taught them to think of themselves as victims or potential crime victims—and to strike out militantly as a first resort against presumed or potential victimizers. As a result the United States has become what it never was in the past (as an ample folklore attests), a nation of cop lovers.

This cultural shift happened quickly. Conceived in the tumult of the 1960s, the changeover was all but complete by the 1980s. The brief and improbable history of how this happened has many twists, turns, and subplots. Enter center stage the figure of the white crime victim.

White Backlash and the War on Crime

The modern "war on crime" was propounded by then-presidential candidate Richard Nixon in 1968.[29] As waged by the Nixon administration, war on crime would serve as an enduring conservative riposte to the war on poverty, as well as a distraction from the war in Indochina. From 1968 on, Nixonian language about crime and punishment strategically tapped and accelerated deeper political trends. It appealed, first, to the rural and small-town values of traditional midwestern conservatives, the mainstay of the Republican Party. It appealed no less obviously to conservative southern Democrats who from the beginning had depicted the civil rights movement as unlawful and disorderly. And it played increasingly well in the North, voicing in politically palatable terms the spread of a white middle- and working-class backlash against civil rights, black power, and the antiwar movement.

"War on crime" became the battle cry of a countercounterculture, shorthand for an ascendant conservatism centered on law, order, and traditional forms of authority. The rise of the religious Right—whose God is not the God of love and whose apocalyptic fantasies involve blood-drenched divine punishment for nonbelievers—was an important part of the changing political picture.[30] Northern secular manifestations of these trends were not much subtler; the rise of "hardhat conservatism" and the defection of blue-collar white ethnics from the Democratic rank-and-file consummated a long-term realignment of the political map.[31]

The veneration of policing and the idealization of tough law enforcement played no small parts in this realignment; they defined a steely "silent majority," caught between campus unrest on the one side and urban disorder on the other. And so a punitive attitude came to demarcate the "middleness" of a new white middle class; it was expressly associated with the patriotism, loyalty, and work ethic of law-abiding citizens.

Soon came the first salvos in the war on drugs, a war that would be waged without quarter, largely against black men, for decades to come. New York's 1973 Rockefeller laws, which applied severe minimum penalties against drug crimes and initiated the expansion of the carceral state, were to prove a sign of things to come.

Cultural Paranoia

The punitive turn that began in the late 1960s continued unimpeded through the mid-1970s, when the new coalition of social conservatives began to consolidate its political gains and modern sex, crime, and drug panics got underway in earnest. Philip Jenkins summarizes this mood swing in *Decade of Nightmares:* the liberal and libertarian optimism of the 1960s gave way to "a more pessimistic, more threatening interpretation of human behavior" and "more sinister visions of the enemies facing Americans and their nation."[32] Signs of this mood swing are everywhere in popular culture. Beginning with the 1974 hit *Death Wish,* the period's vengeance films played to public discontent with high crime rates, perpetually reenacting the same basic plot line: Charles Bronson takes the law into his own hands after the vicious murder of his wife and the rape of his daughter. *Death Wish* and other exploitation films of the period enlisted a familiar sexual spectacle—outrages against girls and women—in the service of right-wing populism; they aligned liberal politicians, civil libertarians, and high-minded elites with the predatory criminal forces that torment Everyman. And in this realignment of values, such films were careful to whiten the vicious criminal, allowing the audience to experience the visceral thrill of vengeance with an untroubled racial conscience.

By 1982 Rambo too had to take the law into his own hands—because the same liberal government authorities who would not let U.S. soldiers win the war in Vietnam also would not acknowledge the continued existence of prisoners of war there. A new spin on the rescue genre, *First Blood,* mass-marketed a profoundly reactionary denial of the U.S. defeat in Vietnam. It also tapped deeper cultural trends. America's long-

drawn howl of anguish about its MIAs—soldiers missing in action—
distilled important elements of the period's growing paranoia:
Government reports concluding that no prisoners of war were still being
held captive in Vietnam were brushed aside as conspiratorial lies, and
few politicians were willing to directly confront these outraged assertions, which were often leveled by groups of Vietnam War vets. But by
this time the malaise of the late 1970s was giving way to the full-throttle
Reaganite 1980s. Fear was finding new rationales, and punitiveness
was more openly expressed.

Mistrust of anonymous, lurking others was underscored by the 1982
Tylenol tampering scares, which also produced a strange effect, illustrative of an emergent psychopathology of spectacular victimization. Seven
people died of cyanide poisoning, all in the Chicago area. But nationwide there were hundreds of faked, staged, bogus, or "copycat" tamper-
ings, in which members of the public sought (and often received) sympathetic media attention by committing acts that were imitations of
crimes publicized in news stories. Meanwhile, the emerging AIDS epidemic was fostering new anxieties involving sex, and ever more bizarre
imaginings of predation proliferated. As I have discussed, the satanic
ritual abuse panics of the period supplied reliable tropes for the routinization of sexual terror in U.S. culture: the victim child, the diabolical
sexual predator, the supposed ordinariness of extraordinary abuse. Such
panics maintained the popularity of the punitive approach even after
the race reaction of the 1960s began to burn out. Sexual fears—some
reasonable, some delirious—would play a pivotal role in conjuring up
sinister enemies, feeding the frenzy for harsh retribution, forging strange
alliances, domesticating and co-opting elements of the Left, and planting the psychological conditions of the state of panic in the seedbed of
the family.

And the war on drugs was heating up. Fanned by malign neglect,
government cutbacks, and inept policing strategies, Reagan-era crack
wars fostered the perception that white middle-class Americans were living in a state of emergency, besieged by hardened incorrigible black
criminals. A string of drug panics featured white children lured off the
path to successful adulthood by nefarious drug dealers and all-powerful
narcotics. "Just Say No" still stands as the Reagan administration's enduring cultural epigram. The era's draconian drug laws represent its institutional legacy, and these rapidly accelerated the growth of the prison
system, which had already begun in the 1970s. Against this backdrop
the victims' rights movement came of age. Nothing has institutionalized

illiberal resentments, righteous anger, and the politics of fear more than this curious movement, which began as one thing and evolved into something quite different.

The Origins of Victims' Rights

Arguably the most successful social movement of the late twentieth century, the victims' rights movement has no single origin, emerging at the confluence of multiple sources. Conditions were uniquely propitious for the emergence of such a movement in the 1960s and 1970s. Crime rates were high, and resentment against criminals was also widespread. Such resentment blurred with white backlash against leftist social movements, but this is where the plot thickens. Paradoxically, leftist social movements—civil rights, the women's movement, gay liberation—provided the model for the political mobilization that also gave rise to victims' rights. The game plan was remarkably straightforward: (1) define an injury; (2) create an identity around this grievance; and (3) mobilize to seek legal redress, material compensation, and protection from the state. The victim of criminal violence, like the victims of Jim Crow or institutional sexism or homophobia, would step out of the shadows to claim rights. Over time redress and protection took increasingly punitive form.

And so the story is complicated—as is the movement's relationship to the state. This complex history has been examined by victims' advocates Marlene Young and John Stein, the journalist Bruce Shapiro, researchers at the progressive think tank Political Research Associates, and others. Consider the four main sources of the victims' rights movement: the welfare state of the 1960s, the women's movement, the self-help movement, and social service activists and organizations.[33]

Despite its future conservative trajectory, the institutional inception of the victims' rights movement was actually positioned in the welfare state of the 1960s, which attempted to address the socioeconomic causes of crime (poverty, institutional racism, alienation) while taking a holistic approach to crime's effects on communities. Originally, aid for the victims of violent crime was conceived as the flip side of attempts to rehabilitate convicts through counseling, education, and job training. As former Supreme Court justice Arthur J. Goldberg put it: "In a fundamental sense . . . [the] one who suffers the impact of criminal violence is also the victim of society's long inattention to poverty and social injustice." California's compensation fund for victims of violent crime, established in 1965, was a leading example of this approach. Similar programs quickly followed in New York, Hawaii, and other states.[34] So began the gradual construction of a new social identity—the crime victim—and its incorporation into the machineries of the state.[35]

Perhaps the most important nongovernmental source of inspiration for victims' rights was the feminist movement of the 1960s and 1970s. Convinced that police, the court system, and social services were unresponsive to women's needs, feminist activists founded rape crisis centers, domestic abuse hotlines, women's shelters, and other initiatives to assist raped and battered women. Much of the rhetoric of the victims' rights movement derives from early feminist work around rape and domestic violence—for example, the assertion that crime victims are victimized a "second time" by their experiences with the police and court system.[36] Rape shield laws set a precedent for later laws protecting accusers while diminishing the rights of the accused, most notably laws allowing children to testify by means of closed circuit television, or allowing parents to testify on children's behalf, in cases of alleged sex abuse. Key provisions in assorted "victims' bills of rights" (discussed later in this chapter) emerge from the antibattery movement. Such moves progressively aligned feminist grassroots efforts with crime control techniques.

The self-help movement of the 1970s also figured prominently in the development of victims' rights. Self-help groups have numerous historical antecedents: small-scale religious congregations, immigrants' mutual aid groups, fraternal orders, and, of course, the twelve-step recovery program of Alcoholics Anonymous. Modern self-help groups provide participants with resources, information, community, peer counseling, and emotional support, as well as an organizational structure capable of expressing political demands. These political demands tend to be of the single-issue sort. As Elayne Rapping has shown, the modern self-help phenomenon follows in the wake of countercultural mobilizations of the 1960s, with their emphasis on organization and immediacy—but without their vision of radical social change.[37] Support groups for the victims of traumatic crimes and their families were an increasingly visible part of the self-help movement during the 1970s, and self-help continues to provide the organizational model for the movement's far-flung base today.[38]

Finally, a new generation of socially conscious service providers and social workers played an important role in the development of the victims' rights movement, facilitating connections between government agencies, feminist groups, and various self-help organizations. Arguably, service providers were the "organic intellectuals" of the movement; they would serve as activists, referrers, intermediaries, and popularizers. Incubated in the New Left, the socially engaged service provider's outlook echoed older generations' traditions of progressive social uplift. As with earlier U.S. movements of social reformers, the new service providers began with laudable goals. They sought to help the victims of various sorts of injuries and to rescue women and children from domestic violence and dysfunctional family lives. They then followed a familiar trajectory for such movements. Emphasizing problems such as crime, prostitution, and the effects of alcohol and substance abuse, many became advocates of temperance and social purity. And like earlier social reformers, the engaged service provider's work over time would become associated with increasingly conservative policies of family monitoring, crime control, and punishment.

Victims' Rights in the War on Crime

These elements became intertwined—at first subtly, then dramatically—with the increasing popularity of punitive anticrime politics. A thumbnail sketch of institutional history provides insight into how this happened.

The first federal instrument for fomenting and funding nascent victims' organizations was the Office for Law Enforcement Assistance, which was organized in 1965, then reorganized in 1968 as the Law Enforcement Assistance Administration (LEAA). An independent agency of the Justice Department, the LEAA dispensed funds and block grants not only to local police departments but also to public defenders and community groups, including women's shelters, domestic abuse hotlines, and victims' services providers. This approach to community-based developments was characteristic of Great Society programs, which simultaneously stimulated, harnessed, subsidized, disciplined, and domesticated grassroots initiatives.[39] This arrangement in turn reinforced the political limitations inherent in liberalism that shaped and constrained New Left social movements from their inception: political demands on the state that take the form of grievances, and state responses that take the form of redress. Perhaps under other circumstances liberal dissident traditions eventually might have pushed the logic of the welfare state in a more consistently social-democratic or democratic-socialist direction. Some elements of the New Left aspired to just that. But by the time rising crime rates produced a politicization of crime issues, the times were already changing again, and the logic of grievance-redress politics was about to take a 180-degree turn. The transition from the original Office for Law Enforcement Assistance to the reorganized LEAA marks a crisis in the liberal welfare state—and, in this crisis, the inception of the punitive state.

In 1968 specters of chaos haunted U.S. cities, and white backlash was in full swing. That year Congress overwhelmingly passed the Omnibus Crime Control and Safe Streets Act. Originally developed by southern Democrats and western Republicans, the bill took aim at liberal Great Society approaches to social problems—which conservatives viewed as having unleashed rampant lawlessness. The bill gained momentum even among northern liberals after the assassination of Martin Luther King, Jr. triggered major urban riots and stoked white fears of crime and unrest, followed by the assassination of Robert F. Kennedy. Johnson overcame his initial reservations and signed the bill into law, attempting to claim its logic (or parts of it) as his own. This would not be the last time liberals capitulated to conservative legislation in the face of crime fears and specters of lawlessness. Jonathan Simon has described how this bill provided a basic blueprint for the subsequent development of the punitive state, positioning its partisans as advocates for the crime victim, who begins to assume a larger role in the imagination of government. Through the newly organized LEAA, the bill pumped federal money into local law enforcement projects—many of which would take the form of victims' rights efforts. As a result "nationalized" crime control would be driven by local initiatives, many of which came from conservative governors. A harbinger of things to come, the omnibus bill attempted to undermine federal court rulings on the admissibility of confessions in criminal cases, and it authorized wiretapping without court order under certain circumstances. Last, the legislation set federal guidelines for gun sales.[40] And so federal crime-control policy was tilted in a generally punitive direction. The still-inchoate victims' rights movement would soon follow suit.

By the mid-1970s the LEAA had become a pointed instrument of the war on crime. The LEAA attributed low conviction rates to a lack of cooperation by victims and witnesses, so it launched demonstration projects designed to get victims and witnesses involved in the war on crime. It also funded conferences for victims' organizations and encouraged the formation of victims' assistance programs nationwide, eventually launching the National Organization for Victims' Assistance (NOVA). Prominent organizations founded during this period of ferment include Families and Friends of Missing Persons (1974), Parents of Murdered

Children (1978), and Mothers Against Drunk Driving (1980).[41] The framing and rhetoric of such organizations resonated with the escalating logic of sex panics: they depicted a heterosexual hearth under siege, innocents snatched from their families by predatory strangers. And they called forth a new normative model of governance: paternal or maternal protection of innocent (although sometimes wayward) children.

The LEAA was disbanded after 1981 budget cuts, but deeply entrenched victims' rights organizations were already successfully securing state and local funding. And by this time these organizations had improvised an enduring political strategy: they were lobbying for the passage of a "Basic Bill of Rights for Crime Victims and Witnesses."[42] This strategy was to prove pivotal in the ongoing conservative reaction to the Warren Court's liberal interpretation of constitutional law. During the 1960s courts had vigorously defended the rights of the accused, drawing clear lines against illegal searches and seizures, harsh interrogation methods, coerced confessions, and abusive policing in general. The unsound notion that large numbers of criminals thereby were escaping justice on "legal technicalities" was a conservative favorite, and by the late 1970s the idea that "criminals" (not "the accused") had "too many rights" proved pivotal in America's turn to the Right. *But what about the rights of victims?* Thus the contrary notion of victims' rights came of age. Recent state-sponsored flyers and posters continue to echo this vague politics of resentment, which pits the rights of crime victims against the rights of the accused: "VICTIMS HAVE RIGHTS TOO!"

Sensing the opportunity to draw the victims' rights movement "securely within the compass of the right," as Bruce Shapiro puts it, the Reagan administration quickly reorganized the federal government's approach to the movement and set up the President's Task Force on Victims of Crime, which produced a report based largely on anecdotal horror stories of "double victimization" and official "unresponsiveness" to crime victims.[43] "Something insidious has happened in America," the report begins; "crime has made victims of us all." The opening statement by the chair pointedly calls for an emotional, not intellectual, approach to crime: "You cannot appreciate the victim problem if you approach it solely with your intellect. The intellect rebels. The important proposals contained here will not be clear unless you first encounter the human reality of victimization." In imperative language she insists: "You must know what it is to have your life wrenched and broken, to realize that you will never really be the same."[44] Such language explicitly adjures the citizen-reader to take on the identity of a trauma-tized victim.

Based in part on this report, Congress passed the Victims of Crime Act in 1984, establishing the Office for Victims of Crime (OVC) in the Justice Department. With a budget today of more than $1 billion, the OVC provides hundreds of millions of dollars each year to broadly distributed elements of the victims' rights movement. The movement's basic components include

- Thousands of grassroots organizations and programs that provide compensation or function as support groups for victims of violent crime and their families

- A variety of government agencies or state-subsidized organizations that provide medical, psychological, and social services for victims and their families

- Organizations, including a few highly visible, well-funded national centers and institutes, that "raise awareness" of victims' issues and "promote compliance" with victims' rights laws.[45] These organizations express political demands on behalf of victims and their families, whom they present as constituents. Such groups include Parents of Murdered Children, MADD, and the Center for Missing and Exploited Children, established at the height of Reagan-era sex panics in 1984.

Bruce Shapiro surveys the results of this reorganization of the government's approach to the movement. In what would prove a stroke of genius, the Reagan administration established funding for the OVC not out of general revenues but out of proceeds from fines and property seizures levied against those convicted of federal crimes. This funding stream for crime victims permanently reverses the holistic logic of Johnson administration programs and gives victims' service providers, whatever their political orientation, an obvious stake in punitive laws.[46] And because it appropriates money for crime victims' services from convicted criminals, this funding strategy also reinforces the privatized model of justice promoted by conservative victims' rights advocates. Under this model redress is not a contract to which society is party and has nothing to do with social redress for victims of racism or poverty; it is a personal, immediate, and moralized relationship between victim and criminal.

This privatized notion of justice is enshrined in victims' rights amendments in various states, which typically include mandates for financial restitution—as though punishment were "payment" and justice a cash transaction. The periodic assertion that vengeance is a basic right of victims reiterates the idea that punishment is a settling of accounts between individuals. And this view is embodied in the movement's frequent assertion that the criminal justice system has "lost an essential balance" that supposedly once existed in the practices of early colonial America, when plaintiffs brought private charges against those they accused of having wronged them. As Shapiro notes, proponents conveniently forget that the system of private criminal prosecution favored the rich—who could afford lawyers—against the poor and encouraged social actors to make criminal accusations against their business or political adversaries.[47]

INSTITUTIONALIZING VICTIMHOOD

To date, all fifty states and the District of Columbia have passed some version of a victims' bill of rights, thirty-three as amendments to their state constitution.[48] These newly minted rights tilt law enforcement practices away from a constitutional emphasis on rights of the accused while embedding a punitive preemptive orientation ever more deeply in institutional practices everywhere.

For example, one provision in a victims' rights bill asserts the victim's right to be protected from the accused. Much of the logic for this measure derives from feminist antibattery efforts that sought to protect from stalking partners or violent husbands battered women who had pressed charges. The concern is a valid one, and this approach may sound reasonable—but codified as legal norm this "right" reverses the traditional presumption of innocence. It assumes, in advance of any trial, that there is a victim and that the accused is the perpetrator, someone who must be held without bail to prevent his doing further harm to the victim. Civil libertarians point out that these assumptions, applied broadly, favor pretrial detention and thus give prosecutors a powerful weapon to wield against the accused. Isolated from friends, family, and social support, incarcerated defendants are more likely to seek a plea bargain or to enter a guilty plea than are those who remain at home awaiting trial.

Other provisions in victims' rights bills assert the right of victims to confer with prosecutors in cases to which they are a party and to be heard at any public hearings regarding sentencing, parole, or release. Advocates of this approach stress the supposed therapeutic benefits of involvement for the victims. In actuality it remains unclear whether such participation accelerates healing or reinforces a sense of victimization. Much remains unclear about the nature of trauma, as well. Trauma is usually associated with violence, but research suggests that some victims of nonviolent crimes such as burglary are also traumatized. Whether the triggering event was violent or nonviolent, most crime victims recover from trauma in a few months, although there is a great deal of individual variation in recovery time.[49] It also remains unclear whether the resulting victim impact statements inflame judges and juries, prodding them to impose harsher sentences. Certainly, the prevailing rhetoric of the victims' rights movement suggests that no punishment is ever sufficiently severe. What is clear is that these provisions shift the work of the justice system, in perilous ways, toward theater, pop psychology, and punitiveness as norm.[50]

Emotional presentencing testimony by victims and their families is now as much a part of regular criminal trials as it is a part of congressional hearings, but the mandatory admission of such testimony strains against one of the most ancient principles of Western law: the idea that law ought to be dispassionate, free of emotion. As Paul H. Robinson has put it, victim influence on sentencing is "inconsistent with our reasons for being so careful to have impartial judges, jurors, and prosecutors. Our notions of fairness and justice demand that such decisions be made by *impartial* decision-makers who will look only to the facts of the case." Justice, moreover, ought not be influenced by whether a crime victim has family members who make impact statements, nor should it be affected by whether the victims and their families are reputable or disreputable, forgiving or vengeful.[51] Presentencing testimony is a recipe for unequal justice.

Wendy Kaminer judiciously sums up the case against victims' rights—the idea that victims ought to occupy the center of attention in court proceedings, the notion that adjudication is a face-off between victim and criminal regarding punishment and restitution:

> The prosecutor and defense are not engaged in a "duel about punishment"; they're engaged in a duel about guilt. Should we determine the restitution owed by the defendant to the victim before we have determined her guilt? What if the victim is lying or mistaken about the identity of the defendant? (Eyewitness identifications, for example, are notoriously unreliable.) What if police falsify evidence against the defendant; what if the prosecutor has concealed evidence of the defendant's innocence?
>
> Defendants occupy the center of attention in criminal trials because they're the ones being prosecuted. The rights conferred upon criminal suspects are

limitations on the power of the state to kill or imprison its citizens. The Bill of Rights reflects the founders' belief that government could not be trusted to exercise its police powers fairly. It reflects the understanding that power is easily abused and that individuals cannot protect themselves against the state without rights that prosecutors are required to respect. Crime victims have a strong moral claim to be treated with respect and compassion, of course; but they should not be imbued with constitutional rights equivalent to the rights of defendants (their liberty and their lives are not at stake), and they should not expect their need to be "healed" or "made whole" by the trial to take precedence over the defendant's right to dispute allegations of guilt.

Kaminer concludes: "It's hard to argue with the desire to reform trials in order to help victims heal—unless you consider the consequences. Because the victims' rights amendment decreases the rights of defendants, it's not simply a grant of rights to crime victims; it's a grant of power to the state. Victims need and deserve services, but with [more than] two million people already behind bars, the state needs no more power to imprison us."[52]

Naturalizing Vindictiveness

Today the victims' rights movement is everywhere. It has an institutionalized and growing presence in law enforcement. It has changed assumptions and practices in the judiciary system. Its rhetoric inflects news reportage and primetime television entertainment. The constitutionally suspect notion that victims have rights as victims has become all but unimpeachable. A victims' rights amendment to the U.S. Constitution has been before Congress since 1996; if passed, it seems likely that it would quickly be ratified by the requisite thirty-eight states and become law.

The results of the deep ideological and institutional entrenchment of victims' rights thus bear closer inspection:

- As a result of its history of state sponsorship and government subsidy of victims' rights measures, the movement has a peculiar relationship to the state. The victims' rights movement lobbies the state that founded and funds it to be more punitive—which, from the traditional civil libertarian view, is presumably what the state, or certain elements of it, wanted all along. Countervailing political organizations devoted to rights of the accused, such as the American Civil Liberties Union, receive no federal subsidy. Thus the victims' rights movement, and its varied components, can only be described as a state-sponsored political movement. This peculiar status builds a profound political imbalance into the workings of the state.

- The skewed relationship of the victims' rights movement to race and class has made it a natural venue for the expression of white resentments against racial minorities. As critics have noted, the typical victims' rights advocate is a middle-class white woman, and the movement's typical poster child is a white child. In fact, surveys by the Bureau of Justice Statistics show that violent crime disproportionately victimizes young, lower-income black and brown men. Forty-nine percent of the murder victims in the United States are African Americans—and 85 percent of these are male.[53] But these are not the "right" victims.

- The movement narrowly defines *victim*. In Europe and other parts of the world, victims' rights movements have typically included, even emphasized, the victims of abuses of state power. As critics have noted, certain forms of criminal victimization are almost never included under the rubric of victims' rights in the United States. These nonvictims include the victims of white-collar crimes, police brutality, prosecutorial vindictiveness, wrongful conviction, and other forms of business or state lawlessness. The U.S. victims' rights approach thus reifies one type of crime (perhaps not the most socially destructive type) to the exclusion of other types. And many in the U.S. victims' rights movement militantly oppose any wider or more holistic approach. Victims of false accusation, prosecutorial overreach, and wrongful imprisonment are not the "right" kinds of victims.

If vindictiveness seems natural, even honorable, today, it is thanks in no small part to the careful placement of white, infantilized crime victims at center stage in the national political drama. In this morality play there can be no mise en scène—no stage setting, no background story, no life history leading up to the event—for the criminal. His role becomes synonymous with crime, which becomes synonymous with evil, which becomes an essential irremediable condition. There can also be no shared interests between victim and victimizer; the former has no interest in the latter's rehabilitation, nor in the amelioration of the social inequalities that structure many crimes. Such a script can serve only reactionary purposes.

Victimization Unlimited

During the 1980s and into the 1990s victimization emerged as a durable new source of identity. As a quasi-religious movement, the new victimology extended an evangelical invitation to every corner of society. On television the relatives of crime victims evangelized the public; their anticrime activism would redeem a terrible loss, and the story of their recruitment to the social movement would also serve as an inspirational example for others to follow. In bookstores the altar call went out through tracts on recovery, self-improvement, addiction, and true crime stories. Nowhere was the call more sweeping than on matters related to sexual victimization. Self-help recovery books invited readers to engage in serious introspection, searching for experiences of childhood sexual victimization. Of course, if every uninvited pinching, fondling, groping, or bit of adolescent horseplay-turned-amour is construed as abuse, the ranks of the abused will be quite numerous. And theories of repressed memories meant that everyone was a potential victim. The results were not only a long season of terrifying madness—the day-care witch hunts—but, in its wake, the consolidation of what the sociologist Joel Best has called "the victim industry."[54]

Spanning law, medicine, education, and media, this industry produces victims in part by defining victimization broadly, in part by inculcating in the public a perpetual sense of insuperable grievance. Best lays out the basic discursive machinery of this industry as a set of indisputable (if not entirely consistent) propositions: Victimization is widespread and consequential. Although straightforward and unambiguous, this victimization often goes unrecognized. Individuals thus must be taught to recognize their own and others' victimization—and claims of victimization must be respected. Last, the term *victim* has "undesirable connotations" and is best replaced with such terms as *survivor, adult child,* or *recovering*.[55] And so the thing itself—victimization, victimhood—is seldom expressly named, although everything in the system will revolve around it. Assorted "therapeutic" practices linked to this closed and self-validating apparatus crystallize and perpetuate the sense of injury. Whereas victims of abuse or violence once were expected to cope, heal, and (in the vernacular) "get over it," the practices of victims' support groups and new therapies associated with the incest survivors' movement urged victims to perpetually retell their experiences, to relive their ordeals, to make trauma an essential part of their identity, and to make these traumatized identities into political subjects. Americans stopped "getting over it"—age-old wisdom for how to deal with unfortunate events—and learned to love trauma.

Such victimization has its privileges. In one's role as victim, one might enjoy the empathy and indulgences of otherwise unreceptive authorities—authorities who have become characteristically more judgmental and less understanding precisely because of the development of new norms associated with ubiquitous victimology. Victimhood too comes as a relief, a disclaimer of personal responsibility at a time when the state is deregulating, privatizing, and progressively shifting the burdens of health, welfare, and economic security onto individuals.[56] And there are other incentives. The victim is the undisputed hero of his or her story. Victims' suffering bestows a sort of awe, an aura, a halo. This narrative, this nimbus, can be leveraged against others.

In her speech before the 1997 Victims' Rights conference, then–U.S. attorney general Janet Reno captured something of this movement's cultural and political capital, the identity work it performs, its place in the prevailing zeitgeist, and especially its sanctification of victimization as American identity. "I draw the most strength from the victims, for they represent America to me: people who will not be put down, people who will not be defeated, people who will rise again and stand again for what is right. . . . You are my heroes and heroines. You are but [a] little lower than the angels."[57]

The liberal hero of yore—the risk-taking individual who takes responsibility for his or her own fate and triumphs over adversity—gave way to the aggrieved victim who perpetually recounts unhappy experiences and calls for the punishment of others. This redefinition of core values did not go unnoticed or uncontested, and by the early 1990s criticism came from both Left and Right. In *I'm Dysfunctional, You're Dysfunctional,* Wendy Kaminer traces the spread of an increasingly irrational therapeutic culture of victimization. Robert Hughes broadly criticizes the victims' rights movement in *The Culture of Complaint,* while Alan Dershowitz takes narrower aim in *The Abuse Excuse.* The title of a caustic, curmudgeonly book by Charles J. Sykes laments the decay of the American character—and now seems almost a omen: *A Nation of Victims.*[58]

The emergent culture of victimization was not without paradoxes, contradictions, and flash points. It embraces a privatized view of justice, so far as the accused is concerned, while dispensing empathy, forbearance, and state largess so far as the victims of crime are concerned.

America's traditional disdain for complainers and malingerers did not disappear; it was folded into new distinctions. The authentic victim will be noble and entirely innocent, and his or her anonymity will prove a key point. Under most rules the "true" or "worthy" victim will refuse the label of victim, and this refusal will allow her or him to stand above those legions who wrongly clamor for recognition, sympathy, or compensation as victims. Such distinction echoes a durable opposition in U.S. history: the "deserving poor" are distinct from the undeserving poor by dint of their honesty, unwillingness to see themselves as oppressed, refusal to accept handouts. Alyson Cole has shown how the political Right has availed itself of these tropes, some new, others recycled, to both criticize "victimism" (the claims of oppressed people to social redress) while taking on a victimist outlook (e.g., white males as the victims of affirmative action).[59]

This redefinition of core values also has not gone unnoticed abroad. "There's power in the victim role," observed a middle-aged Mexican shopkeeper whom I interviewed about her perceptions of U.S. culture. Although she has never been to the United States, she is an avid reader with an alert mind and progressive anticlerical sensibilities. "You are becoming more like us," she continued—and this was not meant as a compliment. Now the shopkeeper drew a broad connection between crime panics, sex panics, and the post–9/11 culture of fear: "You used to be a nation of businessmen; you buried the dead and faced forward to the future. Now you are a nation of commemorators, memorial builders. You cannot let go of your hurts. You cannot stop inspecting your neighbors for signs of transgression. You are becoming a nation of victims."

THE LEFT MAKES A RIGHT TURN?

The Left was scarcely an innocent bystander in the development of new modes of identity based on victimization and trauma. But for the Left culpability is no simple matter. It involves no simple error, no single wrong turn, and quite a few reversals. New Left rhetoric was especially susceptible to capture by the Right in three disparate areas.

Talk about social oppression lends itself to victimization narratives, perhaps more readily than talk about economic exploitation, and all the movements associated with the New Left emphasized the former over the latter. Betty Friedan's classic, *The Feminine Mystique,* published before the emergence of second-wave feminism, provides a template for the rhetoric to come. The notion that women are diminished by the feminine mystique is a sound one, but as Friedan charted the frustration and internalized aggression caused by cultural concepts of femininity, she discerned victims almost everywhere. Men too are "victims of the feminine mystique," she declared. "The child becomes the real victim."[60] Similar language would reverberate in subsequent social movements.

In addition, the liberal political tradition of the United States, with its emphasis on formal equality, rule of law, and legal redress, presupposes that oppression is an unjust or even criminal undertaking. This assumption has shaped leftist social movements, sometimes in subtle ways. For example, Jonathan Simon has suggested that the success of the early civil rights movement turned in part on a certain kind of crime victim narrative. After the assassination of three civil rights workers in Philadelphia, Mississippi, during the voter registration drive in the Freedom Summer of 1964, the federal government began to take a law enforcement approach to the most egregious denials of civil rights, and northern liberals came to see Jim Crow as a system that criminally victimized black people. The concept of justice was enduringly written into subsequent struggles.[61] It is difficult to imagine an alternative strategy in the campaign for human and civil rights, but it is also useful to mark the limits of this orientation. Structural racism in northern cities—where formal equality prevailed—proved more difficult to expose with the crime victim narrative. Indeed, a law enforcement approach to urban riots and disorders marked a sharp turn to the Right among northern whites who had supported civil rights in the South.

Finally, populist rhetoric is a mainstay of leftist politics in U.S. history, and some of the New Left's rhetoric echoed populist themes: its increasing appeal to victimization narratives, the porous nature of its "participatory democracy," the vagueness of its "the people," the generality of its "power elites." Historical precedents might have suggested the exercise of caution. The Populist Party had grown out of agrarian unrest in the 1870s and 1880s to become a left-wing farmer-labor alliance. The movement never recovered from the disastrous consequences of its 1896 national fusion ticket with the Democratic Party under presidential candidate William Jennings Bryan; the fusion ticket undermined alliances among white sharecroppers, small farmers, and black Republicans in the South and strengthened the hand of conservative Democrats there. After the electoral debacle, the populist language of class resentment was quickly redeployed into profoundly reactionary racial politics. Something similar happened in the wake of the 1968 election. Populist motifs and rage against the Establishment were quickly claimed by the Right. By the 1972 Democratic primaries, George Wallace was producing large blue-collar turnouts in northern states by venting vague anger at inept bureaucrats, out-of-touch intellectuals, and culturally different elites.[62]

Blame Game

Historically, leftist social movements have held the politics of complaint in dynamic productive tension with the politics of liberation. They protest the palpable realities of oppression while keeping the promise of freedom in clear view. This is not always a stable mix. In periods when the Left is strong, the liberationist element comes to the fore—perhaps never so dramatically as in the 1960s. When the Left is in decline, when movements stall or lie in ruins, an emphasis on grievance, injury, and resentment comes to the fore. The Left begins to sound dolorous, envious, plaintive, and whiny (as our enemies are quick to point out)—or, worse, the Left takes on a dark, suspicious, accusatory worldview that is older than modern socialism or even liberalism. Call this bitter distillation of resentment and envy victimology in shorthand. It is a politics about which Marx had nothing good to say.

After the decline of 1960s radicalism, a shrinking view of political options implied an ever-darker worldview. Victims of oppression, abuse, or violence came to be seen as heroic—not because they persevere in the face of adversity, nor because they forge alliances with other oppressed groups, nor even because they resist the system that gave rise to injury but rather because of their very condition of having been injured. And in the unheady cultural mix of despair and fear that has prevailed since the end of the 1970s, talk about victimization on the Left joined powerfully with nascent trends on the Right. Positioned at the intersection of street crime and sexual violence, the victims' rights movement was a natural vehicle for these blended transformations. Given the retrograde race/class politics of victims' rights, how rapidly this movement bent diverse strands of liberal, progressive, and leftist activism into a profoundly conservative shape in the modern state becomes all the more striking.

Feminism and the State

Feminists, in particular, displayed a "surprising amnesia" about the history of women's reform movements, as Marie Gottschalk puts it in her book on the rise of the American carceral state. (A similar view has been developed by Kristin Bumiller in her survey of the "feminist alliance with the state.")[63] U.S. history, Gottschalk notes, is "littered with punitive efforts to address violence against women and children that ended up idealizing the nuclear family and motherhood and emboldening political conservatives."[64]

The dangers of viewing rape and domestic violence through a law-and-order lens should have been obvious, and there were other options for promoting women's rights and well-being. In other developed democracies relationships among victims' rights, women's rights, and judiciary procedures took less toxic forms, and women's movements internationally have tended to maintain a critical distance from the power of the state; generally, they have not made harsh criminal penalties a central demand. But conditions in the United States undermined the autonomy and radicalism of rape crisis centers, women's shelters, and other feminist responses to violence against women. The LEAA's decentralized funding stream for victims' rights groups was especially effective at co-opting elements of the women's movement. By dispensing block grants, money for demonstration projects, and other forms of assistance, the LEAA attached strings that drew some independent, grassroots efforts directly into the war on crime. For example, shelters for the battered were required to cooperate with the police and to include representatives of law enforcement on their boards of directors. Rape crisis centers received support on the condition that they work with prosecutors and function increasingly like apolitical service providers.[65]

Ironies abound in this history of co-optation. The early domestic violence shelters and rape crisis centers aimed to bolster women's liberation against the power of the state and the police. Still, a distinctly American variant of communal violence and vigilantism inflected antirape efforts in some cities, even among radicals who avoided complicity with the criminal justice system. Some rape crisis centers published the names and photographs of alleged sexual assailants; other radicals threatened to submit rapists to various forms of public humiliation. Such tactics would later be formalized with public sex offender registries. Race questions too were tortured and contradictory. In part because the early second-wave feminist movement was largely white, its members "tended to play down or ignore how the charge of rape had been used historically to reinforce white supremacy and the color line," as Gottschalk puts it.[66] Liberal white middle-class women were receptive early on to the crime-control approach—in part because they could ignore the different experiences black and brown women had with the police. But later, when rape crisis centers were eventually established in black and Latino neighborhoods, these tended to have even stronger ties to law enforcement than had the earlier white centers. And then there is the all-important question of how to frame the story of violence against women. The growing emphasis on personal horror stories by the antirape and antibattery movements no doubt resonated with feminism's early insight that "the personal is political," and this emphasis no doubt had the effect of prodding legislators to act, but it also individualized the experience of violence and was in conflict with feminism's broader approach to systematic inequalities.[67]

In the end feminism contributed to the development of a specific sort of victims' rights movement in the United States. Mainstream feminists made common cause with law-and-order conservatives, and some in the women's movement assisted the promulgation of unmistakably punitive laws.[68] In many midwestern cities the rightist Women's Crusade Against Crime outflanked the National Organization for Women; the key goal of the former was "to support, assist, and augment the criminal justice system in doing its job." In Washington State women's groups spun a rape reform law as a crime-control bill; the measure passed in 1975 "by riding on the coattails of a new death penalty statute."[69] Nationwide, new laws made it easier to convict men accused of rape or wife battery. Rape shield laws—which were criticized by civil libertarians from the start, and whose breadth and application have been criticized by some feminists—conflicted with the rights of the accused and set judicial practices on a slippery slope. Antiporn laws, antiprostitution laws, laws making it easier to convict those accused of child abuse, laws raising the age of consent, and other local initiatives drew feminists into alliance with archconservatives. All this contributed to a general atmosphere of punitiveness.

When Congress passed the Violence Against Women Act (VAWA) as part of the 1994 Violent Crime Control and Law Enforcement Act, the active involvement of law-and-order feminists in the punitive state seemed unexceptional, natural. Such a law-and-order orientation was not without other consequences. As Gottschalk notes, mainstream feminist groups were comparatively quiet in the debates two years later on welfare reform, despite the reform measure's profoundly antifeminist title, "The Personal Responsibility and Work Opportunity Act."[70] Even nominal progressives might have felt some discomfort when local police departments began sponsoring "Take Back the Night" rallies. By the time the Bush administration invoked women's suffering under the Taliban and, to a lesser extent, under Saddam Hussein's Baathist regime to justify the invasions of Afghanistan and Iraq, the legacies of state-sponsored feminism were glaringly apparent.

Therein lies not a story of historical inevitabilities but a history of missed opportunities. Great Society liberals might have found in crime and social disorder the conditions for a careful defense of the welfare state and a more consistent articulation of social-democratic principles. Some attempted this move—but, mired in the Vietnam War and caught in the unmanageable racial and cultural conflicts of the 1960s, liberals vacillated. Their arguments faltered, their political coalition unraveled. As political tides turned, a punitive and increasingly conservative logic overtook the welfare-state orientation in the war on crime.[71] American feminists might have remained aloof from and critical of the growing crime-control apparatus of the state, like other women's movements abroad. U.S. feminists might have forged alliances with prisoners' rights groups, and they might have taken a skeptical view of punishment. Some did and still do—but in the absence of viable radical, socialist, or social-democratic alliances, a liberal emphasis on formal equality corralled feminist demands into the grievance-redress model and tended to predict a criminal justice approach to violence against women. The mainstream of an increasingly conservative women's movement embraced a punitive approach to rape, abuse, and battery, forging alliances that would reshape U.S. society for decades to come. In hindsight this all has come to seem inevitable.

Is Injury Ennobling?

The idea that injury empowers or gives insight to the injured has proved difficult to resist, even in scholarly works that purport to critique the politics of victimology. Thus Judith Butler wishes to preserve the central role of trauma in the leftist political imagination, even while disavowing its uses by the post–9/11 Right. She writes: "To be injured means that one has the chance to reflect upon injury, to find out the mechanisms of its distribution, to find out who else suffers from permeable borders, unexpected violence, dispossession, and fear, and in what ways."[72] Perhaps—or, rather, one wishes it were so. But a more realistic assessment of both pre– and post–9/11 invocations of trauma might better suggest that the Left reconsider its fixation on injury, its attachment to political strategies based on victimization.

No less resistant to criticism is the idea that empathy with the victim is, or ought to be, the basis for ethical political action. Gillian Rose contests this notion in her final book, a set of challenging reflections on the political uses of injury and grief. In a telling passage, she examines the forms of identification and feeling prodded by the Steven Spielberg movie *Schindler's List,* illustrating how the innocence of the perfect victim is made possible by what she calls "the sentimentality of the ultimate predator."

> In a nature film, we could be made to identify with the life cycle of the fly as prey of the spider, and we could be made to identify with the life cycle of the spider as prey of the rodent. We can be made to identify with the Peking Opera singer who is destroyed by the Cultural Revolution, and we can equally be made to identify with the rickshaw man, for whom the Cultural Revolution was "the beginning of Paradise." It is only the ultimate predator whose sympathies can be so promiscuously enlisted. Only the ultimate predator who can be made to identify exclusively and yet consecutively with one link or another in the life cycle, because she can destroy the whole cycle, and, of course, herself. Since she is the ultimate predator, she can be sentimental about the victimhood of other predators while overlooking that victim's own violent predation; and she may embellish her arbitrary selectivity of compassion in rhapsodies and melodramas.

Rose then deadpans: "It is my own violence that I discover in this film."[73] Whether in Holocaust piety, 9/11 commemorations, or press releases from the victims' rights movement, the representation of violence can foster a violence of representation that parades about as an innocent child while concealing its own violence.

Injury ennobles no one; it makes no one any smarter; it gives no one insight beyond the simple experience of pain. At best, it leads to a blinkered view, in which the world revolves around one's own pain; at worst, to the development of a perverse politics of identity, in which everyone is defined by exquisite experiences of injury and acts politically to extort sympathy. Such identities derive in part from the rhetorical forms of leftist social movements, but they can only be the psycho-logical and organizational building blocks of the punitive state. They assure a constant production of private trauma, a perpetual state of public accusation and grievance, a never-ending agitation for repressive mea-sures. Their main function is to push forward the wheel of punitive governance.

CHAPTER 8

The Victimology Trap

Capitalism, Liberalism, and Grievance

I know you've been told that all this is for your own safety
and protection, but think about it for a minute. Anyway,
when did you get so scared? You didn't used to be easily
frightened.

—Margaret Atwood, "Letter to America"

So far, I have drawn analyses that are largely concerned with form and
function: how institutions of race and sex interact and mutate under
changing conditions; how durable structures (organizational strategies,
legal rationales) perpetuate themselves and replicate in various domains;
and how fears about sex and crime expand, multiply, and progressively
colonize wider social spaces. Two questions of a different slant and scale
have arisen in various ways: What is the connection between the punitive turn, with its expressly authoritarian politics, and the liberal political tradition, with its emphasis on individual rights? And how is the
punitive state related to capitalism, especially the privatized, deregulated variant that has prevailed since the end of the 1970s and is known
as neoliberalism?

CAUSE AND EFFECT

I am scarcely the first to suggest that the dominance of a vengeance
orientation today is linked not only to various forms of conservatism
but also to a genealogy of liberalism. Wendy Brown develops stark claims
in her influential book *States of Injury,* a theoretical broadside against
the politics of victimology she sees as inherent in modern liberalism,

especially some of its feminist variations. Many of my own arguments have echoed Brown's analysis of the paradox of liberal rights. Liberal rights construct freedom as "freedom from encroachment," and this definition entails other political concepts: atomized individuals, "abstract equality," and an "ethos of defensiveness." In the nineteenth century, liberal conceptions of freedom implied "property and personhood" for some and poverty and deracination for others; Brown examines how twentieth-century variations of liberalism, with their emphasis on victimized identities, foster new forms of power and control. Attempts to "outlaw" injury, she reasons, build a certain kind of state and foster certain kinds of identities: they legitimize law and the state as "protectors against injury" while casting "injured individuals as needing such protection by such protectors." Freedom, defined as protection, comes to mean subjection.[1]

Following Brown, Barbara Nelson, and a long tradition of radical criticism, I have tried to show how liberalism is limited from the outset by a tendency to justify government action narrowly as intervention on behalf of the weakest and most vulnerable; it aims to correct worst abuses rather than address the logic of the system as a whole.[2] On U.S. soil this approach fosters the view that individual pathologies are social problems and sometimes promotes narratives of rescue. The affinity of liberal reformers for victimization narratives should be clear, and I have periodically pointed out how the limitations of liberalism set the stage for moral panic. Still, I would caution against an overly schematic view, a sweeping verdict on the place of victimology within liberal political traditions. Even a cursory glance at history shows that the ethos of liberalism takes other forms as well. Nineteenth-century varieties typically did not commemorate victims and laud risk aversion; they celebrated individualism and embraced risk. An important twentieth-century strand advocated the liberalization of statutes against acts that harm no one or are so commonplace that their prohibition invites contempt for the law.[3] And if liberalism begins with the idea that there might be too much law, it might be better to say that victimist statutes, with their mania for exacting detection and excessive punishment, represent a disintegration or involution of liberal norms, not their extension. I have thus tried to show how liberal political traditions, for all their shortcomings, now take abnormal, unhealthy forms.[4]

Others have tried to show that punitive, authoritarian, or undemocratic trends are rooted in changing economic conditions. Recent books and articles have depicted one or more factors as the key motivating force: colluding business interests, the exigencies of unmodified capitalism, or the implications of empire.[5] These arguments express an elemental truth about the relationship of capitalism and coercion—a relationship that even Thomas Friedman, who is no critic of unfettered markets, understood when he quipped: "The hidden hand of the market will never work without the hidden fist."[6] But if these analyses tend to take a narrow view of political economy and how it relates to governance, they also tend to slight the interplay of race, sex, and class competition in U.S. capitalism.

David Harvey's *Brief History of Neoliberalism* seems emblematic of these tendencies. Harvey sets out to show how a large section of the working class acquiesced to laissez-faire economic policies in the 1970s, but he makes scant reference to how white backlash had begun reshaping the political terrain in the 1960s—even when he is broaching such obvious topics as "the urban crisis" or the politics of welfare reform. And when these do appear in Harvey's text, the festering racial resentments and sexual anxieties of culturally conservative sections of the white working class are largely written into a history of capitalist plots and elite manipulations. The result is an insightful study of economic trends combined with a largely fictitious history of social currents.[7]

Not all analyses have been oblivious to the interplay of race, sex, and class competition in U.S. capitalism. Scholars who study the penal system have developed a large body of work connecting neoliberal economic policies to neoconservative social policies by way of race/class dynamics.[8] Some of their models are essentially descriptive. What the legal scholar Mary Vogel calls "public minimalism" echoes the French sociologist Pierre Bourdieu's description of the "involution of the state" under neoliberalism as "regression to a penal state."[9] Others take a roundabout approach to the reverberations of cause and effect in a stratified social system: deregulation and privatization exacerbate social inequalities and therefore also tend to foster more fear of crime.[10] Either way, when parsing race/class dynamics in the penal state, many analyses seem driven by unexamined assumptions about cause and motive: they treat punitive government as a logical or necessary neoliberal strategy for managing racial minorities and the poor.[11]

Actually, the causal connection between neoliberalism and the punitive state seems anything but straightforward. Early neoliberal theories of crime and punishment gave no hint of the carceral state to come, and as late as 1979 Michel Foucault showed that these theories augured a biopolitics quite different from what actually developed. Neoliberal penal policy, Foucault elaborates, "does not aim at the extinction of crime, but at a balance between the curves of the supply of crime and negative demand. . . . This amounts to posing as the essential question of penal policy, not, how should crimes be punished, nor even, what actions should be seen as crimes, but, what crimes should we tolerate?"[12] Such was the tolerant penal logic of neoliberalism, in early form, before notions of risk, cost, and benefit came to be distorted by panic, before neo*conservative* theories inscribed white backlash and moral panic as principles of government.

AGAINST UNEXAMINED ASSUMPTIONS

Let me put my cards on the table: I have no doubt that business elites plot to fleece the public, that money and power distort U.S. elections, and that empire is corrosive of democracy. These effects were well known to socialists, populists, and anti-imperialists more than a hundred years ago and still need to be shouted from the rooftops.[13] I am quite convinced that liberal law legislates formal equality in ways that sustain substantive inequality, and I am certain that the maintenance of social inequality requires various forms of coercion and incurs costs—some obvious, others concealed. Last, I have no doubt that a "purer" form of capitalist culture was planted in the United States than in most other parts of the world, as my colleague Paul Smith succinctly argues in a virtuoso reading of U.S. politics, and that Americans are constantly reckoning, wrestling, with this tradition.[14] These are important conditions, recurring tendencies.

Conditions set limitations; they demarcate a playing field; they might favor this development or that. But they are not in themselves causes. They are the ground on which causes take root. In any event descriptions of the humdrum workings of a social system can scarcely be invoked to explain systemic changes, historic shifts. It cannot be assumed that whatever intensifies capitalism will also necessarily intensify forms of coercion. The point is to show how the implications of liberalism and capitalism were worked out in unpredictable ways under changing conditions: Just how did it come to pass that in the late twentieth century the balance of political forces shifted so markedly in favor of business interests, turned so decisively against the redistributive functions that had defined government legitimacy during the mid-twentieth century? How was consent constructed for this rewriting of the social contract? And is this return to a deregulated and nakedly predatory variant of capitalism a cause or effect of the proliferation of panic, punishment, and related themes in U.S. culture?

MULTIPLE CAUSES AND EFFECTS

The history that I have presented suggests a reworking of the usual causal claims about the relationship between neoliberalism and the punitive state. It begins with a complex picture of daily life under conditions of social inequality: people live out not only the economic predicaments of their class situation but also variously positioned experiences of gender, changing structures of family/kinship, and a racial situation. Within these institutional forms social actors forge sundry identities and participate in multifarious systems of hierarchy and solidarity. These factors all inflect the collective outlook and shape political agency. In giving an account of what happened during a forty-year period, I have tried to be attentive to the interplay of various aspects of social inequality and communal identification.

What happened was not simply the unraveling of the implications of capitalism. Nor could social developments have been predicted from the requirements of class, or the necessities of race/class, or even effects of race and class with sex factored in. Multiple causes were involved with multiple effects to produce novel outcomes. And in this dynamic interplay of causes and effects, the sequencing of events was a key ingredient in the making of the punitive neoliberal state. The actual sequence of events is a staggered one.

The anticrime alarms of the late 1960s. The anxieties involved in these developments were not strictly of an economic or class nature, nor did they emerge from plots hatched by conspiratorial business people; they were linked instead to rising crime rates and urban disorders. These perturbations thus had everything to do with the period's racial conflicts, with the clash of pro- and antiwar positions, and with pitched contests about the structure, meaning, and legitimacy of received authority. That is to say, they were entangled with volatile changes in the institutions of race, sex, and age.[15] The rise of a punitive orientation to governance was planted first in these cultural politics.

This is not to say that economic questions were entirely absent, or that plots were not being hatched. Wherever racial hierarchy touches upon class stratification, economics is implicit, and key institutional actors—a conservative coalition of southern Democrats and northern

Republicans—actively promoted crime panics as a political strategy for peeling white working- and middle-class voters away from the Democratic New Deal coalition.[16] But this is to say that more or less traditional forms of conservatism and political manipulation were in the air. Neoliberalism was but a glint in Milton Friedman's eye, a grand utopian theory still largely restricted to think tanks and scholarly centers.

As events unfolded, a large segment of the white working class was coming to see itself as middle class—and not merely middle class. Positioned between campus radicalism and urban unrest, this middle class was rapidly abandoning its historical role as bearer of enlightened humanitarianism, social tolerance, and progressive reform.[17] The repository of resentment against the changes of the 1960s, this middle class was defining itself in race reaction, sexual anxiety, and a punitive approach to rule breaking.

The sex panics of the mid-1970s. The anxieties involved in these panics built on apprehensiveness about the future of the heterosexual nuclear family and were linked to antigay backlash. No doubt economic troubles flogged everyday concerns about home life. But the institutional actors who promoted the first wave of sex panics (evangelical fundamentalists) hardly possessed a neoliberal economic theory.

By this time anxieties and resentments were driving policy on a number of fronts. Earlier crime panics had reshaped middle- and working-class attitudes toward law enforcement, crime legislation was beginning to be fashioned along punitive lines, and incarceration rates already were rising. Meanwhile, attacks on welfare had become primary weapons in the ongoing political realignment. Aid to Families with Dependent Children and the food stamp program were depicted as transfers of wealth from the white working and middle classes to the nonworking (thus undeserving) black underclass. If such depictions allowed white racial resentments to be reframed as "taxpayer politics," attacks on welfare also forged an enduring link between the politicization of crime and family values politics. Welfare programs were said to encourage profligate sexuality and unstructured forms of kinship, leading to social breakdown, resulting in high rates of inner-city crime.[18]

Against this unsettled backdrop, neoliberal economic theories were rapidly gaining ascendancy in policy circles and among opinion leaders. The Carter administration's limited, small-scale experiments in neoliberal deregulation and budget cutting cannot be linked directly to crime or sex panics of the period, neither as cause nor as effect. But these measures resonated powerfully with the curmudgeonly, parsimonious, and punitive logic of the ascendant conservative coalition. (Large-scale experiments were being conducted abroad, under the structural adjustment policies of the International Monetary Fund, especially in Pinochet's Chile, where wholesale neoliberal reforms flowed from the barrel of a gun.)

Redefinitions of "citizenship," "activism," "advocacy," "social problems," and "government redress" by subsequent crime and sex panics. In this process of redefinition, the racist and homophobic dispositions of the earlier panics became more subtle and less visible, while progressive rhetoric became more pronounced. Liberalism of a certain sort became increasingly complicit with conservative developments, and the emerging political project co-opted elements of the Left, sometimes wittingly, sometimes not. These developments were key to the institutionalization of a new culture of fear in geographies far removed from white racism in the South or backlash from blue-collar ethnics in the North.

Rhetorical forms were an important element in the ongoing transformations. Moral entrepreneurs in emergent social movements were mobilizing supporters with methods of moral suasion historically associated with melodrama: their goal was to produce an unmediated caring relationship with a person who had been victimized and to use this neighborly feeling to rouse unmodulated anger at the perpetrator of injury. Theodor Adorno had once described similar patterns of "identification through idealization" as a "caricature of true conscious solidarity," and Paul Virilio has subsequently described such orchestrations of public affect, which "cripple the world with grief" and pave the way for revenge, as "emotional pollution."[19]

By the time a second wave of sex panics erupted in the 1980s, anxieties had been revved to the point of psychosis. Subjects so positioned began to see threat everywhere and initiated the unending work of securing formerly "open" arrangements, arming the suburbs and planting surveillance technologies everywhere. Citizens, so primed, participated in new modes of vigilance (Neighborhood Watch groups), supported get-tough laws ("zero tolerance"), embraced the Reagan revolution ("get the government off our backs"), tolerated Clintonian neoliberalism ("the era of big government is over"), and so on.

CONTINGENCIES AND AD HOC ARRANGEMENTS IN THE SHUFFLE OF EVENTS

Four general conclusions can be drawn about the history of the neoliberal punitive state in the United States.

- A cultural change (the surge of a punitive outlook) led to a political reorientation (of the white working and middle classes) that preceded the economic shift (the eventual implementation of neoliberal policies).

- This cultural shift proved crucial in the elaboration of real neoliberal policies, which were first planted not in aspirations for abstract freedom or desires for greater efficiency or even business people's yearnings for higher profits but in darker forms of conservatism linked to racial resentments, sexual anxieties, and the entrenchment of white victimist politics.

- These developments are discontinuous: the conflicts that set trends in motion are not necessarily what keep them in motion.

- The sequence of shocks and disturbances that culminated in the present state of affairs cannot be attributed to a singular elite plot to trick and defraud the masses. The masses were actively involved in the production of the present arrangements.

Not that connivance was absent from the scene. Plots and schemes abounded along a series of points where neoliberal economic policies were sutured to punitive governance. Political strategists and think-tank intellectuals labored for many decades to paper over the divisions among various constellations of paleoconservatives, neoconservatives, religious conservatives, libertarians, and neoliberals. But much of their work was at cross-purposes. The neoliberal guru Milton Friedman was not necessarily a social conservative, and Nixon's brilliant political strategist Kevin Phillips was not necessarily a fiscal conservative. The journalist George Gilder was both, and his broadsides did much to popularize a distinctly punitive variant of neoliberalism—precisely because his arguments tapped a social groundswell, fusing white racism with the backlash against feminism and gay rights.[20]

On this shifting social ground moral entrepreneurs were key actors, more so than intellectuals or class elites; the moral entrepreneurs deliberately stoked different kinds of panic at various sites and among various constituencies: southern evangelical churches, northern white-ethnic neighborhoods, far-flung suburbs and small towns. But it was not only rightists who fanned sparks into flames. Some of this activity was stirred by elements of the Left or by salaried professionals who were pursuing strategic goals that had little to do with either neoliberalism or traditional conservatism. Over time a variety of institutional actors sought specific goals at disparate sites; sometimes their strategies competed, and sometimes they converged. The real course of events was a concatenation of cause and effect involving culture, politics, and economics. The route was studded with conflict and accident, plot hatching and opportunism, histrionics and hysteria.

In giving precedence to the cultural and political elements of these events, I do not simply invert the unicausal logic of economic determinism. I am not making a global claim that culture always takes the lead role in setting the course of historical events, only that it sometimes does. Nor do I depict this cultural shift as springing to life ex nihilo. If what I have been describing is the gestation of a new variation of white middle- and working-class biopolitics, then, obviously, this biopolitics is rooted in preexisting institutions of race, sex, and class, not to say federal policies that subsidized suburbanization after World War II. A long history of capitalism—and not only of capitalism but also of various forms of power under distinctly American conditions—is involved in this business. Changing economic conditions are part of the picture. I certainly do not discount the severity of the 1970s economic recession, nor do I minimize its role in convincing policy makers everywhere to pursue strategies of deregulation, privatization, and laissez-faire. Neoliberalism is a global phenomenon, as David Harvey's history shows. But the punitive state is not. And the United States stands alone among industrialized democracies in taking both neoliberalism and the punitive function to extremes. There is a connection or, better yet, there are multiple connections, interlacing causalities, between the two trends.

One might be tempted to say that neoliberalism and the punitive state emerged and developed together. Or one might say that everything that happened was simultaneously cultural, political, and economic. Or one might reflect on capitalism's capacity for thriving on crisis, for incorporating disruptions, after the fact, into its logic. Such descriptions get the picture partly right but at the risk of obscuring crucial points. I stress these points: In the real shuffle of events the emergence of a punitive culture predates the advent of market fundamentalism. The fracturing of the New Deal consensus, which had set modern liberalism on a moderately social-democratic foundation, was a prerequisite for economic deregulation, not its consequence. At every turn along the way, punitive disdain for losers, complainers, and outcasts supplied something of the sink-or-swim ethos that readied the public for the shocks of deregulation. In short, the punitive turn prepared the way for the neoliberal turn, not vice versa.

EFFECTS BECOME CAUSES

Later—or rather, very quickly—the relationship between the one thing and the other became reciprocal. The resulting culture of punishment, whose development occurred alongside the dismantling of the welfare state, came to fit in a deregulated marketplace in a variety of ways: Its increasingly privatized notion of justice mirrors economic privatization. Its ideas about victimization call attention to criminal micropredation at a time of untrammeled economic macropredation. Its ultimate product, the security economy, creates "guard labor" to contain "surplus labor," serving as a kind of Keynesianism in reverse. Punitive culture, an important enabler of the neoliberal turn, will subsequently function as key ballast for the resulting economic system. No doubt such utility is part of what kept the punitive turn going long after the conflicts that gave rise to it had burned out. In this context the boundless rage John and Jane Q. Public vent on shadowy evildoers seems symptomatic of their helplessness in the face of accelerated capitalism.

Marie Gottschalk succinctly captures the essential trade-off involved in the punitive turn: "As social services began to shrink in the 1980s due to the tax revolt, the recession, and the Reagan revolution, services for crime victims . . . expanded."[21] The penal system grew as the welfare system shrank, and in this process the figure of the victim presides over a weird transformation. The notion of victims' rights recalls, in nightmarish form, the logic of welfarism; it even installs a distorted little welfare state in the middle of savage capitalism. Under victim compensation laws, once an injured party can establish that she or he was the victim of a violent crime and, moreover, was "innocent"—did nothing, said nothing, to provoke the assault—she or he becomes eligible to have any resulting medical expenses paid by the state. Crime victims also may be eligible to receive free psychological treatment, job retraining, and other benefits—a sympathetic ear, a hand up, at public expense. This logic, and the material incentives it conveys, curiously conditions rights and entitlements: victims must be innocent, strictly speaking; innocents, and only innocents, deserve help. The citizen is not entitled to social benefits, and does not get sympathy from increasingly punitive authorities—except as a victim. Call this the final ensnarement of the victimology trap.

By various means the punitive state, with its perpetual panics and rages for punishment, meshes with the neoliberal order of unregulated, unmodified capitalism. But I reiterate: the logic of this arrangement is ex post facto, not a priori. Explaining the rise of the punitive neoliberal state requires the thoroughly historicist concepts of accident (things or arrangements that happened but did not have to happen), contingency (events that depend upon other events or on preexisting structures), and conjuncture (events or trends, including accidental or contingent ones, that join together).[22] That is, the development of this state of affairs depends not on one determinant or structural support but on how multiple preexisting elements became subject to various events and how they unfolded. Forms find functions after the fact.

AMERICAN EXCEPTIONS AND CONDITIONS

Nothing ordained that history would follow this course. Nor does anything in the inner nature of liberalism or capitalism predict that sequences of panic would foster a modern culture of fear and induce the resurgence of a punitive orientation in governance. But these changes have played out uniquely on the U.S. political landscape. Recent punitive turns in Europe, even at their worst, do not remotely approach the scale and intensity of the U.S. phenomenon—even though European states too experienced generational turmoil in the 1960s, economic shocks in the 1970s, varying degrees of neoliberal reform in the 1980s, 1990s, and 2000s, and crime spikes at various times. Why the difference? A comparison of U.S. and European practices highlights the aforementioned element of contingency in the making of the punitive state; it shows how capitalism and liberalism come together in deeply planted features of U.S. political life, not as causes but as enabling or constraining conditions against which causes and effects play out.

The humanitarian assumptions and norms of civility embedded in social-democratic welfare states seem to cushion not only against the shocks of economic dislocation but also against the effects of institutional and cultural conflicts. These cushions tend to tamp down panics. In contrast American liberal traditions tend to position well-being as a private matter ("the pursuit of happiness"), not the focus of statecraft. Populist, socialist, and labor movements in the United States have opposed this private conception of good but made little headway; they encountered both cultural obstacles and institutional impediments, including key barriers that were carefully erected by the founders. Under the U.S. constitutional structure, with its separation of powers and its delineation of federal and state governments, it proved impossible to develop a full-fledged welfare state comparable to those that exist in "even the most conservative European societies," as Jonathan Simon has put it.[23] As a result the United States is the more exposed, less "buffered" version of modernity. Barred from making welfare the centerpiece of government, its political elites will often construct their authority as a response to crisis or peril. Moral panic will be a recurring technique for setting tasks and solving problems.

Institutions of government are implicated in other ways, as well. European parliamentary political procedures, which involve multiparty negotiations, compromise, and explicit policies of inclusion, seem to curb public vengefulness and subdue the rage to punish. As the sociologist David F. Greenberg suggests, political actors will be reluctant to rail against folk devils linked to minority groups if next week's legislative session will involve elaborate negotiations with political parties representing those very sectors.[24] In contrast, in the U.S. two-party system the pursuit of a majority vote encourages moderation, but processes that foster genuine inclusion and discourage scapegoating are far more precarious. The democratically expressed will of the majority sometimes becomes the occasion for crackdowns, zero tolerance, and high-minded crusades. Moral panic will seem as American as apple pie.

The less secure, more "atomized" citizen can be induced to roar like a lion against lawbreakers, deviants, and evildoers. There is a connection here among unmodified capitalism, the liberal tradition, a two-party system, and punitive politics. The more secure, more socially embedded citizen appears to be a less "individualist" individual but also a less frightened and less punishing one. There is a connection here between social democracy's "humanization" of society and what Norbert Elias named "the civilizing process."[25]

ARE WE DOOMED, THEN, TO BE AFRAID?

The current shape of U.S. society results neither from immutable laws of capitalism nor from rules of social organization laid down at the time of the founding; its current condition is, rather, the outcome of political struggles about how to reorganize society in the wake of major institutional shifts. The good news, then, is that we are not doomed to be afraid. We do not even have to overthrow capitalism or eliminate empire to reverse the punitive turn. The bad news is that changing course will not be much easier. Deep political structures and enduring American cultural conceits are built into the present arrangements. Fear and punishment have become profoundly embedded in new ways in everyday assumptions and workaday practices.

Conclusion

Whither the Punitive State?

"Papa, what is happiness?" "Living each day with a little less
anguish than the day before."

—Alejandro Jodorowski, *Fábulas Pánicas*

It is said that U.S. politics runs in cycles, with periods of progress and
regress alternating roughly every forty years. These periods are often
marked in presidential terms, and some have heralded the election of
Barack Obama in 2008 as giving closure to a forty-year period inaugu-
rated by the election of Richard Nixon in 1968.[1] I am skeptical of anything resembling a numerological approach to social trends. Still, signs
of change are in the air.

If it now seems that the party of hope and change is displacing the
party of memory and reaction, other matters remain unsettled: Is the punitive turn winding down? If so, will the compromises of rights and procedures that dominated politics of the recent past be discarded or will
they be incorporated into a reform version of the punitive state? Answers
to such questions will likely elude us for many years. In any event judi-
cious authors will avoid prognostication. For now what we can do is demarcate the scope of the punitive state and indicate what might count as
answers to questions about its general direction. In conclusion, then,
I survey the landscape, sum up my findings, and venture a few guesses
about the American present and its contradictory tendencies.

PROGRESS AND REGRESS IN THE AMERICAN PRESENT

Many have noted that the Republican "southern strategy," with its subtle
or not-so-subtle appeals to racism, no longer packs electoral wallop.

Antigay crusades also appear to be losing their power to mobilize voters. Even the politics of fear seems to be losing traction. On this count the repudiation of the most extreme usurpations of power by the Bush-Cheney administration seems striking. The courts repeatedly swatted back against that administration's most egregious examples of executive overreach during the war on terror, and by the end of its second term the Republican administration enjoyed the support of scarcely more than 20 percent of the public.

The long tide of punitive lawmaking also shows signs of abatement. Some prosecutors have brought child pornography or abuse charges against teens for "sexting," the increasingly popular practice of swapping nude or provocative photos by cell phones, but media discussions of the phenomenon have been more subdued than hysterical. Even in conservative states there has been renewed interest in the notion of rehabilitation, at least in the juvenile justice system. Meanwhile, upbeat journalists occasionally produce pieces on the advent of a more rational approach to crime, especially where drug crimes are concerned.[2] Racial sentencing disparities, especially, have become a point of national embarrassment, and in 2007 the United States Sentencing Commission intervened to retroactively reduce the sentences of some (not all) federal inmates convicted on crack-related drug charges, effectively bringing their sentences into closer alignment with those for cocaine charges. In 2009 the State of New York rescinded much of what remained of its 1973 Rockefeller drug laws, with their mandatory minimum sentencing provisions for low-level drug offenders.

More sweepingly, first-term U.S. senator Jim Webb introduced bipartisan legislation that would create a blue-ribbon commission to study the U.S. criminal justice system, which the Virginia Democrat calls a "national disgrace," and to propose broad reforms. With each passing recession and economic downturn, the cost of maintaining a bloated prison system becomes clearer—perhaps especially to fiscally conservative politicians. In recent years, then, the prison system has continued to expand, but its rate of expansion is slowing.[3] It seems probable that high incarceration rates are topping out and will begin to gradually decline.

These and other indicators suggest that key institutional actors are beginning to question the desirability of organizing social relations around panic. However, many assumptions that undergird the punitive state persist, even in policies that seem to initiate important changes. This is especially clear where terrorism is concerned. President Barack Obama retired his predecessor's unilateralist rhetoric, but he has retained nearly all the war powers claimed by George Bush. His administration has squelched inquiries into warrantless wiretapping and torture, ramped up clandestine military actions across the Middle East, rapidly expanded the drone attack program in Pakistan, and authorized targeted killings abroad, including the assassination of a U.S. citizen living in Yemen.[4] Obama launched his presidency by announcing a schedule for closing the Guantánamo camp, a detention center holding "unlawful enemy combatants." But what to do with a dwindling number presumed terrorists still held there? Whatever evidence might be used against them in criminal proceedings is tainted by harsh interrogation techniques and would almost certainly be ruled inadmissible in court. The Obama administration's eventual improvised solution was to propose the development of a "new legal framework" for indefinite detention without trial for terror suspects—a proposal that sounds much like the Bush administration's approach, except that the new policy would detain suspected terrorists on U.S. soil. I underscore the proposal's connection to ongoing erosions of U.S. legal standards: indefinite detention, hitherto applied to some sex offenders after completion of their sentences, is poised to expand to cover a new class of people but without the benefit of any trial.[5] And as debates have roiled around "waterboarding" and other forms of torture, the security paradigm appears to have waxed, not waned, in public opinion. Polls suggest that a majority of Americans think torture is justified if it keeps the country safe. If history is any guide, it seems likely that a broad sector of the public would clamor for extreme measures, for new forms of surveillance and control, in the event of a major new terror attack.

On the broader criminal justice front, it remains unclear whether modest adjustments to some penalties will result in a substantial reduction of the prison population or whether an entrenched punitive system will continue to reproduce comparatively high incarceration rates for the foreseeable future. The good news is that the number of African Americans sentenced to prison or jail declined between 2000 and 2008. The bad news is that the number of whites and Hispanics sent to prison increased rapidly enough to keep the system growing.[6] Some elements of the carceral system appear to have become self-sustaining. Long periods of incarceration for minor offenders logically portend future recidivism, and a "life of crime" may be virtually all that remains now for millions of people who were churned through penitentiaries at a time when vindictive legislatures were shrinking or eliminating prison rehabilitation, job training, and educational programs.

Some reform trends embrace contradictory tendencies. For example, capital punishment is held in increasingly ill repute, but opponents of the death penalty typically offer a questionable alternative: life without the possibility of parole. A life sentence makes little sense in rehabilitation models and carries with it a more subtle underscoring of punitive policies: juries seem more likely to reach a verdict of guilt if they know they are not consigning the defendant to execution. Barring wider systemic reforms, the discontinuation of capital punishment would probably nourish a bloated penal system.[7]

And even while penalties for some drug crimes have become less severe, other penalties are becoming more severe. Penalties for violent crimes, second offenses, and crimes committed with a handgun continue to intensify. Illegal immigration continues to be harshly penalized, and with the deputizing of local police officers to act as extensions of U.S. Immigration and Customs Enforcement, the lives of undocumented workers have never been laid barer to power. New laws prescribe harsher sanctions for sex offenders, including offenders whose crimes were nonviolent, noncoercive, and did not even necessarily involve sex. While some state courts have blocked or modified the implementation of sweeping "child safety zone" laws designed to summarily evict sex offenders from the community, the Supreme Court has upheld public registries, civil confinement, and other extraordinary procedures. It is unclear how the High Court would rule should a variation of Jessica's Law reach its docket.

Meanwhile, public and private surveillance technologies are rapidly expanding and intensifying. Global Positioning System tracking makes possible the broad use of electronic house arrest, effectively offloading the cost of incarceration to the prisoner and his family. Policing continues to expand, even in the face of falling crime rates, as do other institutional mechanisms associated with the perpetuation of what used to be called a police state.

SEX PANIC REDUX

As I have shown, the apparatus of punitive governance is not confined to the problem of racial disparities and is larger than the institution of the prison proper. The punitive state is not a fragile regime, compelled to defend every territory with equal urgency. The regime has put down deep roots in far-flung institutions and social organizations; its logic is woven into a fine cultural mesh that spans politics, policies, technologies, and media. Modifications to the worst excesses of this system will no doubt ameliorate suffering in some measure, but suppression of the most extreme effects at certain sites will not prevent the system's retrenchment at other sites nor its continual deployment on new fronts. Addressing the underlying machineries will require a more thoroughgoing approach.

The sex panics treated in this book are an important part of the picture; they constitute the frontier where the punitive state's line of march seems least obstructed. Their recurrent object of desire and dread, sex, is uniquely susceptible to all the shape-shifting techniques that wrest control from disturbance: projection, condensation, contagion, paranoia.

The basic anatomy of sex panic and its relation to the punitive state will by now be apparent. Successive waves of sex panic have kept sensational crime stories in the news, produced new victim (and villain) identities, legitimized the political expression of rage, spun elaborate webs of legislation, eroded rights of the accused and other norms of democratic law, and driven a culture of fear deep into established institutions such as the family and the school system. By tying together institutional and popular thinking about such esoteric subjects as life, innocence, and risk, sex panics have fostered new social norms and supplied a reliable and reproducible set of tropes for the production of other panics in many domains. In some ways they have accomplished this work rather more intensively than have wider panics about crime.

The history of modern sex panics is complex and episodic. Although today's owe something to earlier sex panics of the 1930s through the 1950s (which likewise borrow from Victorian and Progressive-era sex panics), modern sex panics do not represent a direct continuation of earlier hysterias. And although successive panics build on preceding ones during the present sequence, which began in the mid- to late 1970s, contents have shifted along the way. The earliest episodes in the present sequence took shape during a period of cultural and political retrenchment in the wake of feminism and gay liberation. Subsequent episodes blended feminist logics and religious rationales with the outlook of the helping professions, in the process enlarging the definition of "child sex abuse" while vastly expanding the bureaucratic apparatus designed to detect, administer, and treat it. Later episodes feature scientific-sounding concepts of risk assessment and risk avoidance; new variations on the theme attach powerfully to new technologies and means of communication, both as these embody danger (perils of the Internet) and as they might be used in surveilling miscreants (electronic registries, DNA databases, the Global Positioning System).

The constant element in successive waves of panic is the figure of the imperiled innocent child—a child whose innocence is defined in terms of his imagined sexlessness and whose protection from sex looms as an ever more urgent and exacting demand. The resulting cult of the sacred child becomes larger, more influential, and less questionable in public culture. When New York attorney general Andrew Cuomo says, "There can be no higher priority than keeping our children safe," he succinctly invokes this figure of the child to express, as though it were common-sensical, an unprecedented new rationale of government.[8] In times past governments provided for the collective defense, common good, protection of rights and freedoms, or even for the redistribution of wealth, but the health and welfare of children were largely the responsibilities of parents and kin. Today the figure of the child victim stands at the center of governance. Reciprocally, the state undergoes a conceptual metamorphosis: it becomes the parent figure, not simply in a figural sense ("the motherland," "the fatherland") but in the sense that its practices are increasingly developed and rationalized in terms of an overtly paternalistic logic. This reconfiguration of norms and rationales bears myriad authoritarian implications—more so, I suggest, than do the excesses of the religious right, occasional eruptions of overt militarism, or other commonly perceived threats to civil liberties.

Echoing a number of queer theorists, I refer to "the figure" of the child here (and in other portions of this book) not only because of his sexlessness but also because this child himself is quite often imaginary. This curious fact is of no mean significance, for feats of the imagination become increasingly important in anticipating risks, formulating barriers, and setting the course of government. Under the new logic—which is in step with other risk-averse tendencies in U.S. culture—if a risk can be imagined, then preventative measures must be taken. This working assumption underlies the obsessive-compulsive character of constantly evolving sex crime laws. Even wholly imaginary risks become part of the reckoning. In 2002 the Supreme Court struck down a federal child pornography law that applied even to the depiction of figures who were not real children. More recently, the Court upheld a law designed to circumvent its 2002 ruling. "Fake child pornography" remains nominally protected speech, but the newer law makes its sale or promotion illegal. Thus the depiction of imaginary sexual risks to imaginary children is swept up under laws against pandering.[9] By such mechanisms the phantasmic overtakes the rational in jurisprudence and law.

SHIFTING THE BURDENS OF QUEERNESS AND BLACKNESS

Virtually everyone who has written about the subject has marked connections among changing gender roles and anxieties about the status of the family, gay acceptance and antigay backlash, sexual revolution and sex panic. Cultural dynamics mapped by Gayle Rubin at the peak of the satanic ritual abuse hysterias continue to be reproduced today: certain types of sexual dread are intensifying at a time when other sexual taboos are being relaxed.[10] The one thing is linked to the other in a variety of ways, and these ways seem to reinforce each other. I have tried to understand the relationship between old-style homophobia and contemporary sex panics, a relationship that is partly historical, partly psychological, and partly sociological. I venture a handful of generalizations about the modernization of taboo and the elaboration of new hierarchies.

The intensification of taboos around intergenerational sex, along with the airing of intense anxieties about the sexuality of minors, allows for the expression of ambivalences toward the supposedly more accepted practices—that is, for the expression of homophobia in less overtly homophobic forms. In many current panics the homosexual is the "absent presence," the figure who is never directly invoked but whose spectral existence is what gives meaning to otherwise indecipherable events. These effects are intensified by current political strategies for evading stigma and managing unspoken accusations. When, as the price of entry into the "properly political sphere," mainstream gay rights organizations promote a hypernormal image of homosexuality, maintain silence about sex offender registries and "child safety zones," and—unlike many European gay rights movements—avoid discussions of age-of-consent laws, they reinforce a dynamic that Lee Edelman has described: everyone wants to offload the burden of queerness onto someone else; no one wants to be left holding the stigma.[11]

The redoubling of taboos around age at a time when other taboos have been reexamined, deemphasized, or modified serves wider social functions. It revives the idea that sex is *the* basis for morality, and it disallows on principle the development of what Rubin calls a "concept of benign sexual variation."[12] Extreme scenarios of harm keep sex at the center of public morality and tether law, ever more securely, to functions associated with taboo, dread, and spectacles of punishment. These are no small matters; they circumscribe a crucial feature of our social dispensation. As moral hierarchies based on race or ethnicity have become inadmissible, and as old variants of homophobia have become progressively more unacceptable in polite society, the pivot has turned to new moral hierarchies based on sex. The resulting distinctions have a complex and unstable relationship to racism and homophobia. Stories about black inner-city family pathology (single mothers, supposedly absent fathers) preserve racial hierarchies around sex while also exempting members of the heteronormative black middle class. Public expressions of rage against pedophiles often traffic in homophobic language while similarly exempting what might be called "homonormative" gays and lesbians.

Sexual anxieties, racial animosities, class dynamics, and fear of crime interact in subtle but powerful ways in the construction of the new moral hierarchies. But all is not of one piece in the resulting picture. There are important differences between the psychic and social dynamics involved in sex panics and those at work in crime panics. The generic lawbreaker is black and poor. The pedophile predator is implicitly white, tacitly homosexual. A long history of class antagonisms is implicated here, but these are not struggles of the sort Marx emphasized. The racial dynamic in modern sex panics suggests that bourgeois moral purification, middle-class self-disciplining, and sexual hygiene—mechanisms for the production of a certain kind of "whiteness," more so than tools for either race or class repression—are at stake. Codified as law and disseminated in a wide range of institutions, such reformation projects are no longer the reserve of the white middle classes but have become universal, the key to the gate of an unbrave new world.

If the framing of these dynamics in functionalist language seems to suggest that these are universal tendencies, let me be clear: these trends are not equally distributed in the world today. Americans make sex a key criterion of their moral hierarchy with a zeal that is not equaled in any other industrialized democracy. Whether one takes a more or less benevolent view of sexual variation (as the sexual liberationists did) or a darker, more tempered view of sexuality as a troubled terrain haunted by spooky figures and visited by night terrors (a recurring tendency in psychoanalytic traditions), the American exception is striking.

Consider, in brief, the difference between British and American practices. Such comparison is useful, in part because the two countries share cultural and political traditions, and in part because Britain is one of the few places where modern sex panics have rivaled those in the United States. In fact, modern British sex panics were significantly shaped in the 1990s by child advocates' and social workers' use of an American import, theories of "recovered memories"—which initially convinced authorities that they were on to a vast pedophile ring operating out of schools and care homes for adolescent boys. Richard Webster reports how tabloids raged, thousands were accused, and hundreds of teachers and in-residence care workers were arrested before the mania subsided.[13] As with the U.S. case, the culture of child protection expanded, and the British eventually developed sex offender registries. Yet the differences between the two countries' implementation of such registries are striking. British registries are a closely guarded secret, available only to police, probation officers, social services authorities, and officials of other relevant agencies; American registries post the names, photos, and proximate addresses of sex offenders on the Internet. The British also monitor many fewer offenders than Americans do. In England and Wales the ratio of registered sex offenders to the general population is 46 per 100,000; in the United States the current ratio is more than 4.5 times greater: 228 per 100,000. And the overwhelming majority of British registrants are classified as "level 1" (on a three-level scale); they are said to pose minimal public risk and are subject to minimal supervision.[14] In Britain a culture of deference to expertise favors government restraint and the recognition of a zone of privacy. In the United States the "democratic" impulse favors publication, punishment, and shunning. The rights of victims and imagined future victims obliterate any rights to privacy that ex-offenders might claim.

THE OLD/NEW

In the United States sexual anxieties and fear of crime have come to form a dynamic feedback loop. On the one hand, it seems unlikely that revived sex panics would have put down such deep social roots except in the context of a wider war on crime. On the other hand, it also seems unlikely that crime fears could have become so finely woven into the fabric of everyday life without the element of sex panic.

The resulting system of social control is an amalgam of old and new elements. Its puritanism, its paranoia about strange outsiders, its enactment of dramas of peril and rites of protection are as old as the United States itself; they are deeply embedded in the national psyche.[15] The politics that sustain this system are a logical but not necessary precipitate of socially activist liberalism, whose limiting frames of reference occur and recur here. At the same time the resulting system of social control departs from long-standing liberal traditions that begin with a presumption of innocence, restrain the reach of law, defer to zones of privacy, and resist the application of excessive punishments or the tacking on of ex-post-facto provisions. The victim, who stands at the center of attention, seems an inversion of all that was vital, dynamic, and heroic in liberal individualism. New too is the network of institutions that constitutes the victims' rights movement, which is woven from threads of citizen activism, government, law enforcement, and judiciary practices. This formalized collusion of organized elements of civil society and functions of the state has few clear antecedents on U.S. soil.

In describing this evolving amalgam, I have tried to be sparing in the use of such terms as *archaic, atavistic,* and *primitive*. Everyone uses such terms, of course, and even words like *brutal* and *barbaric*—about which I have been less cautious—carry similar connotations. But the cultural work done by such words is seldom benevolent. We fling the label primitive at practices we do not like in order to convince ourselves that we, and practices we do like, are modern. This conviction that we are civilized typically prepares the way for the unleashing of savage violence, in much the same way that the depiction of abject victimization prepares the way for retaliatory rage. Thus Lévi-Strauss's old quip: "The barbarian is, first and foremost, the man who believes in barbarism."[16] But even this proposition trades in the prejudice it purports to criticize.

As an anthropologist, I am not convinced that "primitive law" in small-scale societies invariably tends toward abbreviated forms and punitive, as opposed to restorative or harmonizing, practices. Quite the contrary.[17] I am also not convinced that the provincial or rustic components of U.S. society are really the primary sources of fear and suspicion, either historically or today. Puritan witch hunters, Ku Klux Klansmen, intrusive social uplifters, and modern panic mongers are invariably middle-class townsfolk or suburbanites with a patina of education.

The problem is that despite their frequently hallucinatory character, the sorts of revitalization movements and moral fortification campaigns I have been describing are perpetual fonts of *modernity* in U.S. history; they often are associated with progress or progressivism in one sense or another. Preaching the virtues of diligence, sobriety, and thrift, nineteenth-century moral reformers also advanced the values of education, science, and sanitation. Railing against alcohol consumption, the temperance movement was an important catalyst for the discussion of social ills, women's suffrage, and government reforms. Anyway, where would one draw the line between the modern and the archaic in public sex offender registries, digital scarlet letters, GPS ankle bracelets, and other new disciplining technologies? One could perhaps invoke Horkheimer and Adorno and say that reason itself has become irrational, that social regress is tied to technological progress because reason has been applied to instrumental tasks in uncritical ways.[18] An old-fashioned premise of this book is that we need to keep track of the difference between rational fears and irrational ones, reasonable precautions and unreasonable ones. A wise person looks both ways before crossing the street; an unsound person stands paralyzed at the intersection with the "walk" sign on and no traffic in sight.

But perhaps Foucault's old saw about nineteenth-century campaigns against masturbation, a linchpin of that century's sexual hygienics, is more instructive. The modern imagination of innocence, like the antecedent prohibition of acts that are not really susceptible to eradication, seems illogical on the face of it but nonetheless produces logical effects: it facilitates the development of new webs of authority, new forms of expertise; it leads to the elaboration of new suspicions, new disciplining institutions, and new subjectivities. The secrecy it forces stimulates the laying of traps and the application of surveillance technologies at new sites. The production of new demonologics, the conjuring of outsized risks and harms—which are not distinguished from actual risks and real harms—is part of this work, but the prohibited act is not so much the enemy of as the support for these procedures.[19] There is a logic to unreason. We have been here before. We shall doubtless visit this place again, when the present manias have passed. The point is to be alert to history while describing emergent phenomena, which never strictly repeat history. Neither fear nor puritanism is new in the United States, but they are stoked in new ways, under new conditions.

Plainly, the logic of sex panic is contagious (or, in the stricter ethnological argot, associative), a word I have not been cautious about using, and this contagion has made sex panic especially effective at reshaping social relations and fostering new institutional arrangements. At the microlevel guilt by association means that accusations of wrongdoing are combustible; they communicate rapidly and spread uncontrollably from person to person in an immediate social medium. Propagated by mass media, sex panics quickly replicate at other sites and "micro" becomes "macro" by dint of mere mechanical repetition. The logic spreads in other ways, too. Sex panics provide a reusable template, a movable type for spelling out the modern punitive state.

WARPS, TWISTS, AND MULTIPLICITIES

The history of the punitive turn is neither singular nor straightforward. Architects of this cultural change worked with preexisting cultural motifs—a vengeance orientation has deep cultural roots in American sexual and racial institutions—but not without transforming those motifs. This cultural change was grounded in preexisting American law and in political ideas about justice—but in reorienting basic concepts, the punitive approach has gathered under its auspices a wide array of laws and practices (e.g., the parole system) whose logic had not always been punitive. The development of a new concept of risk linked to peril, injury, and victimization is an important part of the emerging picture; this rising culture of risk has been partially mapped by sociologists, anthropologists, and legal scholars. But the first thing that will be apparent is that evaluations of risk in the imagination of crime victimization and sex abuse have little connection with cost-benefit models, probabilities, or rational assessments of harm. Rather, the scientific-sounding language of risk in these domains masks the surge of an unmodulated associative logic more properly linked to taboo, pollution, and religious danger. And when *risk* means *danger*, fascination with extremely improbable occurrences and catastrophic outcomes becomes the rule.[20] Panic, in other words, is an inflated, distorted mirror image of the actuarial logic at work in other spheres.

Such twists and warps are crucial to the architecture of the emergent social form. It could be said that the carceral state, the surveillance society, is a conservative political project; it would be more telling to note how liberals played a crucial role in the production of this state of affairs. Alternatively, one might rightly claim that the victimology trap was present in liberal law from the start, but it seems more useful to note that this "trap" could be sprung, elaborated as the punitive state, only under certain specific conditions. Surely, economic conditions are among those conditions: the coarsening of U.S. political culture seems connected to ongoing economic changes, which have made the United States a harsher, less secure place. But this is not to say that neoliberalism caused the punitive turn, a claim that gets the historical sequence backward.

Because this cultural shift has emanated from various sources (racial turmoil, anxieties about the family, sexual dread, material interests, vague feelings of economic insecurity) and has taken up different objects (urban disorder, black recidivists, Latino gangs, white pedophiles) in different locations (ghetto, suburb, workplace, Internet), it has proved able to perpetuate itself, long after the original conditions that initiated it (rising crime rates, urban riots, antigay backlash) have changed. One source of anxiety waxes while others wane; one type of paranoia spirals while others recede from public consciousness. In any event each passing wave of fear perpetuates itself by leaving in its wake new institutions, new laws, and new economic uses. Institutionalization, codification, self-perpetuation: overall, the panic-punitive cultural schema remains intact, intensifies, spreads, and then hardens.

The result, then, is not quite your father's authoritarianism, a new variation on old repressive themes. For the new authoritarianism is seated in institutional structures, means of communication, and mass mobilizations that lack clear analogy in the past. It is woven into a post–civil rights–era political milieu that more or less consistently forbids the public expression of overtly racist or homophobic aims. In fact the new authoritarianism actually derives some of its rhetorics and many of its techniques from that most antiauthoritarian of social movements, the New Left—or, at any rate, from its decaying compromised versions. As a result it can coexist, even thrive, alongside the slow acceptance of gay civil unions and same-sex marriage (which, after all, domesticate and privatize homosexuality) as well as widespread enthusiasm for a black president (so long as he expresses a "postracial," "postpartisan" approach to politics).

AUTHORITARIAN TENDENCIES

A number of social critics, not all on the Left, used the term *fascist* and related vocabularies to describe the alarming usurpations of power that occurred under the Bush-Cheney administration: secret detention, accelerated policies of extraordinary rendition, unrestrained domestic spying, and torture—officially countenanced by a string of dubious legal memos and executive findings. Even if one takes a dim view of the harsh institutions, violent forms of coercion, and extralegal promotion of assassination and torture in U.S. history, it is hard to get around the idea that something went terribly wrong in American society during the first decade of the twenty-first century.

No doubt the development of an increasingly paranoid, irrational, narcissistic, and authoritarian political culture (I borrow these four traits from Theodor Adorno's research on fascist psychological and cultural tendencies in the United States in the 1930s and 1940s) took a great leap forward after the atrocities of September 11, 2001.[21] But, as I have shown, post–9/11 policies have only worked materials already at hand, underscoring victimization narratives, feeding obsessions with infantilized innocence, reinforcing trends toward punitive governance, extending the logic of preemption, and otherwise intensifying notable features of what sociologists call "the culture of fear"—which I have sometimes glossed (the better to underscore both its official standing and its perpetual sounding of alarms) as "the state of panic."

The ultimate form to be assumed by the emergent social and political system remains uncertain. This new, distinctly American system of social control remains a work in progress. What we should call it also seems an open question. Some points, however, seem to me to have been settled. Certainly, national melodramas depicting the siege of the heterosexual nuclear family by shadowy evildoers have a clear political lineage. The term *authoritarian* applies, by definition, to norms that buttress a paternalistic state whose citizens are conceived as imperiled innocents and infantilized victims. Also, a great many techniques used in the management of sex offenders, not to say policies of mass incarceration heavily directed against racial minorities, begin to resemble fascist techniques of coercion. These techniques of social control have demonstrated a tendency to intensify and spread: they attach to ever wider definitions of *sex* and *crime* and ever greater numbers of offenders; similar techniques of control and supervision also have been applied to assorted lawbreakers, illegal immigrants, "enemy combatants," and those accused of harboring terrorist sympathies.

It involves no exaggeration, dysphemism, or analogy whatsoever to say that the United States has become a carceral state, one in which a bloated prison system provides the normative model for governance in general and in which elements of the state collude with civil society to intensify these norms and to feed ever more prisoners into the penal system. Some manifestations of this system are obvious: there are now more prisoners than farmers in the United States. Other manifestations are subtle. Modes of surveillance multiply unobstructed in the community, at schools, in the workplace—and increasingly citizens are primed to crave new techniques of supervision, which are silently disseminated across the landscape.

The suburban consumer chooses this shopping mall over that one because the former's parking lot is watched by closed circuit cameras. The consumer believes that this degree of security is beneficial. The traveler queues up at airport security checkpoints and cheerfully submits to interrogation by Homeland Security upon reentering the country—because these procedures are for the good. The home purchaser chooses this neighborhood over that one because no residents of the former appear in the Megan's Law sex offender registries. The home buyer believes that she has a genuine need to know such information. In order to stay continuously informed, she downloads a popular new iPhone application, the P.O.M. (Peace of Mind) "Offender Locator," which compiles information from sex offender databases to provide the names, addresses, and photographs of registered sex offenders living or working in any vicinity. The prospective homeowner believes that this technology will empower parents to "turn the tables" on predators. Such new techniques of power are embedded in a far-flung series of presuppositions and predispositions; entwined, they construct an expansive new web, a new grid of decentralized supervision and depersonalized control.[22]

The resulting picture of power bears some resemblance to Sheldon Wolin's notion of an "inverted totalitarianism," a system that involves the pursuit of total control but whose form inverts many classical features of totalitarianism. Classical totalitarianism compelled business to serve state interests. In contrast, inverted totalitarianism represents "the political coming-of-age of corporate power": the state promotes business interests. Wolin dubs this unholy union of state and corporation "Superpower," a term that plays off the outward projection and the inward intensification of control in a variety of ways. Old-style totalitarianisms kept the masses perpetually mobilized (for war or for monumental domestic projects) while dispensing with democracy; in the new inverted mode, the whole point is to keep the masses demobilized and enervated. As elections increasingly revolve around peripheral or private, as opposed to public, questions, democracy becomes "privatized and submissive rather than unruly." The political system thus remains formally democratic, but politics is closely managed.[23]

There are problems with the picture Wolin draws. He presents "the culture wars"—for instance, political struggles around abortion and gay marriage—and anticrime politics as part of a strategy of divide and rule. Surely, such politics have such effects, but I should think it more productive to take seriously the institutional interests and social stakes involved in such struggles. These conflicts, after all, stoke the fears that feed the punitive state. They precipitate distorted ideas about victimization, prevention, and common good, and it is around these very notions that the coils of control have spiraled ever tighter for more than three decades. In consequence, the emergent system will be experienced as more totalitarian for some than for others—and some will even find it just, empowering, and liberating. In the end I am less certain that a ruling elite actually seeks "total control" than I am that the mad desire for total security has become widely distributed, poisoning the political system at its most "demotic," a term Wolin draws from the Greek *dēmos*, "the people," and uses to mark the rowdy, contentious nature of electoral democracy. "Superpower" is a formidable nemesis, but nothing is more terrifying than a nation of victims.

And this is key: it is not in the name of steel, will, or strength that the emergent system finds its justification. A recurrent culture of fear provides the crucial nexus of punitive governance at home and irrational imperial adventures abroad. Whether dealing with black urban menace, perverts lurking under the bed, brown border incursions, or far-flung Islamic peril, the most intolerable acts of the United States invariably take shape within a lifeworld dominated by fear. The uniquely self-righteous posture of its leaders, much noted throughout the world, turns on a familiar Victorian story line that is likewise grounded in elaborate mechanisms of dread and projection: the infantilized, imperiled innocent ever in need of rescue. And whether this imagined innocent is fashioned as America's inner child (its true identity) or as the ultimate suffering Other who commands our attention, the result is much the same: a nation conceived at the intersection of puritanism and liberalism is obliged to defend the innocent, punish evildoers, and remake the world according to a moral imperative. It is far from clear that this Great Commission has waned in the age of Obama. It is not clear what forms all this will take in the future.

I have occasionally evoked the term *prefascist* to describe the current social scene, mindful that receptivity to appeals of a fascistic sort is nothing new. Surely, one could argue that experiments in "microfascism" are a recurring feature of U.S. history, with its assorted sex panics, political paranoias, race perils, witch hunts, dietary fads, fitness crazes, social purity movements, mind-control cults, communal purgings, and utopian communities—disparate scenes of fear and loathing, sites where the desire to remake the world so often goes bad. Certainly, political projects of an authoritarian, repressive, or eugenic sort sometimes have taken "democratic" form, defining freedom as the untrammeled expression of the will of the majority or progress as the suppression of political, racial, or sexual minorities. Over time, then, Americans have flirted with various modes of strong-arm rule without ever consummating the marriage. Tendencies and movements of a fascistic sort have waxed and waned throughout much of U.S. history; each of these social currents has had distinctly American characteristics.[24] Key tendencies, as I have mapped them, have been waxing since the 1970s. And that, no matter what you call it, is a long trend.

POINTERS FOR A SOUNDER PUBLIC DISCOURSE

Because the cultivation of panic involves the collaboration of a style of journalism, a type of advocacy, and a mode of political opportunism, and because the punitive state consolidates distorted ideas about risk, justice, and citizenship, rolling back this state of affairs will require changes on a variety of fronts. The legal front alone seems formidable, given the scale of victimist statutes and the scope of punitive laws; true reform would entail the meticulous rewriting of thousands of local and national laws. I offer only a handful of quick pointers here, notes toward the desired cultural shift, brief memorandums to the citizen who would be defined by something more than his or her vulnerabilities.

1. *Take a deep breath*. Panic requires the horror story, the outrage, the depiction of some condition of abject brutalization. A vengeance orientation cannot thrive where the rank exploitation of emotional responses is not respectable. Concerted efforts by scholars, public intellectuals, journalists, and others could begin to make tabloid culture less respectable.

2. *Always insist on hard evidence*. Credulity is implicated at every turn in the development of the culture of fear, and simple skepticism would have put the brakes on any number of sex panics. If a charge sounds too extraordinary to be true, there is at least some chance that it is not true. The accusation begins to lose its magical quality, and public culture begins to return to sobriety, if one simply repeats the formula: "The jury is still out."

3. *Demystify.* Sex and crime panics thrive on the mystification of sex and violence. Much of this mystification takes the form of ideas about innocence: the minor, up to an ever more advanced age,

is innocent of sex; the victim of violence is a victim *only* if she or he is strictly innocent. A demystified approach to sex and violence could cut short the perpetual dragnet for the ultimate predator. It might allow for distinctions between morality and law, whose conflation does much to discredit both. It might even eventually result in more nuanced laws and procedures (e.g., punishments calibrated for varying degrees of infraction, realistic ages of consent).

4. *Be wary of biopolitical monsters.* Or, rather, be wary of the construction of monsters and monstrosity. All human beings are capable of vice and violence. The assertion that some subspecies or other is uniquely and congenitally disposed to commit evil acts sets in motion a series of chain reactions: a tendency to blur distinctions between degrees of harm; an inclination to envelope ancillary acts and dispositions within the category of the monstrous; a propensity to classify more and more people as monsters. A different approach becomes possible if one starts from the premise that the monster is a distorted mirror image or screen projection of collective fears and desires.

5. *Return to basics.* Laws should prohibit, and punish, no more than is strictly necessary. Reasonable people might debate how much is necessary, but they will eschew the emotional blackmail of remote risks to the imagined, anticipated victim. The idea that law exists primarily to correct and to balance is older than the Enlightenment or even classical antiquity; it exists in many cultures.

6. *Forget.* Today we celebrate tireless investigators who never give up on cold cases; we honor family members who never let go the torment of a grievous loss. Such commitment to memory cannot be deemed healthy and should scarcely be extolled. Given all that culturally enjoins us to the memory of victimization, perhaps the forgetting of trauma would be a better course. And given all that would perpetuate endless mourning, let us let grief do its work and be finished, so that we can move on.

7. *Try retrofitting.* It remains unclear whether institutions and infrastructures built around a culture of fear can be retrofitted to serve other purposes. But some attempts seem worth pursuing. What if victims' advocates and child welfare agencies were charged broadly with promoting health, nutrition, exercise, and well-being? What if most prisons were reconfigured, not as sites of perpetual punishment but as temporary places for rehabilitation, higher education, job training, and other socially useful purposes?

8. *Accept some risks.* This will be difficult. For years, institutional actors working in many domains have promoted the unsound notion that no level of risk is ever acceptable. This unrealistic conception has distorted public policies in many ways, and the idea that government exists solely to protect citizens from harm has eclipsed other rationales for statecraft. The punitive state begins to loosen its grip on citizens as soon as we let go of the notion that life ought to be entirely free of risk.

9. *Change the political discourse.* This will be even more difficult. The lack of a sustained radical, socialist, or social-democratic current in U.S. politics means that there are few checks on the escalating politics of individual grievance. Difficulties notwithstanding, a partial remedy seems obvious. If what has eroded civil liberties and democratic norms most dramatically has been the increasingly irrational pursuit of personal security, then perhaps a fitting anti-dote—a logical way to begin to reverse these trends—will lie less in the direct confrontation with excess and unreason than with the promotion of a politics of economic security.

UNPANICKED NOTES ON THE CRISIS

In any event the deregulated and privatized economic regime that was deployed as the cure for Keynesian malaise would seem to be in deep trouble today, and signs of its crisis continue to multiply. Plainly, deregulation and laissez-faire policies have not worked as their Reagan-era advocates predicted: "A rising tide lifts all boats." The wear and tear on U.S. economic performance has become increasingly evident in the first years of the twenty-first century. Speculative booms have been followed by inevitable busts. Outsourcing has relocated industrial production to foreign lands, driving up trade deficits and eliminating union-wage jobs without generating desirable new jobs in the service-information sector. Underregulated markets have produced a series of financial crises and corporate implosions. The dollar continues to take a long-term beating.

If the new system of social control that I have been describing is understood as an eventual coupling of punitive governance with neoliberal economic policies, then the tectonic plates beneath this arrangement would seem set for another shift, another realignment of some sort. What remains unclear is how much longer the present arrangement can last and what will replace it. It is even less clear what social actors will rise to the historical occasion: Technocratic elites, willing to modify only the most extreme manifestations of dysfunction? Citizens, feeling danger and primed for vengeance, who might very well roll forward the wheel of the punitive state? Or some new citizen, ready to break with trends of the past forty years?

The weaknesses of the present system seem glaringly apparent. A public defined by its fears cannot pursue its rational interests. A culture overwhelmed by a sense of its own victimization will become an increasingly unhealthy place to live. A political system that revolves around punishment cannot long remain democratic in any meaningful sense. An economic system that cannibalizes the public good will become poorer, shabbier, and less vibrant over time. An empire positioned at the confluence of these trends will be predisposed toward disastrous undertakings.

Race, Incarceration, and Notification

TABLE I   RACIAL DISTRIBUTION IN SAMPLE OF STATE CIVIL
COMMITMENT PROGRAMS

State (Year Law Passed)	Number Committed	Racial Breakdown by Percentage		
		White	Black	Latino
Arizona (1995)	71	75%	9%	15%
California (1995)	443	63	22	11
Florida (1998)	240	65	34	1
Illinois (1997)	169	70	27	-
Iowa (1998)	65	80	17	2
Kansas (1994)	159	93	3	3
Massachusetts (1999)	105	78	12	6
Minnesota (1994)	342	79	14	3
Missouri (1994)	79	84	14	-
Nebraska (2006)	10	70	10	20
New Hampshire (2006)	0	-	-	-
New Jersey (1998)	342	48	42	10
North Dakota (1997)	37	78	6	4
Pennsylvania (2003)	9	78	11	-
South Carolina (1998)	70	68	32	-
Texas (1999)	66	55	21	24
Virginia (1999)	37	50	44	3
Washington (1990)	167	81	13	1
Wisconsin (1994)	283	69	23	2

NOTE: A majority of those held under civil commitment laws are white. (Because "other" races are not shown, percentages do not add up to 100.)

SOURCE: Based on interviews by reporters Abby Goodnough and Monica Davey of officers of state civil commitment programs for "Doubts Rise as States Hold Sex Offenders after Prison," *New York Times,* March 4, 2007.

TABLE 2   INCARCERATION RATES VERSUS COMMUNITY NOTIFICATION RATES,
SELECTED STATES, 2001

| State | Incarceration Rates, Prisons and Jails, 2001 | | | Sex Offender Community Notification, 2001 | | |
| | Incarceration Rate per 100,000 Population | | | Notification Rate per 100,000 Population | | |
	White	Black	W/B Ratio	White	Black	W/B Ratio
New York	173	1,638	1:9.47	4.7	10.0	1:2.13
Nebraska	229	1,973	1:8.62	6.8	20.4	1:3.00
Kansas	345	2,469	1:7.16	49.6	94.7	1:1.91
North Dakota	189	1,321	1:6.99	8.9	127.7	1:14.35
Colorado	394	2,751	1:6.98	2.8	10.3	1:3.68
Michigan	369	2,247	1:6.09	130.4	184.3	1:1.41
Louisiana	379	2,251	1:5.94	44.9	74.0	1:1.65
West Virginia	294	1,708	1:5.81	45.7	73.4	1:1.61
Kentucky	429	2,392	1:5.58	52.6	121.3	1:2.31
Arizona	544	2,849	1:5.24	26.4	72.4	1:2.75
Texas	640	3,287	1:5.14	90.4	121.6	1:1.35
Montana	417	2,118	1:5.08	22.3	148.6	1:6.67
Tennessee	392	1,991	1:5.08	14.7	26.7	1:1.81
South Carolina	349	1,740	1:4.99	99.9	170.4	1:1.71
Alabama	417	1,877	1:4.50	42.6	88.8	1:2.08
Georgia	519	2,149	1:4.14	45.1	74.9	1:1.66
Mississippi	399	1,645	1:4.12	45.0	71.0	1:1.58

NOTE: African Americans are overrepresented in community notification programs (see "W/B Ratios"). But except in North Dakota and Montana, they are far more overrepresented in prisons and jails. States are presented in order of racial disparities in incarceration rates, from highest to lowest.

SOURCES: Incarceration rates are drawn from Allen J. Beck, Jennifer C. Karberg, and Paige M. Harrison, "Prison and Jail Inmates at Midyear 2001," *Bureau of Justice Statistics Bulletin*, April 2002, 13, National Criminal Justice Reference Service no. 191702. Data on community notification programs and sex offender registration under Megan's Law, adjusted to reflect the rate per 100,000 population, are drawn from Daniel Filler, "Silence and the Racial Dimension of Megan's Law," *Iowa Law Review* 89 (2004): 1535–94. Filler's data sets were collected between August and November 2001.

TABLE 3   INCARCERATION RATES VERSUS SEX OFFENDER REGISTRATION RATES,
SELECTED STATES

| State | Incarceration Rates, Prisons and Jails, 2001 | | | Sex Offender Registration, 2001 | | |
| | Incarceration Rate per 100,000 Population | | | Registration Rate per 100,000 Population | | |
	White	Black	W/B Ratio	White	Black	W/B Ratio
Minnesota	139	1,755	1:12.63	173.2	843.2	1:4.87
Iowa	284	3,302	1:11.63	132.8	611.1	1:4.60
Vermont	218	1,794	1:8.23	210.6	750.9	1:3.57
Virginia	361	2,268	1:6.28	114.3	278.2	1:2.43
North Carolina	265	1,612	1:6.08	65.4	139.4	1:2.13
Oregon	458	2,763	1:6.03	369.6	1139.0	1:3.08
California	470	2,757	1:5.87	215.6	634.6	1:2.94
Indiana	391	2,236	1:5.72	180.1	438.2	1:2.43

NOTE: African Americans are overrepresented in sex offender registries (see "W/B Ratios"). But they are far more overrepresented in prisons and jails. States are presented in order of racial disparities in incarceration rates, from highest to lowest.

SOURCES: Incarceration rates are drawn from Allen J. Beck, Jennifer C. Karberg, and Paige M. Harrison, "Prison and Jail Inmates at Midyear 2001," *Bureau of Justice Statistics Bulletin,* April 2002, 13, National Criminal Justice Reference Service no. 191702. Data on sex offender registration under Megan's Law, adjusted to reflect the rate per 100,000 population, are drawn from Daniel Filler, "Silence and the Racial Dimension of Megan's Law," *Iowa Law Review* 89 (2004): 1535–94. Filler's data sets were collected between August and November 2001.

TABLE 4   COMMUNITY NOTIFICATION PROGRAM ENROLLMENTS COMPARED
WITH PRISON POPULATION AND GENERAL POPULATION BY RACE

State	Community Notification		Prison Population		General Population	
	White	Black	White	Black	White	Black
Alabama	56.6%	43.1%	35.5%	64.2%	71.1%	26.0%
Arizona	83.0	9.3	44.9	14.4	75.5	3.1
Colorado	85.2	14.8	45.3	23.0	82.8	3.8
Georgia	57.5	42.1	34.7	63.6	65.1	28.7
Kansas	87.4	11.1	54.1	35.2	86.1	5.7
Kentucky	83.4	15.6	66.0	32.9	90.1	7.3
Louisiana	54.3	45.5	24.6	75.2	63.9	32.5
Michigan	77.9	19.5	41.7	54.8	80.2	14.2
Mississippi	51.0	47.6	28.2	71.2	61.4	36.3
Montana	81.3	1.8	76.1	1.9	90.6	0.3
Nebraska	80.0	10.8	58.8	25.1	89.6	4.0
New York	62.9	31.3	17.4	50.7	67.9	15.9
N. Dakota	77.9	7.4	68.8	4.5	92.4	0.6
S. Carolina	56.9	42.6	31.1	67.7	67.2	29.5
Tennessee	71.5	26.5	46.9	51.8	80.2	16.4
Texas	81.8	17.9	31.6	41.6	71.0	11.5
W. Virginia	94.5	5.1	83.2	16.0	95.0	3.2

NOTE: A majority of those who are subject to community notification procedures are white, even in states where a majority of the prison population is black.

SOURCES: Data on community notification program enrollments under Megan's Law are drawn from Daniel Filler, "Silence and the Racial Dimension of Megan's Law," *Iowa Law Review* 89 (2004): 1535–94. Filler's data sets were collected between August and November 2001. Information on the racial breakdown of the prison population is drawn from draft data generously supplied to me by the U.S. Department of Justice, "Prisoners under State or Federal Jurisdiction, by Race, 2001." Data on ethnic breakdown for the general population are derived from U.S. Census Bureau, "Race and Ethnicity," 2000, http://factfinder.census.gov.

TABLE 5   SEX OFFENDER REGISTRANTS COMPARED WITH PRISON POPULATION
AND GENERAL POPULATION BY RACE

State	Sex Offender Registrants		Prison Population		General Population	
	White	Black	White	Black	White	Black
California	50.0%	16.5%	28.8%	30.1%	59.5%	6.7%
Indiana	78.8	18.4	55.7	41.1	87.5	8.4
Iowa	89.0	9.2	70.1	22.7	93.9	2.1
Minnesota	77.2	14.7	54.6	36.5	89.4	3.5
N. Carolina	59.2	37.8	32.6	62.1	72.1	21.6
Oregon	92.8	5.4	75.0	11.0	86.6	1.6
Vermont	97.0	1.8	86.9	5.4	96.8	0.5
Washington, D.C.	7.1	89.9	1.7	94.3	30.8	60.0

NOTE: A majority of those who appear in sex offender registries are white, even in states where a majority of the prison population is black.

SOURCES: Data on sex offender registries under Megan's Law are drawn from Daniel Filler, "Silence and the Racial Dimension of Megan's Law," *Iowa Law Review* 89 (2004): 1535–94. Filler's data sets were collected between August and November 2001. Information on the racial breakdown of the prison population is drawn from unpublished draft data generously supplied to me by the U.S. Department of Justice, "Prisoners under State or Federal Jurisdiction, by Race, 2001." Data on ethnic breakdown for the general population are derived from U.S. Census Bureau, "Race and Ethnicity," 2000, http://factfinder.census.gov.

Notes on Method

Participant observation, a cornerstone of research in the interpretive social sciences since the turn of the last century, basically attempts to produce knowledge by imposing analytical discipline on the researcher's observations, experiences, and conversations in some setting. The first product of such research is a set of fieldnotes, which record events, impressions, and interviews. The finished product, derived from such data, is an "ethnography," or text about people or a people. The strength of ethnographic writing derives from the attention it pays to empirical detail, unofficial happenings, and everyday understandings.

Ethnographic methods have been especially productive for research into definable domains (small-scale societies, family life, street-corner society); they would also seem well suited for research into policing, courtrooms, and prisons: What happened? What collective sense or conflicting meanings do participants make of events? How do these events and meanings compare with the official record? How do actions at the microlevel (police work, court hearings) square with social theories of the macrolevel (how wider social, political, or economic systems work)? Yet ethnographies of the U.S. criminal justice system remain relatively rare. Notable among them is Lorna A. Rhodes's *Total Confinement: Madness and Reason in the Maximum Security Prison* (Berkeley: University of California Press, 2004), which examines day-to-day life and routine practices in the prison industry. More common are memoirs of various sorts, among them, prison journals and prison letters. The most famous of these include Jack Abbott, *In the Belly of the Beast: Letters from Prison*; Malcolm Braly, *On the Yard*; and George L. Jackson, *Blood in My Eye*.[1] This book uses a mix of historical, textual, and ethnographic methods, sometimes related in journalistic style. Its overarching sensibility is ethnographic in the sense that it takes news stories, anticrime campaigns, policing, lawmaking, conversations, and events as the material of everyday life, to be aggregated and analyzed in search of larger trends and connections.

The most ethnographic portion of the book, chapter 4, took shape in hindsight; it thus represents an "autoethnographic" account, that is, an account that focuses on the writer's chance experiences rather than developing from a planned research program. Autoethnographic techniques are generally associated with postmodern ethnography, especially its feminist and queer variants, and with good reason: feminism and lesbigay studies have theorized how power operates in personal life, and in autoethnography the writer's subjective experiences become grist for the mill. The pitfalls attendant to these techniques are well known; they include the risk of solipsism, the real possibility of narcissism, and the chance of producing a strictly subjective text whose claims cannot be examined with any sort of tests. While I acknowledge these worst-case scenarios, I take a quirkily traditionalist view of the practice and the problems it entails. First, autoethnography is not autobiography; its proper subject is the social world around the writer, as evinced in the writer's experiences (and sometimes beliefs), not the writer himself. Second, insofar as the techniques of autoethnography reflect one's experiences (and not, say, one's inner psyche), they prove difficult to rigorously distinguish from the techniques of mainstream ethnography. Autoethnographic techniques can be said to be present, even in old-fashioned ethnographies, whenever the anthropologist or sociologist explicitly reflects on how he or she obtained certain data or the conditions under which a particular interview occurred, or when the text attends to accidental but revelatory happenings in the field, especially if these involve the researcher as a socially situated person.

Autoethnographic techniques are implicit in traditional ethnography but have become increasingly explicit since the reflexive turn of the 1970s and are now more or less conventional in contemporary ethnographic work. These include the placement of the author, writing in the first person, in the ethnographic narrative; reflection on how points of biography have shaped the author's research questions; and queries about how one's positioning as a social subject affects both the interpretation and shaping of data.[2]

A WORD ON ETHICAL DILEMMAS AND MORAL HAZARDS

I have thought a great deal about the ethics involved in this book's scattered instances of autoethnographic writing, especially the primarily autoethnographic chapter 4. What could be the implications of writing about so many intimate scenes, so many fraught events? Have I included too many private stories, related too much information? I have no easy answers. Instead, I will try to define the problem as a set of dilemmas, entanglements, and temptations.

My initial reaction is to recoil from the task. Like most anthropologists trained during the 1980s, I have often thought that ethnographic writing involves "stealing" something from someone. This objection can be met but is not easily overcome. Certainly, the notion that anyone can "own" his or her experiences is problematic, as even elementary theories of meaning suggest.

Experience, like meaning, is always between us, not within us, "like an electric spark that occurs only when two different terminals are hooked together."[3] And even if one grants the notion of a "private" experience, the experiences about which the ethnographer is concerned are shared, collective experiences. What I have written about in the major section of chapter 4 happened to Ritchie and to Joe; it happened to me too, and it involved a much wider number of participants. Who "owns" a story coauthored by so many "writers"?

The idea of theft or poaching nonetheless haunts the ethnographic imagination, and for good grubby reason. The ethnographer turns shared experiences into something: a book, promotion, career. The subjects of study, who are usually poor, disadvantaged, or disempowered, are often left with nothing. It seems to me that the charge of theft can be successfully refuted under only two conditions. One is simply giving people their say, and I have tried to give my primary subjects space to talk here, in their own words. (Some might object that I have not given the accusers and the authorities their say, but they have already had their say, and I have been scrupulous in my description of their assertions.) The other condition is that the research brings social benefits to the subjects of study, as opposed to making them more vulnerable. The problem is that any benefits are seldom dramatic or immediate. My hope is that this book will contribute to new conversations about sex, minors, agency, and accusation and that these discussions will eventually promote sounder policies. But I do not see a clear path to this outcome.

A more substantial objection derives not from a conception of experience as a sort of property but from the idea that experience is intersubjective, social. On this count ethnographic writing risks exposing subjects to pain or embarrassment. What hurts, hurts—and retelling it or having it told or retold also hurts. I have pondered the pain chapter 4 dredges up for those of us who lived through the events it describes. Again, this objection is not easily dismissed. For my own part I do not feel especially empowered in revealing that I was a teenage pariah. Ritchie has allowed me to tell his story, but it is clear that he gets no joy from the retelling. I have no idea how countless acquaintances might feel if they recognized their own intimate stories woven into the fabric of my arguments. But ethnographic writing, if it is true to form, is a different kind of retelling than that involved in idle gossip, sensationalist chatter, the police blotter, and other forms of representation intended to shame, scandalize, or humiliate. I have taken pains to avoid embarrassing people. Like literature, good ethnographic writing appropriates happenings but also gives something back to them. Mindful of this, I wrote with two goals in mind. One was compensation—the controlled telling of uncontrollable events gives some sort of satisfaction. The other has to do with an old ethnographic ideal. At their best ethnographic accounts correct and amend the record; they supply knowledge unavailable in the official story, the statistical norm. In uncovering the hidden transcript, I have always tried to recognize the dignity of those about whom I write, even when they find themselves in undignified positions.

In the end I rely on some old-fashioned ideas about writing and representation. The idea of bearing witness has ancient legal and theological roots, and the moral imperative to bear witness is never more pronounced than when it means recounting violence, breaking silences, or saying that which must not be said. Nancy Scheper-Hughes has written eloquently about the practices of "primitive solidarity" and bearing witness in ethnographic research.[4] I tell these stories to counter what was unsaid—unsayable—in the events and to counter the misrepresentations that were produced around unspeakable prejudices. But herein lies a trap, the equally ancient notion that suffering can be redeemed. Everything I have lived or read suggests to me that suffering cannot be redeemed; it can only be endured. If no savior wipes away all tears, if no messiah redeems the past, then amelioration comes only with the passage of time, with forgetting, and with ongoing efforts to build a life with less suffering. "The truth will set you free," they say, but this cannot be true. The truth alone has no such power.

TEMPTATIONS AND RISKS

There are other temptations, and I write both with and against them: the temptation to rouse the reader with emotional stories and to mobilize the specific example as a route to the general rule. These approaches are profoundly embedded in the architecture of ethnographic writing, which tries to elaborate theoretical views from empirical facts, but these approaches are also central to the emotional manipulations of the panic narrative, which tells the personal horror story in order to prod collective action. To the extent that I have worked with the inductive approach, I have tried to find the general in the specific, the truth in the detail, and to explore specific instances as a test of general principles. To the extent that I have worked with the personal horror story, I have done so with the intention of "undoing" it. I hope that I have caused the reader more to reflect than to become emotional, and I trust that in sum I have woven a narrative more substantial than the singular statistically anomalous event. The reader will judge whether my observations of empirical happenings are sufficiently detailed and whether they are sustained by rational reflection on risk, harm, standard procedures, and so on.

I note certain other risks involved in writing of this sort. Narratives sometimes have unpredictable or unintended political effects; more often, pernicious effects are merely attributed to narrative. I have said that minors are imbued with sexual feelings and that the sexuality of teenagers is complex, contradictory, and fraught. I also have observed that minors sometimes do lie about sex and abuse. If such claims now seem controversial in public culture, where the projection of childhood innocence is closely patrolled, it will be clear that I am writing against the prevailing party line. I do not believe that such observations have the effect of putting children at greater risk of abuse. Writing against such claims and arguments, I have tried to give some insight into a small-scale sex panic, linking its development to ideas about childhood (adolescent) innocence, to hypervigilant law enforcement practices, and to patterns that have been widely documented in other sex panics.

No doubt my starting with a denial of adolescent sexlessness and my refusal of a strictly hygienic view of sexuality imply complications for policy, which no longer would be about "protecting innocence" but then could be oriented around other principles: calibrated harm reduction, perhaps, or nurturing well-being. Maybe such reorientation would not be as complicated as some Americans think. Many countries of northern and western Europe seem to have worked out overall approaches that avoid the Scylla of sex panic and the Charybdis of rampant child exploitation. In saying all this, perhaps poorly, I do not minimize the suffering involved in genuine acts of harm; I am simply calling for more rigor and less hysteria in defining terms, calibrating distinctions, and investigating claims (some of which will be false). I have tried to show how hypertrophied conceptions of harm have harmful effects.

Ethical dilemmas cannot be outrun; these are deeply rooted in the nature of human social intercourse. In the end the risks involved in ethnographic representation seem to me to be similar to those involved in any other sort of representation. Saying, observing, and depicting are implicated in power, value, and hierarchy of various sorts. We write, we talk, we try to relate things that happened to ideas about good and right. In writing about injustice or injury, one encounters both moral hazards and ethical imperatives. Such writing need not reproduce the condition of unhappiness, because good representation, as Gadamer says, is not about copying or reproducing but about showing.[5] I hope that I have shown.

Notes

INTRODUCTION

1. I am hardly the first to note this. See James R. Kincaid, *Erotic Innocence: The Culture of Child Molesting* (Durham, N.C.: Duke University Press, 1998).

2. Solomon Moore, "Using Muscle to Improve Health Care for Prisoners," *New York Times*, August 27, 2007, A12.

3. See Barry Glassner, *The Culture of Fear: Why Americans Are Afraid of the Wrong Things* (New York: Basic, 1999), 3, 5, 17, 119; Erich Goode and Nachman Ben-Yehuda, *Moral Panics: The Social Construction of Deviance*, 2nd ed. (Malden, Mass.: Wiley-Blackwell, 2009), ix.

4. Abusive driving was no small matter: before the law's repeal, penalties included the possibility of jail time, and fines ran as high as $3,000. See Tom Jackman, "Hefty Fees in Store for Misbehaving Va. Drivers," *Washington Post*, June 23, 2007, A01; Tim Craig, "Legislators' Short View Killed Va. Driving Fees; Repeal of 'Bad Law' Expected Today," *Washington Post*, March 8, 2008, B01.

5. Al Gore, *The Assault on Reason* (New York: Penguin, 2007), 3–4.

6. See, for instance, Alexandra Juhasz and Jesse Lerner, eds., *F Is for Phony: Fake Documentary and Truth's Undoing* (Minneapolis: University of Minnesota Press, 2007).

7. Margaret Carlson, "A Murder in Boston: Presumed Innocent," *Time*, January 22, 1990, 10–14.

8. "The denunciation of scandal always pays homage to the law" (Jean Baudrillard, *Selected Writings*, ed. Mark Poster [Stanford, Calif.: Stanford University Press, 1988], 173).

9. Florida sets a lower age of consent, sixteen, if the older party is younger than twenty-four.

10. Abby Goodnough, with Christine Jordan Sexton, "Foley Was Sexually Abused as a Youth, His Lawyer Says," *New York Times,* October 4, 2006, A26; user comments, "Foley Unlikely to be Prosecuted; Lewd Internet Messages Too Old," *ABC News: The Blotter,* September 14, 2007, http://blogs.abcnews.com/theblotter/2007/09/foley-unlikely-.html (accessed November 13, 2009).

11. Robert L. Jacobson, "'Meagan's Laws' Reinforcing Old Patterns of Anti-Gay Police Harassment," *Georgetown Law Journal* 81 (1998–99): 2456. See also Laud Humphreys, *Tearoom Trade: Impersonal Sex in Public Places* (New York: Aldine, 1970), 98–99, 101–102; John Hollister, "A Highway Rest Area as a Socially Reproducible Site," in *Public Sex/Gay Space,* ed. William Leap (New York: Columbia University Press, 1999), 59–60.

12. The imaginary child was first described by Lauren Berlant, who shows how this figure grounds ubiquitous "narratives of rescue" under neoliberal capitalism. Drawing on queer theory and psychoanalysis, Lee Edelman sees the imaginary child as central to homophobic culture's collective imagination. See Lauren Berlant, *The Queen of America Goes to Washington City* (Durham, N.C.: Duke University Press, 1997), and Lee Edelman, *No Future: Queer Theory and the Death Drive* (Durham, N.C.: Duke University Press, 2004).

13. James R. Kincaid suggests that innocence itself has been eroticized in what he calls America's evolving "culture of child molesting." The purer the child is imagined to be, the greater the danger of his or her defilement—and the greater the thrill some adults experience in performing rites of protection. See Kindcaid, *Erotic Innocence,* esp. 14–16, 54–55, 102–106.

14. "Parents Search for Children Swept Away," CNN.com, January 10, 2005, www.cnn.com/2005/WORLD/asiapcf/01/05/missing.children/index.html; "Fears Rise of Child Trafficking," Fox News.com, January 4, 2005, www.foxnews.com/story/0,2933,143320,00.html; Kelly Beaucar Vlahos, "Aid Workers: Tsunami Child Exploitation Rare," Fox News.com, July 16, 2005, www.foxnews.com/story/0,2933,162752,00.html.

15. David Usborne, "The Dispossessed of New Orleans Tell of Their Medieval Nightmare," *Independent,* September 4, 2005, A8–9.

16. Joseph R. Chenelly, "Troops Begin Combat Operations in New Orleans," *Army Times,* September 2, 2005, www.armytimes.com/legacy/new/1-292925-1077495.php (accessed November 13, 2009).

17. Terry Klierwer, "Juvenile Sex Cases on Upswing: Young Suspects Put Strain on Montgomery County," *Houston Chronicle,* April 1, 2004, A19.

18. Judith Levine, *Harmful to Minors: The Perils of Protecting Children from Sex* (Minneapolis: University of Minnesota Press, 2002), 46.

19. Ray Rivera, "Council Bans Metal Bats in High School, with Veto-Proof Vote," *New York Times,* March 15, 2007, B12.

20. Associated Press, "Police: Wisconsin College Student's Abduction Story Was a Hoax," *USA Today,* April 2, 2004, www.usatoday.com/news/nation/2004-04-02-missing-student_x.htm.

21. Susan Faludi, *The Terror Dream: Fear and Fantasy in Post-9/11 America* (New York: Metropolitan, 2007), 215–16, 262, 289. See also Faludi, "America's Guardian Myths," *New York Times,* September 7, 2007. Susan Jeffords developed an earlier version of this argument in an essay about what she calls "sce-

narios of protection"; see Jeffords, "Rape and the New World Order," *Cultural Critique* 19 (autumn 1991): 201–15.

22. Gary Younge, "The Good Victim," *Nation,* May 7, 2007, 12.

23. Jonathan Simon situates his discussion of new sex offender laws in a context in which risk assessment and risk management have become central concerns in judicial decision making. See Simon, "Managing the Monstrous: Sex Offenders and the New Penology," *Psychology, Public Policy, and Law* 4, no. 1/2 (1998): 453.

24. Vikki Henlie Sturgeon and John Taylor, "Report of a Five Year Follow-Up Study of Mentally Disordered Sex Offenders Released from Atascadero State Hospital in 1973," *Criminal Justice Journal* 4 (1980–81): 58; Center for Sex Offender Management, "Recidivism of Sex Offenders," May 2001, U.S. Department of Justice, Washington, D.C., www.csom.org/pubs/recidsexof.pdf (accessed November 13, 2009), 9; Karl Hanson and Kelly Morton-Bourgon, "Predicting Relapse: A Meta-Analysis of Sexual Offender Recidivism Studies," *Journal of Consulting and Clinical Psychology* 66, no. 2 (1998), 348–62. On the general use of recidivism statistics to guide policy and punishment, see Roxanne Lieb, Vernon Quinsey, and Lucy Berliner, "Sexual Predators and Social Policy," *Crime and Justice* 23 (1998): 43–114.

25. This is scarcely terra incognita among progressive intellectuals. See, for instance, Corey Robin, *Fear: The History of a Political Idea* (Oxford: Oxford University Press, 2004), and Naomi Wolf, *The End of America: Letter of Warning to a Young Patriot* (White River Junction, Vt.: Chelsea Green, 2007).

26. Glasser, *Culture of Fear.*

27. Thomas Friedman, "9/11 Is Over," *New York Times,* September 30, 2007.

28. Franklin E. Zimring, *The Great American Crime Decline* (Oxford: Oxford University Press, 2007).

29. See, for instance, Michael K. Brown et al., *Whitewashing Race: The Myth of a Color-Blind Society* (Berkeley: University of California Press), 132–60; Michael Tonry, *Malign Neglect: Race, Crime, and Punishment in America* (Oxford: Oxford University Press, 1995); Bruce Western, *Punishment and Inequality in America* (New York: Russell Sage, 2006); Kofi Buenor Hadjor, *Another America: The Politics of Race and Blame* (Boston: South End Press, 1995); Michael Welch, Melissa Fenwick, and Meredith Roberts, "Primary Definitions of Crime and Moral Panic: A Content Analysis of Experts' Quotes in Feature Newspaper Articles on Crime," *Journal of Research in Crime and Delinquency* 34, no. 4 (1997): 474–94; Michael Welch, Eric A. Price, and Nana Yankley, "Moral Panic over Youth Violence," *Youth and Society* 34, no. 1 (2002): 3–30.

30. Terry Thomas, *Sex Crimes: Sex Offending and Society* (Portland, Ore.: Willan, 2005), 1.

31. Faludi, *Terror Dream*; Jeffords, "Rape and the New World Order."

32. "No Easy Answers: Sex Offender Laws in the US," *Human Rights Watch* 19, no. 4(G) (September 2007), www.hrw.org/en/reports/2007/09/11/no-easy-answers; Georgia Harlem, "America's Unjust Sex Laws," *Economist,* August 6, 2009, 9.

33. Steve Herbert and Elizabeth Brown, "Conceptions of Space and Crime in the Punitive Neoliberal City," *Antipode* 38, no. 4 (2006): 755–77; Michael Sherry, "Dead or Alive: American Vengeance Goes Global," *Review of International Relations* (London) 31, supplement S1 (December 2005): 245–63.

34. Jeffrey Weeks, *Sex, Politics and Society: The Regulation of Sexuality since 1800* (New York: Longman, 1989), 13, 232–44; Gail Bederman, *Manliness and Civilization: A Cultural History of Gender and Race in the United States, 1880–1917* (Chicago: University of Chicago Press, 1995).

35. Naomi Klein, *The Shock Doctrine: The Rise of Disaster Capitalism* (New York: Metropolitan, 2007).

36. See Jonathan Simon, "Ghosts of the Disciplinary Machine: Lee Harvey Oswald, Life-History, and the Truth of Crime," *Yale Journal of Law and the Humanities* 10, no. 1 (1998): 75–113.

37. I am skeptical of accounts that trace only the disappearance of *overt* reference to homosexuality from notions of deviance and sex offender laws. See John Pratt, "The Rise and Fall of Homophobia and Sexual Psychopath Legislation in Postwar Society," *Psychology, Public Policy, and Law* 4, no. 1/2 (1998): 25–49 (esp. 45).

38. Stanley Cohen, *Folk Devils and Moral Panics*, 30th anniv. ed. (1972; repr., New York: Routledge, 2002); Jeffrey Weeks, *Sexuality and Its Discontents: Meanings, Myths, and Modern Sexualities* (New York: Routledge, 1985), 44–53; Gayle Rubin, "Thinking Sex: Notes for a Radical Theory of the Politics of Sexuality," in *Pleasure and Danger: Exploring Female Sexuality*, ed. Carole S. Vance, 2nd ed. (London: Pandora, 1992), 267–319.; Estelle B. Freedman, "'Uncontrolled Desires': The Response to the Sexual Psychopath, 1920–1960," *Journal of American History* 74, no. 1 (1987): 83–106; Simon Watney, *Policing Desire: Pornography, AIDS, and the Media*, 3rd ed. (Minneapolis: University of Minnesota Press, 1997), 38–57.

39. Berlant, *Queen of America*.

PART ONE

1. Fredrick Kunkle, "Caught in a Neighborhood Web: Innocent Man Mistaken for Registered Offender," *Washington Post*, May 13, 2006, A01.

2. Roger Caillois, *Man, Play and Games*, trans. Meyer Barash (1958; repr., Urbana: University of Illinois Press, 2001), 81–97, 132–36.

CHAPTER 1. PANIC

1. Stanley Cohen, *Folk Devils and Moral Panics*, 30th anniv. ed. (1972; repr., New York: Routledge, 2002); Jeffrey Weeks, *Sex, Politics, and Society: The Regulation of Sexuality since 1800* (London: Longman, 1981); Erich Goode and Nachman Ben-Yehuda, *Moral Panics: The Social Construction of Deviance* (New York: Blackwell, 1994).

2. Paul Boyer and Stephan Nissenbaum, *Salem Possessed: The Social Origins of Witchcraft* (Cambridge, Mass.: Harvard University Press, 1974); Robert

Griffith, *The Politics of Fear: Joseph R. McCarthy and the Senate* (1970; repr., Amherst: University of Massachusetts Press, 1987).

3. A.F.C. Wallace, "Revitalization Movements," *American Anthropologist* 58, no. 2 (1956): 264–81.

4. A.R. Radcliffe-Brown, "Taboo," in *Reader in Comparative Religion,* ed. William A. Lessa and Evon Z. Vogt (Evanston, Ill.: Harper and Row, 1979), 46–56.

5. Sir James George Frazer, *The Golden Bough: A Study in Magic and Religion,* vol. 9, pt. 6, *The Scapegoat* (1920; repr., New York: Elibron Classics, 2005).

6. See J. Edward Chamberlain and Sander L. Gilman, eds., *Degeneration: The Dark Side of Progress* (New York: Columbia University Press, 1985).

7. Joel Best and Gerald T. Horiuchi, "The Razor Blade in the Apple: The Social Construction of Urban Legends," *Social Problems* 32, no. 5 (June 1985): 488–99.

8. James R. Kincaid, *Erotic Innocence: The Culture of Child Molesting* (Durham, N.C.: Duke University Press, 1998), 93–95.

9. Christopher Diffee, "Sex in the City: The White Slavery Scare and Social Governance in the Progressive Era," *American Quarterly* 57, no. 2 (June 2005): 411–37; Gail Bederman, *Manliness and Civilization: A Cultural History of Gender and Race in the United States, 1880–1917* (Chicago: University of Chicago Press, 1995), 20–22.

10. Cohen, *Folk Devils and Moral Panics.* The term itself was coined a year earlier in Jock Young's study of drug alarms; see Young, "The Role of the Police as Amplifiers of Deviancy, Negotiators of Reality and Translators of Fantasy: Some Aspects of Our Present System of Drug Control as Seen in Notting Hill," in *Images of Deviance,* ed. Stuart Hall (New York: Penguin, 1971), 27–61.

11. David K. Johnson, *The Lavender Scare: The Cold War Persecution of Gays and Lesbians in the Federal Government* (Chicago: University of Chicago Press, 2003). See Neil Miller's account of sexual McCarthyism in Sioux City, Iowa, *Sex-Crime Panic: A Journey to the Paranoid Heart of the 1950s* (Los Angeles: Alyson Books, 2002).

12. Georg Simmel, "The Metropolis and Mental Life," in *The Sociology of Georg Simmel,* ed. Kurt H. Wolff (Glencoe, Ill.: Free Press, 1950), 413–15; Todd Gitlin, *Media Unlimited: How the Torrent of Images and Sounds Overwhelms Our Lives* (New York: Henry Holt, 2001), 36–42.

13. Jean Baudrillard, *Selected Writings,* ed. Mark Poster (Stanford, Calif.: Stanford University Press, 1988), 171.

14. Thomas Shevory, *Notorious HIV: The Media Spectacle of Nushawn Williams* (Minneapolis: University of Minnesota Press, 2004), 4.

15. Paul Virilio, *The Original Accident,* trans. Julie Rose (Cambridge: Polity, 2007), 26, 62.

16. Stuart Hall, Chas Critcher, Tony Jefferson, John Clark, and Brian Roberts, *Policing the Crisis: Mugging, the State, and Law and Order* (New York: Holmes and Meier, 1978).

17. Ibid., 278, 217, 219; Stuart Hall and Martin Jacques, *The Politics of Thatcherism.* (London: Lawrence and Wishart, 1983), 10.

18. It is true that some countries with a minimum legal drinking age of eighteen have higher traffic fatality rates than the United States. But many industrial democracies have set legal drinking ages between sixteen and eighteen—and these generally have significantly lower traffic fatality rates than the United States, whether the rates are measured per million vehicles or per million inhabitants (*OECD Factbook 2009: Economic, Environmental, and Social Statistics*, rev. ed. [Paris: OECD, 2009], 270–71).

19. Joel Best, *Threats to Children: Rhetoric and Concern about Child-Victims* (Chicago: University of Chicago Press, 1990).

20. Orlando Patterson, "The Red Phone in Black and White," *New York Times*, March 11, 2008.

21. Steven Epstein and April N. Huff, "Sex, Science, and the Politics of Biomedicine: Gardasil in Comparative Perspective," in *The HPV Vaccine and Sexual Risk: Citizens and States at the Crossroads of Cancer Prevention*, ed. Keith Wailoo, Julie Livingston, Steven Epstein, and Robert Aronowitz (Baltimore Johns Hopkins University Press, forthcoming).

22. Edgar J. McManus, *A History of Negro Slavery in New York* (Syracuse, N.Y.: Syracuse University Press, 1966), esp. 121–40; William F. Cheek, *Black Resistance before the Civil War* (Los Angeles: Glencoe, 1970), 32; Jill Lepore, "The Tightening Vice: Slavery and Freedom in British New York," in *Slavery in New York*, ed. Ira Berlin and Leslie M. Harris (New York: New Press, 2005), 78; Gunnar Myrdal, *An American Dilemma: The Negro Problem and American Democracy* (1944; repr., New York: Transaction, 1996), 2:561–62, 1356; Jennifer Lynn Ritterhouse, *Growing Up Jim Crow: How Black and White Southern Children Learned Race* (Chapel Hill: University of North Carolina Press, 2006), 36, 72–78; C. Vann Woodward, *The Strange Career of Jim Crow* (1955; repr., Oxford: Oxford University Press, 2002), 86–87; Glenda Gilmore, *Gender and Jim Crow: Women and the Politics of White Supremacy in North Carolina, 1896–1920* (Chapel Hill: University of North Carolina Press, 1996), 88, 117; Lisa Cardyn, "Sexualized Racism/Gendered Violence: Outraging the Body Politic in the Reconstruction South," *Michigan Law Review* 100, no. 4 (February 2002): 675–867.

23. Kristian Williams, "The Demand for Order and the Birth of Modern Policing," *Monthly Review* 55, no. 7 (2003): 1–9; Judith R. Walkowitz, *City of Dreadful Delight: Narratives of Sexual Danger in Late-Victorian London* (Chicago: University of Chicago Press, 1992).

24. Michel Foucault, *The History of Sexuality, Vol. 1: An Introduction* (New York: Vintage, 1980), 122–27. Ann Stoler develops an analysis of the wider sites of European colonialism where the bourgeoisie invented itself at the crossroads of sex and race. See Ann Stoler, *Race and the Education of Desire: Foucault's History of Sexuality and the Colonial Order of Things* (Durham, N.C.: Duke University Press, 1995).

25. One result is that liberal reforms often have conservative consequences, as Barbara Nelson shows in her perceptive study, *Making an Issue of Child Abuse: Political Agenda Setting for Social Problems* (Chicago: University of Chicago Press, 1984).

26. William G. McLoughlin, *Revivals, Awakenings and Reform: An Essay on Religion and Social Change in America, 1607–1977* (Chicago: University of

Chicago Press, 1978); Frank Lambert, *Inventing the "Great Awakening"* (Princeton, N.J.: Princeton University Press, 1999).

27. Jeffrey Weeks, *Sexuality and Its Discontents: Meanings, Myths and Modern Sexualities* (London: Routledge and Kegan Paul, 1985), 44.

28. Bruce Burgett, "Sex, Panic, Nation," *American Literary History* 21, no. 1 (spring 2009): 76. See also Cindy Patton, "Outlaw Territory: Criminality, Neighborhoods, and the Edward Savitz Case," *Sexuality Research and Social Policy* 2, no. 2 (June, 2005): 74.

29. Janice M. Irvine, "Emotional Scripts of Sex Panics," *Sexual Research and Social Policy* 3, no. 3 (September 2006): 82–94.

30. Weeks, *Sexuality and Its Discontents,* 45.

31. Estelle B. Freedman, "'Uncontrolled Desires': The Response to the Sexual Psychopath, 1920–1960," *Journal of American History* 74, no. 1 (1987): 83–106.

32. Ibid., 94, 92–93.

33. Miller, *Sex-Crime Panic,* 22, 79, 85.

34. Freedman, "'Uncontrolled Desires,'" 83–84.

35. Ibid., 88, 95–97; Stephen Robertson, "Separating the Men from the Boys: Masculinity, Psychosexual Development, and Sex Crime in the United States, 1930s–1960s," *Journal of the History of Medicine* 56 (January 2001): 12. On the second wave see also George Chauncey, "The Post-War Sex Crime Panic," in *True Stories from the American Past,* ed. William Graebner (New York: McGraw Hill, 1993).

36. Freedman, "'Uncontrolled Desires,'" 93, 96, 84, 91–92, 101.

37. Ibid., 98–99, and esp. 103–104; Miller, *Sex-Crime Panic,* 81–82.

38. "Queer People," *Newsweek,* October 10, 1949; "The Unknown Sex Fiend," *Time,* February 13, 1950; "Crime in California," *Time,* March 2, 1953.

39. Miller, *Sex-Crime Panic;* John Gerassi, *The Boys of Boise: Furor, Vice, and Folly in an American City* (1966; repr., Seattle: University of Washington Press, 2001, 290.

40. Philip Jenkins, *Moral Panic: Changing Concepts of the Child Molester in Modern America* (New Haven, Conn.: Yale University Press, 1998), 23; Freedman, "'Uncontrolled Desires,'" 92–94, 98, 99, 103–104.

41. Freedman, "'Uncontrolled Desires,'" 95–96, 100. Alfred C. Kinsey, Wardell B. Pomeroy, and Clyde E. Martin, *Sexual Behavior in the Human Male* (Philadelphia: W.B. Saunders, 1948), and Alfred C. Kinsey, Wardell B. Pomeroy, Clyde E. Martin, and Paul H. Gebhard, *Sexual Behavior in the Human Female* (Philadelphia: W.B. Saunders, 1953).

42. Jenkins, *Moral Panic,* 4, 8, 13–15.

43. Freedman, "'Uncontrolled Desires,'" 97–98, 102.

44. Ann Laura Stoler, *Carnal Knowledge and Imperial Power: Race and the Intimate in Colonial Rule* (Berkeley: University of California Press, 2002), 61–62; Siobahn Sommerville, "Scientific Racism and the Construction of the Homosexual Body," in *The Gender/Sexuality Reader: Culture, History, Political Economy,* ed. Roger N. Lancaster and Micaela di Leonardo (New York: Routledge, 1997), 41–56; Jennifer Terry, "Anxious Slippages between 'Us' and 'Them': A Brief History of the Scientific Search for Homosexual Bodies," in *Deviant*

Bodies, ed. Jennifer Terry and Jacqueline Urla (Bloomington: Indiana University Press, 1995), 129–69.

45. Robertson, "Separating the Men from the Boys," 5, 23–25.

46. Foucault, *History of Sexuality,* 41–47, 120–22.

47. Bertram Pollens, *The Sex Criminal* (New York: Macaulay, 1938), 50–51, quoted in Robertson, "Separating the Men from the Boys," 28.

48. Freedman, "'Uncontrolled Desires,'" 96–97, 103–104.

49. Jenkins, *Moral Panic,* 63–64.

CHAPTER 2. INNOCENTS AT HOME

1. Daniel Patrick Moynihan, *The Negro Family: The Case for National Action* (Washington D.C.: U.S. Department of Labor, March 1965). See also Micaela di Leonardo, "The Neoliberalization of Minds, Spaces, and Bodies: Rising Global Inequality and the Shifting American Public Sphere," in *New Landscapes of Inequality: Neoliberalism and the Erosion of Democracy in America,* ed. Jane L. Collins, Micaela di Leonardo, and Brett Williams (Santa Fe, N.Mex.: School for Advanced Research Press, 2008), 202–203.

2. Jeffrey Weeks, *Sexuality and Its Discontents: Meanings, Myths and Modern Sexualities* (London: Routledge and Kegan Paul, 1985), 40.

3. Kevin Ohi, "Molestation 101: Child Abuse, Homophobia, and the Boys of St. Vincent," *GLQ: A Journal of Lesbian and Gay Studies* 6. no. 2 (2000): 195; Lee Edelman, *No Future: Queer Theory and the Death Drive* (Durham, N.C.: Duke University Press, 2004), 112–13.

4. Anita Bryant, *The Anita Bryant Story: The Survival of Our Nation's Families and the Threat of Militant Homosexuality* (Old Tappan, N.J.: Fleming H. Revell, 1977), 114; Hans Johnson and William Eskridge, "The Legacy of Falwell's Bully Pulpit," *Washington Post,* May 19, 2007, A17.

5. D.E. Newton, "Homosexual Behavior and Child Molestation: A Review of the Evidence," *Adolescence* 13 (1978): 29–43; Carole Jenny and Thomas A. Roesler, "Are Children at Risk for Sexual Abuse by Homosexuals?" *Pediatrics* 94, no. 1 (1994): 41–44; M.R. Stevenson, "Public Policy, Homosexuality, and the Sexual Coercion of Children" *Journal of Psychology and Human Sexuality* 12, no. 4 (2000): 8, 15.

6. Howard Snyder, "Sexual Assault of Young Children as Reported to Law Enforcement: Victim, Incident and Offender Characteristics," U.S. Department of Justice, Washington, D.C., July 2000, National Criminal Justice Reference Service no. 182990.

7. "Homosexuality: Gays on the March," *Time,* September 8, 1975; "Chicago Is Center of National Child Porno Ring," *Chicago Tribune,* May 16, 1977, A01; U.S. House of Representatives, *Sexual Exploitation of Children: Hearings before the Subcommittee on Crime of the Committee on the Judiciary* (Washington, D.C.: Government Printing Office, 1977), 205; Philip Jenkins, *Decade of Nightmares: The End of the Sixties and the Making of Eighties America* (New York: Oxford University Press, 2006), 119, 121. See also Philip Jenkins, *Moral Panic: Changing Concepts of the Child Molester in Modern America* (New Haven, Conn.: Yale University Press, 1998), 121–25.

8. Robin Lloyd, *For Money or Love: Boy Prostitution in America* (New York: Vanguard, 1976).

9. Kerwin Kaye, "Male Prostitution in the Twentieth Century: Pseudohomosexuals, Hoodlum Homosexuals, and Exploited Teens," *Journal of Homosexuality* 46, no. 1/2 (2003): 42–46.

10. Philippe Ariès, *Centuries of Childhood: A Social History of Family Life* (New York: Alfred A. Knopf, 1962); George Boas, *The Cult of Childhood* (London: Warburg, 1966).

11. Marie Winn, "What Became of Childhood?" *New York Times Magazine,* January 25, 1981, 68.

12. Debbie Nathan, "Inside the Satan-Scare Industry: The Devil Made Them Do It," *In These Times,* January 1, 2003; Bill Ellis, *Raising the Devil: Satanism, New Religions, and the Media* (Lexington: University of Kentucky Press, 2000); James T. Richardson, Joel Best, and David G. Bromley, *The Satanism Scare* (New York: Aldine de Gruyter, 1991).

13. See, for instance, Ian Hacking's excellent essay, "Kind-Making: The Case of Child Abuse," in *The Social Construction of What?* (Cambridge, Mass.: Harvard University Press, 1999), 125–62.

14. Barbara Nelson, *Making an Issue of Child Abuse: Political Agenda Setting for Social Problems* (Chicago: University of Chicago Press, 1984), 2–3, 15, 17–19.

15. Nathan dissects this trend in "What McMartin Started: The Ritual Sex Abuse Hoax," *Village Voice,* June 12, 1990, 36–44. She marks the denial, then redefinition, of incest, citing a passage by Judith Herman: "Because a child is powerless in relation to an adult, . . . any sexual relationship between the two must necessarily take on some of the coercive characteristics of rape." This equation of a power imbalance with the powerlessness experienced by rape victims has far-reaching consequences, especially in the context of expanding definitions of *child* and *sex.* See Judith Lewis Herman, *Father-Daughter Incest* (1981; repr., Cambridge, Mass.: Harvard University Press, 2000), 27; Florence Rush, *The Best-Kept Secret: Sexual Abuse of Children* (New York: Prentice Hall, 1980), 187.

16. Susan Brownmiller, *Against Our Will: Men, Women, and Rape* (New York: Bantam, 1975).

17. Again, see Nathan's discussion, "What McMartin Started"; Herman, *Father-Daughter Incest,* 27; Diana Russell, *The Politics of Rape: The Victim's Perspective* (New York: Stein and Day, 1979), 117; Diana E.H. Russell, *The Secret Trauma: Incest in the Lives of Girls and Women,* rev. ed. (New York: Basic, 1999), 42 55; David Finkelhor, *Sexually Victimized Children* (New York: Free Press, 1979), 50–52, 55–57.

18. Andrea Dworkin, *Intercourse* (New York: Free Press, 1987), 122. See also Catherine A. MacKinnon, "Liberalism and the Death of Feminism," in *The Sexual Liberals and the Attack on Feminism,* ed. Dorchen Leidholdt and Janice G. Raymond (New York: Pergamon, 1990), 4.

19. Carole Vance, "More Danger, More Pleasure: A Decade after the Barnard Sexuality Conference," in *Pleasure and Danger: Exploring Female Sexuality,* 2nd ed. (London: Pandora, 1992), xviii.

20. Unlike sex panics of the mid-twentieth century, which were largely orchestrated by male conservatives, feminists of a certain sort were centrally involved in the production of the new sex panics. See Estelle B. Freedman, "'Uncontrolled Desires': The Response to the Sexual Psychopath, 1920–1960," *Journal of American History* 74, no. 1 (1987): 96.

21. The mid- to late 1970s, when remnants of the counterculture gazed inward at the life of the psyche rather than outward at the world of social relations, had been a seedbed for implausible new ideas about the self, its shaping, and its actualization. Most notable among the new theories to flourish after 1980 was the psychoanalysis of "repressed" or "recovered" memories. See Wendy Kaminer, *Sleeping with Extra-Terrestrials: The Rise of Irrationalism and the Perils of Piety* (New York: Pantheon, 1999).

22. Mark Pendergrast, *Victims of Memory: Sex Abuse Accusations and Shattered Lives* (Hinesburg, Vt.: Upper Access, 1996); Hollida Wakefield and Ralph C. Underwager, *Return of the Furies: An Investigation into Recovered Memory Therapy* (Chicago: Open Court, 1994).

23. Michelle Smith and Lawrence Pazder, *Michelle Remembers* (New York: Congdon and Lattès, 1980).

24. Maggie Jones, "Who Was Abused?" *New York Times Magazine*, September 10, 2004, 77.

25. Debbie Nathan and Michael Snedeker, *Satan's Silence: Ritual Abuse and the Making of a Modern American Witch Hunt* (New York: Basic, 1995), 67–92. See also David L. Altheide, *Creating Fear: News and the Construction of Crisis* (Hawthorne, N.Y.: Aldine de Gruyter, 2002), 147–49; Mary De Young, *The Day Care Ritual Abuse Moral Panic* (Jefferson, N.C.: McFarland, 2004). Doug Linder, a law professor at the University of Missouri–Kansas City, has written an excellent overview of the trial and compiled a useful source archive: "Famous Trials: The McMartin Preschool Abuse Trials, 1987–90," 2003, www.law.umkc.edu/faculty/projects/ftrials/mcmartin/mcmartin.html.

26. Steven Strasser with Elizabeth Bailey, "A Sordid Preschool 'Game,'" *Newsweek*, April 9, 1984, 38; John Leo, "'Someday I'll Cry My Eyes Out'; A California Case Prompts New Awareness of Child Molestation," *Time*, April 23, 1984, 72–73; "Brutalized: Sex Charges at a Nursery," *Time*, April 2, 1984; "Crime and Punishment," *Time*, May 7, 1984.

27. Nadine Brozan, "Witness Says She Fears 'Child Predator' Network," *New York Times*, September 18, 1984, A21.

28. Elizabeth Holtzman, "To Help Prosecute Child Molesters," *New York Times*, March 28, 1984, A27.

29. "Child Abuse on the Stand," *Newsweek*, June 24, 1985, 39.

30. Nathan, "What McMartin Started," 38.

31. Margaret Talbot, "Against Innocence: The Truth about Child Abuse and the Truth about Children," *New Republic*, March 15, 1999, 27.

32. "A Child-Abuse Case Implodes," *Newsweek*, January 27, 1986, 26.

33. Nathan, "What McMartin Started," 37–38.

34. Talbot, "Against Innocence," 28.

35. Ibid., 30.

36. See Nathan, "What McMartin Started," 36–44.

37. See Bernard Baran Justice Committee, "Thank You for Helping Us Free Bernard Baran," n.d., www.freebaran.org/ (accessed July 1, 2009).

38. See Free the West Memphis Three Support Fund, "An Urgent Message from WM3.org," February 2010, www.wm3.org (accessed July 1, 2009).

39. Nathan and Snedeker, *Satan's Silence.*

40. Elizabeth Loftus, "The Reality of Repressed Memories," *American Psychologist* 48 (1993): 518–37; Elizabeth F. Loftus and Katherine Ketcham, *The Myth of Repressed Memory* (New York: St. Martin's, 1994); Elizabeth Loftus, "Creating False Memories," *Scientific American* 227, no. 3 (September 1997): 70–75; Elizabeth F. Loftus, "Make-Believe Memories," *American Psychologist* 58, no. 11 (November 2004): 867–73; Richard McNally, *Remembering Trauma* (Cambridge, Mass.: Harvard University Press, 2003), 17–18, 245–46; Richard Ofshe and Ethan Watters, *Making Monsters: False Memories, Psychotherapy, and Sexual Hysteria* (Berkeley: University of California Press, 1996).

41. The American Psychological Association's working paper on repressed memories, and therapies designed to elicit them, stresses that "there is a consensus among memory researchers and clinicians that most people who were sexually abused as children remember all or part of what happened to them although they may not fully understand or disclose it." It goes on to invoke research showing how "it is possible to construct convincing pseudomemories for events that never occurred." It concludes that "at this point it is impossible, without other corroborative evidence, to distinguish a true memory from a false one" (American Psychological Association, "Questions and Answers about Memories of Childhood Abuse," n.d., www.apa.org/topics/memories.html [accessed October 5, 2009]).

42. Claudia Dreifus, "Beyond the Bounds of Betrayal: Men Cope with Being the Victims: A Conversation with Richard Gartner," *New York Times,* March 1, 2005, F5; Stephen Kinzer, "In Stunned City, Priest Is Arraigned in Killing of Nun," *New York Times,* April 27, 2004, A16; "Nun Killer: Priest Gets Life for Satanic Ritual Murder of Sister Margaret," *Irish Daily Mirror,* May 13, 2006, A18.

43. Diana E.H. Russell, *The Secret Trauma: Incest in the Lives of Girls and Women,* rev. ed. (New York: Basic, 1999), 39–44, 53, 60.

44. Alec P. Spencer, *Working with Sex Offenders in Prisons and through Release to the Community: A Handbook* (London and Philadelphia: Jessica Kingsley, 1999), 35; Ellen Bass and Laura Davis, *The Courage to Heal: A Guide for Women Survivors of Child Sexual Abuse* (New York: Harper and Row, 1988), 21.

45. The fuzzy categories and forced memory retrieval techniques presented in *The Courage to Heal* have been repeatedly linked to false memories and false accusations. See Loftus and Ketcham, *Myth of Repressed Memory,* 21–22, 26, 53–55, 149–51, and Frederick C. Crews, *Follies of the Wise: Dissenting Essays* (Emeryville, Calif.: Shoemaker and Hoard, 2004), 91–133, 180.

46. Neil Gilbert, "Miscounting Social Ills," *Society,* March–April 1994, 21; Hacking, "Kind-Making," 143–45.

47. Reagan Morris, "Teacher Admits Molesting Pupils," *New York Times,* August 5, 2006, A9; Al Baker, "D.J. Is Arrested over His Threat to Rival's Child," *New York Times,* May 13, 2006, B1.

48. Talbot, "Against Innocence," 29; Joseph Tobin, *Making a Place for Pleasure in Early Childhood Education* (New Haven, Conn.: Yale University Press, 1997), 119.

49. Gayle Rubin, "Thinking Sex: Notes for a Radical Theory of the Politics of Sexuality," in Vance, *Pleasure and Danger,* 267–319.

50. Frederic G. Reamer, "Social Work: Calling or Career?" *Hastings Center Report* 17, no. 1 (February 1987): 14–15; Richard M. Scheffler and Paul B. Kirby, "The Occupational Transformation of the Mental Health System," *Health Affairs* 22, no. 5 (September–October 2003): 178.

51. Margaret Carlson, Jonathan Beaty, and Elaine Lafferty, "Six Years of Trial by Torture," *Time,* January 29, 1990, 26–27; Richard Lacayo, "Law: Sex Abuse or Abuse of Justice?" *Time,* May 11, 1987, 49.

52. Bruce Rind, Philip Tromovitch, and Robert Bauserman, "A Meta-Analytic Examination of Assumed Properties of Child Sexual Abuse Using College Samples," *Psychological Bulletin* 124, no. 1 (1998): 22–53; Bruce Rind, Philip Tromovitch, and Robert Bauserman, "The Condemned Meta-Analysis on Child Sexual Abuse: Good Science and Long-Overdue Skepticism," *Skeptical Inquirer,* July–August 2001, 68–72.

53. Peter J. Boyer, "The Children of Waco," *New Yorker,* May 15, 1995, 44.

54. U.S. Census Bureau, "Household Income Rises, Poverty Rate Declines, Number of Uninsured Up," press release, August 28, 2007; Robert Longley, "Number of Uninsured, Poverty Rate Both Climb," About.com, August 30, 2004, http://usgovinfo.about.com/od/censusandstatistics/a/censusbadnews.htm; U.S. Department of Health and Human Services, "Overview of the Uninsured in the United States: An Analysis of the 2005 Current Population Survey," *ASPE Issue Brief,* September 22, 2005; Erik Eckholm, "In Turnabout, Infant Deaths Climb in South," *New York Times,* April 22, 2007, A1.

55. Hacking, "Kind-Making," 161.

56. David Garland, *The Culture of Control: Crime and Social Order in Contemporary Society* (Chicago: University of Chicago Press, 2001), 106.

57. Judith Levine, *Harmful to Minors: The Perils of Protecting Children from Sex* (New York: Thunder's Mouth Press, 2003); Janice M. Irvine, *Talk about Sex: The Battles over Sex Education in the U.S.* (Berkeley: University of California Press, 2004).

58. Amelia Hill, "'Stranger Danger' Drive Harms Kids," *(London) Observer,* May 23, 2004, 5.

59. Emily M. Douglas and David M. Finkelhor, "Childhood Sexual Abuse Fact Sheet," Crimes against Children Research Center, May 2005, www.unh.edu/ccrc/factsheet/pdf/childhoodSexualAbuseFactSheet.pdf (accessed October 4, 2009).

60. Levine, *Harmful to Minors,* 47.

61. Judith Levine, "A Question of Abuse," *Mother Jones,* July–August 1996. There are recent signs that the zeal to discover and discipline child sex offenders is waning. See Maggie Jones, "How Can You Distinguish a Budding Pedophile from a Kid with Real Boundary Problems?" *New York Times Magazine,* July 22, 2007; Yvonne Bynoe, "Is That 4-Year-Old Really a Sex Offender?" *Washington Post,* October 21, 2007, B04.

62. Brigid Shulte, "For Little Children, Grown-Up Labels as Sexual Harassers," *Washington Post*, April 3, 2008, A01.

63. Carolyn E. Cocca, *Jailbait: The Politics of Statutory Rape in the United States* (Albany: State University of New York Press, 2004), 11. See also Rita Eidson, "The Constitutionality of Statutory Rape Laws," *UCLA Law Review* 27 (1980): 767.

64. Cocca, *Jailbait*, 12–14.

65. Ibid., 18–21.

66. Ibid., 22.

67. Ibid., 22–24. See also Rigel Oliveri, "Statutory Rape Law and Enforcement in the Wake of Welfare Reform," *Stanford Law Review* 52, no. 2 (January 2000): 463–508.

68. Brenda Goodman, "Man Convicted as Teenager in Sex Case Is Ordered Freed by Georgia Court," *New York Times*, October 27, 2007, A9.

69. American Civil Liberties Union, "Limon v. Kansas—Case Background," September 8, 2005, www.aclu.org/lgbt/discrim/11940res20050908.html; Michael Bronski, "The Other Matthew," *Boston Phoenix*, February 20–27, 2003, www.bostonphoenix.com/boston/news_features/other_stories/documents/02704491.htm (accessed October 4, 2009).

70. David T. Evans, *Sexual Citizenship: The Material Construction of Sexualities* (London: Routledge, 1993), 215.

71. Laura Mansnerus, "Eddie Was Murdered. Sam's Doing 70 Years. But Who Is to Blame?" *New York Times*, August 8, 1999, 14NJ:1.

72. William K. Rashbaum and Kevin McCoy, with Lawrence Goodman, "Boy in Sex-Abuse Cycle; Teen's a Kid Killer— & Victim, Say Cops," *New York Daily News*, October 3, 1997, 6; Carol Ann Campbell and Peggy O'Crowley, "Boy's Slaying Shows Internet's Ferocious Side," *(Bergen County, N.J.) Record*, October 3, 1997, A16; Patrice O'Shaughnessy, "Tragic Cycle of Victims: Ex-Cop Sees a Pattern of Sex Abuse, Youngsters and Murder," *New York Daily News*, October 12, 1997. 32; Phyllis Schlafly, "Activist Judges Rule for Special Interests," *Eagle Forum* 38, no. 2 (September 2004), www.eagleforum.org/psr/2004/sept04/psrsept04.html (accessed October 5, 2009); Lance Morrow, "A Boy Dies in the '90s: Nothing Human Is Foreign? Nothing Foreign Is Human? Choose One," *Time*, October 20, 1997, 120; "Spring Trial Date Possible for Teen in Jackson Murder Case," *Asbury Park Press*, December 8, 1998.

73. Suicidal thoughts and hostile behavior are among the rare side effects of some antidepressant drugs. In 2003 the Food and Drug Administration followed British and other health authorities in warning doctors against prescribing Paxil for pediatric depression.

74. Steve Silberman, "Gay Kids in the Real World," *Wired Magazine*, November 4, 1997, www.wired.com/culture/lifestyle/news/1997/11/8246 (accessed October 4, 2009).

75. Cori Anne Natoli, "Slaying Suspect Sought Help from Child-Abuse Group," *(Bergen County, N.J.) Record* , April 5, 1998, A04; Laura Mansnerus, "Thinking about You," *New York Times*, October 17, 1999, 14NJ; 10; Laura Mansnerus, "Teenager Who Killed Boy Defends Molester as Good Role Model," *New York Times*, October 13, 1999, B5.

CHAPTER 3. TO CATCH A PREDATOR

1. JoAnn Wypijewski notes a similar conflation of major, traumatizing crimes with less violent or fleeting offenses in her review of Judith Levine's book *Harmful to Minors, Nation,* May 20, 2002, 24.

2. Brian Dakss, "New, Damning Evidence vs. Jackson?" *The Early Show,* CBS, January 26, 2005, www.cbsnews.com/stories/2005/01/26/earlyshow/leisure/celebspot/main669375.shtml (accessed May 6, 2010).

3. Karen Terry et al., "The Nature and Scope of the Problem of Sexual Abuse of Minors by Priests and Deacons in the United States, 1950–2003," prepared by the John Jay College of Criminal Justice for the U.S. Council of Catholic Bishops, Washington, D.C., 2004, www.bishop-accountability.org/reports/2004_02_27_JohnJay/; for the executive summary, see www.usccb.org/nrb/johnjay-study/exec.pdf.

4. Ibid. See also Karen Terry et al., "2006 Supplementary Report: The Nature and Scope of the Problem of Sexual Abuse of Minors by Priests and Deacons in the United States, 1950–2003," prepared by the John Jay College of Criminal Justice for the U.S. Council of Catholic Bishops, Washington, D.C., 2006, www.usccb.org/ocyp/JohnJayReport.pdf.

5. Philip Jenkins, *Pedophiles and Priests: Anatomy of a Contemporary Crisis* (Oxford: Oxford University Press, 1996), 7.

6. JoAnn Wypijewski, "Priest Abuse and Recovered Memory: The Passion of Paul Shanley," *Legal Affairs,* September–October 2004, www.legalaffairs.org/issues/September-October-2004/feature_wypijewski_sepocto4.msp (accessed November 19, 2009).

7. Ibid.

8. Sacha Pfeiffer, "Famed 'Street Priest' Preyed upon Boys," *Boston Globe,* January 31, 2002, A21; Sally Jacobs, "'If They Knew the Madness in Me': A Search for the Real Rev. Paul Shanley Suggests That He Was Part Hero, Part Horror," *Boston Globe,* July 10, 2002, F1; Wendy Davis, "Memory Questioned in Abuse Case: Lawyer Cites Possible Contradiction," *Boston Globe,* April 8, 2003, B1; Katie Zezima and Benedict Carey, "Ex-Priest Challenges Abuse Conviction on Repressed Memories," *New York Times,* September 11, 2009, A13; "Massachusetts: Court Upholds Ex-Priest's Conviction," *New York Times,* January 16, 2010, A16.

9. Abby Goodnough, "After 2 Cases in Florida, Crackdown on Molesters," *New York Times,* April 30, 2005, A26.

10. I derive these numbers from various studies produced by the Office of Juvenile Justice and Delinquency Prevention and published in *National Incidence Studies of Missing, Abducted, Runaway, and Thrownaway Children (NISMART),* U.S. Department of Justice, Washington, D.C. See, for instance, Heather Hammer, David Finkelhor, Andrea J. Sedlak, and Lorraine E. Porcellini, "National Estimates of Missing Children, Selected Trends: 1988–1999," December 2004, National Criminal Justice Reference Service no. 206179, www.ncjrs.gov/pdffiles1/ojjdp/206179.pdf, and David Finkelhor, Heather Hammer, and Andrea J. Sedlak, "Nonfamily Abducted Children: National Estimates and Characteristics," October 2002, National Criminal Justice Reference Service no. 196469, www.ncjrs.gov/pdffiles1/ojjdp/196467.pdf.

11. Statistical Assessment Service, "Phony Numbers on Child Abduction," STATS.org, August 1, 2002, www.stats.org/stories/2002/phony_aug01_02.htm (accessed October 5, 2009); John D. Whittaker, "Evaluation of Acceptable Risk," *Journal of the Operational Research Society* 37, no. 6 (June 1986): 542.

12. National MCH (Maternal and Child Health) Center for Child Death Review, "United States Child Mortality, 2002," n.d.,www.childdeathreview.org/Nat<#213>l%20Data%20Webpage%202002_files/US2002.pdf.

13. I derive these figures from government documents. The U.S. Department of Health and Human Services provides Child Maltreatment Annual Reports at www.acf.hhs.gov/programs/cb/stats_research/. See also U.S. Department of Health and Human Services, "Child Abuse and Neglect Fatalities: Statistics and Interventions," Child Welfare Information Gateway, April 30, 2010, www .childwelfare.gov/pubs/factsheets/fatality.cfm.

14. See Malcolm Feeley and Jonathan Simon, "Folk Devils and Moral Panics: An Appreciation from North America," in *Crime, Social Control and Human Rights: From Moral Panics to States of Denial, Essays in Honour of Stanley Cohen,* ed. David Downes, Paul Rock, Christine Chinkin, and Conor Gearty (Portland, Ore.: Willan, 2007), 46–48; Office of Justice Programs, "Frequently Asked Questions on AMBER Alert," n.d., U.S. Department of Justice, Washington, D.C., www.amberalert.gov/faqs.htm (accessed September 26, 2006).

15. Howard Snyder, "Sexual Assault of Young Children as Reported to Law Enforcement: Victim, Incident and Offender Characteristics," U.S. Department of Justice, Washington, D.C., July 2000, 10, National Criminal Justice Reference Service no. 182990.

16. Patrick A. Langan, Erica L. Schmitt, and Matthew R. Durose, "Recidivism of Sex Offenders Released from Prison in 1994," U.S. Department of Justice, Washington, D.C., November 2003, National Criminal Justice Reference Service no. 198281.

17. "No Easy Answers: Sex Offender Laws in the U.S.," *Human Rights Watch* 19, no. 4G (September 2007): 31–32.

18. Langan et al., "Recidivism of Sex Offenders." Compare with Patrick A. Langan and David Levin, "Recidivism of Prisoners Released in 1994," U.S. Department of Justice, Washington, D.C., June 2002, National Criminal Justice Reference Service no. 193427. See also Lawrence A. Greenfeld, "Sex Offenses and Sex Offenders: An Analysis of Data on Rape and Sexual Assault," U.S. Department of Justice, Washington, D.C., February 1997, National Criminal Justice Reference Service no. 163392.

19. Anonymous ("Pariah"), "Sexual Fascism in Progressive America: Scapegoats and Shunning," *Counterpunch,* March 4–5, 2006, www.counterpunch .org/pariah03042006.html (accessed October 24, 2009).

20. "No Easy Answers," 31–32.

21. Sociologists and legal scholars have treated the emergence of "risk" as the focus of criminal justice. See Malcolm Feeley and Jonathan Simon, "The New Penology: Notes on the Emerging Strategy of Corrections and Its Implications," *Criminology* 30, no. 4 (1992): 449–74. See also Malcolm Feeley and Jonathan Simon, "Actuarial Justice: Power/Knowledge in Contemporary Criminal Justice," in *The Future of Criminology,* ed. David Nelkin (London: Sage, 1994);

Jonathan Simon, "Managing the Monstrous: Sex Offenders and the New Penology," *Psychology, Public Policy, and Law* 4, no. 1/2 (1998): 452–67; Jonathan Simon and Malcolm M. Feeley, "The Forms and Limits of the New Penology," in *Punishment and Social Control: Essays in Honor of Sheldon L. Messinger,* ed. Thomas G. Blomberg and Stanley Cohen, 2nd ed. (New York: Aldine Transaction, 2003), 75–116; Wayne Logan, "A Study in 'Actuarial Justice': Sex Offender Classification Practice and Procedure," *Buffalo Criminal Law Review* 3 (2000): 593–637.

22. Gayle Rubin, "Thinking Sex: Notes for a Radical Theory of the Politics of Sexuality," in Carole S. Vance, ed., *Pleasure and Danger: Exploring Female Sexuality,* 2nd ed.(London: Pandora, 1992), 267–68, 270.

23. David Garland, *The Culture of Control: Crime and Social Order in Contemporary Society* (Chicago: University of Chicago Press, 2001), 192.

24. Actuarial logic has not served rational aims any better when applied to nonsexual crimes. Malcolm Feeley and Jonathan Simon noted early on how sentencing reforms associated with actuarial techniques "mask significant differences among offenders and offenses" and, in combination with theories of the "underclass," produce policies of mass incarceration; see Feeley and Simon, "New Penology," 461, 467–70. On the anthropological view of risk, see Mary Douglas, *Risk and Blame: Essays in Cultural Theory* (New York: Routledge, 1992), as well as Mary Douglas and Aaron Wildavsky, *Risk and Culture: An Essay on the Selection of Technological and Environmental Dangers* (Berkeley: University of California Press, 1982).

25. Samuel R. Gross, Kristin Jacoby, Daniel J. Matheson, Nicholas Montgomery, and Sujata Patil, "Exonerations in the United States, 1989 through 2003," *Journal of Criminal Law and Criminology* 95, no. 2 (2004): 523–60; Adam Liptak, "Study Suspects Thousands of False Convictions," *New York Times,* April 19, 2004, A15.

26. I am quoting verbatim, as Oprah's show aired, and from the "Watch List" that once appeared on her Web site but has been removed. Much of this quote also appears in "Accused Child Molesters Caught," *The Oprah Winfrey Show,* January 1, 2006, www.oprah.com/world/Accused-Child-Molesters-Caught_1.

27. Anonymous ("Pariah"), "Sexual Fascism in Progressive America."

28. Kurt Eichenwald, "Through His Webcam, a Boy Joins a Sordid Online World," *New York Times,* December 19, 2005, A1; Debbie Nathan, "Hysteria, Exploitation and Witch-hunting in the Age of Internet Sex," *Counterpunch* 14, no. 7/8 (April 2007): 4, 7–8, 5.

29. Eichenwald, "Through His Webcam." Eichenwald elaborates: "On one occasion Mr. Berry was arrested and charged with slamming Justin's head into a wall, causing an injury that required seven staples in his scalp. Although Justin testified against him, Mr. Berry said the injury was an accident and was acquitted. He declined to comment in a telephone interview."

30. Kurt Eichenwald, "Making a Connection with Justin," *New York Times on the Web,* December 19, 2005; Nathan, "Hysteria, Exploitation and Witch-hunting," 5, 8.

31. Kurt Eichenwald, "The Customers: Where the Credit Card Trail Leads," *New York Times on the Web,* December 19, 2005.

32. Eichenwald, "Through His Webcam"; Kurt Eichenwald, "The History: A Shadowy Trade Migrates to the Web," *New York Times on the Web,* December 19, 2005; Joshua Brockman, "Child Sex as Internet Fare, Through the Eyes of a Victim," *New York Times,* April 5, 2006, A20. Brockman's *Times* article leads with the $20 billion claim but does not name the speaker who asserts it. In "Hysteria, Exploitation and Witch-hunting" (11), Nathan identifies Eichenwald as the speaker.

33. Nathan, "Hysteria, Exploitation and Witch-hunting," 3.

34. Ibid., 4.

35. See Garland's discussion of the penal-welfare state in *Culture of Control,* 27–51.

36. See Garland's account of the crisis of penal modernism in *Culture of Control,* 53–73. See Philip Jenkins account of the 1970s, *Decade of Nightmares: The End of the Sixties and the Making of Eighties America* (New York: Oxford University Press, 2006).

37. Mabel Perez, "Sex Offender on Flier Is Apparent Suicide," *Miami Herald-Tribune,* April 23, 2005, YB.

38. Emily Bazar, "Website Led Shooter to Sex Offenders' Homes," *USA Today,* April 18, 2006, 5A.

39. Wendy Koch, "States Get Tougher with Sex Offenders," *USA Today,* May 25, 2006, 1A.

40. *Kennedy v. Louisiana,* 128 S. Ct. 2641 (2008); *Coker v. Georgia,* 433 U.S. 584 (1977).

41. In mid-2010 the Center for Missing and Exploited Children estimated that there were 704,777 registered sex offenders, or 228 per 100,000 people. See "Map of Registered Sex Offenders in the United States," June 14, 2010, www.missingkids.com/en_US/documents/sex-offender-map.pdf. See also Jerry Markon, "Tracking Sex-Crime Offenders Gets Trickier; Violator Registry Is Growing as Tech-Savvy Predators Put a Greater Burden on Officers," *Washington Post,* November 23, 2009, A1.

42. Gallup, "Sex Offenders," June 9, 2005, www.gallup.com/video/16708/Sex-Offenders.aspx (accessed May 15, 2010).

43. Kerra L. Bolton, "Sex Offender Tracking Ramps Up: GPS Monitoring, Other New Efforts Start in January," *Asheville (N.C.) Citizen-Times,* September 14, 2006, A1; Bob Driehaus, "Green License Plates Proposed to Identify Ohio Sex Offenders," *New York Times,* March 7, 2007, A12; Michael Sluss, "Panel Seeks Evidence Castration Is Effective: A Lawmaker Proposes Offering Convicted Sex Offenders Castration and Conditional Release," *Roanoke (Va.) Times,* September 13, 2006, B2.

44. Anemona Hartocollis, "Sex Offenders Held Illegally, Judge Rules," *New York Times,* November 16, 2005, B1.

45. Danny Hakim, "Bills on Workers' Aid and Civil Confinement Pass," *New York Times,* March 7, 2007, B6; Danny Hakim, "State Plan to Monitor Sex Offenders Goes beyond Detention," *New York Times,* March 2, 2007, B1.

46. *Kansas v. Hendricks,* 521 U.S. 346 (1997); Allison Morgan, "Civil Confinement of Sex Offenders: New York's Attempt to Push the Envelope in the Name of Public Safety," *Boston University Law Review* 86 (2007): 1034.

47. Monica Davey and Abby Goodnough, "Doubts Rise as States Hold Sex Offenders after Prison," *New York Times,* March 4, 2007, A1; Monica Davey and Abby Goodnough, "A Record of Failure at Center for Sex Offenders," *New York Times,* March 5, 2007, A1; and Monica Davey and Abby Goodnough, "For Sex Offenders, Dispute on Therapy's Benefits," *New York Times,* March 6, 2007, A1.

48. Estelle B. Freedman, "'Uncontrolled Desires': The Response to the Sexual Psychopath, 1920–1960," *Journal of American History* 74, no. 1 (1987): 83–84, 92–94. See also Chrysanthi Settlage Leon, "Compulsion and Control: Sex Crime and Criminal Justice Policy in California, 1930–2007" (PhD diss., University of California–Berkeley, 2007), 210–14, 245, 265–67.

49. Davey and Goodnough, "Doubts Rise," D13; Davey and Goodnough, "A Record of Failure," A1; and Davey and Goodnough, "For Sex Offenders," A1.

50. Daniel Filler, "Silence and the Racial Dimension of Megan's Law," *Iowa Law Review* 89 (2004): 1588.

51. Ibid., 1553.

52. Jonathan Simon, *Governing through Crime: How the War on Crime Transformed American Democracy and Created a Culture of Fear* (Oxford: Oxford University Press, 2007), 20.

53. William J. Sabol, Heather Couture, and Paige M. Harrison, "Prisoners in 2006," *Bureau of Justice Statistics Bulletin,* December 2007, 7, National Criminal Justice Reference Service no. 219416.

54. On prisons as a form of racial domination, see Loïc Wacquant, *Urban Outcasts: A Comparative Sociology of Advanced Marginality* (Malden, Mass.: Polity, 2008), 2–3, 89–91.

55. See Chrys Ingraham, *White Weddings: Romancing Heterosexuality in Popular Culture,* 2nd ed. (New York: Routledge 2008); Ruth Frankenberg, *White Women, Race Matters: The Social Construction of Whiteness* (Minneapolis: University of Minnesota Press, 1993), esp. 6.

56. Lee Edelman, *No Future: Queer Theory and the Death Drive* (Durham, N.C.: Duke University Press, 2004), 112–13, 132, 149.

57. I draw freely here from Rubin's important essay, "Thinking Sex."

58. Lorna A. Rhodes, "Changing the Subject: Conversation in Supermax," *Cultural Anthropology* 20 (3) (August 2005): 388–411.

59. Giorgio Agamben, *State of Exception* (Chicago: University of Chicago Press, 2004), 14; see also 6–7.

60. Ibid., 2.

61. See Julia O'Connell Davidson, *Prostitution, Power, and Freedom* (Ann Arbor: University of Michigan Press, 1998), and *Children in the Global Sex Trade* (Cambridge: Polity). See also Patty Kelly, *Lydia's Open Door: Inside Mexico's Most Modern Brothel* (Berkeley: University of California Press, 2008).

62. Garland, *Culture of Control,* 180–81.

63. Simon, "Managing the Monstrous," 462–63.

64. See Paul Smith's astute discussion in *Primitive America: The Ideology of Capitalist Democracy* (Minneapolis: University of Minnesota, 2007), 91.

65. Kevin Sack and Brent McDonald, "Popularity of Hallucinogen May Thwart Its Medical Uses," *New York Times,* September 8, 2008, A1.

66. Colorado Department of Public Safety, "Report on Safety Issues Raised By Living Arrangements for and Location of Sex Offenders in the Community," March 15, 2004, report prepared for the Colorado State Judiciary Committees, Denver, 22–25; Minnesota Department of Corrections, "Level Three Sex Offenders Residential Placement Issues," February 2004, Report to the Legislature, St. Paul, 11.

67. Don Thompson, Associated Press, "State Supreme Court Halts Jessica's Law for Four Sex Offenders," *San Diego Union-Tribune,* October 10, 2007, http://legacy.signonsandiego.com/news/state/20071010-1906-ca-sexoffenders .html.

68. Marc Gardner, a defense attorney living in the Bay Area, has written about this case: "When Mooning Is a Sex Crime," *Counterpunch,* November 18, 2008, www.counterpunch.org/gardner11182008.html (accessed March 7, 2009).

69. Monica Davey, "Iowa's Residency Rules Drive Sex Offenders Underground," *New York Times,* March 15, 2006, A1.

70. Denise-Marie Balona and Rebecca Mahoney, "Long Ago Charge to Cost Man His Home," *Orlando Sentinel,* March 21, 2007, B1; "Deltona's Hysteria: Hurting Children with Sex-Offender Law," *Daytona Beach News-Journal,* March 16, 2007, A4; Sarah Kiesler, "Deltona Offender Case Could Impact State," *Daytona Beach News-Journal,* July 15, 2007, C1.

71. John Pain, "Sex-Offender Restrictions Leave 5 Men Living under Miami Bridge," *Washington Post,* April 8, 2007, A13; Robert Samuels, "A Life of Tension, Fear for Sexual Offenders Living under Miami Bridge," *Miami Herald,* May 3, 2009, www.miamiherald.com/460/story/1029919.html.

72. Greg Allen, "Bridge Still Home for Miami Sex Offenders," NPR.com, July 21, 2009, www.npr.org/templates/story/story.php?storyId=106689642 (accessed June 22, 2010); Julie Brown, "Iowa Statute May Provide Answer to Bridge Sex-Offender Saga," *Miami Herald,* July 24, 2009, www.miamiherald. com/2009/07/23/1155178/iowa-statute-may-provide-answer.html; Julie Brown, "Sex Offender Camp beneath Julia Tuttle Causeway Finally Being Dismantled," *Miami Herald,* February 27, 2010, www.miamiherald.com/2010/02/27/ 1502949/sex-offender-camp-beneath-julia.html (accessed May 9, 2010); Julie Brown, "'There Will Be Another Julia Tuttle,' Sex Offender Says," *Miami Herald,* March 6, 2010, www.miamiherald.com/2010/03/06/1515467/there-will-be-another-julia-tuttle.html.

73. Orlando Patterson, *Slavery and Social Death: A Comparative Study* (Cambridge, Mass.: Harvard University Press, 1982); James Waller, *Becoming Evil: How Ordinary People Commit Genocide and Mass Killing* (New York: Oxford University Press, 2002), 237; Avery F. Gordon, "Abu Ghraib: Imprisonment and the War on Terror," *Race and Class* 48, no. 1 (2006): 42–59; Loïc Wacquant, "From Slavery to Mass Incarceration: Rethinking the 'Race Question' in the US," *New Left Review* 13 (January–February 2002): 41–60; "Marion A. Kaplan, *Between Dignity and Despair: Jewish Life in Nazi Germany* (New York: Oxford University Press, 1998), 232–33.

74. Siegfried Kracauer, *From Caligari to Hitler: A Psychology of the German Film,* ed. Leonardo Quaresima (1947; repr., Princeton, N.J.: Princeton University Press, 2004).

CHAPTER 4. THE MAGICAL POWER OF THE ACCUSATION

1. I evoke a passage from Theodor Adorno, *Minima Moralia: Reflections from Damaged Life* (1951; repr., London: New Left Books, 1974), 192–93. Readers will perhaps note that I have been glossing the Frankfurt School's general approach to aesthetics, especially literary representation. See Herbert Marcuse, *The Aesthetic Dimension: Toward a Critique of Marxist Aesthetics* (Boston: Beacon, 1978).

2. Shani D'Cruze, "Protection, Harm, and Social Evil: The Age of Consent, c. 1885–c. 1940," in *Evil, Law, and the State: Perspectives on State Law and Violence,* ed. John T. Parry (New York: Rodopi, 2006), 32–33.

3. For instance, an author recently proposed raising the age of consent to appear in nude videos of the *Girls Gone Wild* variety to twenty-one (Garance Franke-Ruta, "Age of Innocence Revisited: A Lot of Those Girls 'Gone Wild' Are Disturbingly Young," *Wall Street Journal,* May 4, 2007, W11.

4. Lee Edelman, *No Future: Queer Theory and the Death Drive* (Durham, N.C.: Duke University Press, 2004), 112–13.

5. Kevin Ohi, "Molestation 101: Child Abuse, Homophobia, and *The Boys of Saint Vincent,*" *GLQ* 6, no. 2 (2000): 195, 197.

6. Jonathan Simon has suggested that fear of crime serves various interests in plural ways, one of which is to make marginal people powerful players. Nowhere is this potential power more condensed and widely distributed than in sexual accusation and sex panic. See Jonathan Simon, *Governing through Crime: How the War on Crime Transformed American Democracy and Created a Culture of Fear* (New York: Oxford University Press, 2007), for instance, 20–22, 190–91, 250–55. Dorothy Roberts has also written about how residents in poor neighborhoods lodge malicious accusations against each other with Child Protective Services in order to settle personal disputes; see Roberts, "The Racial Geography of State Child Protection," in *New Landscapes of Inequality: Neoliberalism and the Erosion of Democracy in America,* ed. Jane L. Collins, Micaela di Leonardo, and Brett Williams (Santa Fe, N.Mex.: School for Advanced Research Press, 2008), 153–67. See also Dorothy Roberts, *Shattered Bonds: The Color of Child Welfare* (New York: Basic, 2002).

7. Angela Y. Davis, *Arbitrary Justice: The Power of the American Prosecutor* (New York: Oxford University Press, 2007); Edward Humes, *Mean Justice: A Town's Terror, A Prosecutor's Power, A Betrayal of Innocence* (New York: Simon and Schuster, 1999).

8. The disciplining of the Durham prosecutor in the Duke lacrosse team case is instructive: the objects of his vindictiveness were wealthy white students at an elite private university. Comments Stephen M. Gillers, a law professor at New York University who writes on lawyer ethics: "If the same case had involved three poor men, instead of defendants with private counsel and families that supported them financially and publicly . . . , we would not likely see a disbarment, in North Carolina or anywhere. I'd be surprised if there were even serious discipline" (Adam Liptak, "Prosecutor Becomes Prosecuted," *New York Times,* June 24, 2007, WK14).

9. Giorgio Agamben, *Homo Sacer: Sovereign Power and Bare Life,* trans. Daniel Heller-Roazen (Stanford, Calif.: Stanford University Press, 1998).

PART TWO

1. See Naomi Wolf, *The End of America: Letter of Warning to a Young Patriot* (White River Junction, Vt.: Chelsea Green, 2007); Chalmers Johnson, *Nemesis: The Last Days of the American Republic* (New York: Henry Holt, 2006); Charlie Savage, *Takeover: The Return of the Imperial Presidency and the Subversion of American Democracy* (New York: Little, Brown, 2007); and Sheldon S. Wolin, *Democracy Incorporated: Managed Democracy and the Specter of Inverted Totalitarianism* (Princeton, N.J.: Princeton University Press, 2008). See also Joe Conason, *It Can Happen Here: Authoritarian Peril in the Age of Bush* (New York: Thomas Dunne, 2007); Susan Jacoby, *The Age of American Unreason* (New York: Pantheon, 2008); Chris Hedges, *American Fascists: The Christian Right and the War on America* (New York: Free Press, 2007); and John W. Dean, *Broken Government: How Republican Rule Destroyed the Legislative, Executive, and Judicial Branches* (New York: Viking, 2007).

2. Zbigniew Brzezinski, "Terrorized by the 'War on Terror': How a Three-Word Mantra Has Undermined America," *Washington Post,* March 25, 2007, B1.

3. David Garland, *The Culture of Control: Crime and Social Order in Contemporary Society* (Chicago: University of Chicago Press, 2001); Jonathan Simon, *Governing through Crime: How the War on Crime Transformed American Democracy and Created a Culture of Fear* (New York: Oxford University Press, 2007), 250.

CHAPTER 5. ZERO TOLERANCE

1. I draw the phrase "carceral state" from Foucault's "carceral system," which is frequently glossed as "carceral society" (Michel Foucault, *Discipline and Punish: The Birth of the Prison* (New York: Vintage). See also Marie Gottschalk, *The Prison and the Gallows: The Politics of Mass Incarceration in America* (Cambridge: Cambridge University Press, 2006), 1–17; Marie Gottschalk, "Hiding in Plain Sight: American Politics and the Carceral State," *Annual Review of Political Science* 11 (June 2008): 235–60.

2. A punitive approach to crime control tends to produce chronic offending: "Repeated experiences of coercion reinforce social-psychological attributes that make it more likely that an individual will exhibit behaviors that elicit further coercion, which only amplifies the emotional and cognitive traits that produce hostile behaviors" (Mark Colvin, *Crime and Coercion: An Integrated Theory of Chronic Criminality* [New York: St. Martin's, 2000], 1).

3. John van Kesteren, Pat Mayhew, and Paul Nieuwbeerta, *Crime Victimization in Seventeen Industrialized Countries: Key Findings from the 2000 International Crime Victims Survey* (The Hague: Ministry of Justice, Wetenschappelijk Onderzoek—En Documentatiecentrum, 2000), 48; Warren Hoge, "Caught Red-Handed? Let It Be in Finland," *New York Times,* January 2, 2003, A1.

4. I draw current incarceration rates come from the Web site maintained by the International Centre for Prison Studies at King's College, London, www.kcl.ac.uk/schools/law/research/icps (accessed May 18, 2010). On the fall and rise of rates over time, see Jerome S. Bruner, "Do Not Pass Go," *New York Review of Books,* September 25, 2003, 44–46.

5. Nick Cohen, "661 New Crimes and Counting," *New Statesman* 16, no. 764 (July 7, 2003): 18.

6. James Q. Whitman, *Harsh Justice: Criminal Punishment and the Widening Divide between America and Europe* (Oxford: Oxford University Press, 2003).

7. See International Centre for Prison Studies, and the Sentencing Project's Web site at www.sentencingproject.org, as well as the Pew Center on the States, *1 in 100: Behind Bars in America 2008* (Washington, D.C.: Pew Charitable Trusts, 2008).

8. Maurice Merleau-Ponty, "The USSR and the Camps," in *Signs,* trans. Richard C. McCleary (1950; repr., Evanston, Ill.: Northwestern University Press, 1964), 264. The piece, drafted by Merleau-Ponty and endorsed by Sartre, was originally published as an editorial in *Les temps modernes.*

9. Thomas P. Bonczar, "Prevalence of Imprisonment in the U.S. Population, 1974–2001," *Bureau of Justice Statistics Special Report,* August 2003, 1, 5, National Criminal Justice Reference Service no. 197976, http://bjs.ojp.usdoj.gov/content/pub/pdf/piuspo1.pdf; Bruner, "Do Not Pass Go," 44. See also Timothy Egan, "Hard Time: Less Crime, More Criminals," *New York Times Week in Review,* March 7, 1999; Joel Dyer, *The Perpetual Prisoner Machine: How America Profits from Crime* (Boulder, Colo.: Westview, 2000); David Garland, *The Culture of Control: Crime and Social Order in Contemporary Society* (Chicago: University of Chicago Press, 2001).

10. Alex Lichtenstein, "The Private and the Public in Penal History: A Commentary on Zimring and Tonry," in *Mass Imprisonment: Social Causes and Consequences,* ed. David Garland (London: Sage, 2001), 171–78.

11. Michael H. Tonry, *The Handbook of Crime and Punishment* (New York: Oxford University Press, 1998), v.

12. See Henry Ruth and Kevin Reitz, *The Challenge of Crime: Rethinking Our Response* (Cambridge, Mass.: Harvard University Press, 2003), 95–96. Ruth and Reitz see specific periods in the long-term hike in incarcerations: During the 1970s and early 1980s courts began sending more "marginal" felons (burglars, auto thieves) to prison. From the mid-1980s through the early 1990s, the war on drugs was the main engine of prison growth. During the 1990s longer sentences for a variety of crimes continued to fuel the growth of the prison state.

13. Bonczar, "Prevalence of Imprisonment in the U.S. Population," 3.

14. Garland, *Culture of Control,* 178.

15. "U.S. Prison Population Sets Record," *Washington Post,* December 1, 2006, A03.

16. Urban Institute, "Beyond the Prison Gates: The State of Parole in America," November 5, 2002, www.urban.org/url.cfm?ID=900567 (accessed November 16, 2009); Jennifer Gonnerman, "A Beaten Path Back to Prison," *New York Times,* May 8, 2004.

17. The Sentencing Project, "Felony Disenfranchisement Laws in the United States," September 2008, www.sentencingproject.org/doc/publications/fd_bs_fdlawsinusMarch2010.pdf (accessed May 19, 2010); Brent Staples, "How Denying the Vote to Ex-Offenders Undermines Democracy," *New York Times,* September 17, 2004.

18. See Christopher Uggen and Jeff Manza, "Democratic Contraction? Political Consequences of Felon Disenfranchisement in the United States," *American Sociological Review* 67, no. 6 (December 2002): 777–803.

19. A notable exception is Jim Webb, U.S. senator from Virginia and former navy secretary.

20. "To Catch a Predator," *Dateline NBC,* February 20, 2007; Adam Cohen, "What's on TV Tonight? Humiliation to the Point of Suicide," *New York Times,* March 10, 2008;. Brian Stelter, "NBC Settles with Family That Blamed a TV Investigation for a Man's Suicide," *New York Times,* June 26, 2008, C3.

21. James T. Hamilton, *Channeling Violence: The Economic Market for Violent Television Programming* (Princeton, N.J.: Princeton University Press, 1998), 248–49; Steve Macek, *Urban Nightmares: The Media, the Right, and the Moral Panic over the City* (Minneapolis: University of Minnesota Press, 2006), 152–53. See also David Trend, *The Myth of Media Violence: A Critical Introduction* (Malden, Mass.: Blackwell, 2007), 67.

22. Steve Herbert and Elizabeth Brown, "Conceptions of Space and Crime in the Punitive Neoliberal City," *Antipode* 38, no. 4 (2006): 755–77; Michael Sherry, "Dead or Alive: American Vengeance Goes Global," in "Special Issue on Force and Diplomacy," *Review of International Studies* 31 (December 2005): 246–63; Dominic Corva, "Neoliberal Globalization and the War on Drugs: Transnationalizing Illiberal Governance in the Americas," *Political Geography* 27, no. 2 (February 2008): 176–93; Jamie Peck, "Geography and Public Policy: Mapping the Penal State," *Progress in Human Geography* 27, no. 2 (2003): 222–32.

23. William K. Knight, "The Psychology of Punitive Justice," *Philosophical Review* 20, no. 6 (November 1911): 622–35; George H. Mead, "The Psychology of Punitive Justice," *American Journal of Sociology* 23, no. 5 (March 1918): 577–602. See also James Q. Whitman's book on U.S. trends, *Harsh Justice.*

24. Francis Bacon, *The Major Works,* ed. Brian Vickers (Oxford: Oxford University Press, 2002), 347.

25. James Q. Whitman, "What Happened to Tocqueville's America?" *Social Text* 74, no. 2 (2007): 251.

26. Although Alexis de Tocqueville, Ralph Waldo Emerson, and others have expressed these views, they are more rigorously associated with the historian Arthur Schlesinger Jr. Gore Vidal once mocked this view by dubbing Schlesinger "Professor Pendulum." See Arthur Schlesinger Jr., *The Cycles of American History* (Boston: Houghton Mifflin, 1986), 23–48; Gore Vidal, "The Great Unmentionable: Monotheism and Its Discontents," *Nation,* July 13, 1992, 56.

27. I am borrowing here from a book that presents these terms in a way that fudges the difference between them. See Philip Bobbitt's *Terror and Consent: The Wars for the Twenty-First Century* (New York: Alfred A. Knopf, 2008).

28. See Jonathan Simon, *Governing through Crime: How the War on Crime Transformed American Democracy and Created a Culture of Fear* (Oxford: Oxford University Press, 2007), 21–22.

29. Abby Goodnough, "In a Break from the Past, Florida Will Let Felons Vote," *New York Times,* April 6, 2007, A14; American Civil Liberties Union, "Florida Clemency Reform Not All It's Cracked Up to Be, Says ACLU," press release, April 5, 2007; Gregory Lewis, "Panel Agrees to Restore Felon Rights after Completing their Sentences," *South Florida Sun Sentinel,* April 6, 2007; Mary Ellen Klas and Gary Fineout, "Felon Rights on Faster Track," *Miami Herald,* April 6, 2007.

30. "Update Income Limits for Public Defender," editorial, *Sheboygan Press,* February 4, 2008, www.nacdl.org/public.nsf/defenseupdates/Wisconsin020 (accessed November 16, 2009); Spangenberg Group, "Public Defender Application Fees: 2001 Update," 2002, report prepared for the American Bar Association. Wisconsin finally updated its requirements, which had been set in 1987, in 2010.

31. Adam Liptak, "Debt to Society Is Least of Costs for Ex-Convicts," *New York Times,* February 23, 2006, A1.

32. Theodore Caplow and Jonathan Simon, "Understanding Prison Policy and Population Trends," *Crime and Justice 26, Prisons* (1999): 110.

33. Radley Balko, "Overkill: The Rise of Paramilitary Police Raids in America," Cato Institute, July 17, 2006, www.cato.org/pub_display.php?pub_id=6476 (accessed November 16, 2009).

34. Bureau of Justice Statistics, "Compendium of Federal Justice Statistics, 2004," December 2006, 2, National Criminal Justice Reference Service no. 213476.

35. See Samuel R. Gross, Kristen Jacoby, Daniel J. Matheson, Nicholas Montgomery, and Sujata Patil, "Exonerations in the United States, 1989 through 2003," *Journal of Criminal Law and Criminology* 95, no. 2 (2005): 523–60.

36. Four defendants in the Tulia case were ineligible for pardon because the charges against them already had been dropped or because they had been convicted on unrelated charges. See Gross et al., "Exonerations in the United States," 534–35.

37. Gross et al, "Exonerations in the United States," 551.

38. Adam Liptak, "Study Suspects Thousands of False Convictions," *New York Times,* April 19, 2004, A15.

39. Caplow and Simon, "Understanding Prison Policy," 111.

40. "Citizens without Proof: A Survey of Americans' Possession of Documentary Proof of Citizenship and Photo Identification," Voting Rights and Elections Series, Brennan Center for Justice at New York University School of Law, November 2006, www.brennancenter.org/page/-/d/download_file_39242.pdf.

41. Ian Urbina, "U.S. Panel Is Said to Alter Finding on Voter Fraud," *New York Times,* April 11, 2007, A1; Eric Lipton and Ian Urbina, "In 5-Year Effort, Scant Evidence of Voter Fraud," *New York Times,* April 12, 2007, A1; Michael Waldman and Justin Levitt, "The Myth of Voter Fraud," *Washington Post,* March 29, 2007, A19; "The Court Fumbles on Voting Rights," editorial, *New York Times,* April 29, 2008; *Purcell v. Gonzales,* 549 U.S. 1 (2006); *Crawford et al. v. Marion County Election Board et al.,* 128 S. Ct. 1610 (2008).

42. "A Loss for Privacy Rights," editorial, *New York Times,* November 28, 2007.

43. Timothy W. Maier, "Data Missing on Missing Children," *Insight Magazine,* September 23, 2002, 16.

44. Matt Zapotsky, "Cruiser-Top Cameras Make Police Work a Snap: Quick Checks for Violators Improve Officers' Efficiency but Worry ACLU," *Washington Post,* August 2, 2008, A01; Ben Hubbard, "Police Turn to Secret Weapon: GPS Device," *Washington Post,* August 31, 2008, A01; Ellen Nakashima, "Citizens' U.S. Border Crossings Tracked: Data from Checkpoints to be Kept for 15 Years," *Washington Post,* August 20, 2008, A01; Barton Gellman, Dafna Linzer, and Carol D. Leonnig, "Surveillance Net Yields Few Subjects," *Washington Post,* February 5, 2006, A1; Yvonne Zipp, "Courts Divided on Police Use of GPS Tracking," *Christian Science Monitor,* May 15, 2009, www.csmonitor.com/USA/2009/0515/p02s13-usgn.html.

45. Jeremy W. Crampton, "Surveillance, Security and Personal Dangerousness," paper presented to the American Association for the Advancement of Science Annual Conference, St. Louis, February 16–20, 2006.

46. Mark Hugo Lopez, "A Rising Share: Hispanics and Federal Crime," Pew Research Center Publications, http://pewresearch.org/pubs/1124/hispanic-immigrant-crime-report (accessed March 20, 2009).

47. Simon, *Governing through Crime,* 257.

48. Ibid., 17.

49. Ibid., 204–206.

50. Naomi Klein, *The Shock Doctrine: The Rise of Disaster Capitalism* (New York: Metropolitan, 2007), 420.

51. Sarah Jain, "Violent Submission: Gendered Automobility," *Cultural Critique* 61 (2005): 186, 196, 200–201; Randel Hanson, "A Gated Community on Wheels: Sports Utility Vehicles, Privatization, and Global Capital," in *Hummer: Myths and Consumer Culture,* ed. Elaine Cardenas and Ellen Gorman (Lanham, Md.: Lexington, 2007), 3–4, 6–7; Patricia Leigh Brown, "Among California S.U.V. Owners, Only a Bit of Guilt in a New Anti-Effort," *New York Times,* February 8, 2003, A15.

52. "Not even the most inventive reading of Foucault, Marx, Durkheim, and Elias on punishment could have predicted these recent developments—and certainly no such predictions ever appeared" (David Garland, *The Culture of Control: Crime and Social Order in Contemporary Society* [Chicago: University of Chicago Press, 2002], 3).

53. Emile Durkheim, *The Division of Labor in Society* (1893; repr., New York: Free Press,); Norbert Elias, *The Civilizing Process: Sociogenetic and Psychogenetic Investigations,* rev. ed. (1939; repr., Oxford: Basil Blackwell, 1994); John Pratt, "Elias and Modern Penal Development," in *The Sociology of Norbert Elias,* ed. Steven Loyal and Stephen Quilly (Cambridge: Cambridge University Press, 2004), 212–28.

54. My argument here goes beyond conventional sociological work on trust. The attitude I am describing resonates more with the sort of social paranoia that produces lynchings and witchcraft accusations. See, for example, J. David Lewis and Andrew Weigert, "Trust as a Social Reality," *Social Forces* 63, no. 4 (1985): 968–69, 979.

55. Lev Vygotsky, "Chapter 12, Ethical Behavior," in *Educational Psychology*, trans. Robert Silverman (1929; repr., Boca Raton, Fla.: St. Lucie Press, 1997), 227.

56. Michel Foucault, *The History of Sexuality, Volume I: An Introduction* (New York: Vintage: 1980), 135–45. For an overview of bio-power, see Paul Rabinow and Nikolas Rose, "Biopower Today," *BioSocieties* (2006) 1: 195–217. I am referencing the discussion of disciplinary power from *Discipline and Punish: The Birth of the Prison* (New York: Pantheon, 1978). On the admixture of forms, see Gilles Deleuze, "Postscript on the Societies of Control," *October* 59 (winter 1992): 3–7. Special thanks to James Faubion for conversations and readings.

57. Paul Virilio, *The Original Accident*, trans. Julie Rose (Cambridge: Polity, 2007), 58, 16.

CHAPTER 6. INNOCENTS ABROAD

1. Michael Sherry, "Dead or Alive: American Vengeance Goes Global," in "Special Issue on Force and Diplomacy," *Review of International Studies* 31 (December 2005): 246–63.

2. "Afflicted Powers: The State, the Spectacle and September 11," *New Left Review* 27 (May–June 2004): 5–21.

3. Corey Robin, *Fear: The History of a Political Idea* (Oxford: Oxford University Press, 2004), 1–3.

4. "'Bring it Down' Was about a Car, Students' Lawyer Says," CNN.com, September 15, 2002, http://archives.cnn.com/2002/US/09/15/fla.terror.students (accessed September 21, 2009); Tamar Lewin, "Sikh Owner of Gas Station Is Fatally Shot in Rampage," *New York Times*, September 17, 2001, B16.

5. Paul Smith, "Why 'We' Lovehate 'You,'" Contemporary Conflicts, March 26, 2004, http://conconflicts.ssrc.org/USA/smith/ (accessed September 18, 2006).

6. Chalmers Johnson, "Blowback," *Nation*, October 15, 2001, 13–15; Chalmers Johnson, *Blowback: The Costs and Consequences of American Empire* (New York: Henry Holt, 2004).

7. See Michelangelo Signorile, "The Mohamed Atta Files," Newsweek/MSNBC.com, October 31, 2001, www.msnbc.msn.com/id/3067491/ (accessed November 19, 2009).

8. Daniel M. Filler, "Terrorism, Panic, and Pedophilia," *Virginia Journal of Social Policy and the Law* 10, no. 3 (2003): 345, 356.

9. Jasbir Puar provides a photographic negative of the picture I develop here, arguing that homonormative inclusions of the present—the overturning of sodomy laws, the legalizing of gay marriage in some locales—depend on the production of new "queers": terrorist populations, Orientalized bodies. See *Terrorist Assemblages: Homonationalism in Queer Times* (Durham, N.C.: Duke University Press, 2007).

10. Michael Ignatieff, "American Empire (Get Used to It)," *New York Times Magazine*, January 5, 2003. For a critical review see William D. Hartung, "The New Imperialism," *Nation*, February 17, 2003, 5–6.

11. Jane Mayer, "Outsourcing Torture: The Secret History of America's 'Extraordinary Rendition' Program," *New Yorker,* February 14, 2005; American Civil Liberties Union, "Enduring Abuse: Torture and Cruel Treatment by the United States at Home and Abroad", report prepared for the United Nations Committee Against Torture, 2006, www.aclu.org/safefree/torture/25354pub20060427.html (accessed September 19, 2006).

12. Muzaffer A. Chisti et al., "America's Challenge: Domestic Security, Civil Liberties, and National Unity after September 11," 2003, Migration Policy Institute, Washington, D.C.

13. Danny Hakim, "Defendant Is Released in Detroit Terror Case," *New York Times,* October 13, 2004, A16.

14. Neil A. Davis, "Memos Reveal Scope of the Power Bush Sought in Fighting Terror," *New York Times,* March 3, 2009, A1.

15. Frank James, "Immigrant Sex Offenders Targeted," *Chicago Tribune,* February 25, 2005, 1.

16. Deborah Sontag, "Video Is a Window Into a Terror Suspect's Isolation," *New York Times,* December 4, 2006, A1.

17. Elaine Cassel provides a bracing review of these and other cases. See Cassel's *The War on Civil Liberties: How Bush and Ashcroft Have Dismantled the Bill of Rights* (Chicago: Lawrence Hill Books, 2004).

18. Alexander Cockburn, "The Ongoing Prosecution of Sami Al-Arian," *Nation,* July 21, 2008, 9; Associated Press, "Al-Arian Released After 5 Years to Await 2nd Trial," *USA Today,* September 2, 2008, www.usatoday.com/news/nation/2008–09–02-al-arian_N.htm (accessed May 20, 2010).

19. Eli Lake, "The 9/14 Presidency," Reason.com, April 6, 2010, http://reason.com/archives/2010/04/06/the-914-presidency (accessed May 20, 2010).

20. Jack Goldsmith, review of *Crisis and Command* by John Yoo, *New Republic,* February 18, 2010, 33–39.

21. Susan Sontag, "Regarding the Torture of Others," *New York Times Magazine,* May 23, 2004, 25; Eduardo Subirats, "Totalitarian Lust: From Salò to Abu Ghraib," *South Central Review* 24, no. 1 (spring 2007): 174–82.

22. Georges Batailles, "The Link between Taboos and Death," in *Erotism: Death and Sensuality* (San Francisco: City Lights, 1986), 40–48.

23. Hannah Arendt, *Eichmann in Jerusalem: A Report on the Banality of Evil* (1963; repr., New York: Penguin, 1977), 135.

24. Fox Butterfield, "Mistreatment of Prisoners Is Called Routine in U.S.," *New York Times,* May 8, 2004.

25. Amnesty International, *Amnesty International Report 2002—United States of America,* May 28, 2002, www.unhcr.org/refworld/docid/3cf4bco510.html (accessed November 19, 2009); Amnesty International, *Amnesty International Report 2003—United States of America,* May 28, 2003, www.unhcr.org/refworld/docid/3edb47e21a.html (accessed November 19, 2009]. See also various reports by Human Rights Watch, www.hrw.org.

26. Nina Bernstein's reporting on these torture sessions was conveyed to the world under the muted headline, "No Plan to Hurt 9/11 Detainees, Ex-Jailer Says" (*New York Times,* May 5, 2004, B1).

27. Bert Useem and Jack A. Goldstone, "Forging Social Order and Its Breakdown: Riot and Reform in U.S. Prisons," *American Sociological Review* 67, no. 4 (2002): 520–22; M.C. Braswell, R.H. Montgomery Jr., and L.X. Lombardo, eds., *Prison Violence in America* (Cincinnati: Anderson, 1994), 132–33, 141; Daniel Lockwood, "Issues in Prison Sexual Violence," in Braswell, Montgomery, and Lombardo, *Prison Violence in America,* 101.

28. Kate Zernike, "Prison Guard Calls Abuse Routine and Sometimes Amusing," *New York Times,* May 16, 2004, A1.

29. Jean Baudrillard, *Simulacra and Simulation,* trans. Sheila Faria Glaser (Ann Arbor: University of Michigan Press, 1994), 14–16.

30. Patrick McGeehan, "New York Plan for DNA Data in Most Crimes," *New York Times,* May 14, 2007, A1.

31. Nina Bernstein, "Foes of Sex Trade Are Stung by the Fall of an Ally," *New York Times,* March 12, 2008, A1; Danny Hakim and William Rashbaum, "No Federal Prostitution Charges for Spitzer," *New York Times,* November 7, 2008, A1.

32. Scheherezade Faramarzi, Associated Press, "Ex-Iraqi Prisoner Details Humiliation," *(Lakeland, Florida) Ledger,* May 3, 2004, A5.

CHAPTER 7. CONSTRUCTING VICTIMIZATION

1. See Michel Foucault, "Nietzsche, Genealogy, History," in *Language, Counter-Memory, Practice: Selected Essays and Interviews,* ed. Donald F. Bouchard (Ithaca, N.Y.: Cornell University Press, 1977), 139–64.

2. Michael Sherry, "Dead or Alive: American Vengeance Goes Global," in "Special Issue on Force and Diplomacy," *Review of International Studies* 31 (December 2005): 246–63.

3. Early intellectual advocates of the punitive turn include James Q. Wilson, *Thinking about Crime* (New York: Basic, 1975), and Ernest Van den Haag, *Punishing Criminals: Concerning a Very Old and Painful Question* (New York: Basic, 1975). Whereas Wilson set punitive approaches on a utilitarian basis, depicting the criminal as a rational actor subject to the logic of deterrence, Van den Haag emphasized expressive punishment, including corporal punishment, as a positive social good linked to ideas about justice and morality.

4. On crime rates in the 1950s, see Alvin L. Jacobson, "Crime Trends in Southern and Nonsouthern Cities: A Twenty Year Perspective," *Social Forces* 54, no. 1 (1975): 230–33; Drew Humphries and Don Wallace, "Capitalist Accumulation and Urban Crime, 1950–1971," *Social Problems* 28, no. 2 (1980): 179; Gary LaFree, "Declining Violent Crime Rates in the 1990s: Predicting Crime Booms and Busts," *Annual Review of Sociology* 25 (1999): 146–47; David C. Anderson, "The Mystery of the Falling Crime Rate," *American Prospect* 32 (1997): 51, 53; Franklin E. Zimring, *The Great American Crime Decline* (New York: Oxford University Press, 2007): 5–16, 20; David Garland, *The Culture of Control: Crime and Social Order in Contemporary Society* (Chicago: University of Chicago Press, 2001), 14.

5. Todd R. Clear, *Imprisoning Communities: How Mass Incarceration Makes Disadvantaged Neighborhoods Worse* (Oxford: Oxford University Press, 2007);

Joan Petersilia, *When Prisoners Come Home: Parole and Prisoner Reentry* (Oxford: Oxford University Press, 2003).

6. Garland, *Culture of Control,* 55–63. See also Marie Gottschalk, *The Prison and the Gallows: The Politics of Mass Incarceration in America* (Cambridge: Cambridge University Press, 2006), 37–40.

7. Michael Tonry and Joan Petersilia, "American Prisons at the Beginning of the Twenty-first Century," *Crime and Justice* 26, *Prisons* (1999): 3. See also Garland, *Culture of Control,* 32–34.

8. Bruce Western, *Punishment and Inequality in America* (New York: Russell Sage, 2006), 168–88; Franklin E. Zimring, *The Great American Crime Decline* (Oxford: Oxford University Press, 2007), 55; William Spelman, "The Limited Importance of Prison Expansion," in *Crime, Inequality, and the State,* ed. Mary E. Vogel (New York: Routledge, 2007), 150–64.

9. Zimring, *Great American Crime Decline,* 141–42, 61, 107–34.

10. Loïc Wacquant, "From Slavery to Mass Incarceration: Rethinking the 'Race Question' in the U.S.," *New Left Review* 13 (January–February 2002): 41–60.

11. Marc Mauer and Ryan S. King, "A 25-Year Quagmire: The War on Drugs and Its Impact on American Society," September 2007, The Sentencing Project, Washington, D.C., www.sentencingproject.org/doc/publications/dp_25yearquagmire.pdf (accessed September 20, 2009); Human Rights Watch, "Targeting Blacks: Drug Law Enforcement and Race in the United States," May 2008, Human Rights Watch Report, http://hrw.org/reports/2008/us0508/ (accessed September 20, 2009). See also Loïc Wacquant, "From Welfare State to Prison State: Imprisoning the American Poor," *Le Monde Diplomatique,* English edition, July 1998.

12. Mark Dow, *American Gulag: Inside U.S. Immigration Prisons* (Berkeley: University of California Press, 2004).

13. U.S. Department of Justice, Office of Justice Programs, "Prison Inmates at Midyear 2007," *Bureau of Justice Statistics Bulletin,* June 2008, 7, National Criminal Justice Reference Service no. 221944. See also Jonathan Simon, *Governing through Crime: How the War on Crime Transformed American Democracy and Created a Culture of Fear* (Oxford: Oxford University Press, 2007), 20.; Dario Melossi and Mark G. Lettiere, "Punishment in the American Democracy: The Paradoxes of Good Intentions," in *Comparing Prison Systems: Toward a Comparative and International Penology,* ed. Robert P. Weiss and Nigel South (New York: Routledge, 1998), 41–42; Mary Pattillo, David Weiman, and Bruce Western, *Imprisoning America: The Social Effects of Mass Incarceration* (New York: Russell Sage Foundation, 2006), 5–7.

14. Simon, *Governing through Crime,* 21–22.

15. Richard Hofstadter, "The Paranoid Style in American Politics," *Harper's Magazine,* November 1964, 77–86.

16. Bernard E. Harcourt, "The Mentally Ill, Behind Bars," *New York Times,* January 15, 2007. See also Theodore Caplow and Jonathan Simon, "Understanding Prison Policy and Population Trends," *Crime and Justice* 26, *Prisons* (1999): 68.

17. These figures derive from a 1999 U.S. Department of Justice study, Paula M. Ditton, "Mental Health and Treatment of Inmates and Probationers," *Bureau*

of Justice Statistics Special Report, July 1999, National Criminal Justice Reference Service no. 174463. Much higher percentages of inmates with mental illness were subsequently reported by Doris J. James and Lauren E. Glaze, "Mental Health Problems of Prison and Jail Inmates," *Bureau of Justice Statistics Special Report,* September 2006, National Criminal Justice Reference Service no. 213600.

18. "U.S. Prison Population Sets Record," *Washington Post,* December 1, 2006, A03.

19. Even non-Marxist economists acknowledge this basic Marxist principle, elegantly set forth in chapter 25 of Marx's *Capital.* See Carl Shapiro and Joseph Stiglitz, "Unemployment as a Worker Discipline Device," *American Economic Review* 74, no. 3 (June 1984): 433–44.

20. Wacquant, "From Slavery to Mass Incarceration," 53.

21. Sherry, "Dead or Alive," 250.

22. Bruce Western and Katherine Beckett, "How Unregulated Is the U.S. Labor Market? The Penal System as a Labor Market Institution," *American Journal of Sociology* 104, no. 4 (1999): 1040–41.

23. In 2003, the last year for which comprehensive figures are available, federal, state, and local governments spent $185 billion on policing, corrections, and courts. But this figure does not include expenditures on private security, which were estimated to exceed $100 billion in 2000 alone. In comparison the total national defense budget for 2003 was $397 billion. See Kristen A Hughes, "Justice Expenditure and Employment in the United States, 2003," *Bureau of Justice Statistics Bulletin,* April 2006, National Criminal Justice Reference Service no. 212260; James F. Pastor, *Security Law and Methods* (Burlington, Mass.: Butterworth-Heinemann, 2006), 16–17; Office of the Undersecretary of Defense, *National Defense Budget Estimates for FY 2003,* March 2002, www.defenselink.mil/comptroller/defbudget/fy2003/fy2003_greenbook.pdf (accessed May 17, 2008).

24. Peter Wagner, *The Prison Index: Taking the Pulse of the Crime Control Industry* (Northampton, Mass.: Prison Policy Initiative, 2003), www.prisonpolicy.org/prisonindex.html (accessed May 17, 2008).

25. Samuel Bowles and Arjun Jayadev, "Garrison America," *Economists' Voice,* March 2007, 1–7.

26. For a similar argument see Katherine Beckett, *Making Crime Pay: Law and Order in Contemporary American Politics* (Oxford: Oxford University Press, 1997). See also Simon, *Governing through Crime,* and Garland, *Culture of Control.*

27. Garland, *Culture of Control,* 3, 139–65.

28. David Alan Sklansky, "Not Your Father's Police Department: Making Sense of the New Demographics of Law Enforcement," *Journal of Criminal Law and Criminology* 96, no. 3 (2006): 1209–44; Brian A. Reaves, "Federal Law Enforcement Officers, 2006," *Bureau of Justice Statistics Bulletin,* July 2006, 6, National Criminal Justice Reference Service no. 212750, www.ojp.usdoj.gov/bjs/pub/pdf/fleo04.pdf (accessed May 13, 2008).

29. Beckett, *Making Crime Pay,* 10, 31–43, 85–86; Simon, *Governing through Crime,* 24–25, 44; Rick Perlstein, *Nixonland: The Rise of a President and the Fracturing of America* (New York: Scribner's, 2008), 266.

30. Michael Sherry puts it this way: "If the sinful deserved total eradication by God, surely mortals were entitled to deal harshly with them through the law" (Sherry, "Dead or Alive," 253).

31. Kevin Phillips's *The Emerging Republican Majority* (New York: Arlington House, 1969) expressly maps this Nixonian strategy subsequently advanced by the Republican Party. See also Micaela di Leonardo, "White Ethnicities, Identity Politics, and the Baby Bear's Chair," *Social Text* 41 (winter 1994): 174.

32. Philip Jenkins, *Decade of Nightmares: The End of the Sixties and the Making of Eighties America* (Oxford: Oxford University Press, 2006), 11.

33. My discussion of the victims' rights movement draws, in part, from Marlene Young and John Stein, "The History of the Crime Victims' Movement in the United States: A Component of the Office for Victims of Crime Oral History Project," National Organization of Victim Assistance, December 2004, www.ojp.usdoj.gov/ovc/ncvrw/2005/pg4c.html; Bruce Shapiro, "Victims and Vengeance: Why the Victims' Rights Amendment Is a Bad Idea," *Nation,* February 10, 1997, 11–16; Political Research Associates, "Conservative Agendas and Campaigns: Victims' Rights," in *Defending Justice: Activist Resource Kit,* ed. Palak Shah (Somerville, Mass.: Political Research Associates, 2005), 197–214.

34. A.J. Goldberg, "Preface: Symposium on Governmental Compensation for Victims of Violence," *Southern California Law Review* 43 (1970). See also Young and Stein, "History of the Crime Victims' Movement."

35. The invention of this new identity thus serves as the paradigmatic case of what Wendy Brown calls "wounded attachments," an identity whose relation to the state is defined by grievance (Wendy Brown, *States of Injury: Power and Freedom in Late Modernity* [Princeton, N.J.: Princeton University Press, 1995]).

36. Young and Stein, "History of the Crime Victims' Movement"; Political Research Associates, "Conservative Agendas and Campaigns," 199; Patricia Yancey Martin and R. Marlene Powell, "Accounting for the 'Second Assault': Legal Organizations' Framing of Rape Victims," *Law and Social Inquiry* 19, no. 4 (autumn 1994): 853–90.

37. Elayne Rapping, *The Culture of Recovery: Making Sense of the Self-Help Movement in Women's Lives* (Boston: Beacon, 1996).

38. Shapiro, "Victims and Vengeance," 11–16; Lucy N. Friedman, "The Crime Victim Movement at Its First Decade," *Public Administration Review,* November 1985, 790–95. See also María Félix-Ortiz de la Garza and James Sorensen, "A Self-Help Group for Drug-Addicted Clients: Assisted Implementation in Outpatient Treatment," *Journal of Substance Abuse Treatment* 12, no. 4 (1995): 260; Alfred H. Katz, "Self-Help and Mutual Aid: An Emerging Social Movement?" *Annual Review of Sociology* 7 (1981): 129–55.

39. In chaps. 5 and 6 of *The Prison and the Gallows: The Politics of Mass Incarceration* ([Cambridge: Cambridge University Press, 2006], 115–64), Marie Gottschalk examines the implications of federal funding and charts the changing relationship between the state and feminist rape crisis centers and domestic violence projects.

40. Simon, *Governing through Crime,* 89–96.

41. Young and Stein, "History of the Crime Victims' Movement."

42. Political Research Associates, "Conservative Agendas and Campaigns," 200.

43. Ibid.; Shapiro, "Victims and Vengeance," 13.

44. President's Task Force on Victims of Crime, *Final Report* (Washington, D.C.: Government Printing Office, 1983), vi–vii. See also David Garland's discussion, *Culture of Control*, 144.

45. Office for Victims of Crime, "Office for Victims of Crime, Report to the Nation 2005: Fiscal Years 2003–2004," 2005, 9, 12, U.S. Department of Justice, Washington, D.C., National Criminal Justice Reference Service no. 209117.

46. Shapiro, "Victims and Vengeance," 16.

47. Ibid., 18.

48. National Victims' Amendment Constitutional Passage, www.nvcap.org/ (accessed December 28, 2007).

49. See, for instance, Mike Maguire's review of the literature in "The Needs and Rights of Victims of Crime," *Crime and Justice* 14 (1991): 387–98.

50. See Jennifer K. Wood, "Justice as Therapy: The Victim Rights Clarification Act," *Communication Quarterly* 51, no. 3 (summer 2003): 296–311.

51. Paul H. Robinson, "Should the Victims' Rights Movement Have Influence over Criminal Law Formulation and Adjudication?" *McGeorge Law Review* 33, no. 4 (summer 2002): 756–57.

52. Wendy Kaminer, "Victims versus Suspects," *American Prospect,* March 12, 2000, 18. See also Robert P. Mosteller, "The Unnecessary Victims' Rights Amendment," *Utah Law Review* 443 (1999): 443–77.

53. Dan Eggen, "Study: Almost Half of Murder Victims Black," *Washington Post,* August 10, 2007, A04; Erika Harrell, "Black Victims of Violent Crime," *Bureau of Justice Statistics Special Report,* August 2007, U.S. Department of Justice, Washington, D.C., National Criminal Justice Reference Service no. 214258.

54. Joel Best, *Random Violence: How We Talk about New Crimes and New Victims* (Berkeley: University of California Press, 1999), 119–41.

55. Ibid., 103–16.

56. Brown, *States of Injury,* 68–69.

57. Shapiro, "Victims and Vengeance," 11.

58. See Best, *Random Violence,* 93; Wendy Kaminer, *I'm Dysfunctional, You're Disfunctional: The Recovery Movement and Other Self-Help Fashions* (New York: Addison-Wesley: 1992); Robert Hughes, *The Culture of Complaint: The Fraying of America* (New York: Oxford University Press, 1993); Alan Dershowitz, *The Abuse Excuse: And Other Cop-Outs, Sob Stories, and Evasions of Responsibility* (New York: Little Brown, 1994); Charles J. Sykes, *A Nation of Victims: The Decay of the American Character* (New York: St. Martin's, 1992).

59. Alyson Cole, *The Cult of True Victimhood: From the War on Welfare to the War on Terror* (Stanford, Calif.: Stanford University Press, 2007): 1–6, esp. 4.

60. Betty Friedan, *The Feminine Mystique* (1963; repr., New York: W.W. Norton, 1997), 385, 415..

61. Simon, *Governing through Crime,* 107–108.

62. C. Vann Woodward, *Tom Watson: Agrarian Rebel* (1938; repr., New York: Oxford University Press, 1967), 370–74; Michael Kazin, *The Populist Persuasion: An American History* (Ithaca, N.Y.: Cornell University Press, 1998), 195–220, 221–44.

63. Gottschalk, *Prison and the Gallows*, 163; Kristin Bumiller, *In an Abusive State: How Neoliberalism Appropriated the Feminist Movement against Sexual Violence* (Durham, N.C.: Duke University Press, 2008), 2.

64. Gottschalk, *Prison and the Gallows*, 163.

65. Ibid., 133–38, 145–46, 124–28.

66. Ibid., 129.

67. Ibid., 128–33, 124.

68. Ibid., 137. See also Ezzat A. Fattah's preface to his edited collection, *Towards a Critical Victimology* (New York: St. Martin's, 1992), xi.

69. Gottschalk, *Prison and the Gallows*, 124, 131.

70. Ibid., 150–51, 153.

71. Simon, *Governing through Crime*, 13–31. See also Garland, *Culture of Control*.

72. Judith Butler, *Precarious Life: The Powers of Mourning and Violence* (New York: Vero, 2004), xii.

73. Gillian Rose, *Mourning Becomes the Law: Philosophy and Representation* (Cambridge: Cambridge University Press, 1996), 47–48.

CHAPTER 8. THE VICTIMOLOGY TRAP

1. Wendy Brown, *States of Injury: Power and Freedom in Late Modernity* (Princeton, N.J.: Princeton University Press, 1995), 5–6, 27; see also 8 and 21.

2. See Barbara Nelson, *Making an Issue of Child Abuse: Political Agenda Setting for Social Problems* (Chicago: University of Chicago Press, 1984).

3. Lisa Duggan has suggested that Brown's sweeping analysis relies too heavily on extreme examples, such as feminists who are against sex, while ignoring more liberal strands. See *The Twilight of Equality? Neoliberalism, Cultural Politics, and the Attack on Democracy* (Boston: Beacon, 2003), 79–80.

4. Brown does occasionally glance at history; she suggests that ongoing economic changes are connected to feelings of powerlessness and ressentiment that give rise to victim identities and the politics of grievance. (See Brown, *States of Injury*, 68–69.) But her arguments too often evoke a familiar postmodern antipathy to law and the state, a reflexive denial that they can serve any good or useful purposes. Her arguments would be stronger if, contra Nietzsche, she allowed that certain kinds of law serve freedom precisely by restricting the freedom of capital—that is, if she made resort to Karl Polanyi, *The Great Transformation: The Political and Economic Origins of Our Time* (1944; repro., Boston: Beacon, 2001).

5. Sheldon S. Wolin, *Democracy Incorporated: Managed Democracy and the Specter of Inverted Totalitarianism* (Princeton, N.J.: Princeton University Press, 2008), esp. 15–40 and 41–68; Chalmers Johnson, *Nemesis: The Last Days of the American Republic* (New York: Metropolitan, 2006), 13–53; Neal Wood, *Tyranny in America: Capitalism and National Decay* (New York: Verso, 2004),

4–5, 53–54, 62–68; Dennis C. Canterbury, *Neoliberal Democratization and New Authoritarianism* (Burlington, Vt.: Ashgate, 2005), 1–9, 173–75; Matthew Crenson and Benjamin Ginsburg, *Downsizing Democracy: How America Sidelined Its Citizens and Privatized Its Public* (Baltimore: Johns Hopkins University Press, 2002), 1–6, 202–205.

6. Thomas L. Friedman, *The Lexus and the Olive Tree: Understanding Globalization* (New York: Anchor, 2000), 464.

7. David Harvey, *A Brief History of Neoliberalism* (Oxford: Oxford University Press, 2005), 4, 41, 39–55. For a critique of Harvey's approach, see Nancy MacLean, "Southern Dominance in Borrowed Language: The Regional Origins of American Neoliberalism," in *New Landscapes of Inequality: Neoliberalism and the Erosion of Democracy in America,* ed. Jane L. Collins, Micaela di Leonardo, and Brett Williams (Santa Fe: School for Advanced Research Press, 2008), 21–22.

8. Angela Y. Davis, *Are Prisons Obsolete?* (New York: Seven Stories Press, 2003); William Chambliss, "Crime Control and Ethnic Minorities: Legitimizing Racial Oppression by Creating Moral Panics," in *Ethnicity, Race, and Crime: Perspectives across Time and Place,* ed. Darnell Felix Hawkins (Albany: State University of New York Press, 1995), 235–58.

9. Mary E. Vogel, introduction to *Crime, Inequality, and the State* (New York: Routledge, 2007), 17–19, 42; Pierre Bourdieu, *Acts of Resistance: Against the Tyranny of the Market,* trans. Richard Nice (New York: New Press, 1999), 34. The sociologists Katherine Beckett and Bruce Western show that states with tight-fisted welfare policies are likely to have higher incarceration rates than those with more generous policies; see "Governing Social Marginality: Welfare, Incarceration, and the Transformation of State Policy," in *Mass Imprisonment: Social Causes and Consequences,* ed. David Garland (Thousand Oaks, Calif.: Sage, 2001), 35–50. See also Jamie Peck, "Geography and Public Policy: Mapping the Penal State," *Progress in Human Geography* 27, no. 2 (2003): 222–32.

10. Steve Herbert and Elizabeth Brown, "Conceptions of Space and Crime in the Punitive Neoliberal City," *Antipode* 38, no. 4 (2006): 757.

11. Loïc Wacquant, *Urban Outcasts: A Comparative Sociology of Advanced Marginality* (Cambridge: Polity, 2009); Loïc Wacquant, *Prisons of Poverty,* expanded ed. (Minneapolis: University of Minnesota Press, 2009).

12. Michel Foucault, *The Birth of Biopolitics: Lectures at the College de France, 1978–1979,* ed. Michel Senellart, trans. Graham Burchell (New York: Palgrave Macmillan, 2008), 258–59, 256.

13. John A. Hobson, *Imperialism: A Study* (1902; repr., Ann Arbor: University of Michigan Press, 1965), 140–52; Charles A. Beard, *An Economic Interpretation of the Constitution of the United States* (1913; repr., Mineola, N.Y.: Courier Dover: 2004).

14. Paul Smith, *Primitive America: The Ideology of Capitalist Democracy* (Minneapolis: University of Minnesota Press, 2007).

15. I have laid out this history in more detail in *The Trouble with Nature: Sex in Science and Popular Culture* (Berkeley: University of California Press, 2003), 306–21.

16. See, again, Chambliss, "Crime Control and Ethnic Minorities." See also Katherine Beckett, *Making Crime Pay: Law and Order in Contemporary American Politics* (Oxford: Oxford University Press, 1999).

17. See David Garland, *The Culture of Control: Crime and Social Order in Contemporary Society* (Chicago: University of Chicago Press, 2001), 148–50.

18. My thinking is indebted to Jane L. Collins; see Jane L. Collins and Victoria Mayer, *Both Hands Tied: Welfare Reform and the Race to the Bottom in the Low Wage Service Sector* (Chicago: University of Chicago Press, 2009).

19. Theodor Adorno, *The Culture Industry: Selected Essays on Mass Culture,* rev. 2nd ed. (New York: Routledge, 2001), 140; Paul Virilio, *The Original Accident,* trans. Julie Rose (Cambridge: Polity, 2007), 28.

20. Milton Friedman, *Capitalism and Freedom* (Chicago: University of Chicago Press, 1962); Kevin Phillips, *The Emerging Republican Majority* (New York: Arlington House, 1969); George Gilder, *Sexual Suicide* (New York: Quadrangle, 1973); George Gilder, *Naked Nomads: Unmarried Men in America* (New York: Quadrangle, 1974); George Gilder, *Wealth and Poverty* (New York: Bantam, 1982).

21. Marie Gottschalk, *The Prison and the Gallows: The Politics of Mass Incarceration in America* (Cambridge: Cambridge University Press, 2006), 127.

22. Robert B. Marks, *The Origins of the Modern World: A Global and Ecological Narrative from the Fifteenth to the Twenty-first Century* (Lanham, Md.: Rowman and Littlefield, 2006), 10–13.

23. Jonathan Simon, *Governing through Crime: How the War on Crime Transformed American Democracy and Created a Culture of Fear* (Princeton, N.J.: Princeton University Press, 2007), 26.

24. David F. Greenberg takes up Savelsberg's observation that countries vary a great deal in the extent to which political and media actors politicize the issue of crime and call for harsh measures. A "corporatist" political system may be defined as one in which "different sectors of society engage in explicit bargaining and compromise agreements," typically through the major political parties, sometimes brokering deals and exacting concessions behind the scenes. In his survey of wealthy industrialized nations, Greenberg found that the "more corporatist societies are not only less punitive: they are also more egalitarian and have more far-reaching redistributive policies" (David F. Greenberg, "Punishment, Division of Labor, and Social Solidarity," in *Crime, Inequality and the State,* ed. Mary E. Vogel (New York: Routledge, 2007), 567, 568; Joachim Savelsberg, "Knowledge, Domination, and Criminal Punishment," *American Journal of Sociology* 99, no. 4 (1994): 911–43.

25. Norbert Elias, *The Civilizing Process: Sociogenic and Psychogenic Investigations,* 2nd ed. (1939; repr., Oxford: Blackwell, 2000).

CONCLUSION

1. Arthur Schlesinger Jr., *The Cycles of American History* (Boston: Houghton Mifflin, 1986), 23–48; Gary Hart, "America's Next Chapter," *New York Times,* June 25, 2008.

2. Sean D. Hamill, "Students Sue Prosecutor in Cellphone Photos Case," *New York Times,* March 25, 2009, A21; Solomon Moore, "Missouri System Treats Juvenile Offenders with Lighter Hand," *New York Times,* March 27, 2009, A13; Chris Suellentrop, "The Right Has a Jailhouse Conversion," *New York Times Magazine,* December 24, 2006, 47.

3. David Stout, "Retroactively, Panel Reduces Drug Sentences," *New York Times,* December 12, 2007; Andy Furillo, "Big Prisoner Release Plan: Schwarzenegger Proposing to Free 22,000 Low-Risk Offenders Early," *Sacramento Bee,* December 21, 2007, A24; "Prisoners in 2008," *U.S. Bureau of Justice Statistics Bulletin,* December 8, 2009 (revised April 1, 2010), National Criminal Justice Reference Service no. 228417.

4. Eli Lake, "The 9/14 Presidency," Reason.com, April 6, 2010, http://reason.com/archives/2010/04/06/the-914-presidency; Mark Mazzetti, "U.S. Is Said to Expand Secret Military Acts in Midwest Region," *New York Times,* May 25, 2010, A1; Scott Shame, "C.I.A. to Expand Use of Drones in Pakistan," *New York Times,* December 4, 2009, A1; Scott Shane, "U.S. Decision to Approve Killing of Cleric Causes Unease," *New York Times,* May 13, 2010, A1.

5. Sheryl Gay Stolberg, "Obama Would Move Some Detainees to U.S.," *New York Times,* May 22, 2009, A1; Peter Baker, "Obama Faces Pitfalls on Detainees," *New York Times,* May 22, 2009, A1; William Glaberson, "President's Detention Plan Tests American Legal Tradition," *New York Times,* May 22, 2009, A1.

6. "Prisoners in 2008," 5–6.

7. Ashley Nellis and Ryan S. King, "No Exit: The Expanding Use of Life Sentences in America," The Prison Project, Washington, D.C., July 2009. See Alexander Cockburn's caustic commentary on life without parole as an alternative to the death penalty, "A Fate Worse Than Death," *First Post,* April 9, 2009, www.thefirstpost.co.uk/46967 (accessed June 1, 2010),

8. Danny Hakim, "3 Net Providers Will Block Sites with Child Sex," *New York Times,* June 10, 2008, A1.

9. David Stout, "Supreme Court Upholds Law Aimed at Child Pornography," *New York Times,* May 20, 2008; "A Discomfiting Threat to Free Speech," editorial, *New York Times,* May 21, 2008.

10. Gayle Rubin, "Thinking Sex: Notes for a Radical Theory of the Politics of Sexuality," in *Pleasure and Danger: Exploring Female Sexuality,* ed. Carole S. Vance, 2nd ed. (London: Pandora, 1992), 282–83, 297–300, 310.

11. A close examination of Edelman's psychodynamic reading, which maps "queerness" onto negativity, marginality, and the "death drive," is beyond the scope of this conclusion. Here is Edelman's framing: "By denying our identification with the negative of this [death] drive, and hence our disidentification from the promise of futurity, those of us inhabiting the place of the queer may be able to cast off that queerness and enter the properly political sphere, but only by shifting the figural burden of queerness to someone else. The structural position of queerness, after all, and the need to fill it remain" (Lee Edelman, *No Future: Queer Theory and the Death Drive* [Durham, N.C.: Duke University Press, 2004], 27).

12. Rubin, "Thinking Sex," 283.

13. Richard Webster, *The Secret of Bryn Estyn: The Making of a Modern Witch Hunt* (Oxford: Orwell, 2005).

14. David Batty, "Number of Sex Offenders Registered Rises 15%," *Guardian,* July 28, 2004; National Center for Missing and Exploited Children, "Map of Registered Sex Offenders in the United States," www.missingkids.com/en_US/documents/sex-offender-map.pdf (accessed May 25, 2010).

15. Richard Hofstadter, "The Paranoid Style in American Politics," *Harper's Magazine,* November 1964, 77–86; Susan Faludi, *The Terror Dream: Fear and Fantasy in Post–9/11 America* (New York: Metropolitan, 2007); Susan Jeffords, "Rape and the New World Order," *Cultural Critique* 19 (1991): 204–206, 212–14.

16. Claude Lévi-Strauss, *Race and History* (Paris: UNESCO, 1952), 12.

17. See, for instance, Laura Nader, *Harmony Ideology: Justice and Control in a Zapotec Mountain Village* (Stanford, Calif.: Stanford University Press, 1990).

18. Max Horkheimer and Theodor W. Adorno, *Dialectic of Enlightenment* (1947; repr., New York: Continuum, 1990), 30, 36, 41–42.

19. Michel Foucault, *The History of Sexuality, Volume I: An Introduction* (New York: Vintage, 1980), 41–42.

20. Niklas Luhmann, *Risk: A Sociological Theory* (New York: Aldine de Gruyter, 1993), ix–xii; Ulrich Beck, *The Risk Society: Towards a New Modernity* (Newbury Park, Calif.: Sage, 1992), 72–76; Mary Douglas and Aaron Wildavsky, *Risk and Culture: An Essay on the Selection of Technical and Environmental Dangers* (Los Angeles: University of California Press, 1982), 186–87, 193–95; Anthony Giddens, "Risk and Responsibility," *Modern Law Review* 62, no. 1 (1999): 3–4; Sarah S. Lochlan Jain, *Injury: The Politics of Product Design and Safety Law in the United States* (Princeton, N.J.: Princeton University Press, 2006); Garland, *Culture of Control,* 191–92.

21. Theodor Adorno, *The Stars Down to Earth and Other Essays on the Irrational in Culture* (1994; repr., New York: Routledge Classics, 2002).

22. Michalis Lianos proposes that the new technologies and techniques are fostering a "desocialization" of control. See Lianos's "Social Control after Foucault," *Surveillance and Society* 1, no. 3 (2003): 412–30.

23. Sheldon Wolin, *Democracy, Inc.: Managed Democracy and the Specter of Inverted Totalitarianism* (Princeton, N.J.: Princeton University Press, 2008), xiii, 131.

24. See, for instance, Jeff Sharlet, *The Family: The Secret Fundamentalism at the Heart of American Power* (New York: Harper, 2008).

APPENDIX 2. NOTES ON METHOD

1. Jack Abbott, *In the Belly of the Beast: Letters from Prison* (New York: Vintage, 1981); Malcolm Braly, *On the Yard* (1967; repr., New York: New York Review of Books, 2002); and George L. Jackson, *Blood in My Eye* (1972; repr., Baltimore: Black Classic Press, 1990).

2. See Carolyn Ellis and Arthur P. Bochner, "Autoethnography, Personal Narrative, Reflexivity: Researcher as Subject," in *The Handbook of Qualitative*

Research, ed. Norman K. Denzin and Yvonna S. Lincoln, 2nd ed. (Thousand Oaks, Calif.: Sage, 2000), 733–68.

3. See V.N. Vološinov, *Marxism and the Philosophy of Language* (1929; repr., Cambridge, Mass.: Harvard University Press, 1986), 102–103.

4. See Nancy Scheper-Hughes, *Death without Weeping: The Violence of Everyday Life in Brazil* (Berkeley: University of California Press, 1992), 286.

5. Hans-Georg Gadamer, *The Relevance of the Beautiful and Other Essays* (Cambridge: Cambridge University Press, 1986), 128.

Index

Abbott, Jack, 252
Abdel Rahman, Omar, 172
abortion, 40
Abu Ghraib, 174–76, 179–80
abuse: definitions of, 47–48, 57–58, 62, 265
  n.15; family as site of, 42, 83, 272 n.29;
  and human rights violations, 179–80
Abuse Excuse, The (Dershowitz), 205
abusive driving laws, 3, 257 n.4
accusations. *See* presumption of guilt; rights
  of the accused
actuarial logic, 80–81, 238, 271 n.21, 272
  n.24. *See also* risk assessment/
  management
Adam Walsh Act, 87–88
Adorno, Theodor, 220, 237, 240, 276 n.1
Afghanistan War, 170, 211
African Americans. *See* race
Agamben, Giorgio, 94–95, 135
age of consent: and American exception, 67;
  and carceral state, 143; and conflation
  of major and minor crimes, 5, 257 n.9;
  history of, 64–66, 109; proposals for
  raising, 109, 276 n.3. *See also* statutory
  rape laws
age-span provisions, 65, 66, 67
AIDS epidemic, 193
Alcoholics Anonymous, 195
All in the Family, 105
AMBER Alert System, 77–78
American Civil Liberties Union, 70, 150, 202

American exception: and carceral state,
  141–42; and neoliberalism, 222,
  224–25, 291 n.24; and punitive
  governance, 234–35; and September
  11, 2001 terrorist attacks, 168; and
  statutory rape laws, 67–68
American Friends Service Committee,
  183
American Idol, 146
American Psychological Association, 57,
  267 n.41
America's Most Wanted, 68, 87
antidepressants, 70–71, 269 n.73
antifeminist movements, 40
antigang squads, 154
antigay movements. *See* homophobia
antitrafficking movement, 7, 96–97
Al-Arian, Sami, 172–73
Ariès, Philippe, 46
Assault on Reason, The (Gore), 3–4
associative logic, 41, 81, 237–38. *See*
  also conflation of major and minor
  crimes
Atta, Mohamed, 169
Atwood, Margaret, 214
authoritarian populism, 26
authoritarianism, 165, 239–43; and carceral
  state, 240–41, 293 n.22; and economic
  stresses, 215–16; and war on terror, 137,
  240. *See also* rights erosion
autoethnography, 253–55